OneStream Administrator Handbook

MATT HA, ERIC HANSON, JANNESA ZHANG

OneStream Press

Disclaimer

About the Authors

Matt Ha joined the OneStream services team in 2019 with a background in data science and systems implementation. As a Lead Technical Consultant, his main roles are acting as a technical SME and triaging complex technical builds across various projects. He was born and raised in LA but got his degree in Mechanical Engineering in the Bay Area, where he currently lives in an overpriced tiny box. In his free time, you can find Matt backpacking or skiing in the outdoors (depending on the weather), making gifts for friends in his woodshop (i.e., dad's garage), or getting voluntarily beat up at the local jiu-jitsu gym.

Dedicated to my family, friends, and girlfriend Annie, who has been extremely patient in rescheduling date nights so I could meet my chapter deadlines.

Eric Hanson joined OneStream Software in 2021 and currently serves as a Director of North America Consulting Services for the South Region. He started his OneStream career as a Senior Consultant after leaving a customer who had implemented OneStream. Eric has implemented solutions for some of the largest customers at OneStream. He now leads a highly skilled implementation team that focuses on configuring and implementing OneStream successfully for customers.

Firstly, this book is dedicated to my wife (Jessye) and two children (Brant and Owen). All three of you are my pillars of support and love. You have continued to be my support system even when times are hard. Next, the book is dedicated to all of my colleagues at OneStream who have helped make me a better OneStreamer. A specific shoutout to Eric Osmanski, Chul Smith, Sam Richards, Nick Blades, and the entire Services Team. I also owe a debt of gratitude to past colleagues as well (Mark – H, S, A, I, Cynthia, Ana, Melissa, Denna). Next, thank you to Amanda G. for continuing to guide and support me through the process. Finally, this book wouldn't have been possible without my other two authors – Matt and Jannesa – both of whom are two of the smartest and (most importantly) kindest humans on planet Earth.

Jannesa Zhang joined OneStream in 2019. Her experience involves nearly a decade in the EPM and consulting space, where she enjoys enhancing financial processes through software enablement and tackling some of the most complex customer requirements in the consolidations and planning space.

To my family and friends who encourage me to go for it. I am still unclear what "it" is, and I guess I'll figure "it" out.

To my OneStream colleagues who have provided me with overwhelming behind-the-scenes support and encouraged me to be a little better than I am each and every day, and for that I strive to continue and to extend the same goodwill and care to those around me. I want to thank George Waddell for being such a great advocate and providing me with guidance when I was a fresh punk out of college, new to this whole EPM and consulting area, and then convincing me to join OneStream! I want to thank Chul Smith for providing the solid foundation and understanding of OneStream (it also helps that I happened to be staffed on all the projects you were overseeing as architect and had no choice but to share some of your insights ☺). Thank you, Jenn Stemm, for bringing the new-ish hire under your wing and showing me the magical power of establishing clear lines of communication and expectations when the sh$t hits the fan; glad to know I could learn from the best. Thank you, Eric Osmanski; by sheer chance and on my first day with the company, I happened to sit next to you in Boston, and I distinctly remember asking you, "How do I login to OneStream?" – gosh how far I have come with my questions – and I am very appreciative that you still respond to my questions! Finally, Matt Ha and Eric Hanson – I can't believe I bamboozled you into writing a book with me; thanks for being such great sports about it and I hope we can still be friends.

Technical Reviewers

Peter Fugere is recognized as a leader within the corporate performance management (CPM) community, where he has been working to deliver world-class solutions for the past 25 years. He has worked extensively with Oracle Hyperion Financial Management, Oracle Hyperion Planning, Oracle EPM Cloud Financial Consolidation and Close, Oracle Hyperion Financial Data Quality Management, Hyperion Enterprise, Upstream, and SAP BPC (Business Planning and Consolidation) before leaving Hyperion in 2004 to help build another consulting practice. He has published books and written whitepapers on the topic of implementation and best practices. He joined OneStream in 2013, is currently OneStream's Chief Solution Officer, and is responsible for OneStream's "Architect Factory".

Eric Osmanski is the Vice President of Solution Network Architecture where he is responsible for the strategy, planning, and execution of solution development projects, including leading engagements with development partners pursuing similar initiatives. Prior to his current role, he was a Distinguished Architect focusing on the design, development, and maintenance of applications for OneStream's largest and most complex customers.

Chul D. Smith has over 25 years of accounting, finance and IT experience using, maintaining, implementing and supporting consolidation and finance systems as both client and consultant. In 2006, he moved from corporate consolidations in Minneapolis, MN to HFM consulting in Paris, France. In 2007, he relocated to London, England, where he spent the next four years consulting with a small Swedish IBM Cognos Controller consultancy. The use of Controller across Europe expanded his work experience to nine countries in multiple industries.

His 2012 United States homecoming triggered his return to HFM and FDM as a freelance consultant with projects in New York City, Montreal, and Sherbrooke, Quebec. He began working with OneStream XF in 2013, and a year later was hired to join their services team. Today, he's a Distinguished Architect within OneStream's Strategic Customer Advisory team.

Chul holds a Bachelor of Science in Accounting from the University of Minnesota – Carlson School of Management and a non-practicing CPA license in the state of Minnesota.

Errata

Despite best efforts, mistakes can sometimes creep into books. If you spot a mistake, please feel free to email us at **errata@OneStreamPress.com** (with the book title in the subject line).

The errata page for this book is hosted at **www.OneStreamPress.com/Admin**

Version Updates

The OneStream platform is constantly evolving, with each release bringing new features and capabilities. The majority of the material in this book covers the OneStream Platform Version of at least 7.3 while incorporating a few features that are only available with Version 8.0 at the time of writing.

25% OFF VOUCHER

Certification

Validate your technical competence and gain industry recognition with OneStream Software.

In purchasing this book, you are eligible to claim a 25% discount on any OneStream Certification Exam.

To request your voucher, open a case with Credentialing via the ServiceNow Support Portal (https://onestreamsoftware.service-now.com/). Include proof of purchase that contains your name and address, the book title, date of purchase, and proof of payment.

Terms & Conditions:
One (1) certification exam voucher per book. All vouchers per receipt must be claimed at one time; if a receipt is for the purchase of 10 books, all 10 vouchers must be claimed at the same time. Vouchers are valid for post-beta production exams only. This offer is only valid for one year from the purchase date on the invoice or receipt.

 onestream

Contents

Chapter 13: Compliance and Audit   277

Chapter 14: Business as "Usual"   289

1
Introduction

Welcome to the OneStream Administrator Handbook! If you are a OneStream administrator and reading this book, then it likely means one of two things: 1. you are incredibly dedicated and deserve a raise, or 2. something blew up and you are hopelessly desperate. Either way, you're in luck. This book is for the admins – those hapless souls who work tirelessly behind the scenes to keep the machinery running and the end-users happy.

Collectively, this book is a compilation of decades of OneStream expertise from active consultants and ex-admins – people who have been exactly where you are now, and who understand your plight. Whether you're new to OneStream and don't know where to begin, or you're already a veteran and just looking to grab some tips and tricks, we hope that this book will help you on your journey!

Purpose

This book is intended to be used by admins responsible for maintaining existing OneStream applications. Admin tasks can be categorized into three general categories:

1. Fixing issues and correcting unexpected behavior.

2. Updating and extending an existing application.

3. Creating entirely new functionality.

The upcoming chapters will mainly address the first two categories since admins spend most of their time completing those types of maintenance tasks.

While these tasks may seem simple, OneStream applications are often complex, and admins may not be familiar with granular, low-level build details. Because of this, it's often a struggle even to identify a starting point when completing maintenance requests from the business.

This book's goal is to address the most common tasks and topics you might encounter as an admin, driven by true-life use cases. For each topic, we have compiled the relevant pieces of information from various sources that you should consider in your work and called out common pitfalls and 'gotchas'. For example, some of the topics covered include updating security settings for users, debugging common issues when loading data into OneStream, and fixing common compilation errors when writing business rules and Member Formulas.

With this in mind, consider the following situation: it's a Monday morning, and the first thing you see when you log on is an email from an end-user that reads, "Hey, a lot of the cells in this report are flagged as invalid now, but it was working last Friday, can you look into this?"

The issue is that OneStream – as an application – is very interconnected, and so there are dozens of different settings spread across dozens of different screens that could be causing the problem. So, where do you start?

You could search for the keyword "invalid" and scan through the OneStream Design and Reference Guide, *or* you could pull out this book and read the information about invalid intersections. There you would find a list of settings that affect the validity of an intersection (from your cube integration settings to conditional input business rules), which would give you a starting point of things to check right away.

Another important part of being an admin is developing and applying new business processes; for example, this might involve governance and controls. Since every company is different and OneStream is so flexible, there isn't a one-size-fits-all answer to how to build these processes into your application. However, we can offer examples of how other companies and admins have resolved these problems, to give you options as to what might work based on your company's specific requirements.

Scope

Before continuing, let's first set expectations regarding what this book covers and, more importantly, what it does not. The OneStream Administrator Handbook focuses on how to maintain and extend an existing application, not how to design and build an application from scratch. Many of the topics covered here are also covered elsewhere in other resources; the main difference is that we approach these topics from the perspective of the admin rather than the consultant.

For example, when discussing metadata management, this book doesn't discuss how to gather requirements and design your application's dimensionality to address them – that would typically be handled in the initial build by consultants. Instead, this book covers how to update and maintain metadata structures that are already in place.

Contents

Since we fully expect you to reach for this book as an 'as-needed' reference, here is a short summary of each chapter so you can quickly skip to your relevant content.

Chapter	Description
2: Testing	This chapter covers common testing definitions, when to use different testing methods, and OneStream's recommended testing practices.
3: Application Properties	This chapter covers the global properties that are available on the Application tab in OneStream, such as enforcing a Global POV or adding currencies.
4: Metadata Management	This chapter serves as a reference for updating existing metadata members or adding entirely new members. In particular, we focus on how different member settings interact, common mistakes when configuring members, and process recommendations for handling metadata updates.
5: Translation	This chapter covers the foreign currency capabilities that are available in OneStream and goes over common translation-related use cases we have seen for companies.
6: Work the Workflow	This chapter highlights important considerations when setting up existing or new Workflow Profiles, and how different workflow setups can be used to accommodate your business requirements and capture your business's responsibility structure.
7: Data Troubleshooting	This chapter covers techniques for validating and investigating loaded data; in other words, debugging data that is getting imported/calculated, but 'not looking quite right.' This includes topics such as auditing and drill-back techniques, and how to debug data that is not clearing or consolidating as expected.

Chapter	Description
8: Import and Validation Errors	This chapter covers the most common import and validation errors you might encounter when loading data.
9: Constraining and Locking Data	This chapter covers methods for securing your data and guaranteeing data integrity. These methods are separated into two major categories: system-level controls and process-level controls.
10: Business Rules	This chapter covers techniques for maintaining and troubleshooting business rules, as well as best practices to help you write code that is robust, scalable, and easy to maintain.
11: Cube Views	This chapter covers techniques and best practices for maintaining Cube Views, as well as common issues and errors such as no data access.
12: Securing the Pieces	This chapter discusses the administrator's responsibilities regarding security. It also provides a checklist of where the key security configuration properties can be found, as well as common issues such as the inability to open the application or see data. We also briefly cover some common practices for security maintenance and controls.
13: Compliance and Audit	This chapter covers the administrator's roles and responsibilities regarding compliance, which might involve providing audit reports to both internal and external audit departments.
14: Business as "Usual"	This chapter highlights high-level considerations when handling common use cases that occur as a company matures and grows. For example, chart of account changes and historical restatements are two common business problems that might occur even after an application is stable.

Figure 1.1

References

If you are new to the OneStream ecosystem, you'll quickly realize that there's a lot to learn and never enough time. With that in mind, we thought it would be helpful to list various available resources, along with some quick summaries of their contents and when you might reach for them.

Reference	Description
OneStream Design and Reference Guide	The Design and Reference Guide is one of the most useful resources. Use it when you want to confirm what any setting or button docs. It also contains helpful background information on what the various OneStream engines are doing, at a high level, behind the scenes. You can access it through the Help button on the top menu bar of any OneStream application; the PDF version can also be found in the `Documentation` directory of any OneStream installation package.
OneStream Foundation Handbook by The Architect Factory	The Foundation Handbook was written to help consultants with the build and design process. While the Design and Reference Guide generally provides documentation on settings, the Foundation Handbook also gives context and examples of which settings to use and when. It is a great starting point when you are approaching any new topic in OneStream.

Reference	Description
	The purchase of the book also entitles the buyer to a 50% discount on the OneStream Certified Professional (OCP) – Lead Architect Exam.
OneStream Finance Rules and Calculations Handbook by Jon Golembiewski	The Finance Rules and Calculations Handbook offers a deeper dive into business rule writing, with a particular focus on the OneStream finance engine. If you are looking to optimize code and find best practice examples, this is a great resource. It also has sample code for some of the more common calculations you might encounter, which can often give you a good starting point if you're unsure where to start.
OneStream Planning: The Why, How and When by Cameron Lackpour and Celvin Kattookaran	The OneStream Planning book delves into the details of building a Planning application. Since these types of applications are extremely rule-heavy, the book also deals a lot with writing planning-specific rules and provides a wealth of sample code.
OneCommunity	This site is a collection of blog posts, knowledge base posts, and forum threads for the OneStream ecosystem. If you're thoroughly stuck, it's often worth checking if someone has had a similar question to you at some point in the past. You can access the site at: https://community.onestream.com
OneStream Navigator (previously OneStream Academy)	This is OneStream's official repository of courses and video lectures. This is a great way to study various topics; if you're looking to get certified, there are even courses available to prepare you for the exam! You can access the site at: https://onestream.thoughtindustries.com/catalog
Microsoft VB.NET documentation	If you are new to VB.NET, it can be intimidating sorting through the swathe of available resources via Google. These are the official Microsoft VB.NET documentation sites, which we often refer to when writing business rules. Use the .NET API to look at available modules and methods. The Language Reference offers explanations on VB.NET syntax. Finally, the Language Features pages explain the core concepts of the language. Home page: https://docs.microsoft.com/en-us/dotnet/ • Language Reference: https://docs.microsoft.com/en-us/dotnet/visual-basic/language-reference/ • Language Features: https://docs.microsoft.com/en-us/dotnet/visual-basic/programming-guide/language-features/ • .NET Standard Guide: https://docs.microsoft.com/en-us/dotnet/standard/ • .NET Framework Guide: https://docs.microsoft.com/en-us/dotnet/framework/ • .NET API: https://docs.microsoft.com/en-us/dotnet/api/?view=netframework-4.8
OneStream API Details and Documentation	This provides documentation on the namespaces of the OneStream API. This is useful for figuring out the methods available to each engine, and also for seeing the available enumerations you can reference in business rules. You can find the API in the `Documentation` directory of any OneStream installation package (though you do have to dig around a

Reference	Description
	bit). For example, for version 6.6.0, the API can be found at `OneStream_6.6.0/OneStream_Doc_On_Prem_6.6.0/Document ation/OneStreamAPIDetailsAndDocumentation_6.6.0.zip`

Figure 1.2

Disclaimer

While the advice and information in this book are believed to be true and accurate at the date of publication, OneStream Press, the authors, and OneStream Software LLC do not guarantee the accuracy or completeness of any information and are not responsible for any errors or omissions or the results obtained from the use of such information.

We would also like to emphasize that any "best practices" are offered based on our experiences but won't cover every case. In particular, examples given for subjective topics (especially business process-driven topics such as controls and security) are offered to provide you with a general idea of where to start or what is possible. It is up to you – as a world-beating administrator! – to decide whether these examples are appropriate for your company and specific use cases.

With that said, we hope that you find this book helpful in both the short and long term, so let's get started!

2
Testing

Testing is a primary component of any standard **Software Development Life Cycle** (SDLC), and companies often spend millions developing these standards. Following the purchase and start of any OneStream implementation (or enhancements), one of the earliest conversations that needs to happen is how to test the software post-build. This chapter will discuss various definitions of testing and when to use these testing methods, plus some of OneStream's recommended testing practices.

OneStream is committed to the success of all implementations and the success of administrators following implementation. This chapter aims to guide how to test various enhancements found later in this book (and even outside the scope of this book).

Armed with the definitions – and when to use the proper testing method – the administrator can make requested enhancements or changes for any organization. They will be able to test and roll out enhancements properly to satisfy any internal or external audit requirements and, most importantly, provide absolute comfort to the organization that enhancements or modifications will work properly.

Types of Testing

There are many types of testing, and this chapter is not intended to cover every possible testing type or testing scenario. This chapter is intended to capture the most commonly used testing methods, provide a brief descriptive definition, and the best use case for employing the testing type.

The most common types of testing found during a OneStream implementation are:

- Unit Testing
- Integration Testing
- Data Integrity Testing
- Data Validation
- User Acceptance Testing
- Smoke Testing
- Performance Testing
- Regression Testing
- Parallel Testing

Unit Testing

Unit testing is defined as individual component testing, and a tester can utilize very targeted unit testing or component testing. The unit tester should be the person or the team that built the original artifact. One of the main reasons to perform unit testing is to ensure that the artifact is working prior to being reviewed by the customer or end-users. One example of such targeted testing might be validating that the import step is working under the Actuals workflow.

In turn, an example of component unit testing might be where we validate that the user can import data, create a journal, post a journal, and enter data in forms under the Actuals workflow parent.

Both examples illustrate unit testing; however, one is more granular than the other. One specifically targets a very specific step in a workflow, whilst the other targets all the steps under a parent workflow. Whatever the case, though, they are both confined to the workflow section of the application.

Unit testing is commonly seen with business rule writing, where the rule writer will need to find a way to test the output of the business rule. If the writer is testing a seeding rule, they might create an Excel spreadsheet using OneStream's Excel add-in tool. They select the dimensions from which they are copying (from within the application) and then create another column for the targeted location of the seeding rule. The business rule writer can then use Excel math to determine if the seeding rule is working properly and if the writer is selecting all the desired or correct intersections between the source and target values.

Integration Testing

Integration testing is when application components are tested as a group; it is typically conducted after unit testing. As with unit testing, integration testing should be performed by the person or group that built the original artifact to be tested. Integration testing would also be commonly used to test the movement of data within an application or into the application and applied to test the import of data into OneStream via a new connector or flat file upload. It could also be used to test the movement of data from Stage to cube. These are all types of integration testing.

Picture the following. You have tested several individual pieces of OneStream, but you want to test whether the individual components work together. Using the same parent workflow unit testing example referenced above, we will expand this to an integration test example.

We have imported our data, created a journal, posted the journal, and entered forms. Now, we need to validate that everything is consolidating and aggregating properly. This is a great example of integration testing. Integration testing can be expanded even further from this one example. We can layer security validation as well. One can now see the importance of integration testing and how it can be applied.

One other example of integration testing might follow the original implementation. Let's assume the company needs to implement OneStream's People Planning solution. Here, the integration test will check the new connection is receiving data into the People Planning register. In contrast, another integration test will verify the movement of data between the register and the cube or alternate tables.

Data Integrity Testing

Data integrity testing follows the lifecycle of data as it is imported into OneStream to the very top of the consolidation/aggregation. Data integrity testing is typically performed by the person who has built the artifact. This type of testing, however, often works in conjunction with the customer. The company building the artifacts knows how to build, but they may not have the detailed data knowledge that the customer would have. This type of testing becomes critical when a customer has a complex ownership structure or possible elimination issues. For example, if you own Subsidiary A at 100% and Subsidiary B at 50%, you expect only half of Subsidiary B's values to consolidate to the top.

Data integrity testing is similar to integration testing; however, the tester will validate that the end number is the correct resulting number. Integration testing, by comparison, only cares that the data is imported or exported correctly within the application.

Data Validation

Data validation is crucial to testing an application. OneStream often becomes the book of record for a company. The customer will always own both the data from the old reporting system and its movement and transformation into OneStream. Implementation partners support the data validation effort, but the customer has the intimate details of the business that generates the data. For that reason, implementation partners can't own the data validation process. Customers typically assume that the data is clean and organized. However, the implementation often uncovers unique data challenges they hadn't anticipated. These challenges can lead to project delays or missing deadlines. Data validation will always be the biggest unknown variable in a project.

User Acceptance Testing

Though I will attempt to do this section justice, the OneStream Foundation Handbook does an excellent review of user acceptance testing. (See Chapter 2, Methodology and the Project.) I will offer a slightly different spin, but it is worth reading that section as well for additional information.

User acceptance testing, or UAT as it is more commonly known, is the phase of testing where an intended audience (typically selected members from a company or organization) runs through real test scripts for a desired testing result. This type of testing can be very singular or individualistic, or this testing can have a complete end-to-end outcome.

UAT commonly occurs after the completion of the final build items and usually after some end-user training has been delivered. This allows the end-user to know what they are testing and gain familiarity with system navigation. Users are typically given a set of scripts for testing, allowing the natural Software Development Life Cycle (SDLC) to maintain traceability as to what was officially tested.

UAT scripts can be written to be very granular or high-level. It is commonly left up to the customer to determine at what level they prefer the scripts. The customer typically writes the scripts with support from the implementing partner unless otherwise agreed upon. The customer will know from the auditing partners what the key testing components will be (e.g., security; calculations such as the balance sheet being in balance or bringing current year net income into retained earnings).

OneStream typically recommends not focusing so much on basic, native functionalities, but rather to focus on the more nuanced functions of your testing scripts (important for the auditing teams). For example, you might want to redirect any focus on posting a journal (which is basic and inherited functionality) in order to ensure that a recurring journal is set up properly, which is more nuanced functionality within OneStream. Another example is the adding of a dimension member, which is basic functionality, versus a focus on the member that has a Member Formula, and that the Member Formula is producing the expected output. An example of a very granular type of test script can be found in Figure 2.1. An example of a high-level test script can be found in Figure 2.2.

Test Script Number	Step	Test Step Detail	Expected Outcome	Actual Outcome	Tester	Status	Screenshot
1	1	Open the OneStream application.	The OneStream application will load and eventually open.		John Doe		
1	2	Log into the application using your active directory credentials.	The SSO application will automatically pass in credentials, and you will be able to select which application to open. No physical typing of the name and password will be necessary.		John Doe		

Test Script Number	Step	Test Step Detail	Expected Outcome	Actual Outcome	Tester	Status	Screenshot
1	3	Select the Actuals workflow.	Selecting the Actuals workflow will open a menu for 12 months.		John Doe		
1	4	Select Jan.	January will open with options to import, adjust, or enter a journal.		John Doe		
1	5	Select the Import workflow under Jan.	Selecting the Import will open the ability to process and import data.		John Doe		
1	6	Click the Load and Transform button, then click OK.	The load and transform connector will appear to import the data. The data will load to Stage. Note: The import should take roughly 10 minutes, then the screen will automatically transition to the validate chevron.		John Doe		
1	7	Click the Validate button; this will validate the import from the ERP chart and ensure it can map to the new OneStream chart.	The data in Stage will transform the data through the assigned transformation rules. If any kick-outs occur, the chevron will turn red. Note: If no errors or kick-outs occur, this screen will automatically change to the load chevron.		John Doe		
1	8	Click the Load Cube button. This will load	The process chevron will turn green upon		John Doe		

Test Script Number	Step	Test Step Detail	Expected Outcome	Actual Outcome	Tester	Status	Screenshot
		the data into the cube.	loading to the cube.				
1	9	Navigate to the Cube View group called Consolidated Status in the OnePlace tab. Click the report titled Top Consol Status. Right-click on the top member and select consolidate.	The task details will run through a consolidation without any errors.		John Doe		
1	10	Navigate to the Cube View group called Income Statement in the OnePlace tab. Click on the current period income statement report. Validate that the numbers match the expected outcome.	Numbers will match the offline report.		John Doe		

Figure 2.1

Test Script Number	Test Step	Expected Outcome	Actual Outcome	Tester	Status	Screenshot
1	Run the import for the Actuals workflow and validate the data.	Data will be imported, consolidated, and tied to previous reports.		John Doe		

Figure 2.2

Individual UAT Script

During UAT, test scripts might be written to test a very specific component of the system that impacts one user or a group of users only.

An individual UAT script could be something like validating journal creation and posting that it is working with the proper security applied. This type of testing will be very similar to the unit testing mentioned above, but instead will be performed by an actual selected end-user. These types of tests are intended to give comfort to the end-user that the system is working as expected.

End-to-End UAT

End-to-end testing covers an entire process or even the entire monthly close process; detailed coordination, communication, and support are needed to accomplish this type of testing.

OneStream's example of end-to-end testing would look something like the following example. The system administrator imports data into a workflow and notifies the consolidation team that the data is loaded. The consolidation team then validates the numbers, creates journals, and manually enters key metrics not captured in the import. The consolidation team will notify the manager that the journals are ready for review and ready to post. The manager will then post the journals, validate the numbers, and notify the controller that the workflow is ready to be certified. The controller will then certify the workflow – after the proper validation checks – and notify the system administrator the workflow is ready to be locked.

This type of testing takes a significant coordinated effort but can realize real value as it crosses many teams and touches many hands (much like it would if it were truly a month-end process). When possible, it is always recommended to perform at least one of these types of tests, however burdensome they may be, as they create extensive value for the overall testing process. These tests usually highlight possible process issues or point out system problems that would not be caught during normal individual component testing.

Smoke Testing

Smoke testing is validating – at a much higher level – that the system is operating as expected. Smoke tests normally occur after migration (often called **cutover**). Smoke testing is typically performed by the customer following artifact migration and may not be applicable during a brand-new implementation. It will definitely be applicable after the initial go-live and the implementation of any additional enhancements. These smoke tests do not normally validate any data but utilize button clicking to ensure nothing is erroring out after the migration from the UAT environment to a production environment. This type of test will allow the implementor to know if a key component has been forgotten during the migration effort.

For a standard OneStream implementation, it is recommended to test all the buttons on a dashboard. This is typically where a smoke test becomes valuable. As an example, I have just migrated my artifacts from UAT to production and am tasked with smoke testing. I receive an error when I push a button. After investigating, I realize that only half of my dashboard components were migrated, and I am able to quickly correct that before the system goes live.

This type of sanity check is very important but not meant to capture *every* aspect of the testing cycles performed in development or test environments.

Performance Testing

Performance testing is the process of attempting to break the system by running so many jobs or processes in parallel that they overload the physical server's capacity. Much like the end-to-end UAT process, a performance test can often take a coordinated effort. Performance testing typically gives companies the comfort that the hardware purchased – in conjunction with the design and configuration that supports the OneStream environment – is sufficient to support the end-user experience.

Process-Oriented Performance Testing

Process-oriented performance testing runs as many processes as possible – at once – to see how the server is performing. This testing takes a coordinated effort to employ multiple users to click a specific button, which kicks off an intense business rule to load data, consolidate data, and action other tasks at one time. The administrator will typically monitor a diagnostic tool or validate the results afterward.

This type of testing could be automated in some way by creating a business rule to run data management sequences. This type of business rule could limit the number of end-users required to perform this type of testing.

User Load Testing

User load performance-based testing maximizes the number of concurrent users utilizing the system and then adds additional users to perform additional tasks. This isn't necessarily about overloading the system with many processes but testing the end-user experience for latency or lag. Is the end-user having an optimal experience in terms of system performance? Are reports rendering properly in a quick timeframe?

To provide a concrete example of this type of testing, let's assume the GolfStream company (OneStream's demonstration company) is provisioned for 100 software licenses but only 40 concurrent users at any given point in the application lifecycle. It might require the company to coordinate those 40 users effectively and add an additional 20 users to perform ancillary tasks within the system. Under test conditions, the system administrator may monitor diagnostic tools and end-users will report if they experience any latency with rendering or system utilization.

As mentioned above, some of these activities could be replicated by building a business rule to imitate the needs of particular users.

This type of test really gives the entire organization comfort that the system and hardware purchased will be adequate for go-live.

Regression Testing

Regression testing is the revalidation of historical test cases. The most common use for regression testing is during a software patch or update. Typically, after the software is updated, the existing list of scripts from both unit testing and UAT cycles is sufficient for this type of testing. Software updates are not the only occasion for regression testing, though. Often, auditing partners will request these types of tests to be performed annually, and it will solve most of the testing standards around Information Technology General Controls (ITGCs).

Parallel Testing

Different types of software may lead to different definitions of what parallel testing means. OneStream defines parallel testing as running a month-end close process from beginning to end within OneStream and comparing the results between the legacy system and OneStream. This type of testing doesn't necessarily need to be run concurrently with the other reporting or planning system; a customer can opt to have a parallel on historical periods. However, when possible, it is recommended to do at least one parallel testing cycle with your existing reporting or planning system. This type of testing will give absolute comfort that the system is generating the same results and allow a smoother transition from a legacy system to OneStream.

Standard OneStream Implementation Testing Cycle

Standard is such a broad term, and testing is never a one-size-fits-all approach; many factors affect many of the key decisions as to how a company will enter testing cycles. However, when sizing an implementation, implementation partners often have to make some baseline assumptions unless told otherwise by the customer. For example, implementation partners will assume that there will be a constant need for unit testing, and that testing will live alongside the building of application components. Partners will also assume that the customer is satisfied with one UAT cycle, and that two parallel testing cycles will take place.

There are many factors, however, that might increase testing or (conversely) cut testing to the bare minimum. Some companies want great comfort when going live and spend extra time testing; some companies want to be live as soon as possible and are willing to assume the risk of implementation defects or quick fixes in production. Other companies prefer a methodical testing approach and target the most optimal end-user experience. These companies are willing to push go-live to ensure that testing has flushed out any possible issues that could arise.

Conclusion

Testing is more of an art than a science, even though testing is a pass-or-fail exercise. Naturally, the science part really comes to the fore when the tester can see quantifiable results through the passing or failure of individual steps or scripts.

End-users will often explore the system *outside* the bounds of script steps when they participate in testing. This is where implementation defects that are not part of specific scripts are found and fixed. Often, companies will fix processes or find that something needs to be tweaked with this testing; this can be frustrating but leads to a better product overall. This is what makes testing an art… allowing end-users the freedom of application exploration.

Another great element of testing and testing cycles is the feeling of accomplishment. When you enter a testing cycle, the implementer is hopeful that everything works on the first try and there are no implementation defects or issues. This is not an attainable goal! There will always be fixes that need to happen in a testing cycle; it takes multiple testing cycles to finally get a clear and clean cycle.

Testing will set the standard for your implementation, your enhancements, and even minor fixes. Testing is often the project phase for the first impression on an end-user. More testing takes time but will be rewarding in delivering an optimal product in the end.

3

Application Properties

When an administrator is confronted with specific requests – such as adding new currencies or updating the time range or UD descriptions – they will find the settings as part of **Application Properties**. Application Properties can be found within the Application tab of OneStream and provides capabilities such as:

1. Enforcing a POV for all users via Global POV.

2. Enforcing Lock After Certify functionality.

3. Updating the start year or end year of the application.

4. Updating UD descriptions in place of the system default UD1, UD2, UD3, [etc.] classification.

5. Assigning a company logo for reporting (e.g., PDF exports).

6. Adding additional foreign currencies into the application.

7. Enabling workflow channels.

Global Point of View

Global POV is another point of view that is specifically defined in Application Properties for the time and scenario. Every user who accesses OneStream will see what the Global POV is when accessing the Point of View pane.

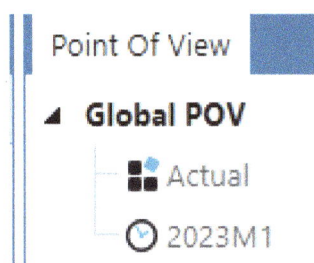

Figure 3.1

In Application Properties, the Global POV is set at the Default Scenario Type. The administrator will see that Global Scenario and Global Time can *only* be updated on the Default Scenario Type. Subsequent Scenario Types will find them non-editable and grey, as reflected in Figure 3.3 for the Administration Scenario Type.

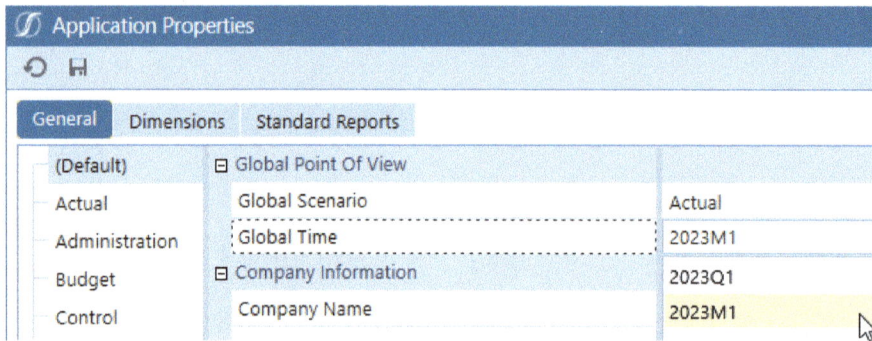

Figure 3.2

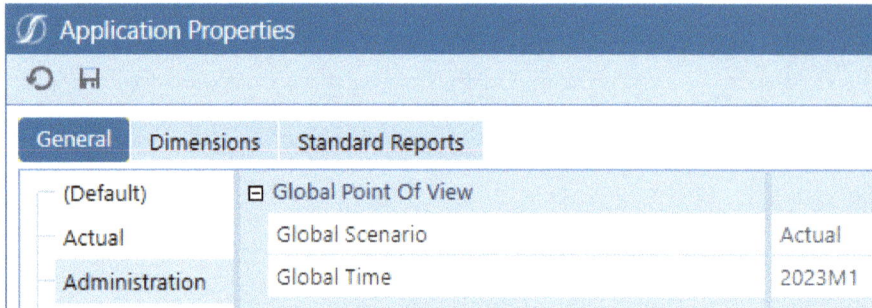

Figure 3.3

A common question we receive on Global POV is, "When would we want to consider using Global POV?" The answer is, "It depends on your company's requirements."

We have seen companies that need to differentiate the use of Global POV versus Workflow POV versus Cube POV for custom business rules. OneStream has specific functions that retrieve the Global POV, as demonstrated in Figure 3.4.

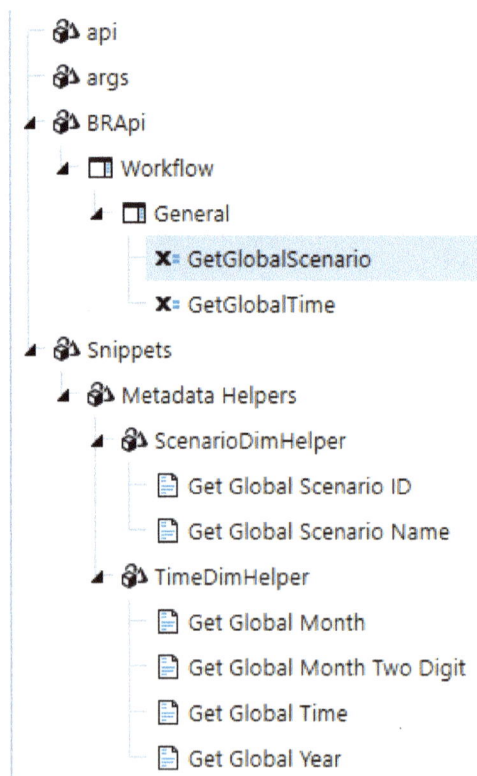

Figure 3.4

Naturally, the next question tends to be, "If we have a Global POV, does this mean that it will be enforced when we use it?" The answer to that is, "You have the option to choose True or False." Business rules can reference Global Time or Global Scenario without needing Enforce Global POV set to be set to True.

However, if there is a need to enforce the Global POV, you will find the setting under the Transformation section. For example, in Figure 3.5, True and False are selectable.

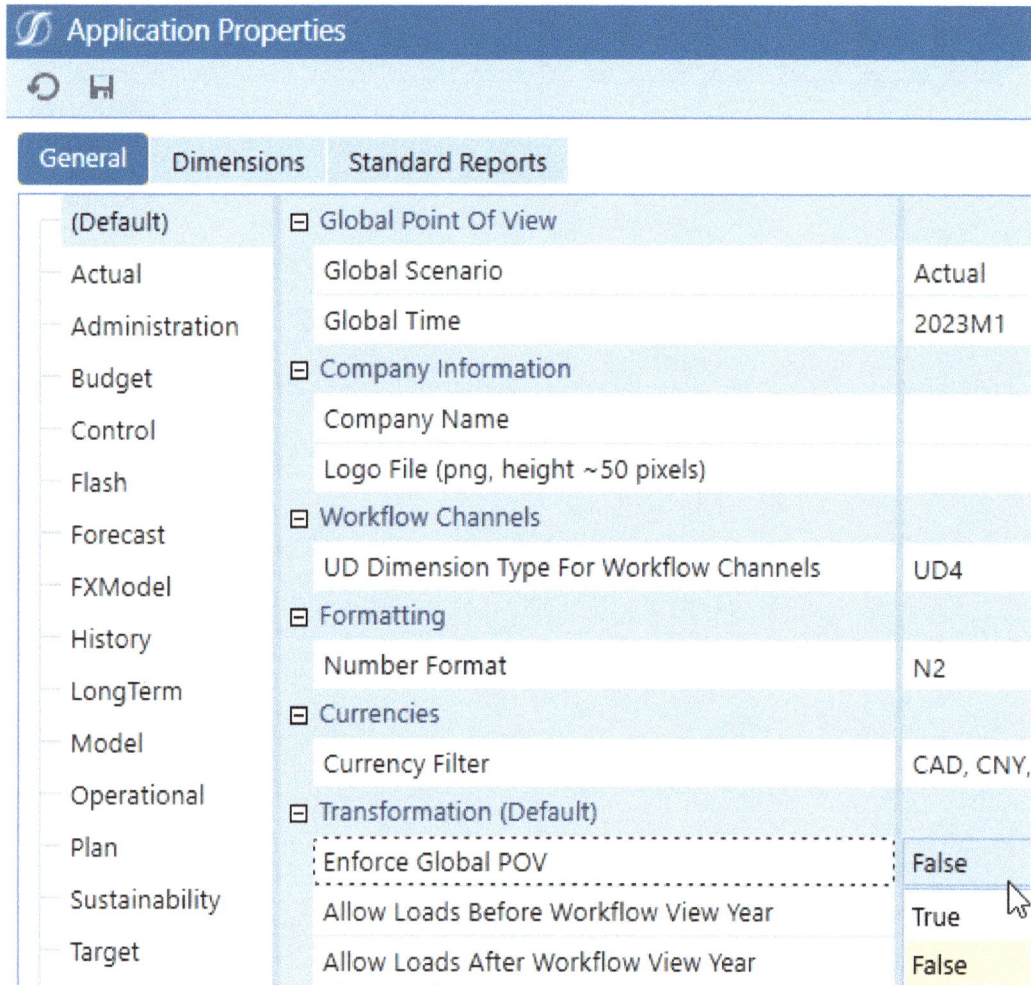

Figure 3.5

Furthermore, the administrator can differentiate whether to enforce the Global POV by Scenario Type. In Figure 3.6, on the Administration Scenario Type, notice that the options are (Default), True, and False. The (Default) setting means that the given Scenario Type will use the selection from Default.

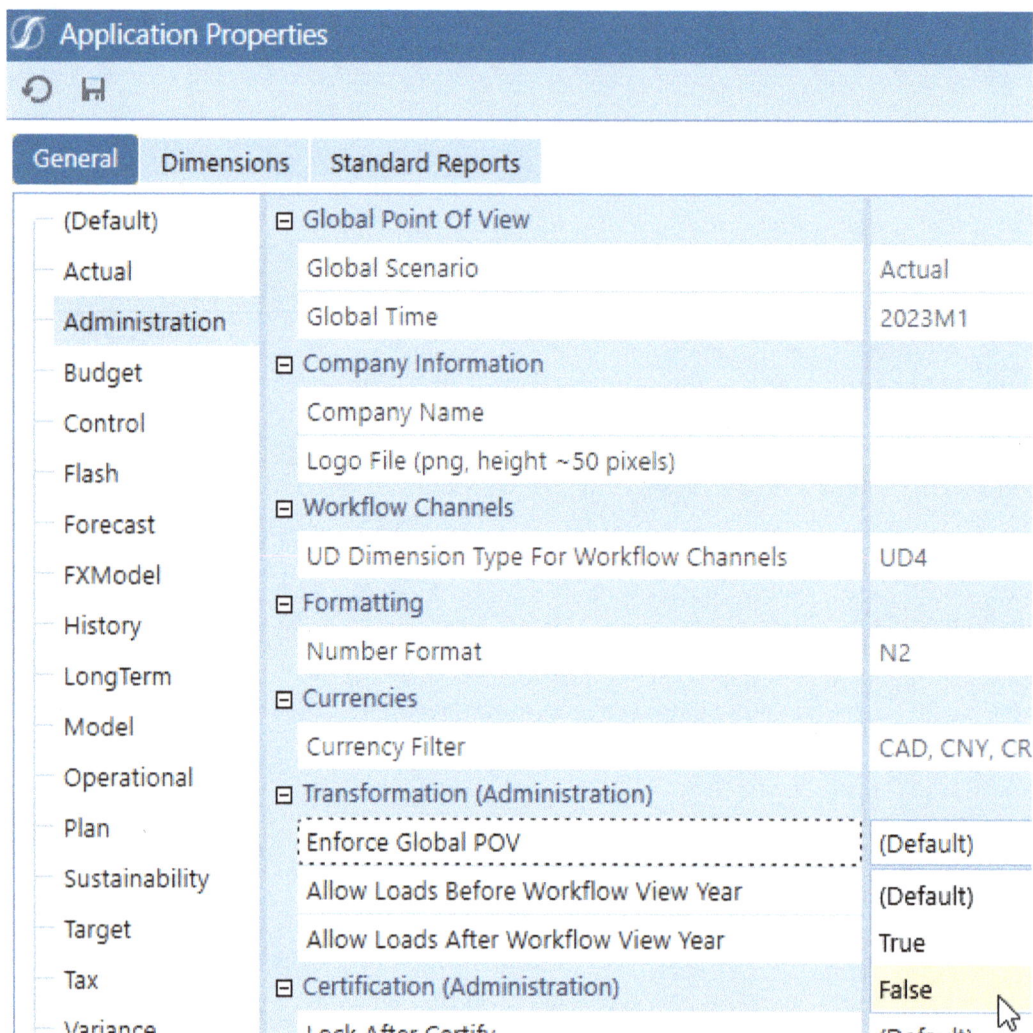

Figure 3.6

If the Enforce Global POV is set to True, this will enforce the current Global Scenario and Time for *all* users. This will specifically impact the Import workflow steps since a True setting will use the Global Time and Global Scenario *instead of* the Workflow Time and Workflow Scenario. In other words, if the user decides to load to a period that is not the Global Time, the import step will load to whatever the Global Scenario and Global Time is, which could be confusing to the end-user (assuming the user was attempting to load to a *different* period).

For example, in my very simple case, I have Global Point of View set to 2023M1 and Enforce Global POV as True.

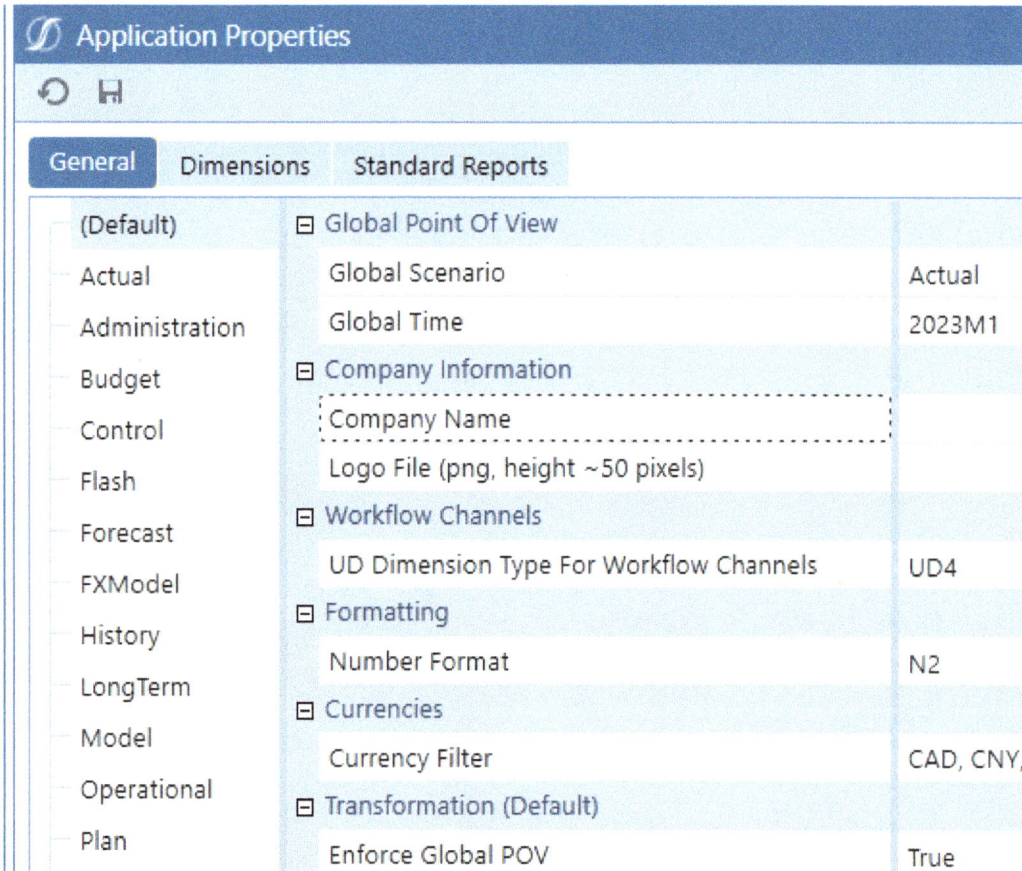

Figure 3.7

If I go to any import step that is *not* on 2023M1 (in this example, 2019M1) and attempt to load a file, I will receive a 'success' message, but nothing will actually show up in the Source Intersections pane for my user's workflow period of 2019M1 (Figure 3.8).

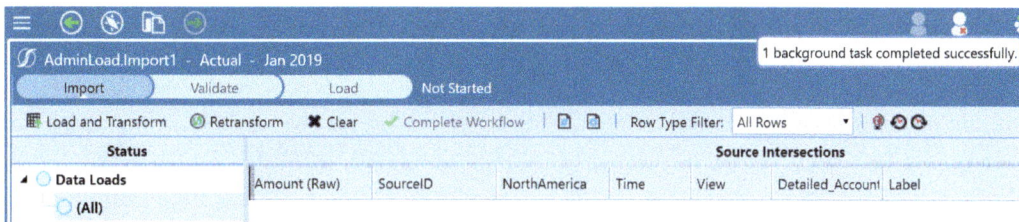

Figure 3.8

But if I go back to 2023M1, I will see my data loaded there.

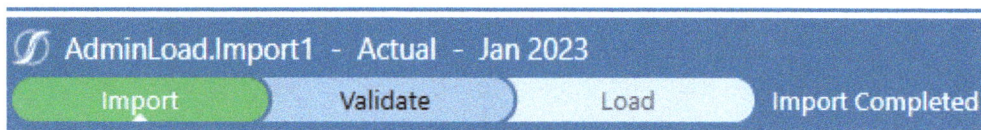

Figure 3.9

However, if Enforce Global POV is set to False, users will continue to use the Workflow POV.

Transformation

In the Transformation section, you will find the Enforce Global POV, Allow Loads Before Workflow View Year, and Allow Loads After Workflow View Year settings.

The Workflow View Year, as the title suggests, refers to the year portion of your Workflow POV.

Figure 3.10

If Allow Loads Before Workflow View Year is set to True, this will allow data loading to time periods before the current workflow year. If this is set to False, data cannot be imported to time periods before the current workflow year. For example, if you had a data file with multiple years that you would like to load prior to the selected workflow year, you may want to update this setting to True.

If Allow Loads After Workflow View Year is set to True, this will allow data loading to time periods after the current workflow year. If False, data cannot be imported to time periods after the current workflow year. For example, if you had a data file with multiple years that you would like to load after the selected workflow year, you may want to update this setting to True.

These settings are also differentiable by Scenario Type. For a specific Scenario Type, the options are (Default), True, or False.

Lock After Certify

If the Lock After Certify setting is True, the system will automatically lock workflow steps that have been certified.

The risk with having Lock After Certify set as True is that administrators may involuntarily participate during the close more often because they have to unlock workflows. This could have a larger impact if users are located around the world and the administrator is in a different time zone. Generally, if this setting is desired, the recommendation is to enable the setting after a few months, as this gives users a chance to learn the process and prevent premature certification.

We need to cover the concept of locking here. Not only does a lock prevent the user from entering inputs directly into the application interface, but it also prevents users from entering inputs via Excel (whether Cube Views into Excel or `XFSubmitCell` formulas).

> **Note:** Lock After Certify works particularly well for workflow steps that have **entity assignments**. However, suppose you have workflow steps without entity assignments, and you need to lock those intersections by Data Unit as well. In that case, this setting will *not* prevent input to the items within those Workflow Profiles. (Remember, you can only assign one entity to one Workflow Input Profile.)

Common Updates

Here are some of the most common updates we have seen administrators handle:

1. Expanding Application Start and End Years.

2. Updating descriptions for UDs.

3. Updating default logos or standardizing the formatting on PDF exports.

4. Adding currencies.

5. Enabling workflow channels.

Expanding Application Start and End Years

To expand the application's start and end years, navigate to the Dimensions tab of Application Properties. The Time Dimension section will have Start Year and End Year.

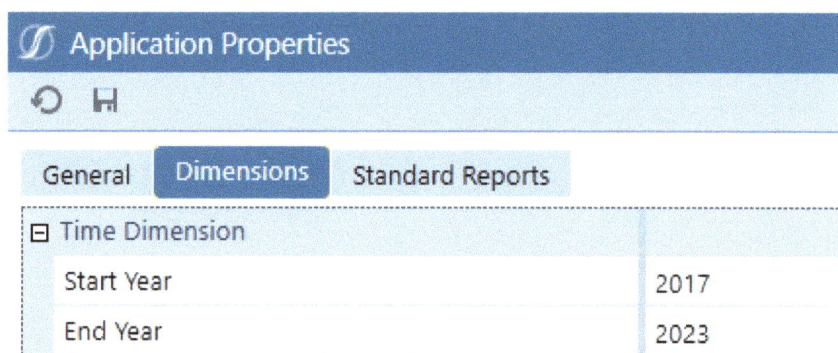

Figure 3.11

Limiting the time ranges a user can select for the Time dimension can be particularly useful. For example, let's say you have had OneStream since 2010, and – as it is now 2024 – the 2010-2018 data does not really 'matter' to users as they are not referenced in reports. Updating the Start Year to 2019 sets accessible time members to 2019 onwards for user reporting. OneStream maintains the data for the years before 2019 if they have already been loaded, of course.

Updating UD Descriptions

UD dimensions can be updated with custom descriptions. The descriptions will display as part of tooltips and are viewable in the POV, dimension library, Cube View Member Filters, drill down dimension headers, and the Excel add-in/Spreadsheet.

Below is an example of UD1-UD3 having descriptions, while UD5-UD8 do not.

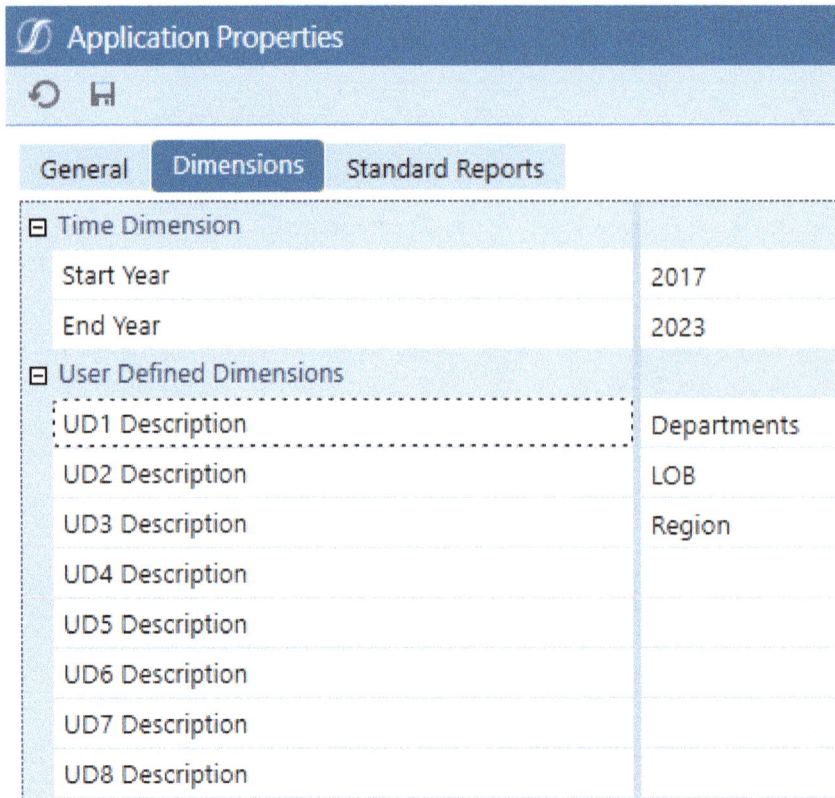

Figure 3.12

Below is an example of what the UD1-UD3 looks like to the user on the Excel add-in.

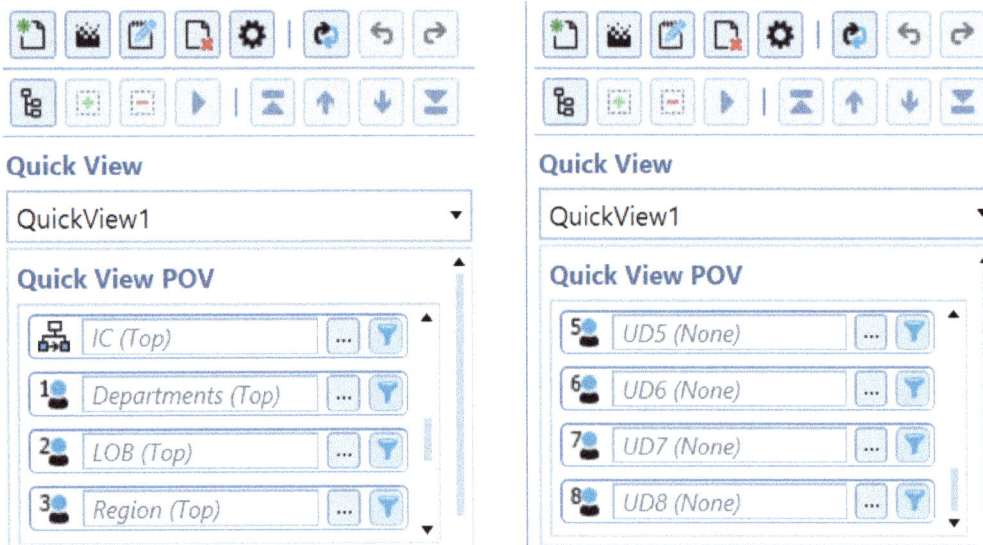

Figure 3.13

Updating Standard Logos or Standardizing Format

You can only add logo files on the `Default` Scenario Type under the Company Information section; there is only one logo for all reports.

In my example, I am using GolfStream, where I have the logo saved as `GolfSTream_GetBackToTheGreen_small.png`.

Figure 3.14

In my `Default` scenario, I have updated Company Name and the Logo File accordingly, as shown in Figure 3.15.

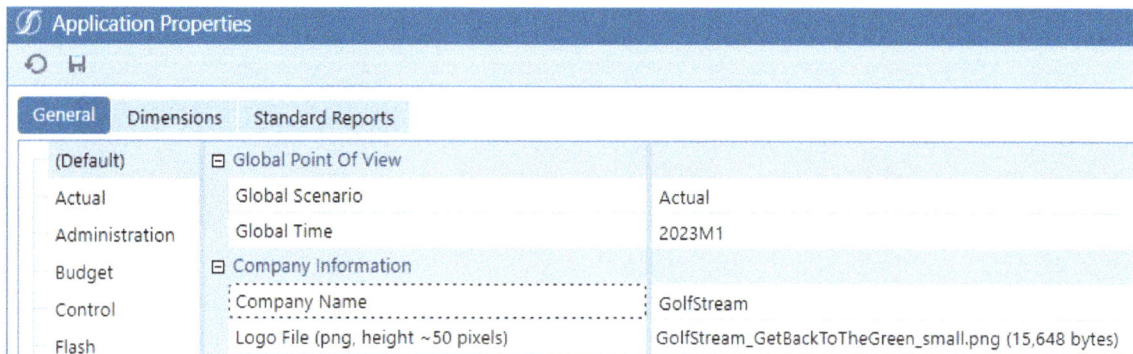

Figure 3.15

Now, when I run any Cube View in the application and export it as a PDF, the logo will be in the top left. Furthermore, there is a Standard Reports tab, which can be used to standardize the formatting for PDF exports. This can be found in Application Properties on Standard Reports (Figure 3.16).

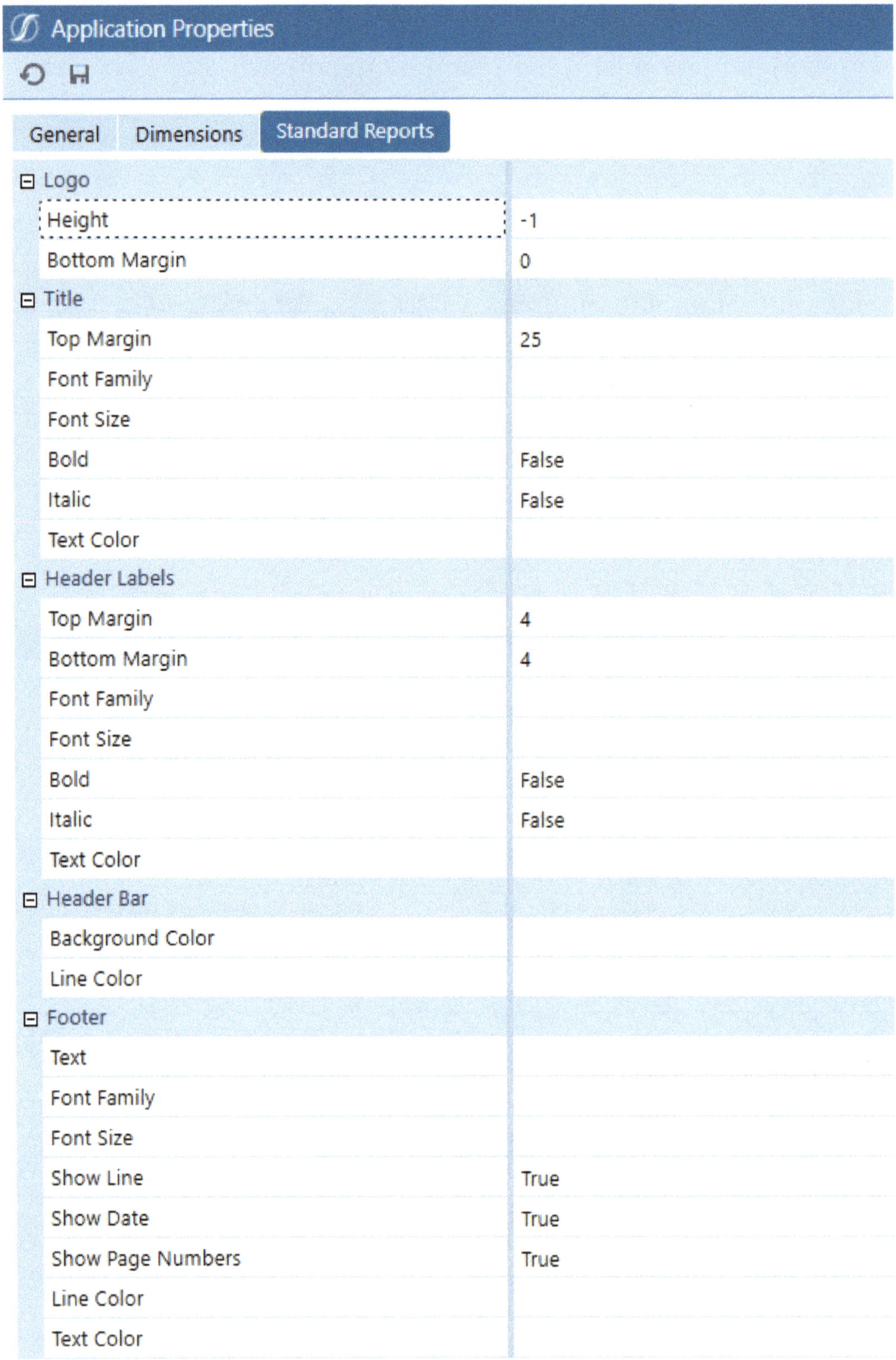

Application Properties	
↺ 💾	

General	Dimensions	**Standard Reports**

⊟ Logo	
Height	-1
Bottom Margin	0
⊟ Title	
Top Margin	25
Font Family	
Font Size	
Bold	False
Italic	False
Text Color	
⊟ Header Labels	
Top Margin	4
Bottom Margin	4
Font Family	
Font Size	
Bold	False
Italic	False
Text Color	
⊟ Header Bar	
Background Color	
Line Color	
⊟ Footer	
Text	
Font Family	
Font Size	
Show Line	True
Show Date	True
Show Page Numbers	True
Line Color	
Text Color	

Figure 3.16

If I change the Title Text Color to BlueViolet (as per Figure 3.17), subsequent reports will have the title as Blue Violet, as we see in Figure 3.18.

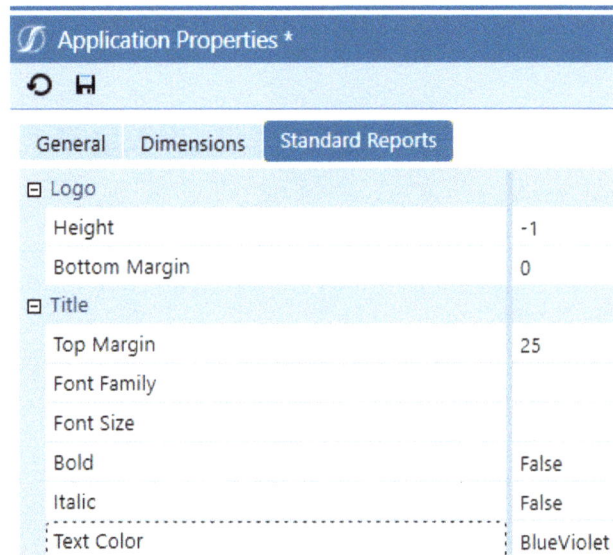

Figure 3.17

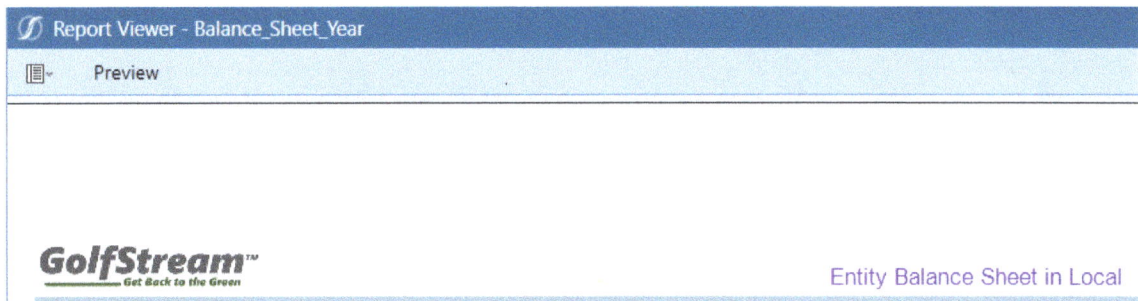

Figure 3.18

Adding a Currency

If your company has companies that utilize various currencies, you can add a currency through Application Properties on the General tab.

You can only add currencies on the Default Scenario Type under Currencies. The system automatically makes the other Scenario Types' Currency Filter non-editable while displaying the list of currencies that was selected from the Default Scenario Type.

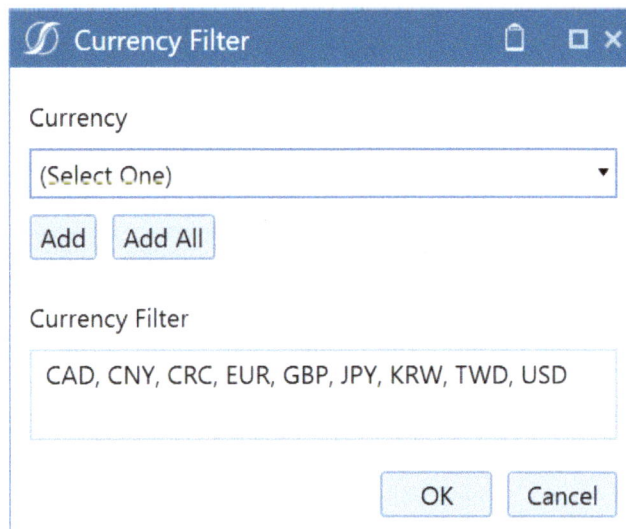

Figure 3.19

After adding these currencies, you can select from the drop-down for Currency on the base entity, as presented in Figure 3.20.

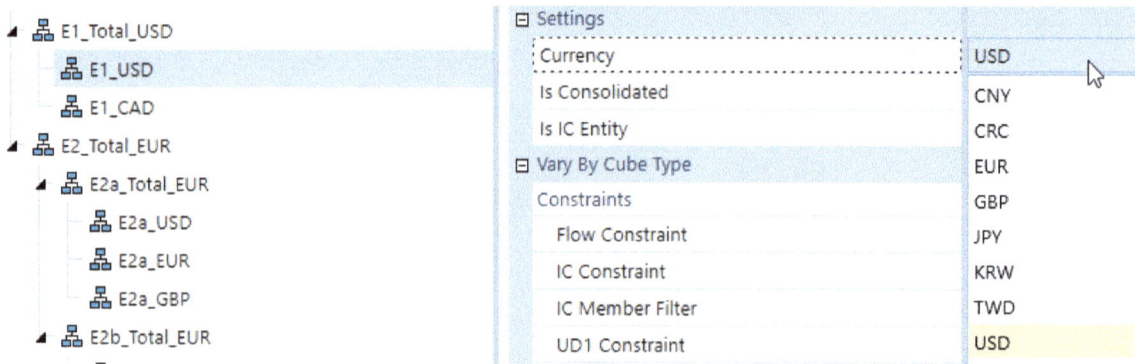

Figure 3.20

You will also see the currencies on the out-of-the-box FX Rates grid, as per Figure 3.21.

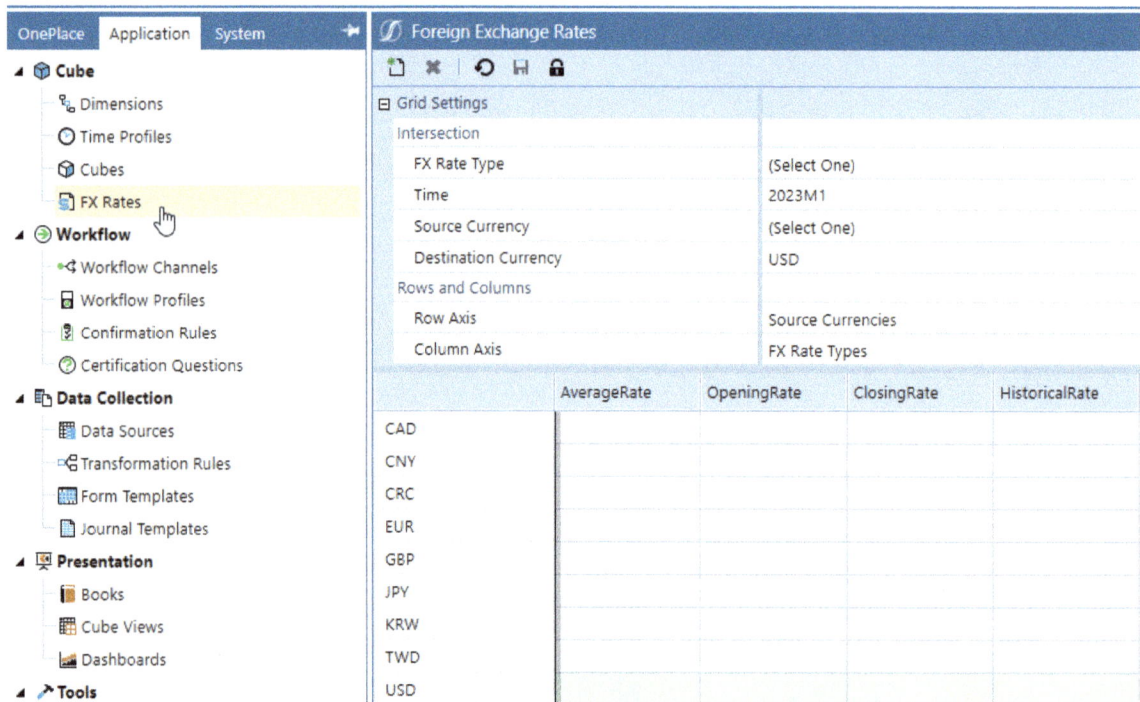

Figure 3.21

The list of currencies will also be part of the Flow dimension drop-down for Flow members with Flow Processing Type as Is Alternative Input Currency or Is Alternate Input Currency for All Accounts. Notice in Figure 3.22 that the drop-down for Alternate Input Currency is the list from Figure 3.19.

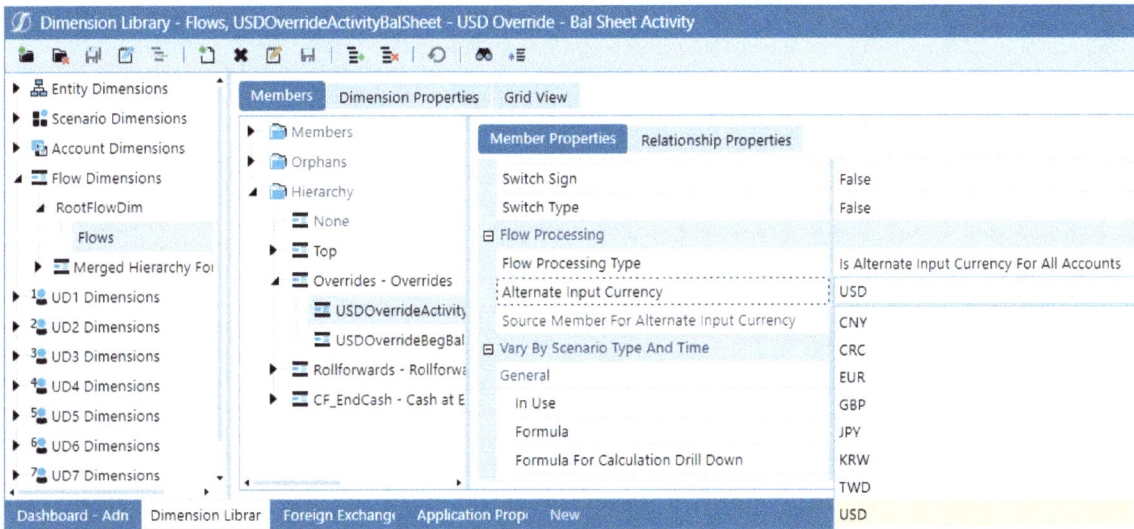

Figure 3.22

Enabling Workflow Channels

If your company chooses to use workflow channels based on UD, this is where you enable a UD workflow channel. Remember, you can only choose one UD. Refer to the workflow section of this book for further details on workflow channels.

If a specific UD dimension is not chosen – in other words (Not Used) is selected – this means that the application will use Account for workflow channels.

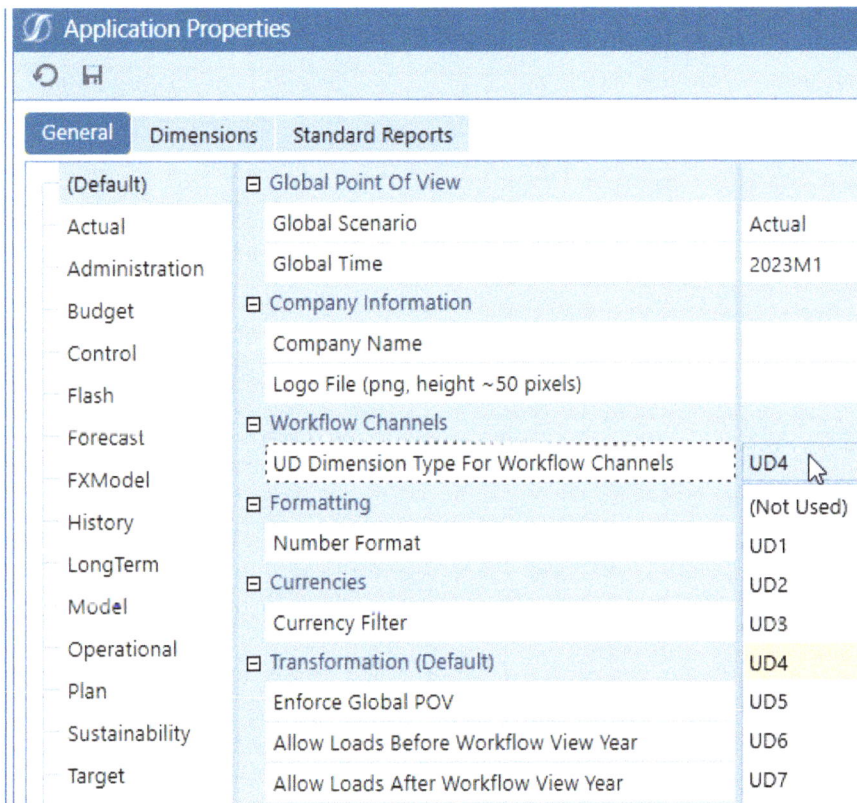

Figure 3.23

Conclusion

This short chapter covered common cases within Application Properties, including the use of Global POVs, application start and end dates, and workflow channels.

We also covered properties that can vary by Scenario Type (e.g., Enforce Global POV, Allow Loads Before Workflow Year, Allow Loads After Workflow Year, Lock After Certify), plus properties that can only be set on the default Scenario Type, which impact all Scenario Types (e.g., Global POV, calendar range, UD descriptions, standard logos, currency, workflow channels).

If you come across a setting on Application Properties that was not covered in this chapter and you suspect that you need to update it – but want to double-check how this setting is being used – refer to the OneStream Design and Reference Guide, as well as other materials covered in Chapter 1 of this book.

4

Metadata Management

In OneStream, metadata configuration refers to the configuration of your dimensions and members. It's hard to overstate how important metadata design is – it determines what intersections are valid for storage in your cube and is the core of your OneStream application. Well-designed metadata structures ensure data quality and make everything – from maintenance to reporting – simpler and more intuitive.

That said, this book is intended primarily for admins maintaining existing applications rather than consultants and partners handling the initial build. If you'd like to read more on what constitutes good metadata design, and how to build your extensibility from scratch, refer to the OneStream Foundation Handbook, specifically Chapter 3 on Design.

If you're reading this chapter, your metadata structures are more than likely already in place and (hopefully) relatively stable. So, this chapter serves as a reference for admins updating or adding new metadata members, creating new member structures, or modifying cube settings. Some of the main topics we discuss are:

1. Data Units and the importance of extensibility.

2. How different settings interact.

3. Common mistakes when configuring members.

4. Process recommendations and case studies on how to handle metadata updates.

Data Units and the Importance of Extensibility

Just because the design is done, you can still make mistakes with metadata changes that impact application performance. This section serves as a reminder of the important foundational topics to consider while maintaining your application (taken largely from the OneStream Foundation Handbook).

Data Unit Definition

You often hear the term "in-memory," but what does it mean, and why is it important? Analytic applications are tasked with processing and enriching large volumes of source data with the expectation the data will be turned into information that can quickly and reliably be analyzed by users. The OneStream financial analytic engine delivers information to users by keeping blocks of data (Data Units) in-memory and making them available – through fast access – to end users.

Here are the dimensions behind a Data Unit cube. These dimensions define each Data Unit.

- Cube

- Entity

- Parent

- Consolidation

- Scenario

- Time

These six dimensions *define* the Data Unit; the other twelve dimensions are *part of* the data unit.

The Data Unit consists of the stored data records for the above combination of dimensional intersections. Only base records of the 12 dimensions are stored in the database. Parent members of dimensions within the Data Unit are calculated only in-memory, and do not exist in the database. This is not necessarily true for any dimension outside the Data Unit. For example, the entity parent's data is stored. When you reference any combination of these dimensions, a "Data Unit" is created in the server's memory. The server calculates parent members of Account, IC, Flow, and User-Defined – dynamically – and generates a small cube of this data. The greater the size of the Data Unit, the larger the strain placed on the system.

The combination of these six values represents a storage key/cluster for a group of related data cells. The best way to visualize this is to think of how it would be presented in Excel. The storage cluster represents the Excel file name or bucket (Cube, Entity, Parent, Consolidation, Scenario, and Time), and each row of the spreadsheet contains the Data Unit's stored detailed intersections (View, Account, Flow, Origin, IC, UD1-8).

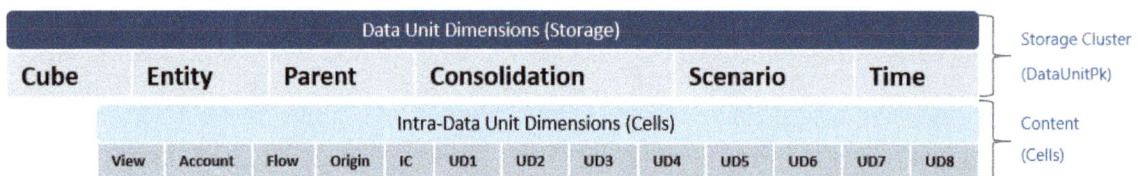

Figure 4.1

Notice here the dimensions that define the Data Unit are what we would expect to be **dense dimensions**. Dense dimensions are populated at, or close to, 100%. We would expect one would load data to every entity or close to it. The dimensions that are part of the Data Unit are typically what we would call **sparse dimensions**. Not only are they not all commonly used for every intersection, but combinations of these dimensions create gaps. You could use all the products for the Inventory Account, but products for the Deferred Tax Asset do not make sense.

Data Unit performance is driven by populated intersections, not intersections. If you have five billion combinations and only load a few thousand base records, the performance should be extremely fast.

> **Note:** Since the Entity defines the data unit, you need to consider dimension changes by Entity.

Stored versus Derived Data

In-memory data represents the cells of information that users have imported, inputted, and/or calculated as stored information. As this stored information is changed and written to the relational database store, the in-memory version of the data is refreshed and synchronized across all application servers that are in use to deliver information to the users who are working with the data.

It is very important to understand that the stored data that is loaded into memory only represents a fraction of the potential cells that the OneStream financial analytic engine can deliver to the end user. This means that many of the cells that a user requests are derived at the time they are requested using **Calc-On-The-Fly-Aggregation**. This is a critical concept that must be understood when designing OneStream analytic applications. Without the combination of in-memory data – combined with Calc-On-The-Fly-Aggregation – it would be impossible for a financial analytic application to perform.

Multi-dimensional applications are based on combinations of metadata structures called dimensions. The combination of dimensions is referred to as a cube. The potential number of cells in any given cube is the factorial of all the members in each dimension (200 Entities * 1,000 Accounts * 100 Cost Centers = 20 million cells).

As you can see, factorial math is a powerful force, and a tiny three-dimensional model can quickly reach 20 million cells. A standard cube in OneStream contains 18 dimensions, which means even a cube with a small number of members in each dimension will potentially reach billions or trillions of cells. With this potential volume of data, it is not possible to store all combinations of cells and achieve the performance levels that users expect from an analytic application. Consequently, the OneStream financial analytic engine uses a combination of stored and in-memory cells to deliver information.

Usage

With this understanding of the Data Unit storage key and content structure, we can gain some insight into how the OneStream in-memory analytic engine works with blocks of data (Data Units). Many of us have encountered a massive spreadsheet (e.g., large .xlsx files with formulas and more than a million rows in the spreadsheet), and just opening the spreadsheet on a local computer takes a long time. In addition, you typically see formulas and recalculations slow down dramatically. A typical OneStream application contains thousands of Data Units that must be managed (Create, Update, Delete, Read) within the computational resource constraints of the servers running the application and the physics boundaries of factorial math.

The more dimensions that are used within a OneStream application, the easier it is to create large Data Units when parents are consolidated or aggregated. Consider that when this Data Unit is loaded into memory to create the multi-dimensional view of the data, there is a tremendous amount of processing that needs to happen. When we look at data in a report, we can see that it uses 'by' dimensions. Accounts 'by' Cost Center 'by' Location 'by' and so on... Each of those subtotals by each dimension is calculated using a complex proprietary process. Each added dimension and increase of data volume yields a model that will impact performance.

Another concern is that one of the easiest ways to create a data explosion that results in large parent Data Units is to create a model that has a content cell dimension (intra-Data Unit dimension) that is unique to the entity at the base level. For example, if a customer dimension is used, and customers are unique for each entity in the Data Unit storage key, then each parent entity that is consolidated or aggregated will have all unique customer data below the parent in its Data Unit. This type of design always results in large Data Units and usually means that the wrong dimension is being used as the entity that controls the storage block.

Data Unit Explosion

Multi-dimensional analytic models are based on the combinations of member values in structures called dimensions. In OneStream, these structures are called cubes and cubes contain many Data Units which hold the detailed cells that result from the intersection of members in the dimensions that belong to the cube. (Think of cubes as an outline structure that defines the dimension structures to combine).

What is Data Unit explosion, and why should a OneStream administrator care about this phenomenon? Data Unit explosion describes a situation where a high number of potential cells in a cube become populated. You are thinking to yourself, the main reason that we are creating a cube is to fill it with data. However, you must always be respectful of the power of factorial math. As soon as you design a cube that utilizes multiple members in two or three customer dimensions, the potential number of cell combinations that could contain data within a given Data Unit will easily hit the billions, and it is not uncommon to see potential cell counts in the trillions.

Example: Simple Five Dimension Cube

1. 100 Accounts
2. 100 Flow Members
3. 100 UD1 Members
4. 100 UD2 Members
5. 100 UD3 Members

10 billion Potential Cells Per Data Unit (*Factorial: 100 x 100 x 100 x 100 x 100*)

The simple example above demonstrates how easy it is to create a substantial number of potential cells in each Data Unit. This example only combines five dimensions with 100 members each, and the potential cell count for each Data Unit in the cube is ten billion cells.

Also, remember that each cube holds many Data Units, so the overall model always hits trillions of potential cells when you add up all the potential cells across all the Data Units. Hopefully, this tiny cube structure demonstrates just how quickly potential cells add up because of factorial math.

Having many potential cells is not a problem; in fact, every practical OneStream model has many potential cells in each Data Unit. The OneStream analytic engine is built to handle very large models, and it is very efficient at finding the cells within a model that have data. The ratio of cells that have data to potential cells in the Data Unit is used to calculate the **data density ratio** (stored cells / potential cells). In most cases, the ratio of cells containing data to potential cells is low. Because of this fact, the OneStream engine must be exceptionally good at finding cells that have data with a vast population of potential cells (**spare data filtering**).

On the other hand, Data Unit explosion refers to the situation where many potential cells are loaded with data. This always results in a model performance problem. Why? Is the OneStream engine not able to scale? The answer is physics limitations. OneStream supports the largest possible model configurations in the analytic software market (18 dimensions per Data Unit), but at a certain point, data cell volume will overcome the performance capabilities of the fastest multi-thread CPUs and algorithms. Therefore, it is important to understand how model design and data density impact the performance of your design.

Now that we have a foundational understanding of Data Unit explosion, let us examine the root causes of this phenomenon. There are three primary causes of Data Unit explosion.

1. An incorrect Dimension selected as the Entity dimension, resulting in too many dimension combinations within the intra-dimension members. This situation usually results in many potential cells in a single Data Unit that is then directly loaded from a source system, which results in excessive data cell population and poor performance.

   An example might be putting a dense dimension – like Product – in the Entity dimension.

2. **Formula spray** is another cause of data explosion. This situation occurs when a rule writer erroneously creates a looping construct that iterates many potential cells in one or more Data Units and populates the cells with data, creating high data density. This type of data explosion is kept to a minimum by the OneStream engine due to formula expression constraints, but it is still a potential problem in situations where large allocation rules are being used. Allocation rules tend to spray data to many cells; in many circumstances, they spray insignificant "Near Zero" values to many cells.

   Please take the time to define all dimensions in rules, as undefined dimensions could write to all members.

3. **Entity-To-UDx Distinct** relationships are another cause of data explosion at parent Data Units. If any UD member is the only value for a single base entity, then there is no collapsing of data rows during the consolidation/aggregation process. This means that each row of a base entity that is added to a parent will become a unique row in the parent. A

typical example of data explosion caused by Entity-To-UDx distinct relationships is found when a company uses different cost centers for each legal entity. This situation results in all parent entities containing all cost center combinations of all base members below the parent. This creates massive Data Units at the parent level and should be avoided by creating common UDx members that represent a summary of the distinct items (**grouping**). The distinct UDx members should be moved to an Entity dimension and a separate model should be built to update and analyze the detail items. (This is the advantage of OneStream's shared metadata / multi-model capabilities.) The details can then be pulled into the primary cube at the summary level, thereby preventing data explosion.

This is created when extensibility is not configured correctly.

Adding a Dimension

The first thing to check is whether the dimension already exists someplace. It is always recommended to try to avoid having users select multiple dimensions for the same dimension type. In other words, one conceptual dimension to one dimension type.

I, generally, would not put rollforwards in User-Defined 1, and Cash Flow movements in User-Defined 2. Both are rollforward adjustments but for different accounts and are related. I would think carefully about having adjustments broken out in one dimension, and a data source in another. Firstly, not only can this confuse the end-users, but it can make reporting more difficult. It undermines the benefit of extensible dimensions. You could create a relationship between dimension types and use them in other ways for future applications.

Another example of this is when people want to put accounting function as the Account dimension and break accounts across Account and User-Defined (UD), by placing operating expense accounts in the User-Defined dimension. I'll define function here to be like a department; for example, Accounting, Sales, Legal, etc. Accounts in this example are natural accounts, like Salary, Bonus, etc. The other choice is to put all of the natural accounts in the Account dimension, and function in the User-Defined dimension. The first thing to understand is that both options provide the exact same detail. There is no benefit for either with respect to the level of detail.

So, why would I choose one over the other? There are some questions to ask. What does the client currently use? Do they only use function? If this is the driver of reporting – and the users mostly expect it – then having the dimensions split won't confuse the end-users, just the opposite. Another question to ask here is whether functional income statement is used for other scenarios. If end-users never break out expenses for Budget and Forecast beyond that function, asking them to add a natural account might be a non-starter. The point here is that while there is no clear right or wrong, there are guiding principles that will help you understand the right choice for any design.

Once you have the dimensions defined, what cube should you assign them to? Your application, if designed properly, should give you a guide for where to add it. Below is a good example of what an application might look like. Do the dimensions only appear where needed? Child cubes should have more detail that is sparse; parent cubes have denser, smaller dimensions.

Dimensions	Cube 1 (Financial Data)	Cube 2 (Planning)	Cube 3 (Subsidiary)
Time Periods	X	X	X
Years	X	X	X
Scenarios	X	X	X
Flow	X	X	X
Accounts	IFRS	Only salary-relevant	Mgt COA
Entities	X	X	X

Dimensions	Cube 1 (Financial Data)	Cube 2 (Planning)	Cube 3 (Subsidiary)
UD1 Products	-	X	-
UD2 Projects	-	-	X

Figure 4.2 (from the OneStream Foundation Handbook, page 64)

Cube Options

So, let's look at the cubes. Assuming you're the administrator of an existing application and are tasked with adding a cube for a specific business process, you have a number of options. Each has advantages and disadvantages to your design.

Paired Cubes

Paired cubes are combinations of cubes that allow for some special situations. For each cube, there will be a second dimension that has its hierarchy but uses the base members of the first Entity dimension as its base members. For each cube in the original design, you would create two cubes. All dimensions must be the same except for the Entity dimension. One cube has the base Entity's dimension; the second has the Hierarchy dimension. Then the cubes must be linked, by making the cube with all base entities the child of the other. This effectively creates a base cube with all entities for its parent. Users would only ever be in the parent cube, so they do not see all entities. While this will not remove the need to copy the data, all data could be copied by a data management job rule. The linking of cubes must then be done by rules.

Specialty Cubes

Specialty cubes are basically monolithic cubes but are much more limited in purpose. They would be used as administrator cubes (drivers cubes, overrides, or equity control) or specialty apps (process control). The benefit of putting these cubes as standalone is simplicity of security. They can easily be separated from the rest of the application.

Some Other Cube Design Considerations

You might ask, 'How many cubes can I have? This seems like a lot.' Having more cubes will not slow the application. You should not worry about adding cubes. Remember to think of the process as the end-user. A high number of cubes will mean more maintenance, but it should not be a deterrent. The gains in performance – while hard to estimate – will justify the needed support.

Cube Integration

Often, you will have to move data between the applications. Fortunately, OneStream gives us some great options. You will have the ability to connect the cubes by creating **linked cubes** via the Entity dimension. Conversely, you could use rules to copy data. You can even update the Workflow to pull data from one cube to another using rules. Then you can drill on the data by using the formula for calculation drill down to specify how a user can drill. The rule is simple, too. All of this is covered in the Rules chapter of the OneStream Foundation Handbook.

You can also use OneStream as a data source. Why would you want to do that? Because you could summarize or remap data and allow people to drill from one cube to another with the benefit of the mapping. If data is being transformed, it would be helpful for users to see this in the system. Since it is how other data sources are mapped, it can be a great way for the user to copy the data, as they will be familiar with it.

You need to be careful if you create too many copies of the data. This is important to understand… *cubes can reference other cubes*. You do not want to copy data unnecessarily. Also, copying data creates timing differences. By using a rule to copy at a parent level, and drilling to the detail in another cube, data synchronization will be faster, and you have mitigated the timing difference.

When Should I Use Extensibility? ALWAYS

All applications should be built using extensibility, or at the very least, you should have a particularly good reason for not doing it. One of the biggest complaints of customers that have had the solution longer than a year or so is they wished they thought more carefully of the future. Extensibility gives you the advantage of flexibility. It also will help if you find yourself with a performance issue. Specifically, the use of multiple cubes and creating breaks in dimensions when possible. To understand why, remember what the Data Unit and a good Data Unit design is.

This benefits the client in multiple ways:

1. Performance.

2. Flexibility – the multiple cube approach gives clients the possibility to make changes to the design for new dimensions, added models, or performance changes.

The application will perform better when using extensibility. When you watch consolidation times by entity, you will see the base entities moving very quickly, and as the consolation moves up to the top, it slows down significantly. There are two primary reasons for this; first, for each child entity below a parent, the processor can use a processor thread to aggregate that data. At the base of the hierarchy are many child entities, and so many threads can be used. At the top parent, there may only be a couple of child entities, so only a couple of threads can be used. Second, the data set for parent entities is naturally denser as the data consolidates at the higher levels. By using extensibility, you can design smaller Data Units for the parent entities. This dramatically improves consolidation times.

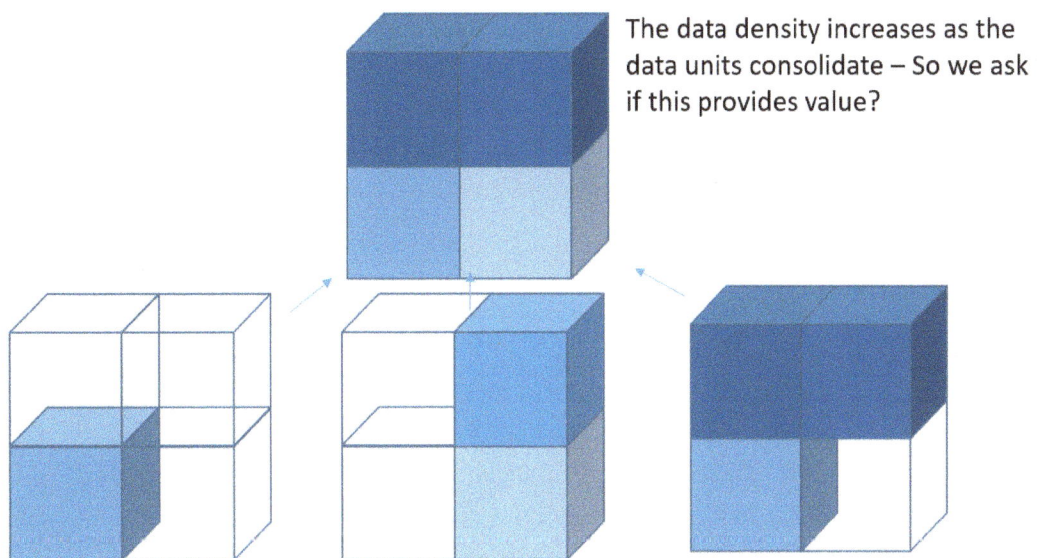

The data density increases as the data units consolidate – So we ask if this provides value?

Figure 4.3 (from the OneStream Foundation Handbook, page 66)

In the example above, each cube represents a Data Unit. The three base units are not completely full for every possible intersection. Because they do not have overlap, the Data Unit for the parent entity is completely full and would perform the slowest. So, we ask ourselves here if there is anything to be gained by aggregating the detail to that parent Data Unit. Can we get the same reports from the child Data Units?

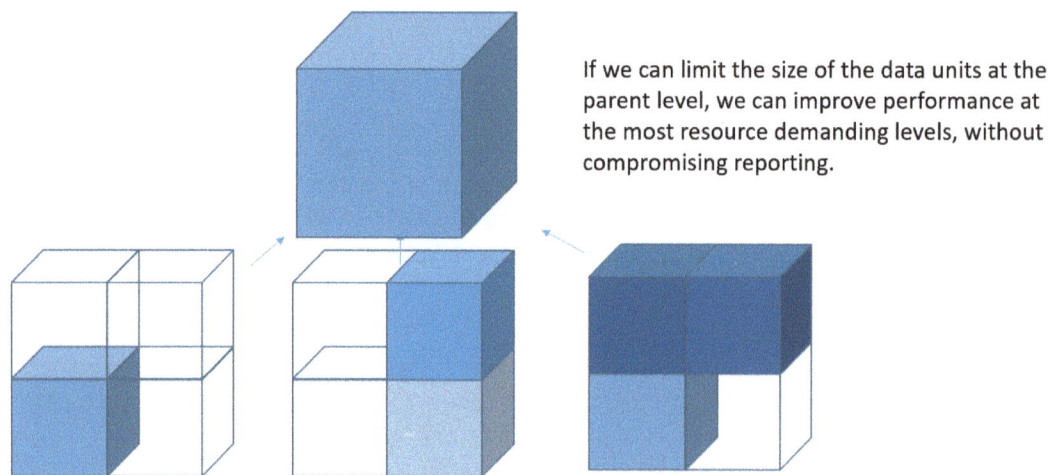

If we can limit the size of the data units at the parent level, we can improve performance at the most resource demanding levels, without compromising reporting.

Figure 4.4 (from the OneStream Foundation Handbook, page 67)

With many members in UD, there is an opportunity for invalid data cells to get populated. This could be from poorly written rules that allowed for the population of those members or allowing end-users to load zeros. By limiting the available cells by base cube, you can minimize this risk.

Typical symptoms of application design problems, or memory configuration problems, are almost certainly due to a server that is too busy swapping Data Units in and out of memory. Customers may – at times – attempt to stop or "kill" a running report by ending the execution of the client, restarting the client, and launching another report. This action, however, does not stop the server from pursuing its query but instead results in an even longer queue of activity requested of the already overloaded OneStream server.

Another reason to use extensibility is that it allows for flexibility by giving a way to add dimensions or new members more easily without impacting the entire user base. You must remember that changing the dimensions on the cube will require dropping the tables for the cube and creating a complete rebuild. This is especially problematic if the data is Actuals, as all the history of loading and Workflow sign-off could be lost. This would mean the data will likely need to be reconciled all over again, and this will require some significant re-work.

What Makes an Application Large?

People may be concerned about how big their application is getting, with all the Cubes and tables, so I want to give some context. Each option below has a cost and benefit.

- Look for Data Units that exceed 1 million records. While OneStream can handle much higher volumes than this, these are large enough to warrant inspection and review of the design.

- More cubes could create integration points but – as per our example – is likely the best design.

- More dimensions – less is better where possible, but you should consider ensuring that reporting requirements are met.

- The database structure depends on a client's reporting / analytical needs.

Some guidelines for numbers of members are as follows:

Dimension	Small Application	Medium Application	Large Application
Accounts – members	500 or less	5000 or less	20,000 or less
Accounts – levels	<5	<8	<12
Custom 1	<100	<10,000	<100,000
Custom 2	<100	<10,000	<100,000
Custom 3	<100	<10,000	<10,000
Custom 4	<100	<10,000	<10,000
Entities	<1000	<10,000	<50,000

Figure 4.5 (from the OneStream Foundation Handbook, page 64)

Configuring Cubes

This section covers how to configure cubes with your desired dimensions. OneStream is strict in what it allows you to do once data is loaded, in order to prevent accidental damage to your data integrity. Because of this, it's important to sort out metadata early in the build to avoid running into roadblocks down the line. In the following sections, we explain what behaviors are allowed and what workarounds are available if you do happen to find yourself "stuck" due to the current configuration.

Setting Default Cube Dimensions

In OneStream, your data model is defined by the metadata assigned to the cube. One way to think about metadata grouping is that members are grouped into dimensions, and dimensions are grouped together into cubes.

When assigning dimensions to a cube, you can assign different dimensions to the same cube depending on the Scenario Type. For example, you might assign `Accounts_Actual` to the Account dimension for the Actual Scenario Type and assign `Accounts_Plan` to the Account dimension for the Plan Scenario Type, as shown in the figure below. This feature of OneStream is the basis for extensibility.

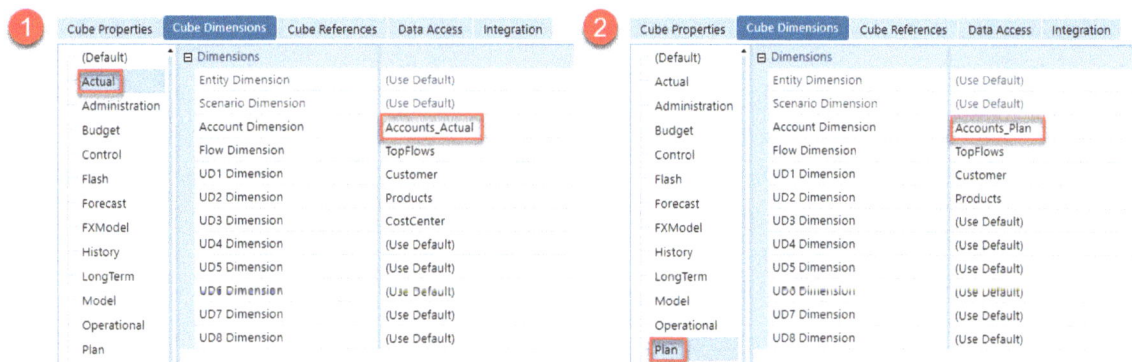

Figure 4.6

Whatever dimensions you assign to the Default Scenario Type will flow down to all other Scenario Types unless you override those dimensions explicitly on those Scenario Types. While you can technically assign any dimension on `Default`, good practice is generally to *assign only the entity and scenario and leave all other dimensions as root*, as shown below. This will give you the most flexibility in the future.

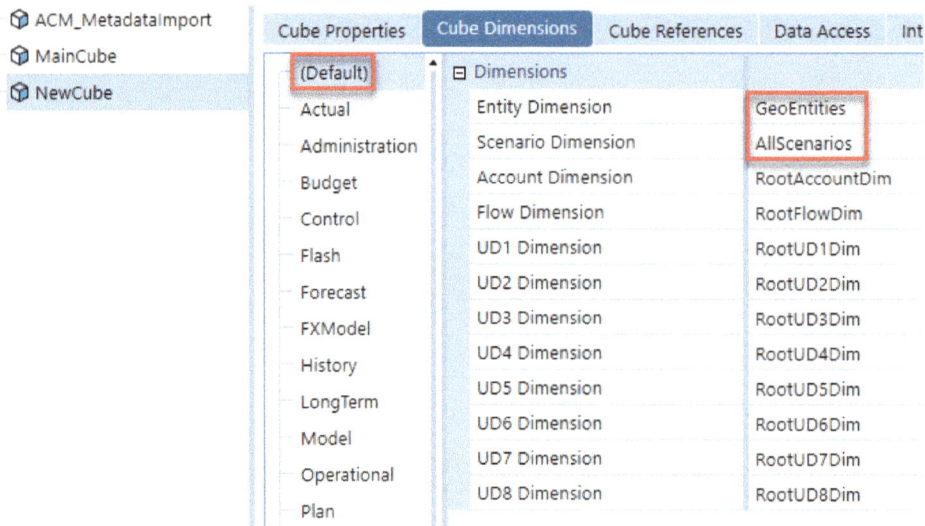

Figure 4.7

To understand why this is, let's cover what happens if you instead choose to assign a dimension to the Default Scenario Type. In this case, as soon as you load data to the cube, OneStream will no longer allow you to change a dimension on the Default Scenario Type; this is to protect you from orphaning data. For example, if I wanted to change the Entity dimension from `GeoEntities` to `LegalEntities`, OneStream would throw the error shown in Figure 4.8. To bypass this error, your only option would be to wipe all data from the cube before reassigning dimensions.

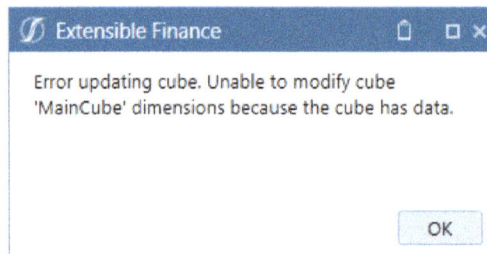

Figure 4.8

As a caveat, OneStream will technically allow you to change dimensions on the Default Scenario Type even when there is data loaded, but only if the dimension is originally root. However, this again is not recommended, as the change will then flow to all other Scenario Types.

You will have more options for adjustment in the future if you assign dimensions on specific Scenario Types instead. We'll discuss this further in the following sections.

Changing Dimensions on a Cube

Suppose you want to change the `UD3 Dimension` for the `Actual` Scenario Type from CostCenter to Function, as shown below.

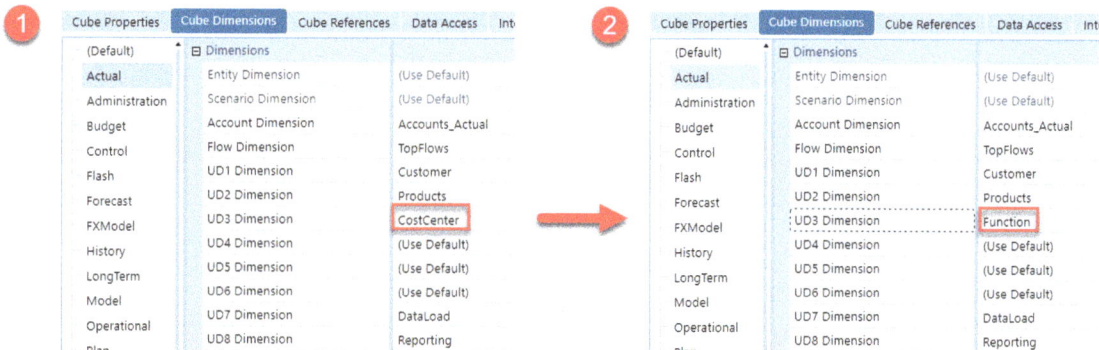

Figure 4.9

OneStream would allow this, provided there is no data in this cube stored for this specific Scenario Type. If there is data, then you will see the following error. In this case, your only option would be to wipe all data from the `Actual` Scenario Type for this cube, though you wouldn't have to clear data from any of the other Scenario Types.

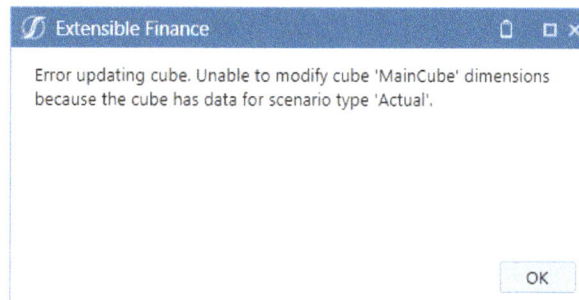

Figure 4.10

Let's cover two edge cases. First, if a dimension was originally set as (Use Default) and the Default Scenario Type was set to root, OneStream will still prevent you from updating that dimension – you would see the same error as above. Second, if you had assigned the dimension as Root on the Actual Scenario Type when first setting up the Cube, then OneStream would allow you to update the dimension even after data is loaded to a scenario with the Actual Scenario Type.

Disabling Dimensions on a Cube

To disable a dimension for a Scenario Type, navigate to the Integration tab on your cube settings, then set the Enabled field to False for the desired dimension. This is typically done when setting up a new cube. By disabling a dimension here, OneStream will not require you to specify transformations for the UD3 dimension; all data will instead be loaded to None by default.

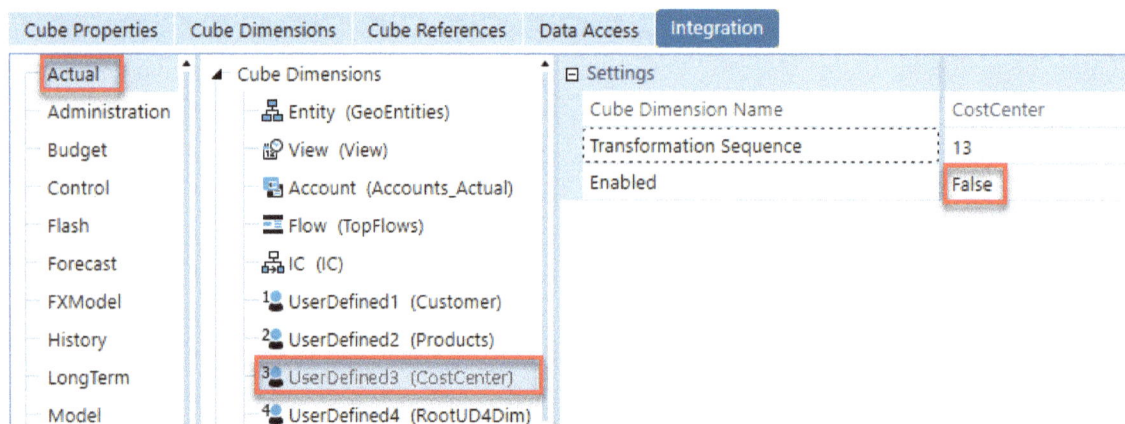

Figure 4.11

Technically, OneStream will allow you to disable a dimension on the Integration tab after data is loaded, although this is not common. However, doing so does not delete pre-existing data from these intersections, nor does this make these intersections invalid for this Scenario Type.

If you want to truly make all UD3 intersections invalid, then you will have to clear data from the Scenario Type and set the dimension to Root on the Cube Dimensions tab. There are some other methods for constraining data, but this section specifies how to handle this purely by configuring your cube.

Dimension Member Management

This section covers how to modify member metadata and lays out the restrictions you must be aware of when doing so.

Creating and Cloning Members

The Design and Reference Guide provides a detailed description of all the properties that you can set on members. However, OneStream has a lot of settings, and it can be difficult to parse which settings are the most important. With that in mind, we figured it would be helpful to compile a list of the properties you should always spot-check whenever you create or clone members. These are the properties that have the potential to create huge headaches for you when troubleshooting if set incorrectly and are easy to gloss over (especially when cloning members).

Entities

Here are the properties you'll want to review. For more details on these settings, refer to the section entitled Consolidation Settings.

- **Is Consolidated**: Check that this isn't unintentionally set to False. If it is set to False, then the values for this entity will not roll up to its parent when a consolidation is triggered, which will obviously affect the top entity total.

- **Percent Consolidation**: This setting is in the Relationship Properties tab. If this is set to 0, then even if the entity's Is Consolidated setting is set to True, the values for this entity will not roll up to its parent.

    Also, note that an entity can have different **Percent Consolidation** values for each of the hierarchies it is in, so you'll have to check this if you ever add an entity into an alternate hierarchy. It's common to copy an entity from a non-consolidating hierarchy and paste it into a consolidating hierarchy, whilst forgetting to update the Percent Consolidation to a non-zero value in the consolidating hierarchy.

Scenarios

Here are the properties you'll want to review:

- **Scenario Type**: The first thing you will want to check (as most rules in the system will key off Scenario Type). It's common to clone a scenario and leave it as the incorrect type.

- **Workflow Tracking Frequency** and **Input Frequency**: If these are set incorrectly, data cannot be loaded or entered to certain periods. For more details, check the OneStream Design and Reference Guide and Chapter 9 of this book – Constraining and Locking Data – where we cover this in more detail.

- **Number of No Input Periods Per Workflow Unit**: Technically, this doesn't constrain data from being entered outright or calculated to these periods. However, you'll want to check this setting for plan and forecast scenarios since this property is often referenced in business rules and NoInput rules to prevent data from being entered into Actual periods. (For example, you might see a NoInput rule which prevents input into the first three periods of a 3+9 forecast, with the three periods being specified in the no input periods).

- **No Data Zero View**: This controls how OneStream will derive values when it finds a period with NoData. If set incorrectly, income statement accounts might aggregate through a year incorrectly. See Chapter 7 on Data Troubleshooting for more details.

- **Clear Calculated Data During Calc**: This is True by default and should almost always be left as True. If this is set to False, data will not clear during the Data Unit Calculation Sequence, likely leading to an accumulation of stale data and a debugging nightmare.

Accounts

Here are the properties you'll want to review:

- **Account Type**: The most important setting for financial accounts. Setting this to Asset or Liability will flag the account as a balance sheet account, while setting it to Revenue or Expense will flag the account as an income statement account. This will affect how this account aggregates, translates, and more. See Section: Common Setting Interactions and Errors for more details.

  If the account is a non-stored dynamically calculated member, then this should be set to DynamicCalc. Forgetting to do this will result in the dynamic calculation not running in Cube Views, with OneStream treating it as a stored member instead.

- **Formula Type**: For stored Member Formulas, this should be set to a formula pass.

- For dynamically calculated members, this must be set to DynamicCalc (along with the account type). A common mistake is to set DynamicCalc on only one of account type or formula type but forget the other.

- **Is Consolidated:** If it is set to False, then even if a base entity has values for this account, you will not see values for this account at the parent entity. This can mislead you into thinking your consolidation isn't working.

  By default, this is set to Conditional (True if no Formula Type (default)). A common mistake is to leave this as default when making an account a stored member with an attached Member Formula. In this case, the formula would run and calculate the value at the base entity, but the value won't be consolidated up to the parent entity. If the amount should be consolidated, then this must be set manually to True.

- **Aggregation Weight**: This setting is in the Relationship Properties tab. If this is set to 0, the values for this account will not aggregate up to its parent. An account can have different aggregation weight values for each of the hierarchies it is in, so you'll have to check this if you ever add an account to an alternate hierarchy.

Flows

Here are the properties you'll want to review:

- **Switch Sign** and **Switch Type**: These settings work in conjunction with account settings. We shall discuss this further later in this chapter.

- **Formula Type**: See the description in the Accounts properties section above.

- **Is Consolidated:** See the description in the Accounts properties section above.

- **Aggregation Weight:** See the description in the Accounts properties section above.

UD Members

Here are the properties you'll want to review:

- **Formula Type**: See the description in the Accounts properties section above.

- **Is Consolidated:** See the description in the Accounts properties section above.

- **Aggregation Weight:** See the description in the Accounts properties section above.

Renaming Members

OneStream allows you to rename a member, even if data is loaded to it. In the OneStream database, records stored to that member will now reference the new name, so you lose no data by renaming members. However, a catch is that hardcoded references to the member in Cube Views, transformation rules, dashboards, and business rules will not get updated and must be updated manually.

A constraint to keep in mind is that member names must be unique within a given *dimension type*. For example, you cannot create a member named Cash in both the Accounts_Plan and Accounts_Actual dimensions since they are both Account dimensions. You could, however, create a member named Top in each of your dimension types, since there would only be one Top member for each type.

Deleting Members

OneStream does not allow you to delete members that have data loaded to them. If you attempt to do so, you'll see the following error. The only way to get around this is to clear all data from this member and then try again.

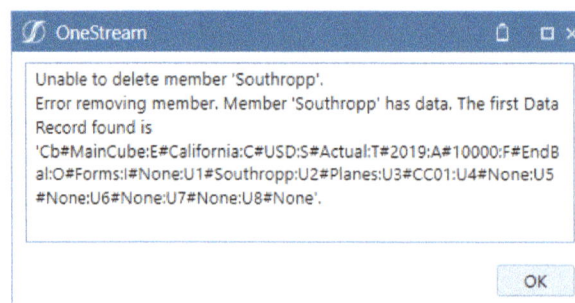

Figure 4.12

Orphaning Members

Whenever you create a member, you must specify its parent. Even if you create a member and place it in no hierarchy, OneStream, by default, will place the member as a child of the root member in a given dimension type.

If you remove all of a member's relationships so that it has no parent(s) (not even root), then that member becomes orphaned and will appear in the Orphans dropdown in a dimension.

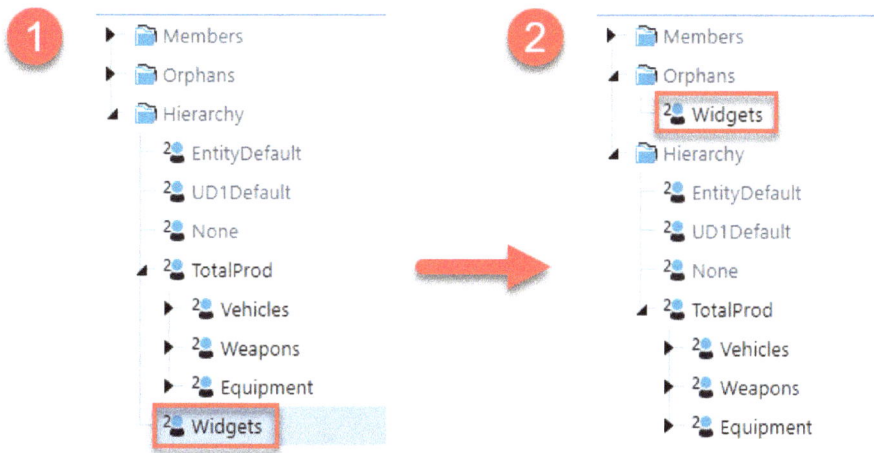

Figure 4.13

If this happens, data can still be loaded to this member, but its values will not be aggregated up to any parents. Furthermore, the member will not appear anywhere in the application. For example, if you tried to search for `Widgets` in the UD2 hierarchy, OneStream would show zero results.

Typically, members end up orphaned when metadata is loaded and relationships are unintentionally dropped. However, orphaning a member, while not recommended, can be an alternative to deleting it since this avoids clearing all of the member's data.

Moving Members Across Dimensions

OneStream does not allow you to move members between dimensions by default, nor does it allow you to create a member with the same name in a different dimension (within the same dimension type). However, there are a couple of common workarounds.

How to Move a Base Member

To move a base non-entity member, your first thought might be to delete the member and recreate it in the new dimension. However, this would require you to wipe the member's data first. If you want to retain this data, then a common workaround is to rename the member first and then create a new member. For example, suppose you want to move the `Widgets` member from `SubProducts` to `Products`.

1. Rename `Widgets` to `Widgets_Old` in the `SubProducts` dimension.

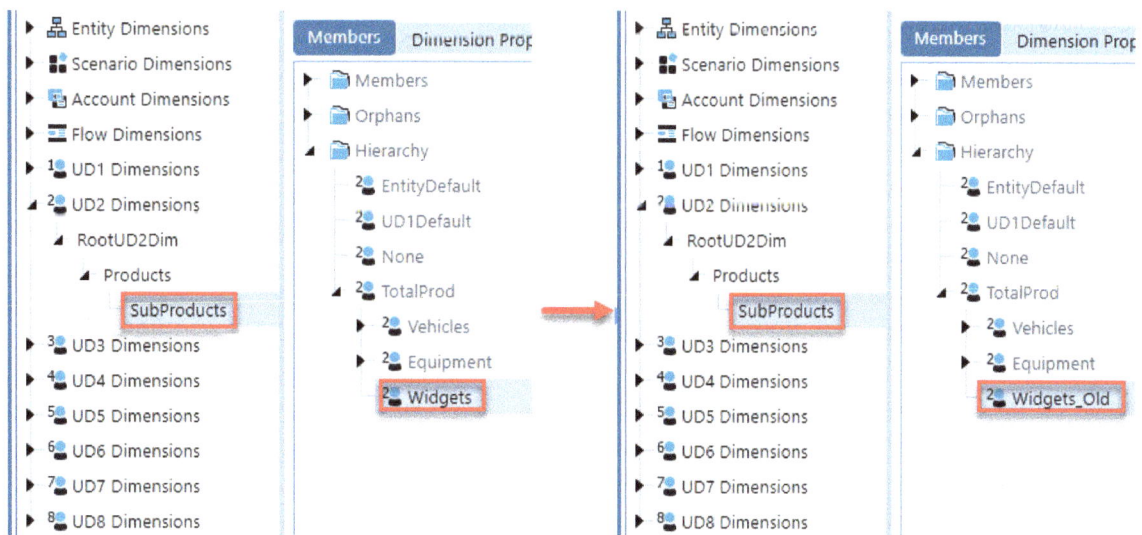

Figure 4.14

2. Create a new member named `Widgets` in the new dimension.

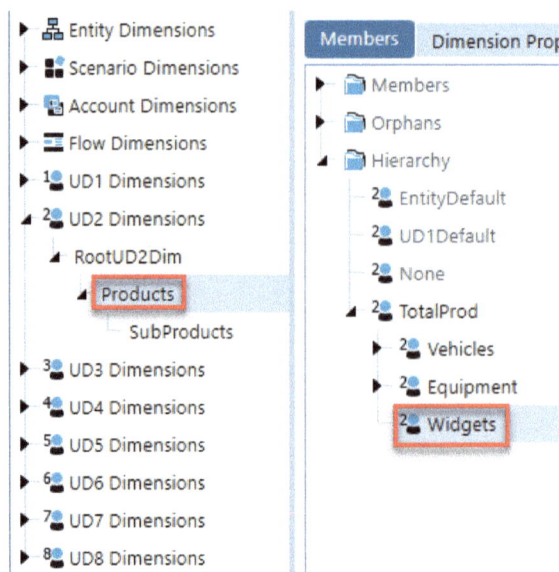

Figure 4.15

3. Create a business rule to copy data from `Widgets_Old` to `Widgets`.

4. You can then either orphan `Widgets_Old` or write an ad hoc business rule to wipe data from `Widgets_Old` before deleting it.

How to Move a Parent Member

Unlike base members, non-entity parent members do not have data stored to them directly in the database, and so can be deleted more easily. However, OneStream prevents you from deleting members with children, even if the children are in an extended dimension. If you try, you get the following error:

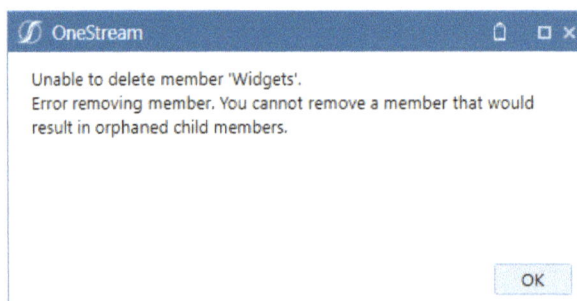

Figure 4.16

To get around this, you can orphan the child members first, and then delete the member before recreating it in the new dimension. For example, suppose you want to move `Widgets` down a level from `Products` to `SubProducts`.

1. First, orphan the children of `Widgets` by removing their relationships to `Widget`.

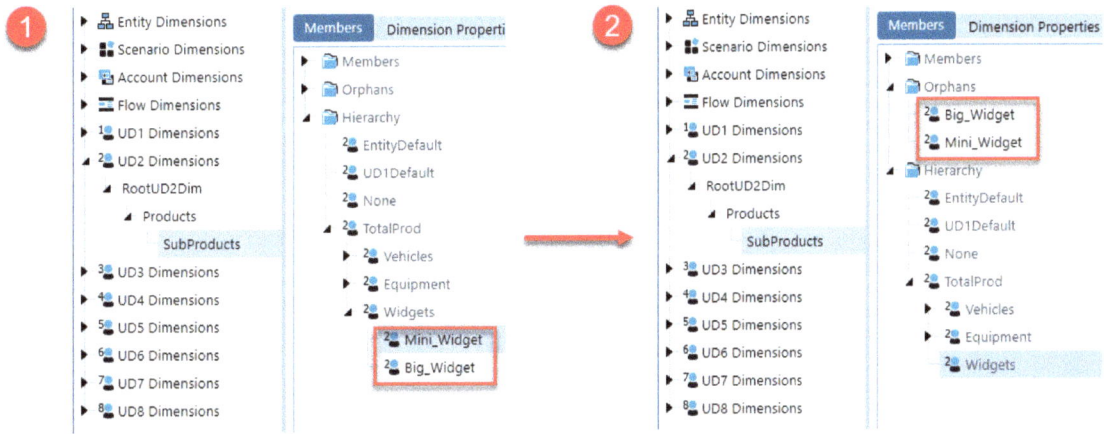

Figure 4.17

2. Delete Widgets in the Products dimension (i.e., the parent dimension).

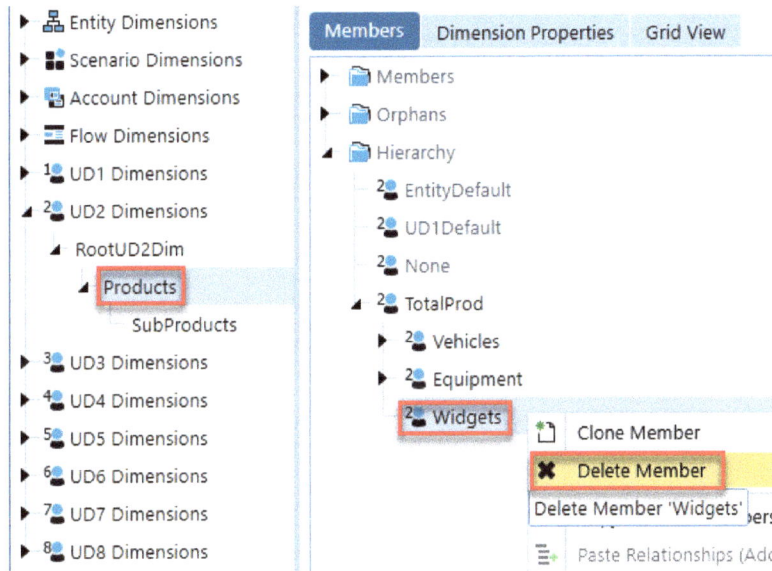

Figure 4.18

3. Recreate Widgets in the SubProducts dimension (i.e., the child dimension), and then add back the child relationships of Widgets. The data for Big_Widget and Mini_Widget will now roll up to Widgets automatically, as with any other aggregation.

You can see here that Widgets is now black in the SubProducts dimension, which indicates that it is a member of SubProducts and is not inherited from Products.

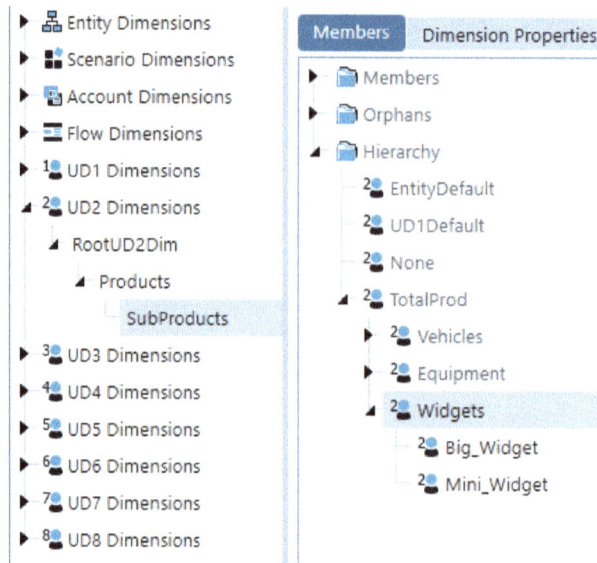

Figure 4.19

Common Setting Interactions

No setting in OneStream functions in isolation. To get your desired behavior, you will almost always need to use a combination of settings, which are often spread across many screens. In this section, we discuss common use cases and group the settings that work together to affect your desired behavior.

Consolidation Settings

Consolidation settings are spread across different members, all of which affect how data is consolidated. For values to be consolidated up from base entities, the following settings must be configured as follows:

- Entity Is Consolidated property must be set to True.

- Entity Percent Consolidation property must be some non-zero value for the entity hierarchy that is being consolidated.

- Account Is Consolidated property must resolve to True.

- Flow Is Consolidated property must resolve to True.

- UD members' (UD1-UD8) Is Consolidated property resolves to True.

> **Note:** For non-Data Unit dimensions (Account, Flow, and UD), the Is Consolidated property is set to Conditional (True if no Formula Type (default)) by default. If your member is flagged as a stored Member Formula, then you must explicitly set this property to True; otherwise, the member will not be consolidated.

This covers just the baseline settings for values to be consolidated. For more details on how to control and customize consolidation behavior (e.g., you might want to have your consolidation take intercompany eliminations into account), refer to Chapter 4 on consolidation in the OneStream Foundation Handbook.

Account Setting Interactions

This section covers how different settings interact to control how accounts are aggregated, translated, and derived.

Account Type and Aggregations

When OneStream aggregates base account members to parent account members, it automatically accomplishes this based on account type. We call this financial intelligence.

To illustrate this, consider the following example in the screenshot below. In the database, Revenue (which has an account type of revenue) is stored as 100, while COS (which has an account type of expense) is stored as 20. When OneStream aggregates to the parent GrossMargin, OneStream will subtract COS from Revenue.

This means OneStream recommends you do not store book values in the database. You can allow OneStream's financial intelligence to take care of this for you. Providing a trial balance report with book signs (revenues and liabilities/equity in credits) can easily be accomplished in a Cube View.

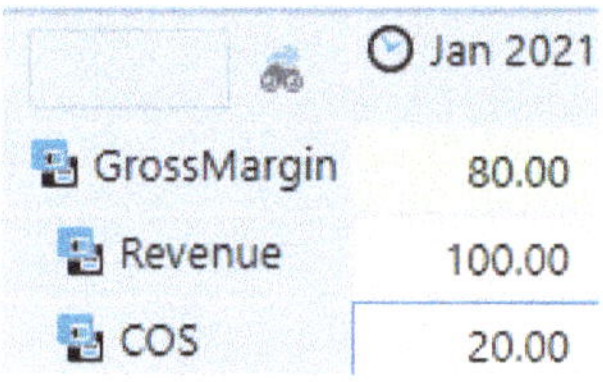

Figure 4.20

A quick tip is that if you would like to see your expense accounts as negative in your reporting, you can use the Cell Format field in your Cube View Properties to control how values are displayed based on the account type, or use a dynamic reporting member which flips signage, depending on the account type.

Account Type and View (YTD versus Periodic)

The account type controls how data is retrieved and stored in conjunction with views.

Read

From a system perspective, OneStream only stores YTD amounts in the database. When you query intersections using other views like Periodic, MTD, or QTD, OneStream will derive the correct amount based on the YTD amount; the Account Type setting affects how these alternate views are derived.

For balance sheet accounts where Account Type is set to Asset or Liabilities, periodic amounts are simply derived as the same as the YTD amount. For example, if you load $100 to YTD for M1, then the M1 periodic value will be derived as $100.

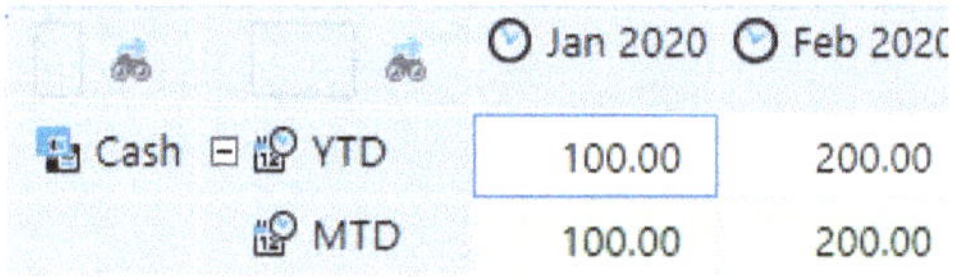

Figure 4.21

For income statement accounts where Account Type is set to Revenue or Expense, periodic amounts are computed as activity by subtracting the prior month and current month's YTD amount. For example, if you load $100 to YTD for M1, and $150 to YTD for M2, then the M2 periodic amount will be derived as $50.

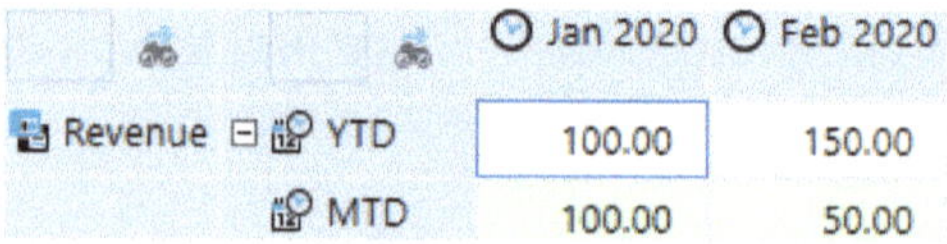

Figure 4.22

Write

In addition, when you input or calculate to periodic, OneStream will derive the YTD value to store, based on the account type.

For balance sheet accounts where Account Type is set to Asset or Liabilities, if you input to periodic, then OneStream will store that amount as the YTD amount in the database.

For income statement accounts where account type is set to revenue or expense, if you input to periodic, then OneStream will sum the entered periodic amount to the prior month's YTD amount to get the YTD amount to store for the current month.

> **Note:** This is the default behavior of these account types. You can override this behavior, causing balance sheet accounts to behave like income statement accounts and vice versa by using the switch type setting on a Flow member.

Account Type and FX Rate Type

US GAAP specifies that balance sheet accounts must be translated using closing rates, while income statement accounts must be translated at average rates. To accommodate this, OneStream lets you specify **direct FX rates** (for assets and liabilities) and **periodic FX rates** (for revenues and expenses) on the Cube Properties tab on each cube. By default, balance sheet accounts are translated using the direct method, while income statement accounts are translated using the periodic method.

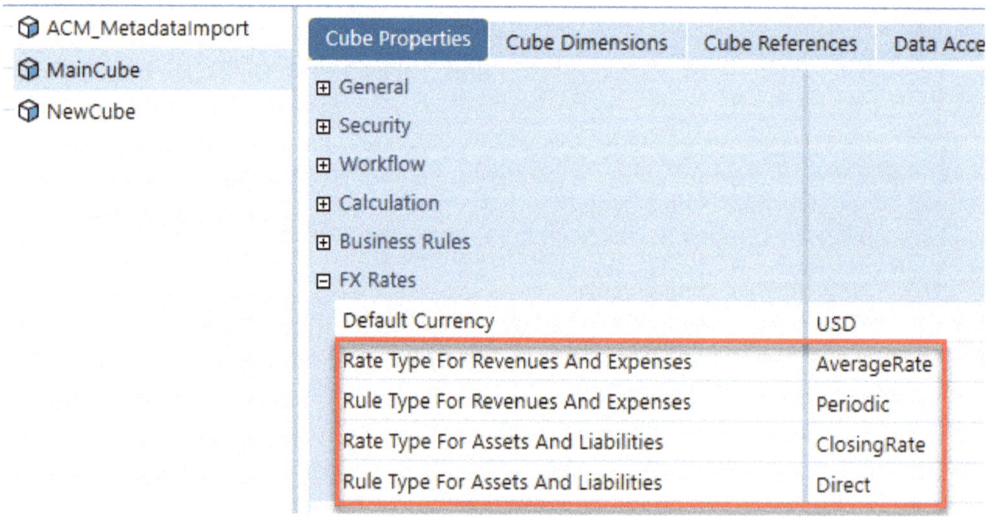

Figure 4.23

You can also override these rates on the Member Properties tab of each scenario.

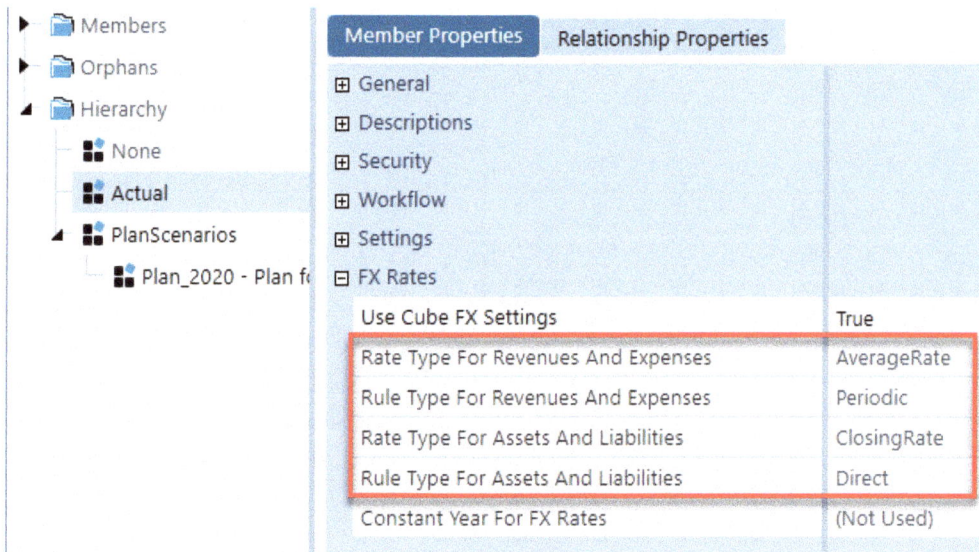

Figure 4.24

For more details on the OneStream translation algorithm and settings, refer to Chapter 5: Translation.

> **Note:** This section references US GAAP, but keep in mind that GAAP and IFRS allow the direct method to be used for income statement accounts.

Scenario and Account NoDataView Settings

When you load data to a period and the next period has no data, OneStream must determine how to interpret that no data period. There are four main settings that control this behavior:

- Scenario No Data Zero View for Adjustments and No Data Zero View for NonAdjustments properties.

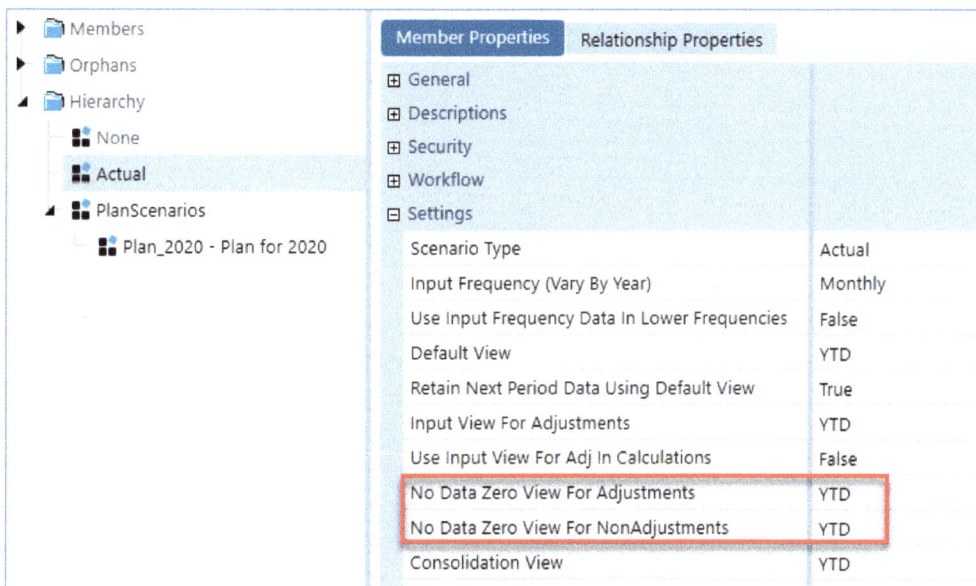

Figure 4.25

- Account No Data Zero View for Adjustments and No Data Zero View for NonAdjustments properties.

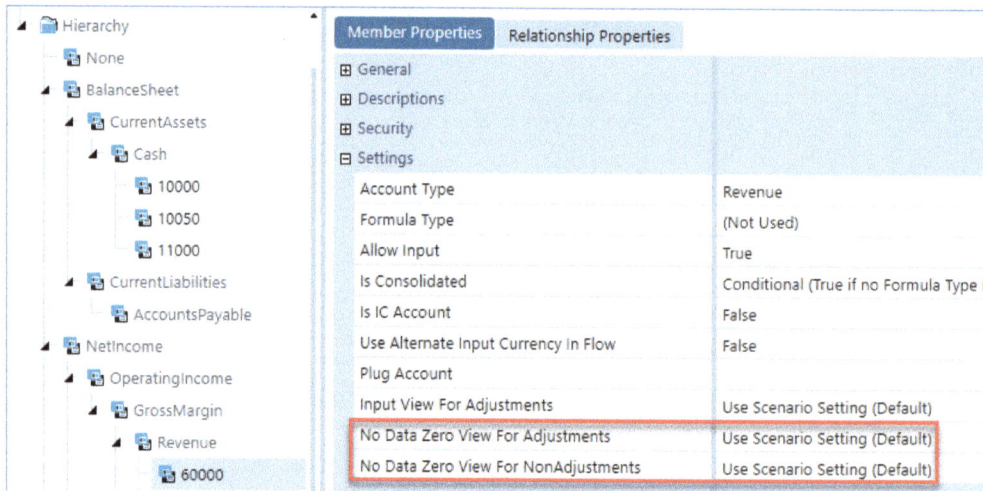

Figure 4.26

You can think of the scenario NoDataView settings as the global setting. By default, accounts will use the scenario setting, but you can override the NoDataView settings on each specific account, though this is generally not recommended as it can complicate troubleshooting.

If you set a NoDataView property to YTD, then OneStream considers NoData to mean that the YTD amount for that month is 0. For balance sheet accounts – where YTD and periodic amounts are the same – this is intuitive. For income statement accounts, OneStream will store a YTD value of 0 to the database and derive the periodic amount for the month to cancel out the previous month's YTD amount.

For example, consider the following example in the screenshot below. Here, suppose that the NoDataView for the Adjustments scenario property is set to YTD. For the balance sheet cash account, OneStream derives the M2 YTD amount as 0, and the periodic amount reflects this. For the income statement revenue account, OneStream again derives the M2 YTD amount as 0, but must derive the periodic amount to be -$100 to cancel out the M1 $100 YTD amount.

Figure 4.27

If you set a NoDataView property to Periodic, then OneStream considers NoData to mean that the periodic amount for that month is 0. Again, for balance sheet accounts where YTD and periodic amounts are the same, this doesn't really matter. For income statement accounts, because you are writing to the periodic view, OneStream will derive the YTD amount to store as the prior month's YTD amount summed with the assumed 0 periodic amount for the current month.

For example, consider the following example in the screenshot below. The data in M1 is the same as in the previous example, but this time, the NoDataView for the Adjustments scenario property is set to periodic. For the income statement revenue account, OneStream assumes that the M2 Periodic amount is 0. It then derives the M2 YTD amount to be $100 (the prior month's YTD amount + this assumed $0), which gives $100. In other words, OneStream has assumed no *activity* and carried the prior month's YTD balance forward.

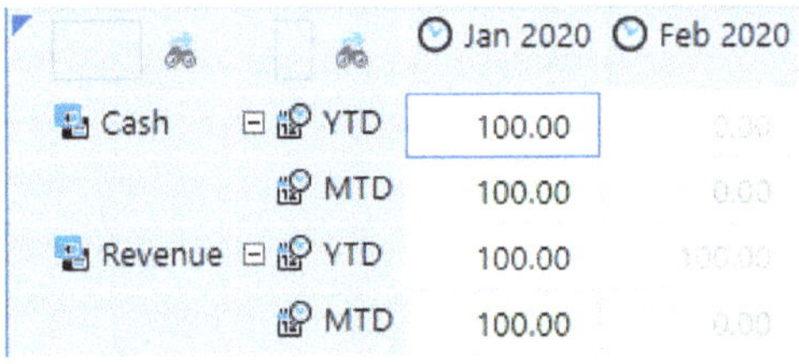

Figure 4.28

Account Type and Flow Switch Settings

Switch Sign

As discussed in the section on account type and aggregations, OneStream will automatically apply financial intelligence so that asset and revenue accounts are treated as positive, and liability and expense accounts are treated as negative during aggregations to parents as well as calculations. If you set a Flow's Switch Sign property to True, OneStream will leave the account type alone, but will override the sign of the current account during aggregations and calculations.

To illustrate this, consider the following example in the screenshot below. Suppose we've set the SwitchSign Flow member's Switch Sign property to True. OneStream will now flip the sign of the expense account to be -$20, and then subtract that amount from the Revenue amount of $100 to get $120.

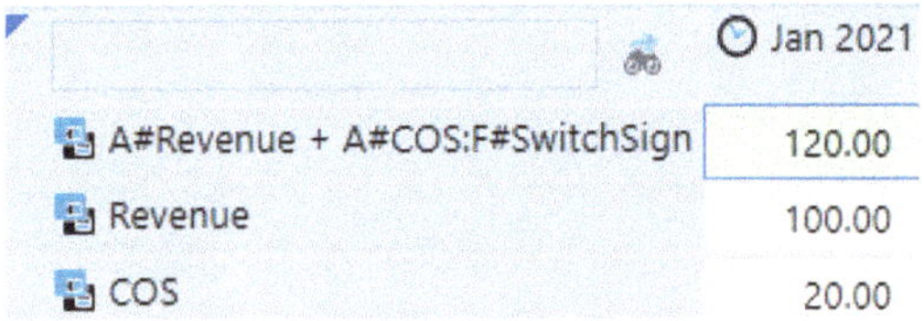

Figure 4.29

This can be useful in combination with the Flow's Aggregation Weight property for cash flow calculations and aggregations.

Switch Type

As discussed in the Account Type and View section, balance sheet accounts are treated as YTD accounts, while income statement accounts are treated as periodic accounts. This means that the periodic amounts for balance sheet accounts will be the same as the YTD amounts, whereas the periodic amounts for income statement accounts reflect that period's activity. If you set a Flow's Switch Type property to True, then for that Flow member, this behavior is reversed: balance sheet accounts will instead be treated as periodic accounts and income statement accounts will be treated as YTD accounts.

Using this property changes how account/flow combinations behave and are translated, as discussed in the Account Type and FX Rate Type section, as well as how NoData cells are derived, as discussed in the Scenario and Account NoDataView Settings section.

This is particularly useful for cash flow calculations, where you want to treat balance sheet account activity as periodic instead of YTD. See the Cash Flow section in the Consolidation chapter of the OneStream Foundation Handbook for more details.

Member Calculation Settings

Stored Member Formula

Here are the properties that must be configured on a stored Member Formula. Formulas for stored Member Formulas are subs and do not expect any return objects but contain `api.Data.Calculate` and `api.Data.SetDataBuffer` calls to calculate cells and store them in the database.

- **Account Type (Account Members only)**: This property is only present on accounts and not on UDs. Members with stored Member Formulas can hold data, and so their account type should reflect the correct financial account type to ensure that they aggregate up to their parent accounts correctly.

- **Formula Type**: For stored Member Formulas, this should be set to a formula pass. This controls the order that this Member Formula will execute, relative to other Member Formulas.

- **Is Consolidated**: Again, it's important that if you want the calculated member to consolidate, this must be set to True.

- **Formula**: Business rule containing `api.Data.Calculate` and `api.Data.SetDataBuffer` calls to calculate and save data to the database.

- **Formula for Calculation Drill Down**: Business rule containing logic to populate drill down results on cells generated.

The following screenshot shows sample settings for an account with a stored Member Formula.

Settings	
Account Type	Revenue
Formula Type	FormulaPass1
Allow Input	True
Is Consolidated	Conditional (True if no Formula Type (default))
Is IC Account	False
Use Alternate Input Currency In Flow	False

Figure 4.30

Something else to keep in mind is that stored Member Formulas will use the active scenario's Default View property when calculating, if you do not explicitly specify the view member.

Dynamic Calculation

Here are the properties that must be configured on a `DynamicCalc` member. Formulas for a `DynamicCalc` must return a `DataCell` object from a `GetDataCell` call; this cell is what is displayed in your Cube Views.

- **Account Type (Account Members only)**: Set to `DynamicCalc`. Forgetting to do this will result in the dynamic calculation not running in Cube Views.

- **Formula Type**: Set to `DynamicCalc`.

- **Formula**: Business rule containing `api.Data.GetDataCell` call.

- **Formula for Calculation Drill Down**: Business rule containing logic to populate drill down results on the returned cell.

The following screenshot shows sample settings for a `DynamicCalc` member.

Settings	
Account Type	DynamicCalc
Formula Type	DynamicCalc
Allow Input	True
Is Consolidated	Conditional (True if no Formula Type (default))
Is IC Account	False
Use Alternate Input Currency In Flow	False

Figure 4.31

Alternate Hierarchies

Alternate hierarchies are extremely flexible, powerful tools within OneStream. This section covers how to create them, as well as two common situations where you might want to leverage them.

How to Create Alternate Hierarchies

Creating alternate hierarchies is simple. The idea is that you can share a member across multiple hierarchies. For example, suppose you want to build out a CorporateReporting hierarchy in your Entity dimension.

Add child members to CorporateReporting by copying them and pasting them under Corporate Reporting. These child members now belong to both the NA and Corporate Reporting hierarchies.

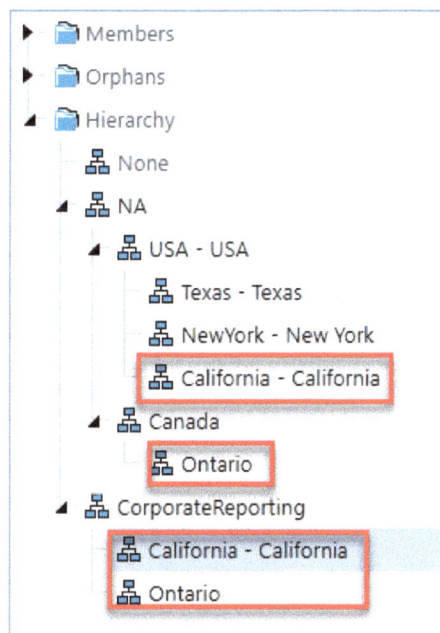

Figure 4.32

> **Note:** Make sure to use the Paste Relationships (Add) option, instead of the Paste Relationships (Move) option.

Review the Percent Consolidation property for entities and the aggregation weight property for non-Data Unit dimensions like Account or Flow to ensure that your child members will roll up to the parent as expected.

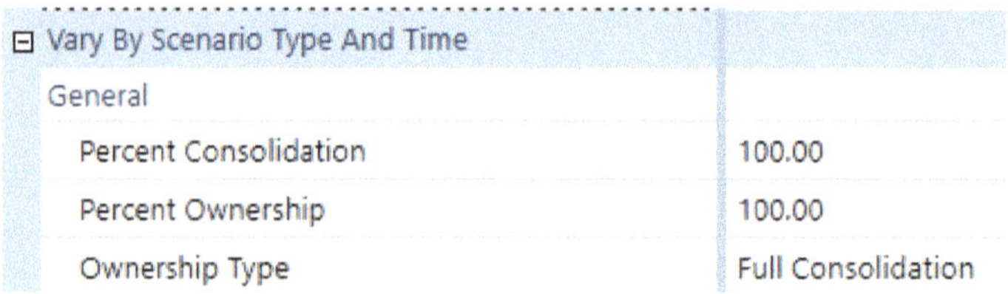

⊟ Vary By Scenario Type And Time	
General	
Percent Consolidation	100.00
Percent Ownership	100.00
Ownership Type	Full Consolidation

Figure 4.33

Use Case 1: Alternate Reporting Structures

There are many ways to get alternate reporting in OneStream. For example, suppose you have alternate GAAP and non-GAAP corporate account structures that you need to support. Let's discuss three different approaches and explain why **alternate hierarchies** is the cleanest option.

Cube View Math

One approach is to do this purely in Cube Views using Cube View math. This would mean cherry-picking accounts one by one, and then using a combination of CVR and CVC functions and `GetDataCell` calls to manually sum accounts and create your report lines.

While this would work, it quickly becomes difficult to maintain and troubleshoot since you end up with a mess of function calls that you can only see by clicking into each row in the Cube View designer. If you've been working with OneStream for any amount of time, there's a fair chance you've run into Cube Views that look something like this, where you have a large number of rows that each have a single cherry-picked account, and rows that have CVR functions to add up each row.

Figure 4.34

On top of how difficult the Cube View is to build and maintain, this approach is generally not recommended since hardcoding accounts means that any changes to your metadata structures will *not* get reflected in your Cube Views, and you'll have to update these Cube Views manually. Since you could be responsible for hundreds of Cube Views, there's a good chance that one of these changes will get missed, and you'll only find out when users are putting in tickets complaining that reports – which worked a week ago – are not working anymore!

Dynamic Reporting Members

Another way to do this would be to create DynamicCalc reporting members in your Account dimension to represent each of your account roll-ups, and then reference these dynamic members in your Cube View. This approach suffers from the same issues as the previous approach, as you'll have to manually update the business rules driving these DynamicCalc formulas manually if any of your members change.

Alternate Hierarchies

As a general principle, OneStream best practice is to enforce metadata-driven design: this means designing your system to be driven dynamically by your metadata as much as possible. Alternate hierarchies are a perfect example of this, since changes in your metadata automatically flow into your report. For example, imagine if the previous Cube View looked like this instead… much better.

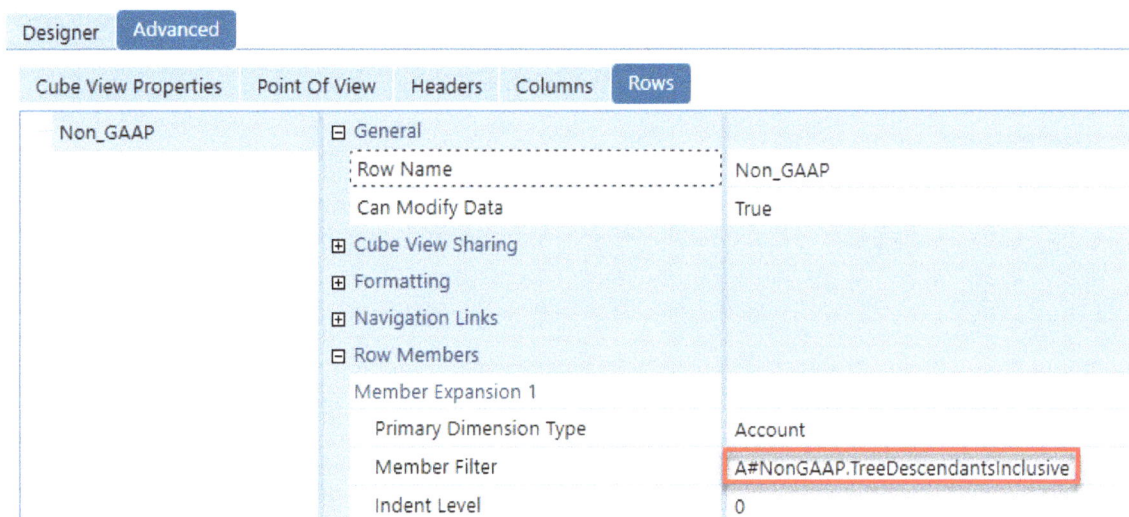

Figure 4.35

Now, if any members are changed, the Cube View will automatically update to allow you to see the updated hierarchy – no changes needed. This also leverages OneStream's built-in aggregation logic so that you can see your parent account values without updating any CVR math. Another advantage is that if you need to maintain this structure, you can simply go to the Account dimension and see the structure in its entirety.

Use Case 2: Grouping Members for Business Rules

Again, whenever possible, you want your metadata to drive your application. For example, suppose you have a business rule that allocates to a subset of your capital expense accounts.

You could hardcode these accounts in your business rule, but another approach would be to create a structure that reflects this business use case directly in your account structure.

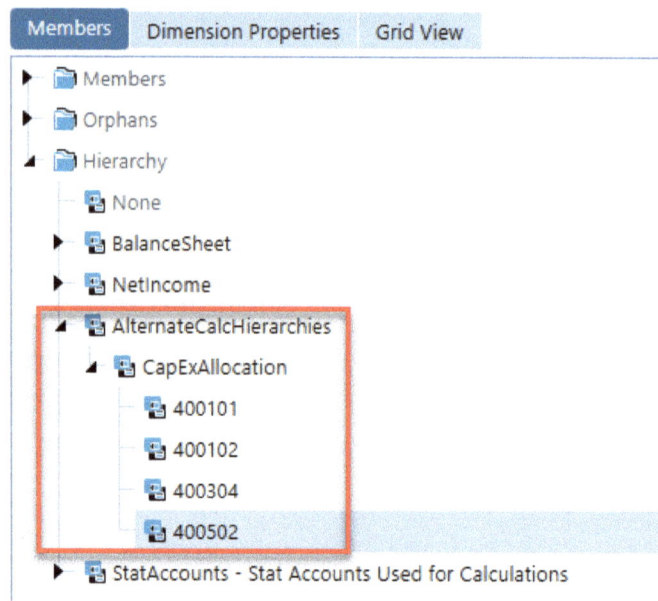

Figure 4.36

Now your rule could reference the `CapExAllocation` hierarchy, looping through the member list defined by `A#CapExAllocation.Base`. If you're doing a percentage of the total, this makes it easy since you can simply do something like `A#400101/A#CapExAllocation`.

Text Fields

This section covers two use cases for the Text Field properties on members (i.e., Text 1 – Text 8). Similar to alternate hierarchies, text fields are a great example of metadata-driven design. The biggest advantage to text fields is that you can do maintenance directly on members and have those changes dynamically affect business rules, reports, and other objects that reference these fields.

How to Reference Text Fields

Before going over use cases, let's quickly cover how you can reference text fields in different locations in your application. Hopefully, this might give you some ideas on where you might use text fields in your application.

Member Filters

Text fields can be referenced in Member Filter expansions, specifically in `Where` clauses, to restrict your resulting member list. This can be used anywhere you use a Member Filter, from Cube Views to Member Filter arguments in business rules. For more details, see the section on Member Expansions in the OneStream Design and Reference Guide.

Figure 4.37

Note: OneStream expects a space before and after the `=` in the `Where` clause. Without it, OneStream doesn't return anything.

Member Text Properties in Business Rules

There are two main method calls to get the text field value of a member:

- If you are in a finance business rule, the recommended way is to use the finance `api` object directly:

```
api.Account.Text(ByVal MemberId As Integer, ByVal
textPropertyIndex As Integer, Optional ByVal varyByScenarioType As
Integer, Optional ByVal varyByTimeId As Integer
```

- If you are not in a finance business rule, then you'll have to invoke the `BRApi.Finance` namespace:

```
BRApi.Finance.Account.Text(ByVal si As SessionInfo, ByVal MemberId
As Integer, ByVal textPropertyIndex As Integer, ByVal
varyByScenarioType As Integer, ByVal varyByTimeId As Integer)
```

> **Note:** We use the Account class here, but you will need to use different API calls depending on the dimension type of the member you're trying to query (e.g., `api.Entity.Text`).

Here is an example of how it is used in a business rule.

```
Dim accText1 As String = api.Account.Text(api.Pov.Account.MemberId, 1)
```

While not necessary, if you are planning on referencing a text field in a business rule, it's recommended to add your text fields in a `NameValuePair` format (with key-value pairs being delimited by commas, and keys and values separated by `=`). Here's an example of what this format would look like in a text field.

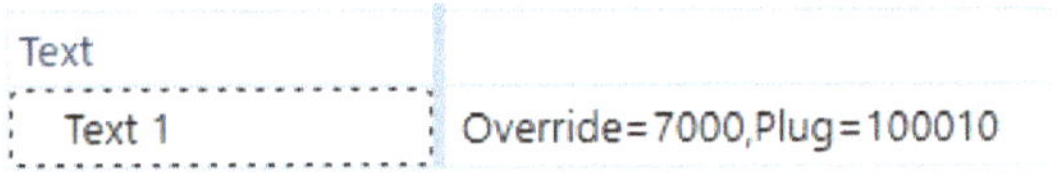

Figure 4.38

This has a few distinct advantages:

1. It allows you to use a single text field for storing multiple values. Keep in mind, though, that you should still use different text fields for different use cases (it's not a good idea to jam all of your values into a single text field, even if you can).

2. It makes parsing values out of the text field simpler and easier to read in business rules.

3. It gives context as to what the text field is being used for.

In your business rule, you can then parse this text field using the OneStream API without doing any convoluted string parsing.

```
Dim accNVBuilder As New
NameValueFormatBuilder(api.Account.Text(api.Pov.Account.MemberId, 1))
Dim accOverride As String = accNVBuilder.NameValuePairs.XFGetValue("Override")
Dim accPlug As String = accNVBuilder.NameValuePairs.XFGetValue("Plug")
```

Workflow Text Properties in Business Rules

Although this section is mainly focused on setting Text 1 fields on members, Workflow Profiles also have four text fields that can be referenced in business rules.

There are two main method calls to get the text field value of a Workflow:

- If you are in a finance business rule, the easiest way is to use `api` directly:

```
api.Workflow.GetWFText1()
```

- If you are not in a finance business rule, it is slightly more complicated. Here is an example:

```
Dim wfText1 As String = BRApi.Workflow.Metadata.GetProfile(si,
"profileName").GetAttributeValue(ScenarioTypeID.Actual,
SharedConstants.WorkflowProfileAttributeIndexes.Text1)
```

> **Note:** If you want to get different text fields, you must change the `WorkflowProfileAttributeIndex`. Also, notice that because Workflow Profile text fields are assigned by Scenario Type, you must specify the `ScenarioTypeID` in the arguments.

Use Case 1: Reporting

You can use text fields to dynamically pull a set of members in a Cube View. For example, you might want a report that displays all of your capital expense accounts. Instead of hardcoding each account in your Cube View rows, you can use a single Member Filter expansion to pull all accounts that have a Text 1 field value that equals CapEx. This is an alternative to using alternate hierarchies, and might be more appropriate if you don't need members to aggregate to a parent.

This is a good approach since all of your maintenance lies in your metadata and not in your Cube View. If you want to flag a new account as a capital expense account, you only have to add CapEx to its Text 1 field.

Use Case 2: Calculations

You can use text fields whenever you 1. want to limit calculations to run on specific members, or 2. want your calculations to do specific things to members based on their text field values.

Specify Forecast Methodologies

Suppose your business would like to plan accounts using different methodologies.

To accommodate this, you can assign each subset of accounts a dedicated Text field value which specifies their calculation methodologies, as shown in the table below.

Text Field	Calculation
StraightLine	Calculate next period based on constant growth rate.
MovingAvg	Calculate next period as prior period multiplied by 5-year average YoY growth.
LinRegression	Calculate next period with statistical voodoo magic.

Figure 4.39

Your business rule could then be partitioned out to execute the different calculations on different member lists, which filter accounts based on the dedicated Text field.

Cash Flow Mappings

Suppose you have your rollforward hierarchy in your Flow dimension, but you need to map these rollforward members into your cash flow hierarchy in a dedicated UD dimension.

To accommodate this, you can assign each rollforward Flow member a dedicated Text field value which specifies which cash flow member it should be allocated to. The advantage of this approach is that the Flow member and its target are contained together; if a Flow member must be remapped, then you only have to modify that specific member's Text field. It's also simple to create a report that lists all of the mappings.

While you could maintain this mapping in the cash flow rule directly, it is not as intuitive, as you would have to remember where this mapping is defined in the business rule. In general, a good guiding principle is to *keep as much maintenance outside business rules as possible*.

For more details on actually implementing a cash flow design, refer to the OneStream Foundation Handbook.

Limit Planned Depreciation Amounts

Suppose you are planning your depreciation expenses. From an accounting perspective, it doesn't make sense for these depreciation expenses to exceed their corresponding assets. Because of this, your users might make a request to modify your plan calculations to respect this constraint.

To handle this, you can link each depreciation account to its corresponding asset account by adding the asset account to one of the Text fields available on the depreciation account. In your rule, you can then add a condition to limit the value of a depreciation account to not exceed the value of the asset account in its designated Text field.

Metadata Management Controls

Metadata is the foundation of your application; it drives reporting, data loads, and almost every other aspect of your system. This is why metadata control management is key for our internal and external auditing partners.

If your business is at the end of its implementation, or is several years into a mature application, it is expected to have multiple controls and practices concerning the management of metadata. This section highlights how OneStream can help automate or facilitate standards to achieve this goal.

Suggested Processes and Controls

OneStream offers the ability to do detailed reporting and help with audits around metadata. This section will help the company with auditing controls and reporting against changes.

Audits

Whether a company is a private company or a publicly traded company, there will be some type of auditing standards required against metadata and the management of metadata. OneStream does a great job of tracking and tracing all the changes to metadata (and other parts of the application). OneStream has standard audit tables that have no impact on existing performance; they are standard with the OneStream application and not something that can be turned on or off. Each section of the application has its own audit table. For dimensions, there is an audit table that tracks the changes. This table is called `AuditDim`.

Though OneStream can't define a process for a company, it can assist in transitioning its old auditing processes to be comparable within OneStream. These processes could be the actual movement of metadata, the tracking of changes, or even month end close. The most common audit practices track the approval of specific metadata changes related to sensitive financial information. However, there are outliers to this that want approval for every type of change for all dimensions. Also, typically during the monthly closing cycle, a company will have documentation to prove that approvals and changes align.

Metadata Reports

OneStream offers a variety of detailed metadata reports. The most commonly used are the Application Reports. As you can see from the screenshot from our GolfStream demo application (Figure 4.40), Application Reports offer three metadata reporting options.

The reports in the Metadata Analysis group offer some detail about orphaned members, the numbers of members for a parent, and cube maintenance details for 30 days. The Orphaned

Members report becomes particularly useful if you have a member you can't seem to find in the hierarchy. This report will tell you which members are currently sitting as orphaned (and a company should really determine if they should exist as orphans). Usually, OneStream recommends a very limited number of orphaned metadata. There are some use cases that could be needed or warranted.

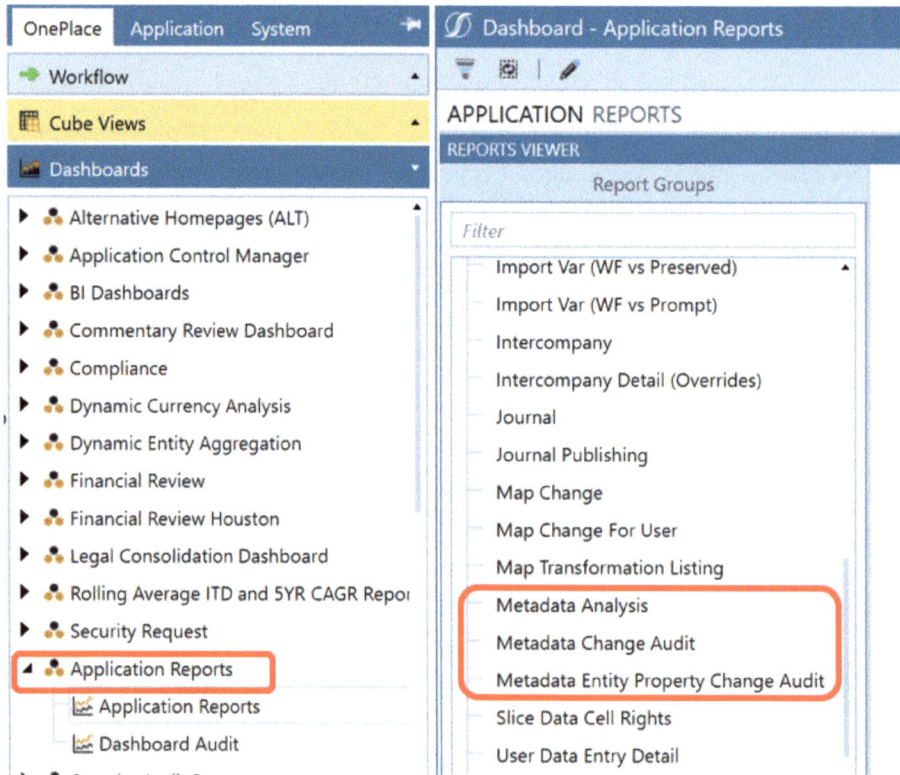

Figure 4.40

The Metadata Change Audit group contains the key reports for the company's auditing partners. As one can see from the screenshot in Figure 4.41, these reports offer a variety of functionality around changes and are intended to work in conjunction with each other to provide a complete change history of a member.

- The Member Changes Audit will allow an admin to know that something has changed.

- The Member Formula Changes Audit report will allow an admin to know when specific formulas have been altered on the metadata member.

- The Member Changes Detail report will list any changes that occurred on the metadata member.

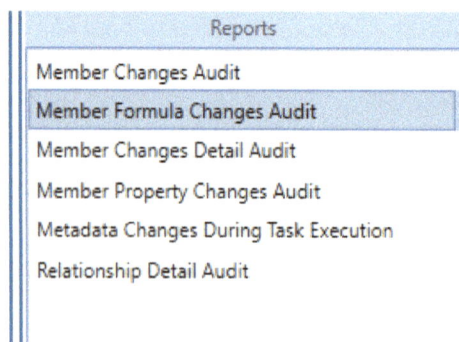

Figure 4.41

Finally, the reports in the Metadata Entity Property Change group will show any changes – adds, updates or removals – to entity structures, although these reports will not show any changes to the actual properties on the Member Properties tab.

Change Requests

Once an application is stable and metadata is not changing regularly, businesses often want to implement a system that allows users to submit metadata change requests.

One option to handle these types of requests is to implement the **Help Desk**, which can be found in the OneStream MarketPlace. This provides an out-of-the-box solution where users can submit change requests as tickets, which can go through an approval workflow. This also provides an audit trail on approved and rejected metadata changes.

Automation

Every OneStream administrator should want the system to be as automated as the company will allow it to be. This enhances not only system usage but allows the admin to have time to do other meaningful tasks (rather than focusing on mundane system moves). **Application Control Manager** or ACM can be found in the MarketPlace for OneStream. ACM is designed to support and manage user change requests for both security and metadata. Though ACM has a significant amount of configuration at the start, the long-run benefit is a truly automated function for metadata. At a high level, the end-user can request a new account, a different user can approve the account, and finally – upon approval – the account will be created in the correct hierarchy. Having this type of construct in place will make all auditing partners happy by having full traceability from request to approval and finally to creation.

Conclusion

OneStream as a tool is extremely flexible, but that comes with a trade-off, as there are countless ways to approach problems and business needs. OneStream has thousands of settings, and it might seem overwhelming to figure out which settings interact and in what ways, especially if you're only just getting introduced to the software. We hope this chapter will provide that context for you and make your life a little easier when managing metadata and maintaining your application.

5
Translation

Translation, in this context, is defined as taking a local currency amount and applying a foreign currency rate to arrive at a translated value in a given reporting currency. This chapter covers common foreign currency capabilities that are available to you in OneStream; by the end of the chapter, you will be equipped with a general understanding of various translation-related needs.

First, we will cover what and how to use rate types conceptually as part of the Background section of this chapter, and then how rates are used in OneStream as part of the Foundational FX Properties section.

Specifically, in Foundational FX Properties, we will cover the locations within the application where you would consider updating settings to allow for certain translation capabilities, such as handling intermediary parents, currency translation adjustment (CTA), overrides, and input currencies.

Then, we will combine what we learned as a use case on the pros and cons when you want to implement the ability to report actuals using prior year rates. Finally, we will end the chapter with various ways to load and view FX rates as part of the Loading FX Rates and Viewing FX Rates sections.

Background

Foreign currency exchange (FX) rates are rates used to convert one currency to another. This is common for companies that have various currency reporting requirements. For the purposes of this chapter, our terminology will be:

- **Functional currency**, which will be used synonymously with local currency. Functional currency is defined as the main currency in which a company conducts its business. The currency setting on the entity member within OneStream is commonly referred to as "local currency", which corresponds to functional currency.

- **Transactional currency**, which will be used synonymously with input currency. Transactional currency is defined as the currency for payments, and the transactional currency can be different from the functional currency of the company. It is most common to have transactional currency captured in the ERP (Enterprise Resource Planning) system, while OneStream handles the functional currencies for consolidation and close processes.

- **Reporting currency** is the currency used to prepare financial statements. Within OneStream, the reporting currency is typically the top parent's currency (e.g., USD), while the subsidiaries or remaining companies will commonly use their local currencies for reporting. This chapter will cover the implications of using `C#Local` versus enabling every currency for reporting purposes.

- **Periodic** is defined as the activity that happens for a given period. For the purposes of this chapter, the examples provided will be in relation to a given month in a monthly application.

Direct Versus Periodic Rule Types

In OneStream, we have rule types to dictate how an account should be translated. The rule types are **Direct** and **Periodic**. These rule types are set on the cube(s) or scenario(s) and used in conjunction with rate type settings to determine account translation behavior.

Direct translation refers to the translation of ending balances. Periodic refers to the translation of the periodic (e.g., monthly) activity amounts, which are then appended to the existing amounts. Direct translation is commonly applied on balance sheet accounts, while Periodic translation is applied to income statement accounts.

Periodic (usually P&L-related)

	Jan	Feb	Mar
Exchange Rate (USD:Currency)	0.5	0.6	0.7
Local amounts as YTD	100	300	600
Local amounts as Periodic	100	200	300
Translated to USD as YTD	100*(1/0.5) = 200	200*(1/0.6) + 200 (from Jan) = 333.33 + 200 = 533.33	300*(1/0.7) + 333.33 (Feb) + 200 (Jan) = 428.57+333.33+200=961.90

Figure 5.1

Direct (usually balance sheet-related)

	Jan	Feb	Mar
Exchange Rate (USD:Currency)	0.5	0.6	0.7
Local amounts as YTD	100	300	600
Local amounts as Periodic	100	200	300
Translated to USD as YTD	100*(1/0.5) = 200	300*(1/0.6)=500	600*(1/0.7)=857.14

Figure 5.2

Rate Types

FX rates can be tracked in a variety of ways as **rate types**. To put this into context, we can start with a non-business-related example.

Let's say you are traveling for your next vacation in a European country that uses euros, and you are based in the United States. In preparation for your trip, you pull up the latest currency rates for that country. Each day, the rate changes a little bit; this is the daily rate. You decide that you need to exchange your US dollars to euros at some point and decide that – at the end of the month – you will exchange your dollars for whatever the rate is on that end-of-month day. This end-of-month rate is commonly referred to as the **ending rate** or **closing rate**. Ending rate or closing rate or spot rate will be used synonymously within this chapter. You can think of closing rate as a rate type within OneStream.

The OneStream application comes with out-of-the-box FX rate types:

- ClosingRate
- AverageRate
- OpeningRate
- HistoricalRate

ClosingRate is commonly used for balance sheet account translations, while AverageRate is used for P&L account translations. OpeningRate, depending on your company's circumstances, could be used for related acquisitions, and HistoricalRate is used for historical rate overrides in lieu of historical balance amount overrides.

Depending on your company's requirements, you might need to add additional translation capabilities that may involve adding new FX rate types. For example, there may be the need for new FX-related reporting, such as actuals at plan rates, actuals at last year's actuals rates, plan at last year's actual rates, etc.

You can create additional FX rate types to represent PlanRate, PlanAverageRate, ForecastRate, etc., via the FX Rates button.

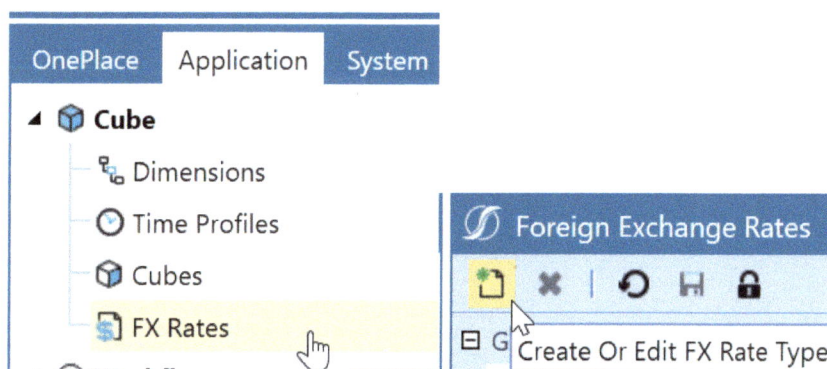

Figure 5.3

If you were to opt for this, keep in mind the number of scenarios you may need as you update your FX rate types by scenario. Below are some general steps to be aware of if you decide to leverage FX rate types by scenario:

1. Apply the FX rates to the appropriate scenarios and update the scenario settings.

    a. Use Cube FX Settings = False

    b. Rate Type for Revenues and Expenses: [NEW RATE TYPE]

    c. Rule Type for Revenues and Expenses: Periodic

    d. Rate Type for Assets and Liabilities: [NEW RATE TYPE]

    e. Rule Type for Assets and Liabilities: Direct

2. After setting Cube FX Settings to False, select your custom FX rate type. In Figure 5.4, the new rate types are AverageRatePY and ClosingRatePY.

⊟ FX Rates	
Use Cube FX Settings	False
Rate Type For Revenues And Expenses	AverageRatePY
Rule Type For Revenues And Expenses	Periodic
Rate Type For Assets And Liabilities	ClosingRatePY
Rule Type For Assets And Liabilities	Direct
Constant Year For FX Rates	(Not Used)

Figure 5.4

Foundational FX Properties

This section covers all the FX-related properties found in OneStream. You may find this section useful if translation-related questions or issues come up. Within OneStream, translation-related capabilities are found through a combination of cube properties and metadata properties, set on the Scenario, Account, Entity, and Flow members.

Cube Properties

This section covers FX-related settings found on Cube Properties, the FX Rates section, and the Cube Translation Algorithm Type setting.

FX Rates

We have a dedicated FX Rates section with settings on the cube to specify how we want to translate our assets and liabilities, as well as our revenues and expenses.

Cubes - Corporate

ACM_MetadataImport	Cube Properties	Cube Dimensions	Cube References	Data A...
Asia				
Corporate	Business Rule 8			(Not Used)
Europe	⊟ FX Rates			
NA	Default Currency			USD
XFW_PCM	Rate Type For Revenues And Expenses			AverageRate
	Rule Type For Revenues And Expenses			Periodic
	Rate Type For Assets And Liabilities			ClosingRate
	Rule Type For Assets And Liabilities			Direct

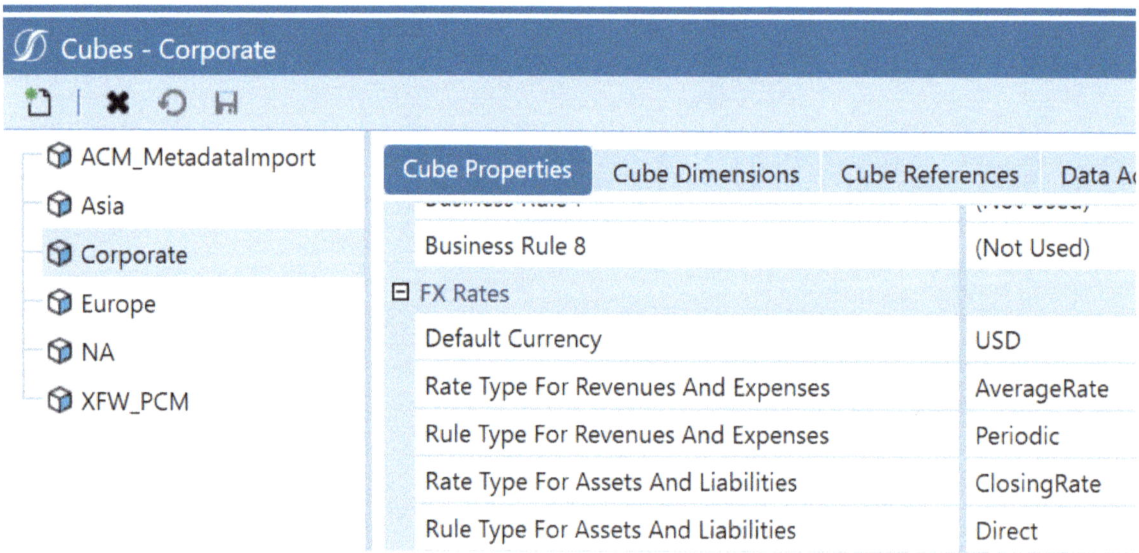

Figure 5.5

On the accounts, we tag each member according to account type (e.g., asset, liability, revenue, expense).

The Account Type and the Switch Type from the Flow member will indicate what rate type and rule type will be used, based on the cube settings above in Figure 5.5 or the scenario settings in Figure 5.7, assuming that cube settings are not used (e.g., Use Cube FX Settings is set to False). OneStream allows for custom translations if these out-of-the-box settings are not sufficient for your processes.

Cube Translation Algorithm Type

The Cube Translation Algorithm Type is a specific setting found on the Cube Properties tab.

There are three choices: Standard, Standard Using Business Rules For FX Rates, and Custom.

The navigation path is Application > Cubes > *Select your Cube.* On the Cube Properties tab, scroll down to Calculation:

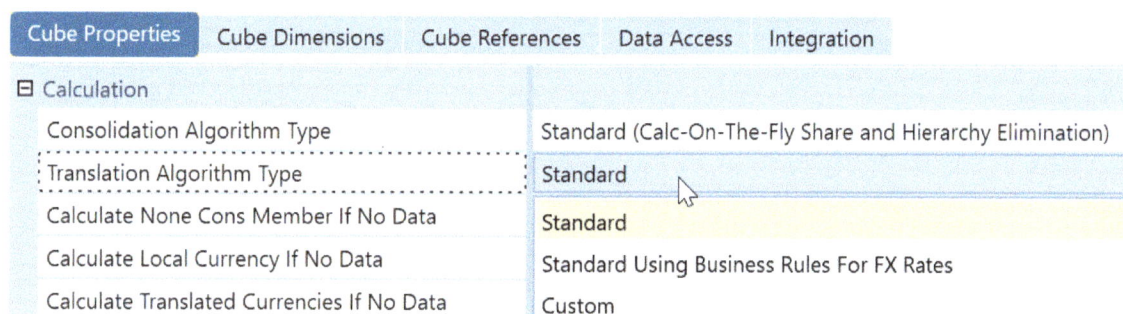

| Cube Properties | Cube Dimensions | Cube References | Data Access | Integration |

⊟ Calculation	
Consolidation Algorithm Type	Standard (Calc-On-The-Fly Share and Hierarchy Elimination)
Translation Algorithm Type	Standard
Calculate None Cons Member If No Data	Standard
Calculate Local Currency If No Data	Standard Using Business Rules For FX Rates
Calculate Translated Currencies If No Data	Custom

Figure 5.6

Standard

This is the default out-of-the-box setting. When your cube is set to Standard, the system will use the settings found in FX Rates (part of Cube Properties) with the combination of the metadata properties on Scenario, Account, Entity, and Flow.

Standard with Business Rule

Standard with Business Rule not only tells the system to leverage the settings found in FX Rates (part of Cube Properties) with the combination of the metadata properties on Scenario, Account, Entity, and Flow but also to use a finance rule, which is commonly attached to the cube.

Custom

The translation process will be entirely handled by the business rules assigned to the cube. This means the system will not take the standard settings into consideration unless specified in the business rule. An example of this situation would be the need for an extensive currency analysis, involving a dedicated UD dimension for currencies.

Metadata Properties

This section covers the FX-related properties for metadata. Because every data point is associated with a cube and an intersection, it is important – when it comes to troubleshooting translation-related issues – that you investigate not only the cube properties but also the properties related to the Scenario, Account, Entity, and Flow dimensions.

Scenario

Within the scenario's Member Properties, there is a dedicated FX Rates section.

- **Use Cube FX Settings**
  - If set to True, subsequent selections are grayed out, and the scenario member will use whatever rate types are assigned at the cube, as represented in Figure 5.7.

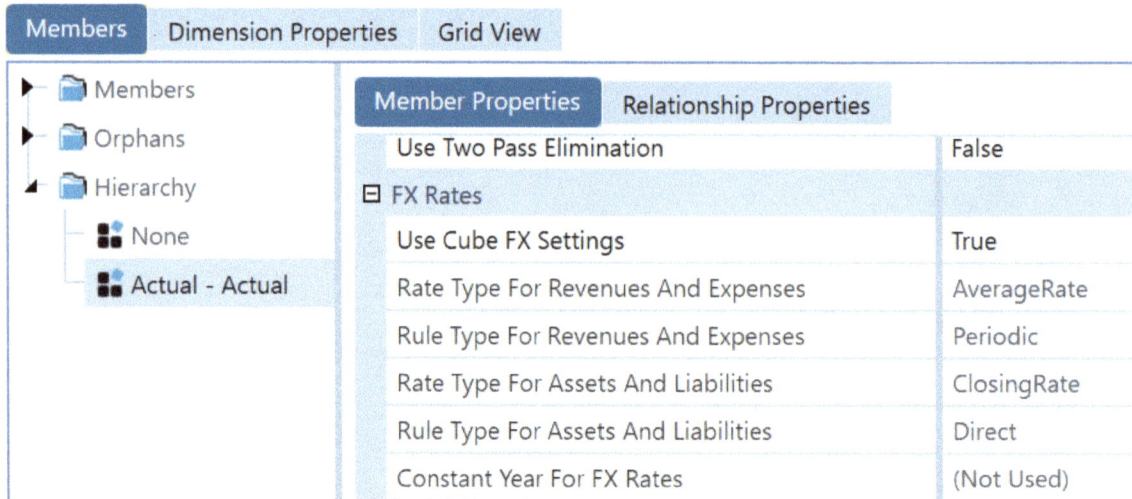

Figure 5.7

- o If set to False, the subsequent selections become available, and you can select what Rate Type and calculation to use for revenue, expenses, assets, and liabilities. This is useful if you opt to use different FX rate types for that scenario.

Entity

The common entity setting for FX is Currency. This currency will typically represent the entity's local currency.

Figure 5.8

There may be instances when you need additional settings adjusted, such as parent entities, which you want to view in a foreign currency, and equity pickup.

Intermediary Parents

For the purposes of this section, an intermediary parent is defined as a parent entity that is not the top consolidated entity, and the intermediary parent's local currency is not the same local currency as the top consolidated entity or that of the application's default currency. The reason why this currency distinction is important is that when we have intermediary parents with differing currencies, this can create confusion for users who view the consolidation status of these entities.

Figure 5.9 represents such an example. Eb2_Total_EUR represents the intermediary parent where its local currency is EUR, which is different to the top consolidated entity, Total_USD, and the application default currency of USD.

When a user consolidates at Total_USD, the user may then see that Eb2_Total_EUR and the other intermediary parents, E2_Total_EUR, E2a_Total_EUR have a status of TR,CN.

Total_USD	CN
E1_Total_USD	OK
E1_USD	OK
E1_CAD	OK
E2_Total_EUR	TR,CN
E2a_Total_EUR	TR,CN
E2a_USD	OK
E2a_EUR	OK
E2a_GBP	OK
E2b_Total_EUR	TR,CN
E2b_USD	OK
E2b_EUR	OK

Figure 5.9

First, we need to cover how OneStream performs calculations and consolidations and how that can create user confusion.

When you perform a calculation on a Data Unit, OneStream will run all business rules attached to the Data Unit's cube and will run all Member Formulas for the Data Unit's Scenario Type; this is all performed on the currency specified on the Data Unit. Remember that a Data Unit comprises of Cube, Entity, Parent, Consolidation, Scenario, and Time.

When you perform a consolidation on a parent entity, OneStream will iteratively calculate each child entity at its local currency, translate it to its parent's currency, and then consolidate the child entity's values up to the common parents. If you have an application with no rates, there is effectively no out-of-the-box translation.

Back to what is presented in Figure 5.9. If we have the following rates in Figure 5.10 and we enter 100 as the local currency amounts in Figure 5.11, what happens?

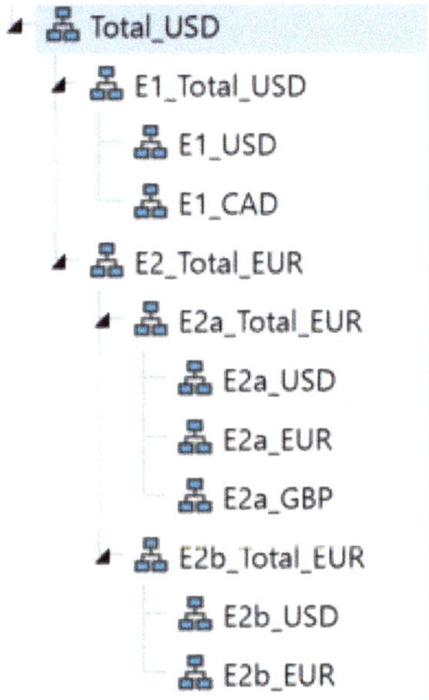

Total_USD
- E1_Total_USD
  - E1_USD
  - E1_CAD
- E2_Total_EUR
  - E2a_Total_EUR
    - E2a_USD
    - E2a_EUR
    - E2a_GBP
  - E2b_Total_EUR
    - E2b_USD
    - E2b_EUR

Closing Rate	CAD	1.24290
	CNY	6.42330
	CRC	6.42330
	EUR	0.81987
	GBP	0.72338
	JPY	110.87100
	KRW	1,065.64100
	TWD	29.40050
	USD	1.00000
Average Rate	CAD	1.24343
	CNY	6.42654
	CRC	0.00150
	EUR	0.81990
	GBP	0.72400
	JPY	110.93200
	KRW	1,065.56242
	TWD	29.42647
	USD	1.00000

Figure 5.10

	Local	USD
Total_USD		
E1_Total_USD		
E1_USD	100.00	100.00
E1_CAD	100.00	
E2_Total_EUR		
E2a_Total_EUR		
E2a_USD	100.00	
E2a_EUR	100.00	
E2a_GBP	100.00	
E2b_Total_EUR		
E2b_USD	100.00	
E2b_EUR	100.00	

Figure 5.11

If we were to manually calculate the output, we would expect the following:

At E2_Total_EUR:	At E2a_Total_EUR:	At E2b_Total_EUR:
<table><tr><td>E2_Total_EUR</td><td></td></tr><tr><td>E2a_Total_EUR</td><td></td></tr><tr><td>E2a_USD</td><td>100.00</td></tr><tr><td>E2a_EUR</td><td>100.00</td></tr><tr><td>E2a_GBP</td><td>100.00</td></tr><tr><td>E2b_Total_EUR</td><td></td></tr><tr><td>E2b_USD</td><td>100.00</td></tr><tr><td>E2b_EUR</td><td>100.00</td></tr></table>**Total at E2_Total_EUR:** 477.32 EUR converted to USD is 582.19 USD. The 477.32 EUR is from 295.33 (E2a_Total_EUR) + 181.99 (Eb2_Total_EUR).	<table><tr><td>E2a_Total_EUR</td><td></td></tr><tr><td>E2a_USD</td><td>100.00</td></tr><tr><td>E2a_EUR</td><td>100.00</td></tr><tr><td>E2a_GBP</td><td>100.00</td></tr></table> - E2a_USD (USD to EUR): 81.99 EUR (100/1.2197) - E2a_EUR (EUR): 100 - E2a_GBP (GBP): 113.34 (100/0.88313) - **Total at E2a_Total_EUR:** 295.33 EUR	<table><tr><td>E2b_Total_EUR</td><td></td></tr><tr><td>E2b_USD</td><td>100.00</td></tr><tr><td>E2b_EUR</td><td>100.00</td></tr></table> - E2b_USD (USD to EUR): 81.99 EUR (100/1.2197) - E2b_EUR (EUR): 100 - **Total at Eb2_Total_EUR:** 181.99 EUR
At E1_Total_USD: <table><tr><td></td><td>Local</td></tr><tr><td>Total_USD</td><td></td></tr><tr><td>E1_Total_USD</td><td></td></tr><tr><td>E1_USD</td><td>100.00</td></tr><tr><td>E1_CAD</td><td>100.00</td></tr></table> - E1_USD: 100 - E1_CAD: 80.46 (100/1.2429) - **Total at E1_Total_USD:** 180.46		

Figure 5.12

Thus, at `Total_USD`, we would expect to see 762.65 (582.19 + 180.46) USD. However, when we run a consolidate in OneStream, notice – as per Figure 5.13 – what happens…

			Local	USD
Total_USD	OK	Total_USD	762.64	762.64
E1_Total_USD	OK	E1_Total_USD	180.46	180.46
E1_USD	OK	E1_USD	100.00	100.00
E1_CAD	OK	E1_CAD	100.00	80.46
E2_Total_EUR	OK	E2_Total_EUR	477.31	582.18
E2a_Total_EUR	OK	E2a_Total_EUR	295.33	
E2a_USD	OK	E2a_USD	100.00	100.00
E2a_EUR	OK	E2a_EUR	100.00	
E2a_GBP	OK	E2a_GBP	100.00	
E2b_Total_EUR	OK	E2b_Total_EUR	181.99	
E2b_USD	OK	E2b_USD	100.00	100.00
E2b_EUR	OK	E2b_EUR	100.00	

Figure 5.13

Although status appears to be OK, the USD values are not populated for the intermediary parents. There are several instances where the USD value is missing, so what has happened?

The answer has to do with the steps associated with a consolidate.

Let's say you run a consolidate at `E#E2a_Total_EUR:C#Local`. Here, the system will run six **Step Type calculations** as presented in Figure 5.14. You can view each of the step types through detailed logging.

		Step Type	Description
	⚠	Calculate None	Cb#Europe:E#E2a_USD:C#None:S#Actual:T#2018M1
	⚠	Calculate Local	Cb#Europe:E#E2a_USD:C#USD:S#Actual:T#2018M1
	⚠	Translate Cons Member	Cb#Europe:E#E2a_USD:C#EUR:S#Actual:T#2018M1
	⚠	Calculate OwnerPreAdj	Cb#Europe:E#E2a_USD:P#E2a_Total_EUR:C#OwnerPreAdj:S#Actual:T#2018M1
	⚠	Elimination	Cb#Europe:E#E2a_USD:P#E2a_Total_EUR:C#Elimination:S#Actual:T#2018M1
	⚠	Calculate OwnerPostAdj	Cb#Europe:E#E2a_USD:P#E2a_Total_EUR:C#OwnerPostAdj:S#Actual:T#2018M1

Figure 5.14

- **Calculate None:** kicks off the `CalculateNoneConsMember` step, which is the `CreateDataUnitCache`, which will initiate `ReadDataRecordsForDataUnit`.

- **Calculate Local:** `CreateDataUnitCache`, which will initiate `ReadDataRecordsForDataUnit`, Calculate Cons Member, `SaveWritableDataCache`.

  o **Calculate Cons Member:** this will look familiar as this is the order of operations performed in the consolidation engine, which is part of DUCS (Data Unit Calculation Sequence).

    1. Clear previously calculated data for the Data Unit (based on StorageType, will not clear durable data).

    2. Run scenario formulas, if any.

3. Run reverse translations, if any.

4. Execute Business Rules 1 and 2 as assigned to the cube.

5. Formula Passes 1 through 4 (Account formulas, then Flow formulas, then UD formulas) as assigned to the member on the formula.

6. Execute Business Rules 3 and 4 as assigned to the cube.

7. Formula Passes 5-8 (Account formulas, then Flow formulas, then UD formulas) as assigned to the member on the formula.

8. Execute Business Rules 5 and 6 as assigned to the cube.

9. Formula Passes 9-12 (Account formulas, then Flow formulas, then UD formulas) as assigned to the member on the formula.

10. Execute Business Rules 7 and 8 as assigned to the cube.

11. Formula Passes 13-16 (Account formulas, then Flow formulas, then UD formulas) as assigned to the member on the formula.

- o Notice how Figure 5.15, found in the application's detailed logging, supports the DUCS described above.

		Step Type	Description
		ClearCalculatedData	Cb#Europe:E#E2a_USD:C#USD:S#Actual:T#2018M1:V#YTD
		Execute Formula Pass	Formula Pass 1 For Account Dimension Type
		Execute Formula Pass	Formula Pass 1 For Flow Dimension Type
		Execute Formula Pass	Formula Pass 2 For Flow Dimension Type
		Execute Formula Pass	Formula Pass 3 For Account Dimension Type
		Execute Formula Pass	Formula Pass 5 For Flow Dimension Type
		Execute Formula Pass	Formula Pass 7 For Flow Dimension Type
		Execute Formula Pass	Formula Pass 8 For Account Dimension Type
		Execute Formula Pass	Formula Pass 8 For Flow Dimension Type
		Execute Business Rule	Cash_Flow

Figure 5.15

- Translate Cons Member: will go through the same step type iteration as Calculate Local, as presented in Figure 5.16. Within Translate Cons Member is a Calculate Cons Member; the system will go through the same order of operations (DUCS) in the consolidation engine, as presented in Figure 5.17.

		Step Type	Description
▤	⚠	CreateDataUnitCache	Cb#Europe:E#E2a_USD:C#EUR:S#Actual:T#2018
▤	⚠	ClearCalculatedData	Cb#Europe:E#E2a_USD:C#EUR:S#Actual:T#2018M1:V#YTD
▤	⚠	GetDataBufferForCurrency	Cb#Europe:E#E2a_USD:C#USD:S#Actual:T#2018M1
▤	⚠	Calculate Cons Member	Cb#Europe:E#E2a_USD:C#EUR:S#Actual:T#2018M1
▤	⚠	ConvertDataBufferToDataCells	Cb#Europe:E#E2a_USD:C#EUR:S#Actual:T#2018M1:V#YTD
▤	⚠	SaveWritableDataCache	Cb#Europe:E#E2a_USD:C#EUR:S#Actual:T#2018M1

Figure 5.16

		Step Type	Description
▤	⚠	ClearCalculatedData	Cb#Europe:E#E2a_USD:C#EUR:S#Actual:T#2018M1:V#YTD
▤	⚠	Execute Formula Pass	Formula Pass 1 For Account Dimension Type
▤	⚠	Execute Formula Pass	Formula Pass 1 For Flow Dimension Type
▤	⚠	Execute Formula Pass	Formula Pass 2 For Flow Dimension Type
▤	⚠	Execute Formula Pass	Formula Pass 3 For Account Dimension Type
▤	⚠	Execute Formula Pass	Formula Pass 5 For Flow Dimension Type
▤	⚠	Execute Formula Pass	Formula Pass 7 For Flow Dimension Type
▤	⚠	Execute Formula Pass	Formula Pass 8 For Account Dimension Type
▤	⚠	Execute Formula Pass	Formula Pass 8 For Flow Dimension Type
▤	⚠	Execute Business Rule	Cash_Flow

Figure 5.17

In Figure 5.17, the system is essentially taking E2a_USD:C#Translated as E2a_USD:C#EUR. In other words, at E2a_Total_EUR:C#EUR, the system performs the following:

- Calculate E2a_EUR:C#Local as E2a_EUR:C#EUR
- Calculate E2a_USD:C#Local as E2a_USD:C#USD
- Calculate E2a_GBP:C#Local as E2a_GBP:C#GBP
- Translate E2a_EUR:C#Translated which is E2a_EUR:C#EUR
- Translate E2a_GBP:C#Translated which is E2a_GBP:C#EUR
- Translate E2a_USD:C#Translated which is E2a_USD:C#EUR

Thus, the expected end result will be local calculated and consolidated. Any local currency will be populated in the equivalent reporting currency (e.g., if local is USD, you will see the same amount in USD. If local is EUR, you will see the same amount populated in EUR). Because E2a_Total_EUR's local currency is EUR and the base members roll up to this parent, the consolidation will translate the base's local currencies to EUR, as depicted in Figure 5.18.

	Local	USD	EUR		Local	USD	EUR
Total_USD				Total_USD			
E1_Total_USD				E1_Total_USD			
E1_USD				E1_USD			
E1_CAD				E1_CAD			
E2_Total_EUR				E2_Total_EUR	295.33	.	295.33
E2a_Total_EUR				E2a_Total_EUR	295.33		295.33
E2a_USD	100.00	100.00		E2a_USD	100.00	100.00	81.99
E2a_EUR	100.00		100.00	E2a_EUR	100.00		100.00
E2a_GBP	100.00			E2a_GBP	100.00		113.34
E2b_Total_EUR							
E2b_USD							
E2b_EUR							

Figure 5.18

> **Note:** USD is not calculated because USD is not the first parent's local currency; thus, it is not part of the consolidate calculations. If you need USD to appear for the base entities that roll-up to the non-USD intermediary parent, you will need to run a Translate or Force Translate.

If you were to toggle to the `Calc Status` at `C#USD`, you would notice that a translation is needed.

Total_USD	OK
E1_Total_USD	OK
E1_USD	OK
E1_CAD	OK
E2_Total_EUR	OK
E2a_Total_EUR	TR
E2a_USD	OK
E2a_EUR	TR
E2a_GBP	TR
E2b_Total_EUR	TR
E2b_USD	OK
E2b_EUR	TR

Figure 5.19

A Translate or Force Translate will lead to three additional steps:

1. Translate to `E2a_EUR:C#USD`

2. Translate to `E2a_GBP:C#USD`

3. Translate to `E2a_USD:C#USD`

If we have intermediary parents where their local currency is not the same as the top consolidated parent or application default currency, is this a problem? The answer is… it depends, based on who and how users are consuming the data.

- If users will always use `C#Local` and know that – behind the scenes – the values reflected are the entity's local currency, then we don't need to do much.

- If users are viewing the intermediary parents in a different currency – and only that portion of the hierarchy – then it is not so much of a problem on their side. It might be more problematic on the consolidated/corporate side if there is the requirement to have everything in a different reporting currency.

Let's say that we need *everything* in a reporting currency of USD. We have a few options (again, this is not an exhaustive list, but it should give you a good starting point).

Option 1: Keep the structure as is, but you will need to add additional translation steps at the base entities followed by translation steps on the parent entities.

	Local	USD
Total_USD	762.64	762.64
E1_Total_USD	180.46	180.46
E1_USD	100.00	100.00
E1_CAD	100.00	80.46
E2_Total_EUR	477.31	582.18
E2a_Total_EUR	295.33	360.21
E2a_USD	100.00	100.00
E2a_EUR	100.00	121.97
E2a_GBP	100.00	138.24
E2b_Total_EUR	181.99	221.97
E2b_USD	100.00	100.00
E2b_EUR	100.00	121.97

Figure 5.20

Pros

- You will get expected results.

Cons

- The translation steps will be additional processing and will take additional time on top of your normal consolidation. This might be cumbersome if you have several base entities and parents. In other words, you need to run a translate and also a consolidate.

- Your calc status might still look wonky at USD.

Total_USD	CN
E1_Total_USD	OK
E1_USD	OK
E1_CAD	OK
E2_Total_EUR	TR,CN
E2a_Total_EUR	TR,CN
E2a_USD	OK
E2a_EUR	OK
E2a_GBP	OK
E2b_Total_EUR	TR,CN
E2b_USD	OK
E2b_EUR	OK

Figure 5.21

- You will need to be mindful of your overrides and the number of accounts that you want to view in this currency.

- If this entity structure is the primary structure, and the only structure, AND you do not want to use an alternate structure where the intermediary parents' currency aligns to the consolidated's currency, you might end up having to write a custom business rule with translation in it. There are additional steps needed, such as creating a sub-set of stat accounts to hold the overrides, changing their adjustment type to data entry, assuming you do not plan to use journals on those accounts and then the testing that comes with these changes. Honestly, even though I present this as an option, it is not the most ideal or performant option.

Option 2: Set the primary hierarchy to have the intermediary parents' local currency the same as the top consolidated member or the application's default currency. Create an alternate hierarchy with specific nodes for your reporting purposes. In other words, if you were using a USD application with USD as the primary reporting currency, the primary hierarchy would have these intermediary parents as USD, while there would be an alternate hierarchy with the foreign currency. You may have a situation where you only need a sub-consolidation in foreign currency rather than seeing the top of the house in multiple currencies.

Pros	Cons
• You will get the expected results. • Users who need to look up intermediary parents in a different currency will continue to be able to do so.	• Another hierarchy to maintain. • Consolidate on both hierarchies (although this can be handled as one step via a data management job).

Option 3: Have only one hierarchy where the intermediary parents are USD. Forget the original structure of the non-USD intermediary parents!

Pros	Cons
• Your calc status report is no longer wonky.	• You do not satisfy the reporting requirement to be able to view the intermediary parent in another currency. Even though this is an option, it is not a valid or viable option if you must have this reporting requirement.

Option 4: Auto translation currencies set on the entity. Values computed with the auto translation currencies do not consolidate (e.g., provide translated eliminations at the base entity, which is then consolidated up to the parent entity).

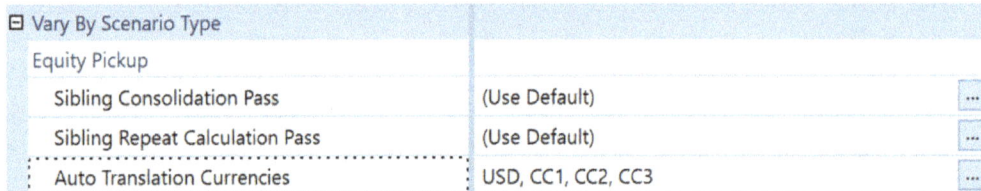

⊟ Vary By Scenario Type	
Equity Pickup	
Sibling Consolidation Pass	(Use Default) ⋯
Sibling Repeat Calculation Pass	(Use Default) ⋯
Auto Translation Currencies	USD, CC1, CC2, CC3 ⋯

Figure 5.22

Pros	Cons
• You will be able to quickly review the results in the specified currency at the base entities.	• The amounts reflected are not the same amounts as a true consolidation (e.g., elimination) and will not consolidate up. This setting is truly for reporting purposes and does not change what the consolidation engine is doing. • If you have this applied to several entities and you have a large Cube View, this may significantly increase your Cube View runtimes. • Does not enable the ability to enter overrides on parents (e.g., equity).

Auto Currency Translation

Auto currency translations can be used for equity pickup calculations when an entity needs to be translated to a sibling holding company's local currency during a consolidation. The use of auto currency translation with equity pickup requires the use of a custom finance rule that has the equity pickup logic. Auto currency translation settings may also be used to automatically translate certain entities to a specified currency for reporting needs and the only benefit is really at the base entities; if there is a need to look at parent entities in foreign currencies at the consolidated amounts (e.g., eliminations taken into consideration), this setting is not a viable option.

- Be mindful of the number of entities that will use auto currency translation functionality, as this will impact performance on both the calculation/consolidation side as well as on the reporting side.

- Auto currency translation will affect dynamic calculations. For example, if you have A#Headcount as a dynamic calculation, then the output will reflect the translated amount. A better approach for handling calculated accounts that should not be translated is to write it as a stored calculation, using a Member Formula with the appropriate FormulaPass and account type assigned.

To add auto translation currencies:

1. Navigate to Application > Cube > Dimensions > *select relevant Entity dimension > select relevant Entity member*.

2. On the Member Properties tab, scroll down to Vary by Scenario Type.

3. Click on the ellipse's icon next to Auto Translation Currencies.

4. If Scenario Type is applicable, then assign by Scenario Type. In the Stored Value row, enter the three-letter currency. Multiple currencies can be separated by a comma.

Vary By Scenario Type		
Equity Pickup		
Sibling Consolidation Pass	(Use Default)	...
Sibling Repeat Calculation Pass	(Use Default)	...
Auto Translation Currencies	USD, CC1, CC2, CC3	...

Figure 5.23

Scenario Type   (Default Scenario Type) ▼

Stored Items	Derived Property Value	
(Default Time)	Scenario Type	(Default Scenario Type)
All Items	Time	(Default Time)
(Default Time)	Derived Value	USD, CC1, CC2, CC3
	Stored Property Value	
	Scenario Type	(Default Scenario Type)
	Time	(Default Time)
	Stored Value	USD, CC1, CC2, CC3

Figure 5.24

Flow

There is a specific setting called **Switch Type** under the settings section for each Flow member.

If Switch Type is set to False, this tells the system to use the account's account type to determine which rate type and rule type to use for translations. If Switch Type is set to True for the given Flow member, then the account at this Flow member will have the account type "switched"; in other words, if my account's account type is Asset and the Flow member's Switch Type is True, then the system will use the Revenue and Expenses Rate Type and Revenue and Expenses Rule Type for translations.

FX

Commonly, there will be an FX hierarchy within the Flow dimension (highly recommended) to ensure that FX components are captured. This FX node captures the differences in the translation rates (e.g., average rate versus closing rate) between the components of a balance sheet account (e.g., beginning balance, activity, and ending balance).

Flow settings, in my experience (and at a minimum), usually include the following FX members:

1. **FXOpen**: a Member Formula that calculates the FX on the opening balance.

2. **FXMovement**: a Member Formula calculated as the difference between current closing rate and current average on the movement amount.

3. **FXOverrideBalance**: a Member Formula that calculates the FX on ending balances that have been overridden.

4. **FXHistOverrideMovement**: a Member Formula that calculates the FX on movements that have been overridden.

5. Members under FX will have the following settings:

    a. Switch Sign = False

    b. Switch Type = True

Refer to the Blueprint application for these Flow examples.

Account

The account's Account Type – in conjunction with the Switch Type on the Flow member – will dictate how translation will be handled based on the FX Rate Type defined in the cube (Application > Cubes > *Select your Cube* > on the Cube Properties tab, scroll down to FX Rates) unless otherwise specified in the scenario's FX rates.

⊟ FX Rates	
Default Currency	USD
Rate Type For Revenues And Expenses	AverageRate
Rule Type For Revenues And Expenses	Periodic
Rate Type For Assets And Liabilities	ClosingRate
Rule Type For Assets And Liabilities	Direct

Figure 5.25

In our above Cube Properties example, this means that accounts with account type of Revenue or Expense will use AverageRate and the Periodic calculation, while accounts with account type of Asset or Liability will use ClosingRate and the Direct calculation, assuming that Switch Type on the Flow member is set as False.

Below is the account type associated with the account member.

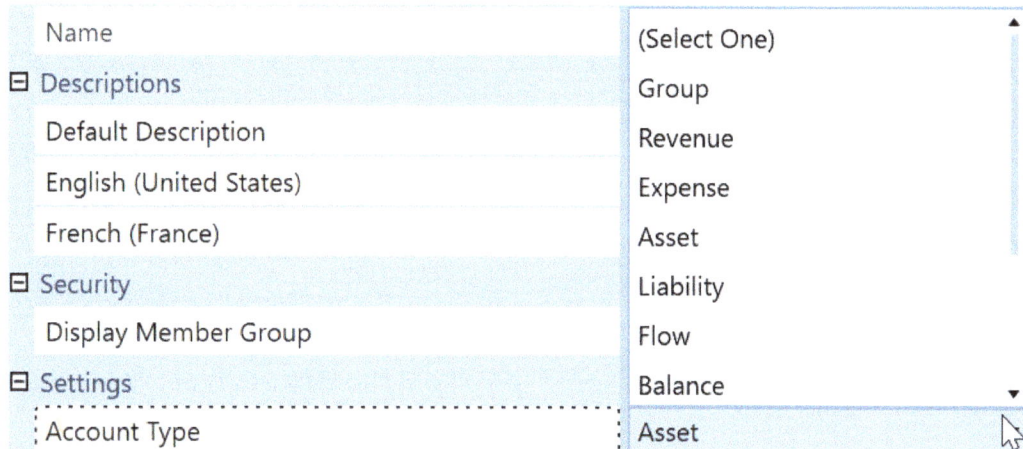

Figure 5.26

Non-Translating Accounts

Accounts that should not be translated should have the account type: Flow, Balance, Balance Recurring, or Nonfinancial. Thus, the amounts at C#Local and C#[Reporting Currency] will be the same amount output.

In the example below, I have account 110005 set to Balance. After I run a consolidate, the USD amount is the same as local.

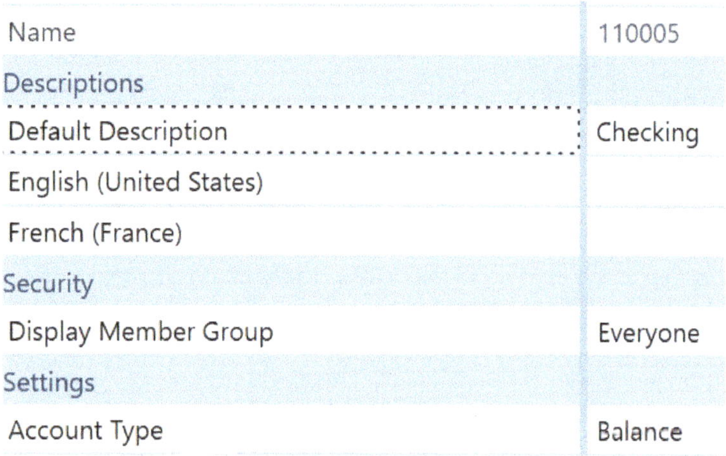

Figure 5.27

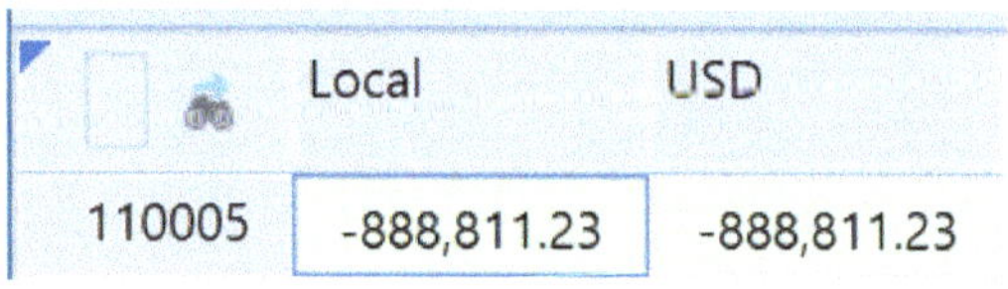

Figure 5.28

> **Note:** The account type, Group, is used as a label, simply to group a number of accounts together.

CTA (Currency Translation Adjustment)

CTA stands for currency translation adjustment. Its purpose is to capture the FX differences between the average and closing rates – per period – as P&L accounts are translated using the average rates, while balance sheet accounts are translated using the closing rates.

If you have an application with translations already enabled, you will already be aware of the CTA and relevant FX Flow members. If you have an application where you would like to enable OneStream's translation capabilities, then CTA will be an account member with a Member Formula. The two common logic approaches that I have seen:

1. **Plug Calculation:** Total assets - total liabilities and equity (since net income would roll into retained earnings, this difference would be CTA).

2. **True FX Calculation**: uses the Flow dimension FX hierarchy, in which the FX differences are already calculated.

Both will end up with the same result.

Refer to the Blueprint application for a CTA example.

Currency Overrides

I like to think of currency overrides as an accounting or consolidation process where you want to use an already defined amount or rate in lieu of the current translated amount or current rates.

Assuming you are managing an application that does not have currency overrides enabled, and you would like to start using OneStream for your override submissions, there are two common options to handle overrides:

- Out-of-the-box property settings on the Flow members.

- Using Member Formulas on the Flow member that represents the currency override, and text fields on the identified override accounts.

Currency overrides are handled by a combination of the Account and Flow dimensions. However, the first step is to gather your override requirements. Is there a need to have both rate and amount overrides, or is one or the other sufficient?

Out-of-the-Box Settings for Amount Overrides

OneStream provides out-of-the-box capabilities to set up amount overrides. However, it is important to note that the out-of-the-box settings assume you only need one currency override, not multiple currency overrides. These out-of-the-box settings are found in the **Flow Processing** section of a Flow member's properties.

Flow processing types include:

- Is Alternate Input Currency: indicates dollar override. If you opt for this setting, the relevant accounts must be flagged as True for Use Alternate Input Currency In Flow.

- Is Alternate Input Currency for All Accounts: all accounts will be able to use this alternate currency. This setting follows the rules of constraint. If the Flow member is set to True for Is Alternate Input Currency for All Accounts, and accounts have constraints set for the Flow dimension, the Flow member is required to be a member of the constraint.

- Translate using Alternate Input Currency, Input Local: will override the translated value with the amount inputted at the local currency level.

- Translate using Alternate Input Currency, Derive Local: will override the translated value and change the local currency value to be derived based on the local currency rate. A use case for this setting would be input currencies (refer to next section).

Additional settings under Flow processing include:

- Alternate Input Currency: contains a list of all available currencies for the source value override. If this Flow member has a USD override, then it should be set to USD. If the override is a EUR override, then it should be set to EUR.

- Source Member for Alternate Input Currency: Define the actual Flow member to override the value for the current Flow member.

Option 1: Your override member's Flow Processing Type is set to Is Alternate Input Currency and the Alternate Input Currency is defined as presented in Figure 5.29.

Flow Processing	
Flow Processing Type	Is Alternate Input Currency
Alternate Input Currency	USD
Source Member For Alternate Input Currency	

Figure 5.29

You will need to make sure your relevant account's Use Alternate Input Currency In Flow is set to True.

Members	Dimension Properties	Grid View	

Member Properties	Relationship Properties	
Id		15728786
Name		32000
Descriptions		
Default Description		APIC
English (United States)		
French (France)		
Security		
Display Member Group		Everyone
Settings		
Account Type		Liability
Formula Type		(Not Used
Allow Input		True
Is Consolidated		Condition
Is IC Account		False
Use Alternate Input Currency In Flow		False
Plug Account		True

Members tree:
- ▶ Members
- ▶ Orphans
- ▲ Hierarchy
  - None
  - ▲ TrialBalance - Trial Balance
    - ▶ IncomeStatement
    - ▲ BalanceSheet
      - ▶ Assets - Assets
      - ▲ LiabAndEquity - Liabilities and Equity
        - ▶ Liabilities - Liabilities
        - ▲ Equity - Equity
          - ▶ Stock - Total Stock
          - ▲ APIC - Additional Paid in Capital
            - 32000 - APIC
          - ▲ RE - Retained Earnings
            - ▲ REBegBal - Retained Earnings: Beg
              - 33000 - RE Beginning Balance

Figure 5.30

If you have an ending balance member, you will also need to ensure that its Flow Processing Type is set to Translate Using Alternate Input Currency, Input Local as shown in Figure 5.31, and its Source Member For Alternate Input Currency is set to the override member as presented in Figure 5.32.

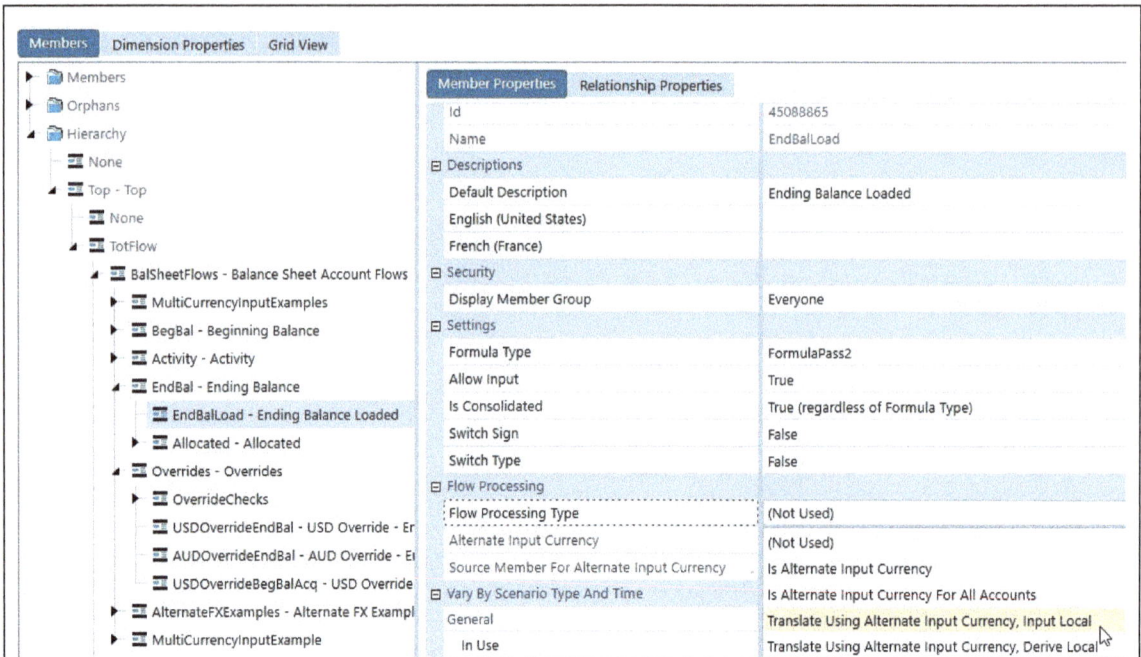

Figure 5.31

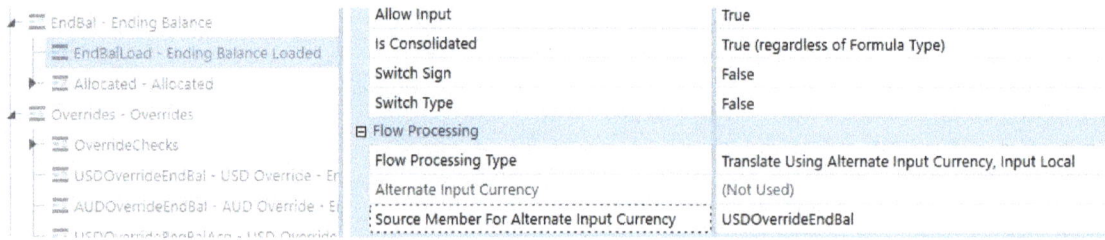

Figure 5.32

Pros	Cons
• A combination of Is Alternate Input Currency on the Flow override member and the individual setups on accounts restricts the number of accounts that are valid for overrides.	• These settings are only good for a single override. In other words, if you have multiple currency overrides, this option is not viable. • Additional effort or maintenance is needed for setting updates in the Account dimension.

Option 2: The override member's Flow Processing Type is set to Is Alternate Input Currency For All Accounts, as presented in Figure 5.33. The steps involved are similar to those of Option 1, except you do not need to go to the Account dimension to update the member's Use Alternate Input Currency In Flow as long as the Flow member is part of the Flow constraint. You will need to ensure your Ending Balance Flow member's Flow Processing Type is set to Translate Using Alternate Input Currency, Input Local, and its Source Member For Alternate Input Currency is set to the override member.

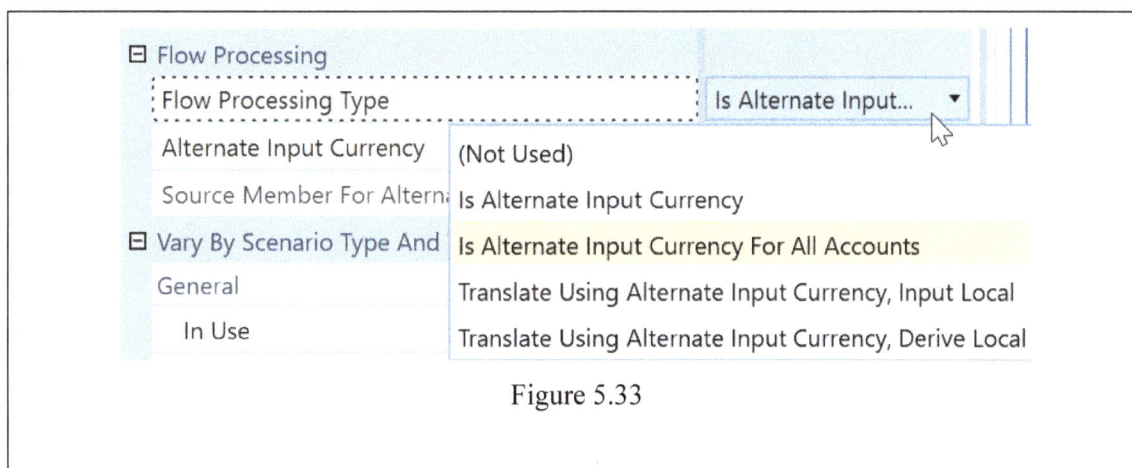

Figure 5.33

Pros	Cons
• Reduces efforts needed to update settings in Accounts dimensions for override accounts.	• These settings are only good for a single override. In other words, if you have multiple currency overrides, this option is not viable. • Additional considerations for controls if you do not want users to be able to enter overrides for all accounts.

Rate Overrides

There are no out-of-the-box settings to facilitate rate overrides. If you need to use rate overrides and you cannot use amount overrides, then you will need to leverage business rules or Member Formulas.

Member Formulas and Text Fields

The use of Member Formulas and text fields is the most common approach for currency overrides as they allow for multiple currency overrides. For accounts that are considered eligible for overrides, we commonly recommend using a text field with something like `Override`. The override logic is then handled on the Flow members, such as `USDOverrideEndBal` and `EndBalLoad` from the Flow dimension.

Refer to the Blueprint application for a CTA example.

Input Currencies

As mentioned in the introduction to this chapter, transactional currency will be used synonymously with input currency. While it is common to have transaction currency captured in the ERP, there may be cases where there is a requirement (or need) to handle transactional currency reporting and local currency translations within OneStream.

This next part is based on a real-life story where a company had such specific reporting needs. In this case, `S#Actual` is actual rates applied to local currency amounts, and this view is commonly compared to `S#Actual_Budget`, where the amounts are transactional (input) currencies with a constant (budget) rate. The company's ERP has both local currency amounts and transactional currency amounts.

You can either consider the use of a UD dimension with custom translation rules or leverage flow settings. This section covers leveraging flow settings to handle transactional and local currency within the OneStream application, which eliminates the need for custom rule writing.

- Enable currencies within the application.

- In the Flow dimension, create a grouping (e.g., `Total_TC`, `Tot_TC`, `TC_Total`; again, whatever makes sense to you and/or the users) that is a sibling to your top member (Total equivalent), which will present the total transactional (input) currencies.

In the screenshot below, there is a suffix of _TC to represent the transactional/input currency, but you can just name them as the currency (e.g., without the suffix). In other words, you simply need something within the Flow hierarchy to discern which grouping of currencies represents the translation of transactional currencies versus local currencies.

Figure 5.34

Transaction currencies (e.g., AED_TC) will be where the data is loaded. Each transactional currency member in the Flow dimension will have the following settings:

o Flow Processing Type is set as Is Alternate Input Currency for All Accounts.

o Alternate Input Currency as the *relevant currency*. For example, if the Flow member (e.g., CNY_TC) represents CNY transaction currency, then the alternate input currency is CNY.

- In the Flow dimension, create a grouping (e.g., Total_LC, Tot_LC, LC_Total; whatever makes sense to you and/or the users to represent local currencies) in the Flow hierarchy. This node can be a sibling to your ending balance member.

Underneath this grouping, create all the members that will represent the transactional (input) currencies that will be translated to local currency.

Figure 5.35

Each member under the total local currency section will have the following settings:

o Flow Processing Type is set as Translate Using Alternate Input Currency, Derive Local.

o Source Member For Alternate Input Currency will be the corresponding transactional currency member in the Flow hierarchy.

- Ensure that FX Rates are entered.

> **Note:** Remember that OneStream will leverage triangulation. As a result, you only need one rates table (e.g., all currencies relative to USD), and the system will derive the remaining translations (e.g., USD to EUR, etc.).

- Create a Cube View where you can view the transactional currency and local currency to validate the output is correct. Suggested setup:
    - Columns: entity and C#Local, C#USD, etc.
    - Rows: account and the Flow members for transactional currencies and local currencies.
    - For reporting purposes, the appropriate combination of dimensions will be the equivalent of F#Tot_LC: C#USD (where F#Tot_LC represents the sum of all the currencies translated to the local currency), or F#Tot_LC:C#EUR.

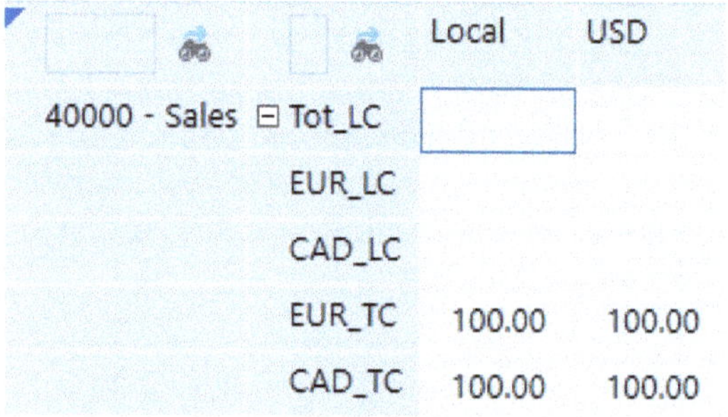

			Local	USD
40000 - Sales	⊟ Tot_LC			
	EUR_LC			
	CAD_LC			
	EUR_TC		100.00	100.00
	CAD_TC		100.00	100.00

Figure 5.36

In my example above, I have a USD entity in which I enter 100 to EUR_TC and CAD_TC. Upon save, the same amounts will show up in USD since the entity's local currency is USD (C#Local as USD = C#USD). Again, for reporting purposes, the intersection should be the equivalent of F#LC_Total: C#USD. After a consolidate, notice that the local amounts are derived in EUR_LC and CAD_LC. The rates used were 1.25 for CAD and 1.229 for EUR, so the expected amounts are 125 and 122.90 USD, respectively, for a total of 247.90 USD (Figure 5.37).

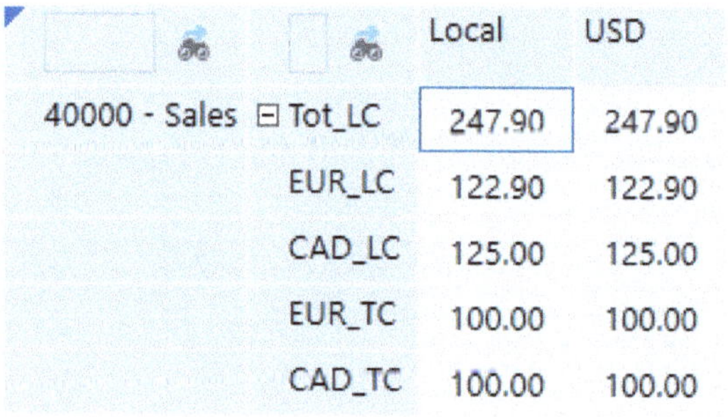

			Local	USD
40000 - Sales	⊟ Tot_LC		247.90	247.90
	EUR_LC		122.90	122.90
	CAD_LC		125.00	125.00
	EUR_TC		100.00	100.00
	CAD_TC		100.00	100.00

Figure 5.37

Note: With this real-life story, we leveraged Scenario Types to further differentiate between the scenarios; here, one scenario (`S#Actual`) took the local balances from the ERP file, while another scenario (`S#Actual_Budget`) took the transactional balances from the ERP file.

If you are considering the use of input currencies, we recommend bringing in the right personnel to help you determine how to implement transactional currencies, especially if your application already has existing data.

Reporting Actuals with Prior Year Rates

Now, following everything we have covered so far, let's assess the ability to report actuals using prior year rates. What functionalities within OneStream will support this requirement, and what functionality should we be using?

I have worked on several engagements where there were only a handful of requirements, such as "The ability to report actuals with prior year actual rates" and "The ability to report actuals with budget rates" and that was all this user base needed. As a result, I leaned towards one choice (in this case, it was additional FX rate types). I have also worked on a case where several scenarios were needed to handle all sorts of FX-neutral reports, and because this application was large and administrator-heavy, I leaned towards another choice (in this case, it was standard with business rules and attaching translation logic to the cubes).

At the end of the day, my goal in this section is to provide you with a high-level assessment of the pros and cons associated with each of the functionalities but, ultimately, it will be up to your company stakeholders, consulting partners, and you – as the administrator – to assess and arrive at an informed conclusion. As always, the list below is not exhaustive, but I do hope it will provide you with a foundation to get started.

Additional FX Rate Types and Standard

You could create additional FX rate types like `AverageRatePY` and `ClosingRatePY` and continue to leverage the standard Cube Translation Algorithm Type for your given scenario(s). The primary changes would be:

- Adding FX rates and entering the FX rates.

- Creating the necessary scenarios. Then, within the scenario's member properties, under the FX Rates section, you would set Use Cube FX Settings to False and update to use these FX rate types.

Below is a table of the pros and cons associated with the creation of FX rate types.

Pros	Cons
Standard translation functionality is maintained.	You need to create several FX rate types.
Rates are explicit and defined by each rate type.	Increased efforts to input, copy, or load the same set of rates across multiple rate types for each currency.
If you are using FX rate types for additional translation capabilities, you will not need to change the Cube Translation Algorithm Type.	

Figure 5.38

FX Rate Types and Standard with Business Rules

The Cube Translation Algorithm Type of Standard with Business Rules is particularly useful for custom translations where you want to leverage existing rates that are already entered into the application and you do not want redundant FX rate types. For example, if you want a scenario that represents actuals with prior year rates, you decide to use the ClosingRate or AverageRate with the already entered rates to T#[last year] instead of creating a new FX rate type and entering last year's rates into T#[this year].

In order for this to work, you will need to…

- Write the finance business rule to support your custom translation requirements.

- Update the Cube Translation Algorithm Type to Standard with a Business Rule.

- Assign the finance business rule to the cube at the beginning of the processing sequence (e.g., Business Rule 1-3, depending on how custom your application is).

  o We commonly see the custom translation rule assigned as Business Rule 1, but again, I want to highlight the unique circumstances in which you might want to assign it in a different order. For example, I was on an engagement that consisted of non-controlling interest calculations and a custom elimination which needed to be populated at base entities. As such, this particular application had the non-controlling interest calculation as Business Rule 1, the custom elimination as Business Rule 2, and the custom translation as Business Rule 3.

- Create the necessary scenarios.

- Consider the Flow's switch type implications with the account type. Do you want the Flow member to have Switch Type as True, or should it be False?

Below is a table of the pros and cons associated with using Standard with Business Rules.

Pros	Cons
Standard translation functionality is maintained.	Requires rule writing.
Reduced maintenance on the number of rate types.	It may be difficult for the user to understand *where* the rate originates.
Reduces manual efforts to enter the same rates across several rate types.	

Figure 5.39

Loading FX Rates

This section covers the various ways to input FX rates into the OneStream application. The most common methods include:

1. Entering directly into the FX rates grid.

2. Submitting through Excel.

3. Using a direct connect.

FX Rates Grid

The navigation path is Application > Cube > FX Rates. This is the out-of-the-box method where you select your views and FX rate type and enter the rates. With this FX grid, you can:

1. Create new FX rate types to represent various FX situations (e.g., PlanAverageRate, PlanClosingRate).

2. FX rates are entered into this grid by FX rate type.

3. FX rate types can then be applied to scenario members.

4. FX rate types can be further differentiated by Scenario Type and/or cubes to govern how translation should be handled.

The FX grid provides the flexibility to select how you want to see your FX rate type, time, source currency, destination currency, row axis, and column axis. A question we often get asked is, "What is the optimal default display?" Generally, the answer is something along the lines of, "Whatever combination makes sense for you!" but an example view that I personally like to use is shown below.

This example displays time across the rows, with destination currencies in the columns. Notice how I have Source Currency selected specifically as USD. Thus, the rates displayed are USD:destination currency. In other words, 1 USD:1.2429 CAD.

	CAD	EUR	GBP	JPY	KRW	TWD	USD
2018							
2018H1							
2018Q1							
2018M1	1.2429	0.819873739	0.72337963	110.871	1,065.641	29.4005	
2018M2	1.2588	0.889679715	0.716281069	107.97	1,078.4747	29.2458	
2018M3	1.2933	0.810766986	0.715512307	106.0468	1,069.9418	29.1991	
2018Q2							
2018M4	1.2732	0.814995925	0.710277719	107.6562	1,068.0452	29.3767	
2018M5	1.2866	0.845809016	0.742390497	109.6882	1,076.6595	29.8673	
2018M6	1.3125	0.856237692	0.752219046	110.0638	1,094.3552	30.0848	
2018H2							
2018Q3							
2018M7	1.3133	0.855798032	0.759762954	111.521	1,122.2029	30.5429	
2018M8	1.3042	0.866025808	0.776518093	110.9965	1,120.427	30.7039	
2018M9	1.3034	0.857118368	0.765345171	112.0974	1,119.82	30.7253	
2018Q4							
2018M10	1.3004	0.870473538	0.768521365	112.7218	1,131.615	30.8823	
2018M11	1.3205	0.879971841	0.775193798	113.338	1,125.345	30.806	
2018M12	1.3426	0.875810124	0.789639924	112.1994	1,122.4244	30.7822	

Figure 5.40

> **Note:** If there is no FX rate entered/loaded for an existing currency, then the translation will not occur. In other words, you will see the local currency amount but no amount in USD; check your FX grid to see if you have a rate there.

To prevent changes to entered FX rates, administrators or users who have access to the FX grid can lock by the FX rate types and the time. OneStream recommends that the administrator manages the locking of FX rate types.

> **Note:** If you don't see the lock icon – as per the screenshot below – you likely have an older version of OneStream. This is a relatively recent feature that was made available after 6.0.

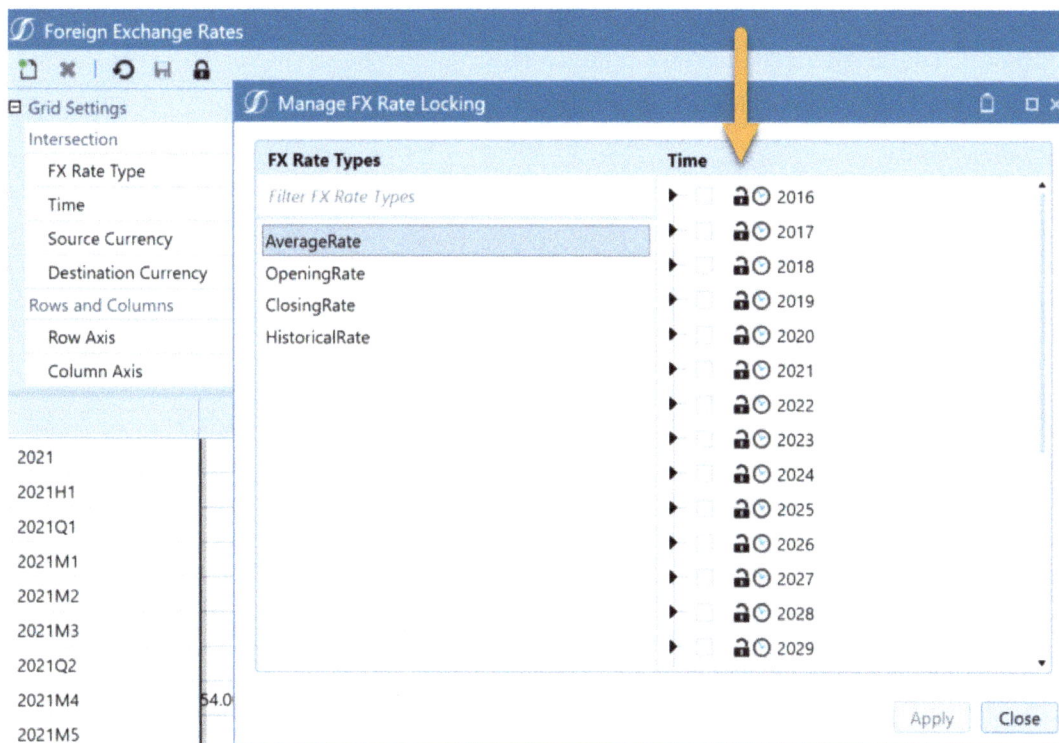

Figure 5.41

Excel or Spreadsheet with Submit Cells

To submit rates in Excel, use: `XFSetFxRate(value, storeZeroAsNoData, fxRateType, time, sourceCurrency, destCurrency)`.

Example: `=XFSetFxRate(1.4,TRUE,"AverageRate","2021M4","USD","CAD")`. When the user clicks Submit Sheet, this will update the FX rates in the system.

> **Note:** The rate entered should be read as `source:destination`. In other words, if the source is USD and destination is CAD, then it is USD:CAD, which is 1 USD = 1.4 CAD

Direct Connect

A custom connector rule is written to directly pull the FX rates from the source system or web service like Thomson Reuters. Typically, this would require a support ticket and, depending on the contracts, someone can assist with getting you started with the integration.

Viewing FX Rates

There are various ways to enable the viewing of FX rates. The common one is the out-of-the-box FX rates grid, but a familiar ask is to limit a person's ability to modify FX rates. Thus, this section covers the common methods for users to view FX rates:

1. FX Rates Grid

2. Excel or Spreadsheet with Get Cells

3. Cube Views using dynamic reporting members

Chapter 5

FX Rates Grid

The FX rates grid is where you can view FX rates after you load them. The navigation path is the same as we saw with loading rates, namely: Application > Cube > FX Rates. Here, the user can make selections to FX rate type, time, source currency, destination currency, row axis, and column axis.

Excel or Spreadsheet with Get Cells

To retrieve rates and view them in Excel, use:

```
XFGetCalculatedFxRate(displayNoDataAsZero, fxRateType, time,
sourceCurrency, destCurrency)
```

Example: `=XFGetCalculatedFxRate(TRUE,"AverageRate","2021M4","CAD","USD")`

Cube Views Using Dynamic Reporting Members

If you need users to view FX rates, but they do not have the relevant security rights to directly access the FX grid, one method would be to use a UD dimension (hopefully you have reserved your UD8 for reporting calcs) where you bring the UD8 member in as a Cube View.

> **Note**: There is a pane that provides you with all the available functions needed to write your rule. As you can see, we have various `GetCalculatedFxRates`, and if you click on one of them, you get a sample of what you need to define. So, in the example below, we need to determine the `rateType` and then fill in the parameters for `GetCalculatedFxRate`. The parameter for the source currency is `api.Entity.GetLocalCurrency.Id`, and the destination is `api.Cons.GetCurrency(api.Pov.Cons.Name).Id`.

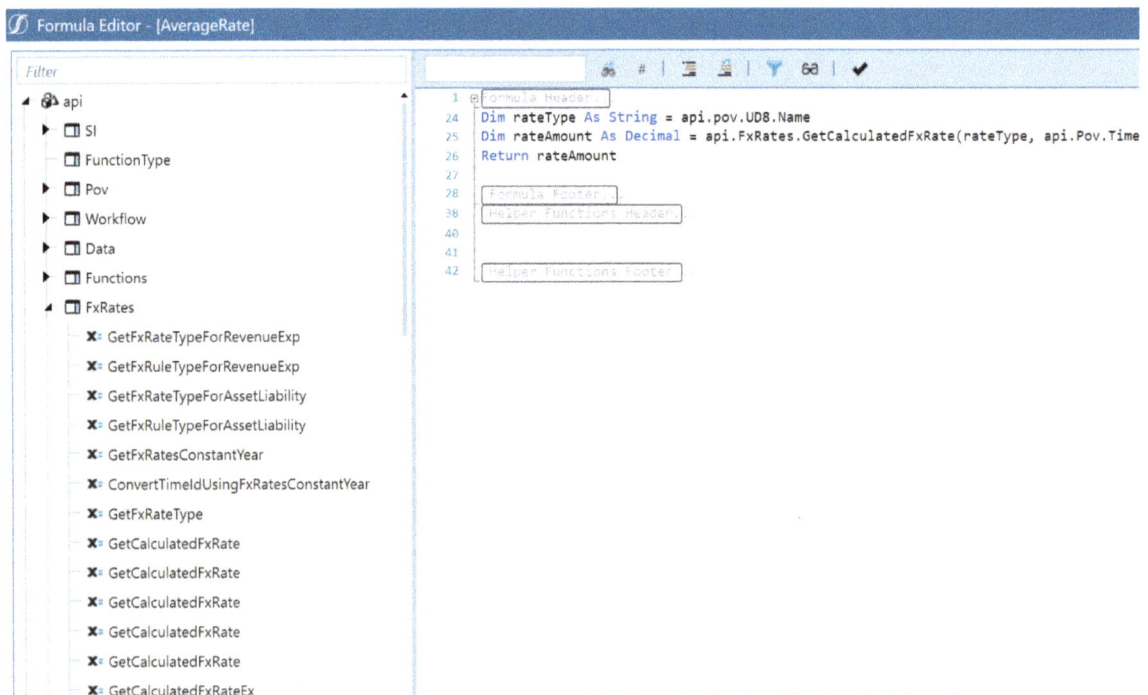

Figure 5.42

Then, on the Cube View, populate the default members (hint: account doesn't really matter) and set the Row Expansion to the UD8 and Currencies.

90

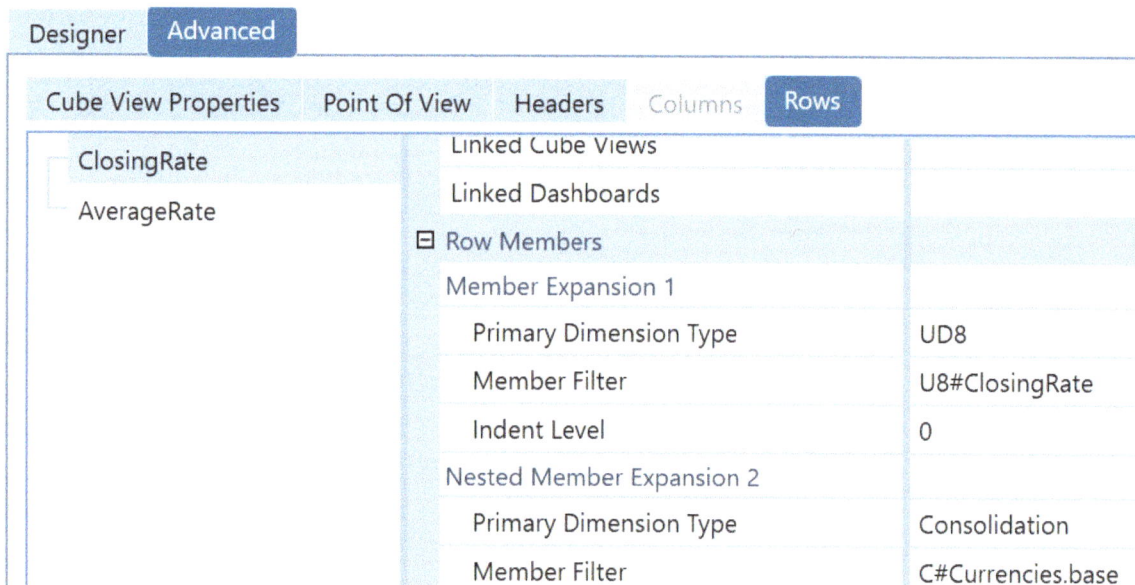

Figure 5.43

This Cube View assumes the user accessing it is viewing currency rates in relation to the entity's local currency. This explains why – in the UD8 Member Formula – the example specifically identified the source currency to be the entity's local currency. In other words, the rates will be [selected entity's local currency]:[destination currency].

		Jan 2018	Feb 2018	Mar 2018	Apr 2018
Closing Rate	⊟ CAD	1.71818	1.75741	1.80752	1.79254
	CNY	8.87957	8.82098	8.82920	8.86512
	CRC	8.87957	8.82098	0.00000	0.00000
	EUR	1.13339	1.24208	1.13313	1.14743
	GBP	1.00000	1.00000	1.00000	1.00000

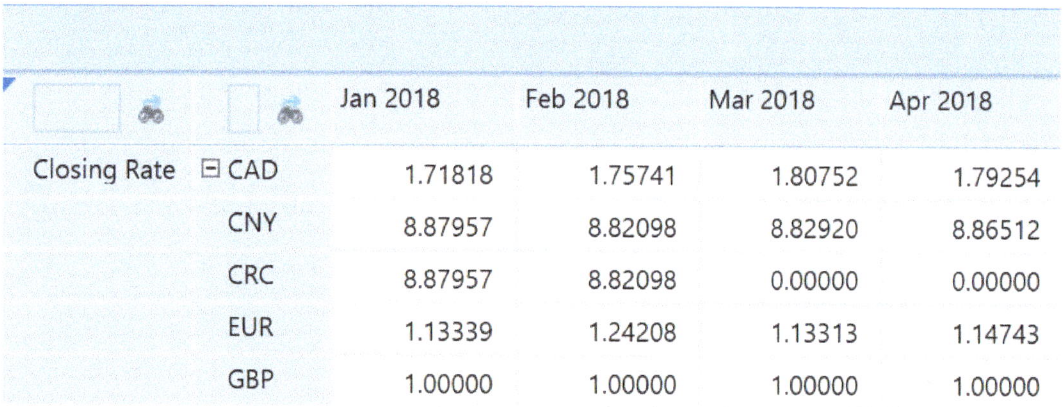

Figure 5.44

It looks like someone forgot to load CRC rates for March and April 2018 ☺.

Conclusion

This chapter was all about where an administrator can enable translations in the OneStream application. The translation process is dependent on the properties found on the Cube, Scenario, Account, Entity, and Flow, as they are all interrelated. Specific translation features that OneStream handles include handling intermediary parents, auto currency translations, CTA (currency translation adjustment), overrides, and transactional currencies.

Translation depends on the rates captured in the system; in other words, if there is no rate entered for a given period, then the local amount will not translate for that given period. The most common methods to enter FX rates include the out-of-the-box FX rates grid, an Excel submission, or through a direct connect.

Chapter 5

Depending on your company's security and reporting requirements, the most common ways FX rates can be viewed include the out-of-the-box FX rates grid, Excel with the `get` formula, or Cube Views with the use of dynamic reporting members.

6

Work the Workflow

The purpose of this chapter is to highlight important considerations when it comes to setting up existing or new Workflow Profiles and how specific workflow steps should be used. At first, the concept of a workflow can be a little daunting, but you may change your mind once you understand its primary function. This chapter covers workflow considerations, especially if you are tasked with expanding functionalities within OneStream.

Workflow Profiles are foundational to OneStream, such that they are covered extensively in the OneStream Foundation Handbook and the Design and Reference Guide. The question, then, is why does this chapter exist?

This chapter exists to re-arrange the information in a way that makes sense to the administrator. For example, what happens if I set up a workflow as X instead of Y? The answer may not be obvious, so we have it covered here. Thus, the organization of this chapter is as follows:

- Background information on the workflow engine and workflow Data Unit (also known as workflow clusters).

- The importance of workflow suffixes, and where you can find and apply them.

- Workflow Profile types, and how each one can be used.

- Examples of using the process step, and ways to set up calculation definitions.

- Security naming recommendations for Workflow Profile groups.

- Workflow channels and troubleshooting workflow channels.

- Locking workflows.

- Common tips and troubleshooting for workflows.

Background

Workflow Engine and **Workflow Data Units** are methods within OneStream that control how data is loaded into the application. For more information, there is a great section in the Design and Reference Guide that covers Workflow Profile data loading behaviors.

Workflow Engine

An extremely important concept in OneStream is that the workflow engine orchestrates all input data entering the application; it is responsible for clearing, loading, and locking all incoming data. Data for any Origin member (Import, Forms, and Adjustments) must pass through the workflow engine, and is always tagged with the workflow that owns it.

When data is loaded to Stage via an Import workflow, the data is tagged with your active Workflow POV. To see the data tagged to the Workflow POV, you can drill down into a cell in OneStream, right-click on the intersection, and select Load Results For Imported Cell to see which workflow the cell was loaded from. In Figure 6.1, you can see that this cell came from loading two separate workflows. You can use the Navigate to Source Data button to navigate to these workflows directly.

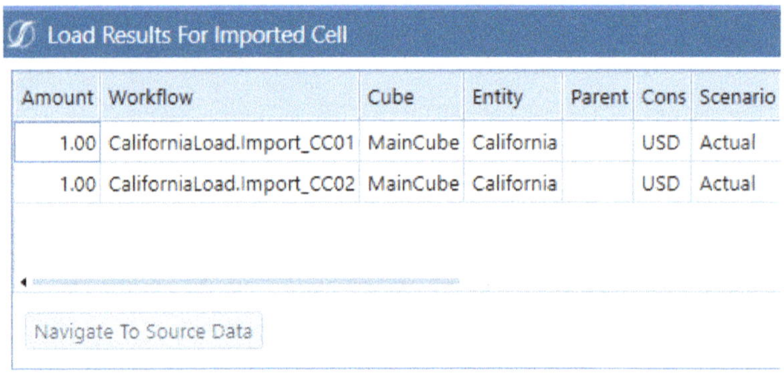

Figure 6.1

It is not obvious, but all inputted forms and adjustment data are also tagged with an owning workflow. This is true regardless of whether you used a Cube View that was *not* linked to any workflows, or even an Excel submission template.

In Figure 6.2, below, the ownership is determined by looking at each intersection's entity, and seeing which workflow that entity is assigned to. Again, you can drill down into a cell, select Audit History For Forms or Adjustment Cell, and then click the View All Impacted Workflow Units button.

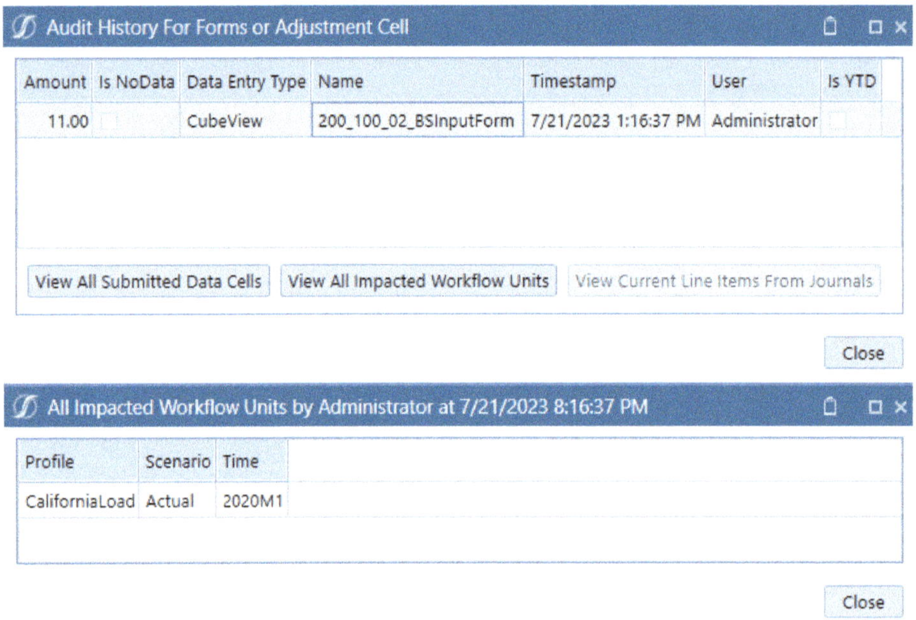

Figure 6.2

This is important to point out because it is often a misconception that workflows are just a way to create a process flow for users. Workflows are more than that; they serve as the backbone of OneStream. Workflows let you impose strict controls on what data can enter your system (preventing the dreaded garbage-in, garbage-out model). They ensure data integrity because you can track down and flush stale data when loading new datasets and lock down datasets to prevent them from being accidentally modified. Finally, they give you a seamless audit trail, so you can always figure out where your data came from.

Workflow Data Units (Workflow Clusters)

This section covers the three basic Data Units that OneStream uses to partition data when performing any sort of work:

1. Cube Data Unit

2. Workflow Data Unit

3. Workflow Channel Data Unit

The concept of Data Units serves as an important foundation for the remaining sections of this workflow chapter. It is integral that you understand which actions affect which types of Data Units, so you can be sure you are not clearing more data than expected, or you are only calculating the subset of data that you want to affect.

The **Cube Data Unit** is the largest unit of work and is comprised of the six Data Unit dimensions (Level 1): Cube, Entity, Parent, Consolidation, Scenario, and Time. The finance engine acts on this level, clearing and loading by entire cube Data Units.

There is a more granular Data Unit called the **Workflow Data Unit** (also known as workflow cluster), which also includes the Account, Flow, View, Origin, and Intercompany dimensions (Level 2). Earlier, we discussed how all input data is tagged with your active Workflow POV. This POV includes your workflow name, Scenario, and Time, which comprises a **Workflow Cluster Primary Key**. When you initiate a load from an Import workflow, the workflow engine will first find and clear any previously loaded data with the same workflow cluster key.

Finally, the **Workflow Channel Data Unit** builds on the workflow Data Unit even further by including a User-Defined dimension (Level 3). Each application can only use a single dimension for workflow channels. By default, workflow channels will apply to accounts. If you select a different dimension for workflow channels, then the workflow channels will also apply to that dimension.

Figure 6.3 is an illustrative example of how the dimensions are sorted by the cube Data Unit, workflow Data Unit, and workflow channel Data Unit.

Level 1 Cube Data Unit (Cube, Entity, Parent, Consolidation, Scenario, Time)	Level 2 Workflow Data Unit (Account, Flow, View, Origin, Intercompany)	Level 3 Workflow Channel Data Unit (UD1-UD8)
Cb#MgmtRpt	A#100	Example: UD1#000
E#Entity1	F#EndBalInput	UD2#None
P#Top	V#YTD	UD3#None
C#Local	O#Import	UD4#None
S#Actual	IC#None	UD5#None
T#20XXM1		UD6#None
		UD7#None
		UD8#None

Figure 6.3

When the workflow engine loads data, it will go through these Data Units and your workflow configuration to determine how the data set should be processed (such as cleared and/or overridden). We discuss these topics further in the workflow channels section of this chapter.

Workflow Suffixes

Workflow suffixes are text strings added to the Scenario Types within OneStream. This section covers the functionalities that adding workflow suffixes will provide, such as streamlining your Workflow Profiles by Scenario Type and providing entity assignments by Scenario Type. We will walk through examples of results when implementing workflow suffixes.

Top Cube Settings

First, workflow suffixes are applied on cubes that have Is Top Level Cube For Workflow set as True. To find this setting, you will need to navigate from the Application tab and click on Cubes. Select the relevant cube, which in Figure 6.4 is Corporate, and click on the Cube Properties tab.

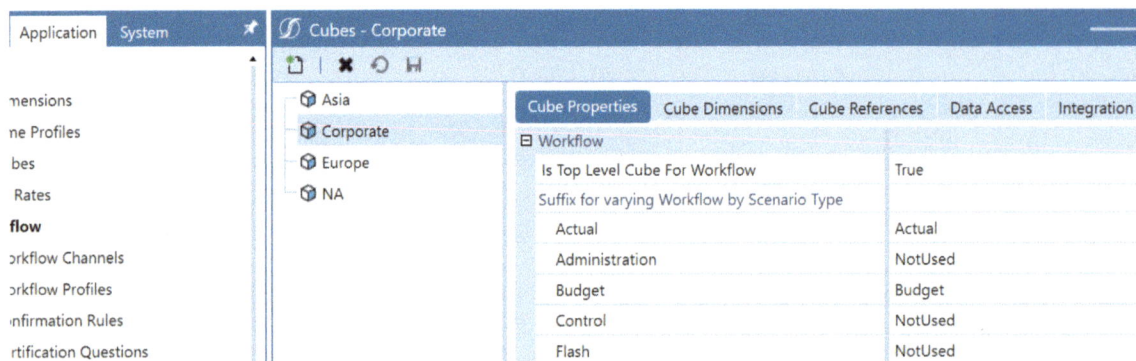

Figure 6.4

In Figure 6.4, notice that workflow suffixes are already assigned to the Scenario Types. For example, Actual has an Actual suffix, while Administration has a NotUsed suffix.

Ensure that your application has workflow suffixes assigned; in other words, any Scenario Types that are *in use* should *not* be blank. You will notice in Figure 6.4 that NotUsed is assigned to some Scenario Types like Control and Flash – this is optional for Scenario Types not in use. Alternatively, you can leave unused Scenario Types blank until you need to use them, at which point, I recommend adding a relevant suffix.

By adding these suffixes, you create a layer of organization for your Workflow Profiles where you can toggle by suffix. For example, if you want one workflow hierarchy dedicated to consolidation, accounts reconciliation, or some other process that is heavily reliant on Actuals data, then tag all the relevant Scenario Types with Actual. By tagging your Scenario Types with the appropriate suffix, you will then be able to see these Scenario Types under the relevant cube root Workflow Profile name.

This is a benefit as you are now specifically choosing which Scenario Types should be valid per cube root Workflow Profile name. Said differently, without the suffixes, you end up having to click through every Scenario Type and somehow track which steps are valid for which Scenario Types.

Cube Root Workflow Profile Name

A cube root Workflow Profile name is created based on the suffixes entered in the Cube Properties of your top-level Cube. In this section, we will walk through the steps and outcomes when updating the suffixes.

Let's assume that we have already created a Workflow Profile hierarchy for Actual, and we now want to create another workflow hierarchy dedicated to Budget.

1. When you want to create a new cube root Workflow Profile name, the system pulls in the suffixes that you defined from Cube Properties for the cube that has True set for Is Top Level Cube For Workflow. Figure 6.4 showed the Corporate cube as the top-level cube and the suffixes are Actual, Budget and NotUsed. Thus, in Figure 6.5, the selection choices

will be the cube name plus the suffixes, which in our case are Corporate_Budget, Corporate_Forecast, and Corporate_NotUsed.

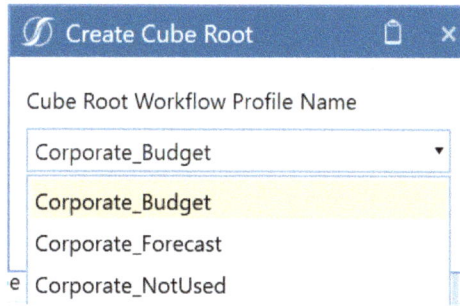

Figure 6.5

2. As such, when you are ready and need another workflow hierarchy for a different Scenario Type, you are able to do so. From Figure 6.5. I can create a Corporate_Budget as another cube root Workflow Profile. The result is Figure 6.6.

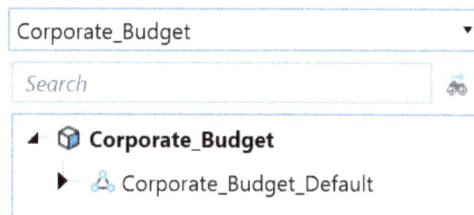

Figure 6.6

I can now manage and separate two *completely different* processes for workflow and view the relevant Scenario Types associated with the given Actual and Budget workflow suffix. This is the benefit mentioned in the previous section; you can toggle between the suffixes and view just the Scenario Types associated with that suffix.

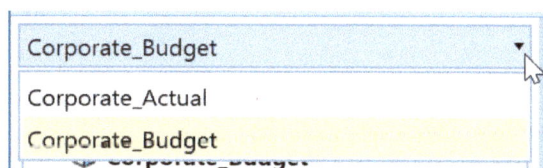

Figure 6.7

The distinction between the workflow hierarchies via the suffixes will allow for entity assignment flexibility. Entity assignment is important as it can be used to control who should be handling what entities throughout the workflow process.

Suffixes Provides Entity Assignment Flexibility

Assigning suffixes provides you with greater flexibility for the entity assignment as you can vary your entity assignments among your cube root Workflow Profiles. This section covers an example of how the same entity is available between two cube root Workflow Profiles.

In Figure 6.8, notice in the Corporate_Actual structure that E101 is already assigned.

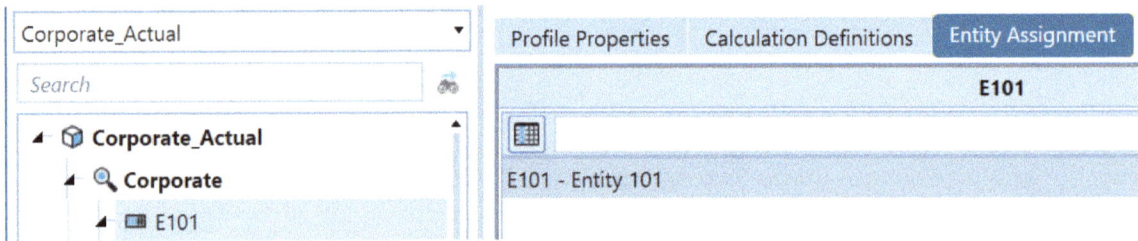

Figure 6.8

Now, when I go to `Corporate_Budget`, notice that `E101` is *also* available to assign (Figure 6.9).

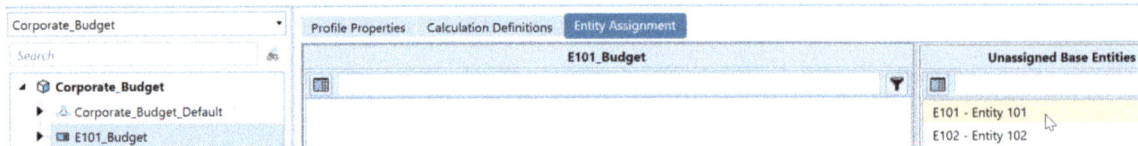

Figure 6.9

Without suffixes, you might run into a situation where you are limited to how entities can be assigned across your business processes. For example, if you have your consolidation team in OneStream, they may be the only folks who should handle *all* entities, and perhaps you have all the entities assigned to their Workflow Profiles. Then, if you try to incorporate your budget team into OneStream and the budget team is responsible for only a *handful* of entities, you will not be able to use the same entities if both Actual and Budget Scenario Types are using the same cube root Workflow Profile. You might now be wondering how to update your suffixes… we will cover this over the next sections!

Not Starting Out with a Suffix and Now You Want to Add Suffixes

If you notice that your current application has Scenario Types as blank, you may be wondering about the repercussions. As already mentioned, a lack of suffixes becomes problematic from the administrator's perspective when you start to expand the application to enable more capabilities involving the use of entity assignments. Furthermore, as an administrator, you will have to keep track of which Scenario Type to update your workflows with, as you may not be able to use the Default Scenario Type.

For example, if you have a Load_Entities import step for Actual and Budget processes in the same cube root Workflow Profile, then you will have to be explicit on your Actual and Budget Scenario Types for security groups and settings.

Users will not necessarily see the impact, but you will whenever you want to update your Workflow Profiles. To add suffixes later, especially if the Scenario Type already *has data*, you will receive an error message (Figure 6.10) when you try to update directly on Cube Properties.

Let's say I have data in a scenario member tagged with the Administration Scenario Type and my Administration does not have a suffix. When I try to add a suffix of _Actual, I will receive an error message.

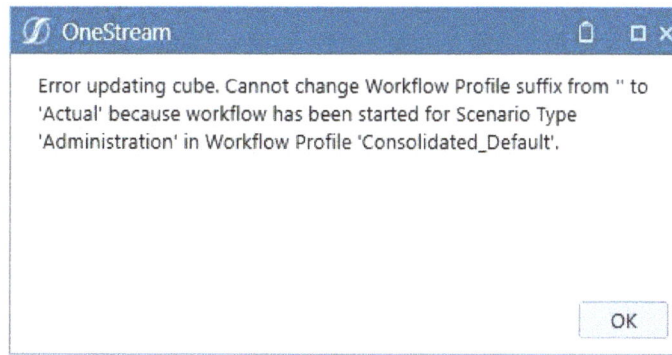

Figure 6.10

So, you may be wondering, how do I get around this error and add a suffix to a Scenario Type that has data? We have a few options to handle this:

1. Clear everything in these Scenario Types and add your suffixes to the Scenario Types, then reload to the Scenario Types.

2. Add suffixes to any remaining Scenario Types that do not have data. You will simply have to make a note, going forward, that for the Scenario Types *that do have data*, you will have to manage them all under the same cube root Workflow Profile.

3. Go to the scenario members with the affected Scenario Type and change the Scenario Type to another Scenario Type that does not have data. Go back to Cube Properties and update the Scenario Type's suffix. Return to the scenario member and add the original Scenario Type.

    a. In our example, Figure 6.11, the Administration Scenario Type does not have a suffix, but we have data loaded to it.

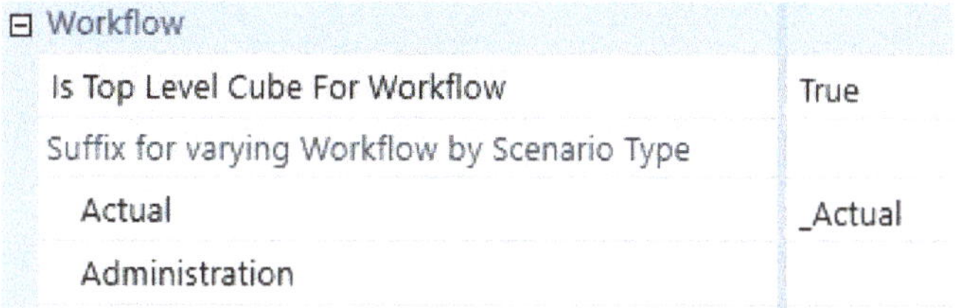

Figure 6.11

    b. I try to add _Actual to Administration, and I get the error message seen in Figure 6.10.

    c. I go to my scenario member, Actual, which is tagged as Administration in Figure 6.12, and change it to a Scenario Type that does not have data (e.g., Forecast) as reflected in Figure 6.13.

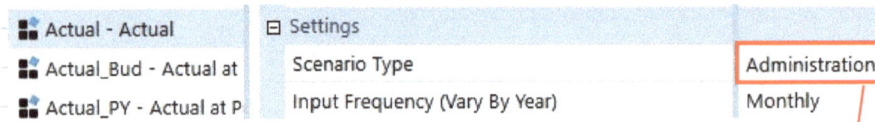

Figure 6.12

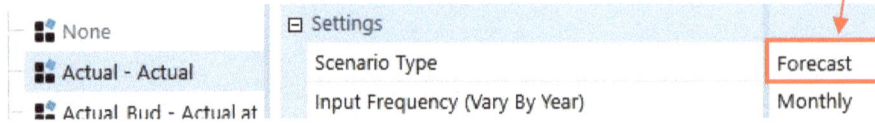

Figure 6.13

d. Now I go back to Cube Properties and update the Scenario Type's suffix to _Actual, and the update is successful.

⊟ Workflow	
Is Top Level Cube For Workflow	True
Suffix for varying Workflow by Scenario Type	
Actual	_Actual
Administration	_Actual

Figure 6.14

e. I return to my scenario member, Actual, and update the Scenario Type from Forecast to Administration.

You might be wondering, "The last option is the preferred way, right?" and the answer is the classic "It depends!" There are pros and cons to each option, reflected in the following table, and – depending on your business needs and where you are in your process – a different option may be preferable.

Options	Pros	Cons
Clear everything in these Scenario Types, add your suffixes to the Scenario Types, and reload to the Scenario Types.	Start anew with the suffix setup for all Scenario Types.	Depending on the volume of data to reload, a complete reload could take time.
Add suffixes to any remaining Scenario Types that do not have data.	Allows remaining unused Scenario Types to be used for future functionalities.	Existing Workflow Profile maintenance may be higher if several Scenario Types have data.
Go to the scenario members with the affected Scenario Type and change the Scenario Type to another Scenario Type that *does not have data*.	Does not need a data clear or data reload. You can still drill down from the cube and get to the load file/load results for the imported cell.	All existing scenarios referencing the Scenario Type must be updated to another Scenario Type that does not have data, and then must be updated back after the suffix is added.

Figure 6.15

Adding Existing Suffixes to New Scenario Types

You can add suffixes and update (or change) suffixes to Scenario Types that do not have data. By adding an existing suffix for a new Scenario Type, the new Scenario Type becomes an option for your workflow hierarchy. In the example below, I'll update the Administration Scenario Type from NotUsed in Figure 6.16 to Actual in Figure 6.17.

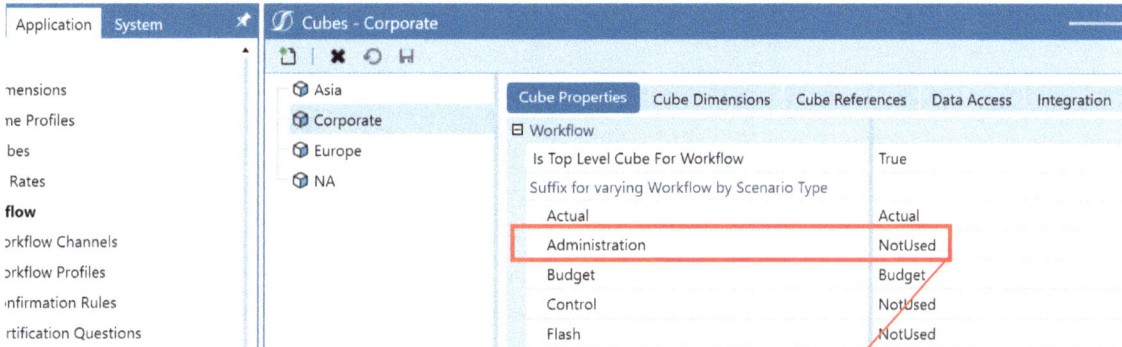

Figure 6.16

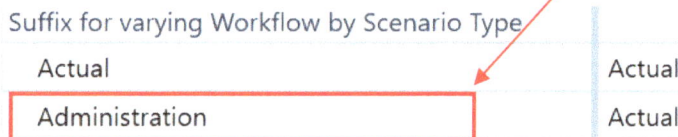

Figure 6.17

Figure 6.18 represents the before change (Administration as NotUsed), in which the Administration was not initially part of the `Corporate_Actual` cube root Workflow Profile.

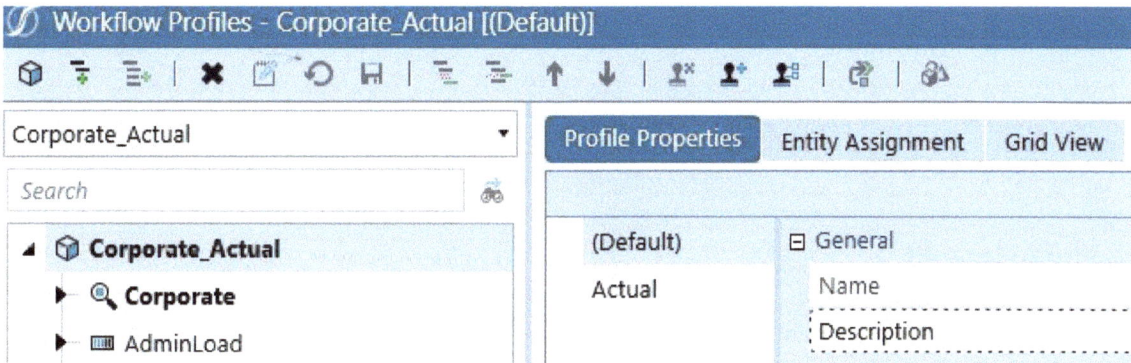

Figure 6.18

After updating Administration to Actual, when I navigate to my Workflow Profile and select my cube root Workflow Profile of `Corporate_Actual`, `Administration` is now part of the selection.

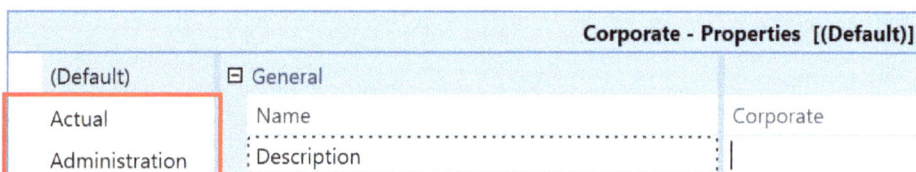

Figure 6.19

Chapter 6

If I want to undo this, I can, because the Administration Scenario Type does not have data. I'll go back and update Administration to SomethingElse.

⊟ Workflow	
Is Top Level Cube For Workflow	True
Suffix for varying Workflow by Scenario Type	
Actual	Actual
Administration	SomethingElse

Figure 6.20

Then, returning to my `Corporate_Actual` cube root Workflow Profile, `Administration` is no longer part of the selection, as shown in Figure 6.21.

Profile Properties	Entity Assignment	Grid View	
		Corporate_Actual - Properties [(Default)]	
(Default)	⊟ General		
Actual	Name		Corporate_Actual
	Description		

Figure 6.21

Workflow Profile Types

Workflow Profile types in OneStream are base input, parent input, and review. Base inputs are primarily used for imports, form inputs and journals; parent inputs are dedicated parent inputs (e.g., inputs to parent entities, which will primarily be journal entries made to the parent entity); and then review would be for review purposes.

Base Input

Base inputs, by default, contain at least the Import, Forms, and Adj steps. Base input represents the three methods in which we can get data into OneStream: data load, user input, or journals. This section will cover the common types of loads on – specifically – the Import step, such as a central load, entity-specific load, and then a combination load.

Central Loads

A central load refers to an import that targets all the entities. In other words, it's a designated step to load data for the entire organization. For this type of load, you should ensure that Load Unrelated Entities = True, and it is recommended to set the specific step's workflow name to either Central Import, or Central Form Input, or central journal input. In this case, you would not necessarily need to assign all the entities to this step unless you have a specific business case to do so.

Entity-Specific Loads

Entity-specific loads commonly require entity assignments, such that the user who accesses the import step would only be able to load that assignment of entities. When entity-specific loads are present, it is important to consider the use of workflow suffixes, which we covered in the earlier sections of this chapter.

> **Note:** Entity assignment only allows for one base input. If you assign Entity 1 to Base Input 1, Entity 1 will no longer be available as a valid selection for any remaining base inputs you have in your given cube root Workflow Profile structure. This also allows for the "locking" of data; once a profile step with entity assignments is marked complete and locked, this prevents further user input for those entities.

Combination of Central and Specific Loads

This section covers instances where you have several import steps where one handles the load of all entities, and the remaining steps are subsets of entities. Depending on how you answer the questions below, you might want to consider the use of workflow channels, and you can refer to the Workflow Channels section of this chapter.

This is where things get fun. Here are some questions to answer when determining how you could design your workflow:

1. Between the central load and specific loads, are there intersections of account/entity that could overlap? And, if so, which members overlap? What dimension is the differentiator?

    a. Overlap, in this sense, means data records that have the same members. For example, one record could be Entity 1 and Account 100 with Line of Business as Operations. Another record could be Entity 1 and Account 100 with a Line of Business as Non-Operating. These two records have overlap, referencing both Entity 1 and Account 100.

2. If there are identified overlapping intersections, which import should the system take (e.g., last load wins)? Or do we need all these intersections (in other words, no load should override or clear the other; we need to append)?

    a. Append refers to adding on to the existing records.

    b. Should we consider workflow channels, or do we need to rethink how we set up the Workflow Profile structure?

3. To which import step will you assign the entities?

I'll walk through the thought process behind the above questions, and how these questions were addressed in the below real-life example.

A client provides a data file and – under certain compliance requirements – the load needs to be completed within a specific time frame. Due to the sheer volume of data, a technical decision was made to parse the file through designated Workflow Profiles with assigned entities. This was fine and dandy until, one day, the client decided to add additional functionalities that included a detailed slice of accounts data (e.g., think PP&E with some of the activity explained in addition to the original load to ending balance). The following day, someone commented, "Hey, what happened to the data loaded yesterday? The data's disappeared."

1. Since the client had already confirmed that the original import worked as expected via data validation, and data disappeared, the situation suggested that there were overlapping records, which the system was clearing based on which import step was recently loaded.

    a. The overlap was entities and the specific PP&E accounts. The differentiating dimensions were the UD dimensions and Flow.

2. The next step was to determine whether clearing should be the expected behavior, going forward, between the two import processes. The client confirmed that both import processes needed to have both sets of data, which meant no clearing, and we were – in fact – "appending".

    a. The next assessment was whether it was possible to re-arrange the import steps, which for the users' specific responsibilities did not make sense. Because the differentiator was the UD and Flow dimensions, the recommended step was to implement Workflow Channels using a specific UD dimension.

3. Was it possible to reassign the entities in the workflow structure? The answer was no, which furthered our recommendation to implement workflow channels.

Load Overlapped Siblings

The Load Overlapped Siblings setting is specifically found on the base input step. It is a boolean setting of True or False. If it is set to True, the system checks for overlapping Data Units. If it is set to False, the last processed channel will overwrite the prior load. Refer to the Design and Reference Guide – it has a great section that describes Workflow Profile data loading behaviors!

You want this setting as True if you have multiple steps under your given base input and you anticipate and/or know multiple import, forms, or adj will have overlapping Data Units. Otherwise, if you have one base input with several import steps, in which each import is distinct (e.g., Import 1 is always Entity 1, 2, 3; Import 2 is always Entity 4, 5, 6), then set the Load Overlapped Siblings to False, as this will improve performance speeds.

Parent Input

This is specifically for topside adjustments and a parent input step helps differentiate things – especially if there are inputs for forms that are at the parent entity level. By parent entity level, I truly mean the parent entity, where you want that parent to reflect X amount regardless of the base members. Refer to the Business as "Usual" chapter in this book, where we cover using a base to represent the parent (versus at the parent level).

Difference Between Base Input and Parent Input

Base input gives you the standard Import, Forms, Adj; parent input, by comparison, only gives you Forms and Adj. Why? Parent input assumes you want to input data to a parent entity, which you can do as a form input or a journal, but not as a data load.

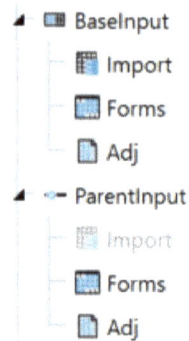

Figure 6.22

Review

Literally, a step to review, confirm, and certify the results. The review profile type can also be used to group the base inputs and parent inputs in a logical structure.

There is a property called **Named Dependents** on the review Workflow Profile type. You can set this property to include non-descendant Workflow Profile entities. A named dependent relationship is used to accommodate situations such as having a single base input profile type used to load data for the entire organization, but the individuals responsible for a subset of those entities have a different workflow and sign-off process. Thus, you can have a review step that depends on a different workflow.

Default Workflow

Do you see `Golfstream_Default` with the triangle icon (Figure 6.23)? *Do not* load data to this. It's mentioned in the out-of-the-box Design and Reference Guide, but I'll say it here, too; its sole job is to establish the default relationship between the workflow structure and unassigned entity members within the cube that the cube root profile was created to control. To prevent inadvertent human error, I recommend the following:

1. Leverage a **DO_NOT_USE structure** if you don't already have one. This can be used for default Workflow Profiles, discontinued Workflow Profiles, archives, etc.

    a. If you have historical entities, consider adding the structure under `DO_NOT_USE` with the assigned historical entities. In other words, do not let the entities remain unassigned in the `_Default` profile.

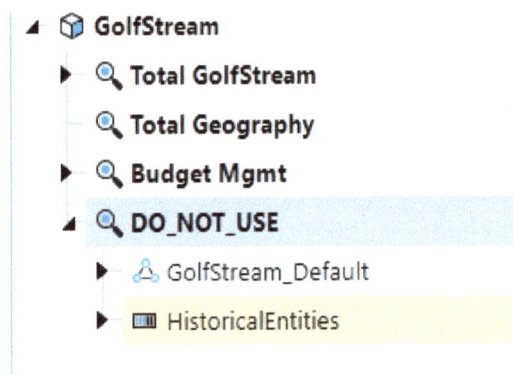

Figure 6.23

2. If you ever get an error on the default Workflow Profile (e.g., when copying data via a data management job), check your entity assignments. If entities were in use at any point and are no longer used, reassign these entities to an archive or historical workflow parent (e.g., `HistoricalEntities` in the example above).

    a. Default Workflow Profile should only be used for new entities or entities that have never been assigned, and which do not need to be assigned to other Workflow Profile steps. In other words, if the entity started out in default, was moved to a step, and subsequently discontinued, then depending on the workflow setup, either the entire step gets moved to under `DO_NOT_USE` or the Entity is reassigned to the `HistoricalEntities` step.

Does a Profile Need a Process?

Process indicates to the system that additional calculations need to be run on the given Workflow Profile step. These processes include consolidate, translate, calculate, and custom calculations.

To level set, the process step is part of the Workflow Profile name. You could have an import step where you set the Workflow Profile name as the typical Import, Validate, Load, or you could set it up with Import, Validate, Process instead.

⊟ Workflow Settings	
Workflow Channel	Standard
Workflow Name	Import, Validate, Load
Workspace Dashboard Name (Custom Workflow)	Import, Validate, Load
⊟ Integration Settings	Import, Validate, Load, Certify
Data Source Name	Import, Validate, Process
Transformation Profile Name	Import, Validate, Process, Certify
Import Dashboard Profile Name	Import, Validate, Process, Confirm
Validate Dashboard Profile Name	Import, Validate, Process, Confirm, Certify

Figure 6.24

Does a profile need a process step? Most likely, yes, if users need to see the calculated, translated, or consolidated data for their entities, such as:

- Utilize the IC matching report.

- Users need to run confirmation rules.

- Run data management jobs (e.g., custom calculate, like seeding).

- Consolidate with the click of a button.

Calculation Definitions

Calculation Definitions is a tab found on the base input Workflow Profile. This is where you set up your consolidate, translate, calculate, or your custom calculations. This section will cover a standard setup, which I am defining as the out-of-the-box selections available to you when you create a new calculation definition row, and custom, where you might have to use a custom rule attached to a data management sequence.

Standard

I am defining standard as the standard functionalities provided when you add a new row to calculation definitions. These standard functionalities include:

- **Entity:** select the entity you want to be processed.

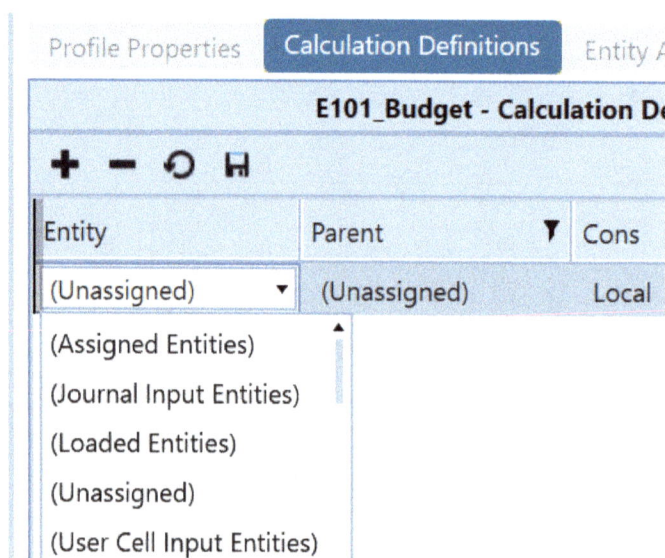

Figure 6.25

- **Parent:** if relevant. This might be useful to define in situations where you have base entities under multiple different parents or hierarchies in your main entity dimension.

- **Cons:** select your consolidation member. The most common I see include local or a reporting currency such as USD.

- **Calc Type:** what you want run for the row.

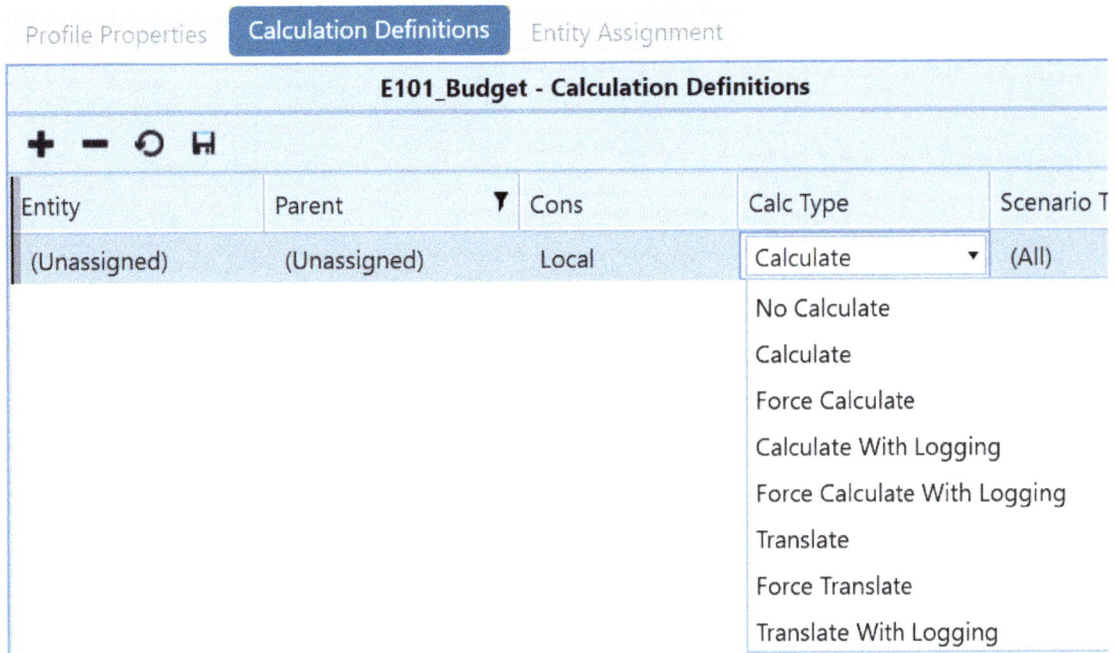

Figure 6.26

- **Scenario Type Filter:** if you only want the process to run on specific Scenario Types.

- **Confirmed:** you *must* check this if you want your confirmation rules assigned to this workflow to be run.

- **Order:** if there is an order of operations associated with your calculation definitions for this specific Workflow Profile type.

- **Filter Value:** commonly used for custom processes, like triggering a data management sequence, as explained in the next section.

Custom

I am defining custom as a process that is not considered "out-of-the-box" or, in other words, additional logic is needed. For these instances, we commonly leverage an event handler such as a DataQualityEventHandler. This section will cover a high-level walkthrough on a basic setup to associate a data management step to your calculation definition.

Create a DataQualityEventHandler rule in the Extensibility Rules folder. You will have to specifically select DataQualityEventHandler.

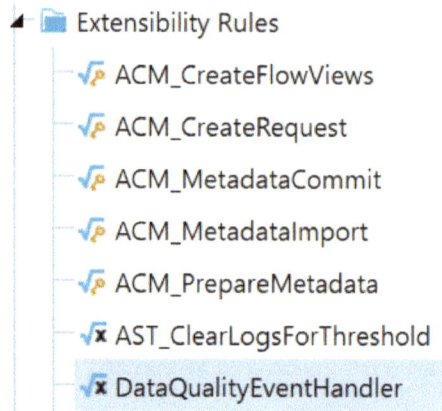

Figure 6.27

1. Create your business rule. I have an example, below, where I want to use a custom calculation that should only run for calculation definitions where I have the calc type defined as No Calculate.

```vbnet
Public Function Main(ByVal si As SessionInfo, ByVal globals As BRGlobals, ByVal api As Object, ByVal args As DataQualityEventHandlerArgs) As Object
    Try
        'Define a switch to control event processing, since many of these are reference examples we do not want them to run all the time
        Dim processEvents As Boolean = False

        'Set the default return values
        Dim returnValue As Object = args.DefaultReturnValue
        args.UseReturnValueFromBusinessRule = False
        args.Cancel = False

        'Evaluate the operation type in order to determine which subroutine to process
        Select Case args.OperationName
            Case Is = BREventOperationType.DataQuality.ProcessCube.NoCalculate
                'Execute a Data Management job after process cube runs
                Me.XFR_HandleProcessCubeNoCalculate(si, globals, api, args)
        End Select


        Return returnValue
    Catch ex As Exception
        Throw ErrorHandler.LogWrite(si, New XFException(si, ex))
    End Try
End Function
```

Figure 6.28

2. In my private sub, called XFR_HandleProcessCubeNoCalculate:

```vbnet
Try
    'Get the DataUnitInfo from the Event arguments so that we can get the name of the DataManagement sequence to process.
    Dim calcInfo As DataUnitInfo = DirectCast(args.Inputs(2), DataUnitInfo)
    If Not calcInfo Is Nothing Then
        'Make sure that a Sequence name as assigned to the filter value of the Calc Definition of the executing Workflow Profile
        If calcInfo.FilterValue <> String.Empty Then
            'Now, execute the DataMgmt Sequence that was specified in the FilterValue (In a background thread)
            BRApi.Utilities.StartDataMgmtSequence(si, calcInfo.FilterValue, Nothing)
        End If
    End If

Catch ex As Exception
    Throw ErrorHandler.LogWrite(si, New XFException(si, ex))
End Try
```

Figure 6.29

3. Then, I go into Data Management, create my sequence, and assign any rules that need to be run for a specific workflow. For example, I have a Workflow step where I want to copy journals from one cube to another.

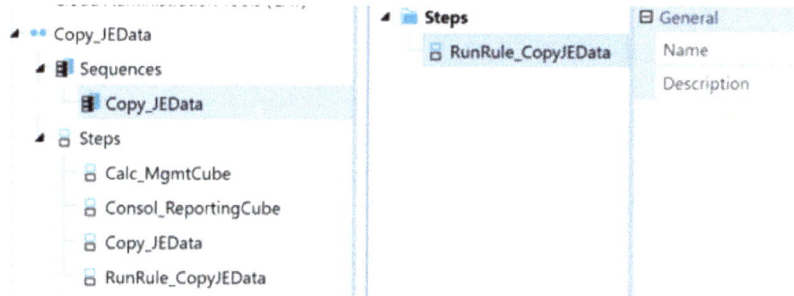

Figure 6.30

4. Then, in my Calculation Definitions, I update the Filter Value to be the name of the data management sequence, Copy_JEData.

	Parent	Cons	Calc Type	Scenario Type Filter	Confirmed ▼	Order ▼	Filter Value
jal_Current	(Unassigned)	Local	Consolidate	(All)		10	
nal Input Entitie	(Unassigned)	Local	No Calculate	(All)		20	Copy_JEData

Figure 6.31

If I Set My Calculation Definition to Consolidate and Confirmed, Does My Workflow Name Really Need to Have Process?

Your calculation definition will not run if Process is not explicitly defined in your workflow name. It is mentioned in the Reference Guide, and I will mention it here again. Calculation definitions determine the type of calculation or consolidation that will occur when a user selects Process Cube. You only have Process Cube if your workflow name has Process as part of it (as shown in Figure 6.32). The confirmed check box only indicates to the system what entities should be run by the confirmation rules.

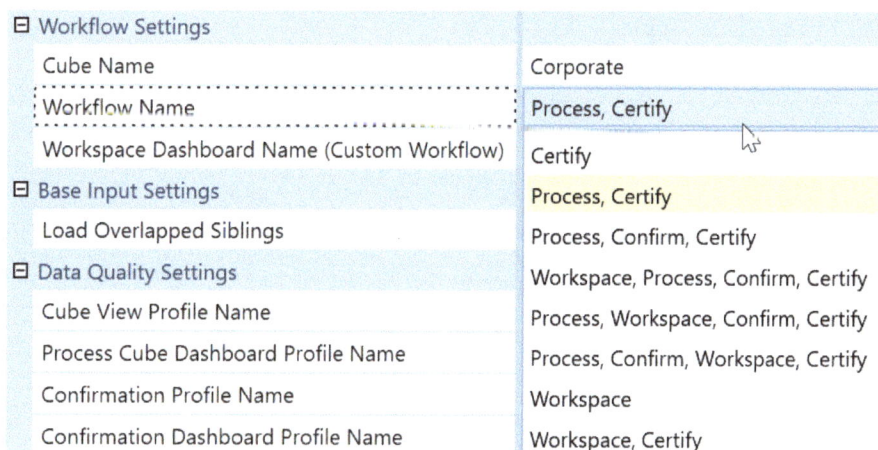

Figure 6.32

Workflow Security Groups

Security is everyone's "favorite". At a high level, you will see a dedicated security section for your Workflow Profile step. In layman's terms:

- **Access Group:** can view this step from OnePlace.

- **Maintenance Group:** who should edit the properties associated with this step. I hope you set this to administrators…

- **Workflow Execution Group:** the group that completes the tasks in the workflow. Commonly, access group and workflow execution group are the same but, again, this property exists to handle exceptions.

- **Certification SignOff Group:** signs off on the workflow.

> **Note:** Nest security groups where possible – less is more! Don't overengineer security!

For those who are on versions 8.0+, there are additional capabilities related to the use of journals. Now, you can specify whether users are able to post or approve their own journals or require the journal template associated with the step.

	Houston.Journals - Properties [Actual]
Name	Houston.Journals
Description	
⊟ Security	
Access Group	Houston Combined Access
Maintenance Group	Houston Maintenance
Workflow Execution Group	(Use Default)
Certification SignOff Group	(Use Default)
Journal Process Group	(Use Default)
Journal Approval Group	(Use Default)
Journal Post Group	(Use Default)
Prevent Self-Post	(Use Default)
Prevent Self-Approval	(Use Default)
Require Journal Template	(Use Default)

Figure 6.33

For the sake of simplicity, here is a general or suggested naming convention for workflow to help you keep security a little more organized:

- Workflow prefix examples
  - WF_Access = Workflow Access
  - WF_Execute_ = Workflow Execution
  - WF_Certify = Workflow Certification
  - J_Process = Journal Process
  - J_Approve = Journal Approve
  - J_Post = Journal Post
- Entity prefix examples
  - E_View_ = read group for given entity (e.g., E_View_Frankfurt)
  - E_Write_ = write group for given entity

- Scenario prefix examples

    o S_ = denotes scenario-specific security (e.g., S_Write)

Workflow Channels

Workflow channels are primarily used to further define how to handle clear, load, and lock data to a more granular level. Workflow channels are created as what I'd like to think of as "labels" that represent some grouping between some base input step (Import, Forms, Adj) and metadata such as accounts or UD members. You can create these "labels" in workflow channels (Application > Workflow > Workflow Channels).

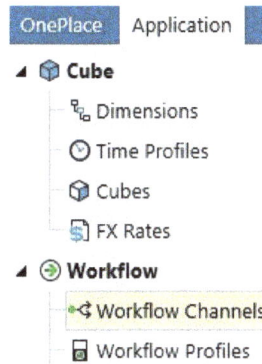

Figure 6.34

Out-of-the-box, we have Standard, NoDataLock, and AllChannelInput as workflow channels.

- **Standard:** this is the default for every Workflow Profile step creation. This assumes you have not implemented workflow channels.

- **NoDataLock:** this is a setting available on the dimensions. In other words, you will not find this as an option for Workflow Profile steps.

    o NoDataLock takes the specified account or UD member out of the workflow process. You are telling the system that this member can be used across multiple workflow Import/Forms/Adj steps.

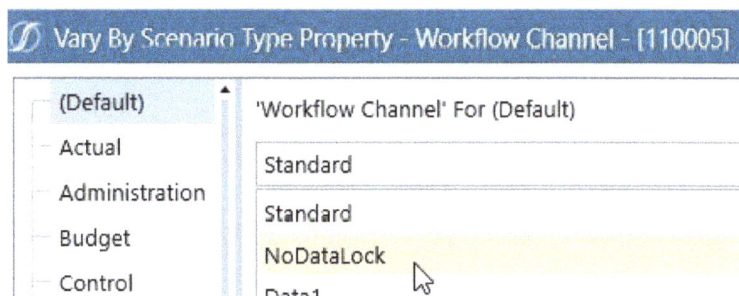

Figure 6.35

Chapter 6

- **AllChannelInput:** this is the `NoDataLock` equivalent for the Workflow Profile step. In other words, you will not find this as an option on dimension properties.
  - Limits the workflow process on certain metadata (e.g., entity) if another workflow step has a specific channel assigned. The `AllChannelInput` focuses on the workflow Data Unit (Level 2) but looks specifically at the Origin dimension.

When to Consider Using an Account Workflow Channel

You may want to use workflow channels on accounts if there is a need to lock certain accounts based on your close days or overall process (not just limited to consolidation and close, you could have very specific steps on the planning side!).

Account Channel example: on day 3 of close, you want to complete the trial balance and lock it down for adjustments, but you still want the ability to submit the statistical accounts by day 5 (both trial balance and statistical accounts are in the Account dimension). You would set up two workflow channels:

- Supplemental accounts workflow channel
- Trial balance workflow channel

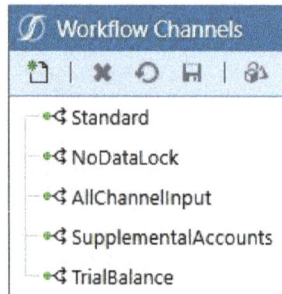

Figure 6.36

In the Account dimension, we would assign the `TrialBalance` workflow channel to the base balance sheet and P&L accounts, and supplemental accounts workflow channel to the base supplemental account members.

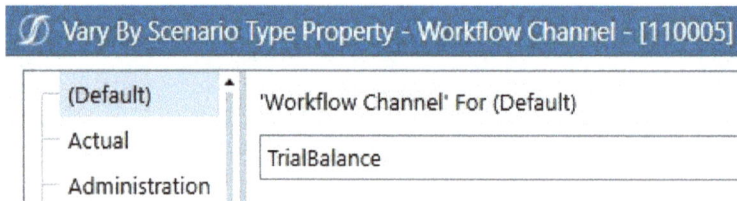

Figure 6.37

Then, on the Workflow Profiles, the workflow channels would be assigned to the relevant step.

- Let's say we load in the trial balance and supplemental accounts through an import step.
  - The trial balance import step would have workflow channel, `TrialBalance` assigned.

Profile Properties	Calculation Definitions	
		BaseInput.Import - Properties [(Default)]
(Default)	⊟ Workflow Settings	
Actual	Workflow Channel	TrialBalance
	Workflow Name	Import, Validate, Load

Figure 6.38

- o The supplemental import step would have workflow channel, Supplemental, assigned.

- Let's say users then go in and review the output and make additional adjustments – whether through forms or journals – and there are no intersection restrictions for users to make these updates.

  - o Forms and Adj steps would have AllChannelInput assigned.

Profile Properties	Calculation Definitions	
		BaseInput.Forms - Properties [(Default)]
(Default)	⊟ Workflow Settings	
Actual	Workflow Channel	AllChannelInput
	Workflow Name	Form Input

Figure 6.39

When to Consider Using a UD Workflow Channel

Will the application contain several integrations and/or Import/Forms/Adj steps that share the same intersections in the cube Data Unit (Level 1) and workflow Data Unit (Level 2)?

Level 1 Cube Data Unit (Cube, Entity, Parent, Consolidation, Scenario, Time)	Level 2 Workflow Data Unit (Account, Flow, View, Origin, Intercompany)	Level 3 Workflow Channel Data Unit (UD1-UD8)
Cb#MgmtRpt	A#100	Example: UD1#000
E#Entity1	F#EndBalInput	UD2#None
P#Top	V#YTD	UD3#None
C#Local	O#Import	UD4#None
S#Actual	IC#None	UD5#None
T#20XXM1		UD6#None
		UD7#None
		UD8#None

Figure 6.3 (shown again)

If yes, then will a UD dimension be used to differentiate the data types or data sources?

If the answer to both of the above is yes, you may want to consider using channels, more specifically, a UD workflow channel. If you do consider using a UD workflow channel, it is very important to be mindful of which UD you ultimately end up selecting because setting a UD for workflow channels will be application-wide and *cannot* vary among cubes and Scenario Types. The use of a UD workflow channel is to control data input access and *does not* allow you to certify up to the workflow hierarchy by channel.

Where to Get Started

There are three main areas to apply your workflow channel updates: Workflow Channels, Application Properties (especially if you decide to use a UD channel), and your account and/or UD metadata.

General Account Channel versus UD Channel Setup

In general, to set up an account workflow channel:

1. Create your workflow channels as part of Application > Workflow > Workflow Channels.

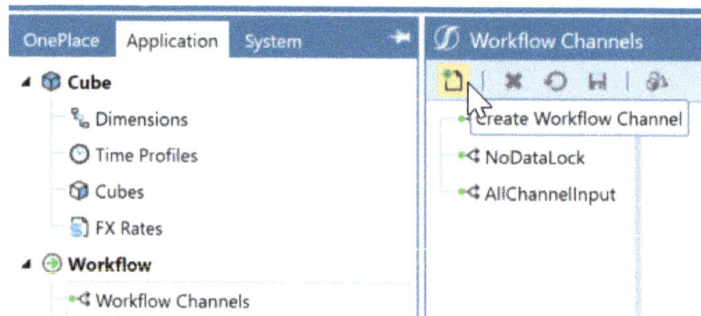

Figure 6.40

2. Apply the workflow channels to the relevant account members.

3. Apply the workflow channels to Workflow Profile steps.

In general, to set up a UD workflow channel:

1. Create your workflow channels as part of Application > Workflow > Workflow Channels.

2. Go to Application Properties > UD Dimension Type for Workflow Channels.

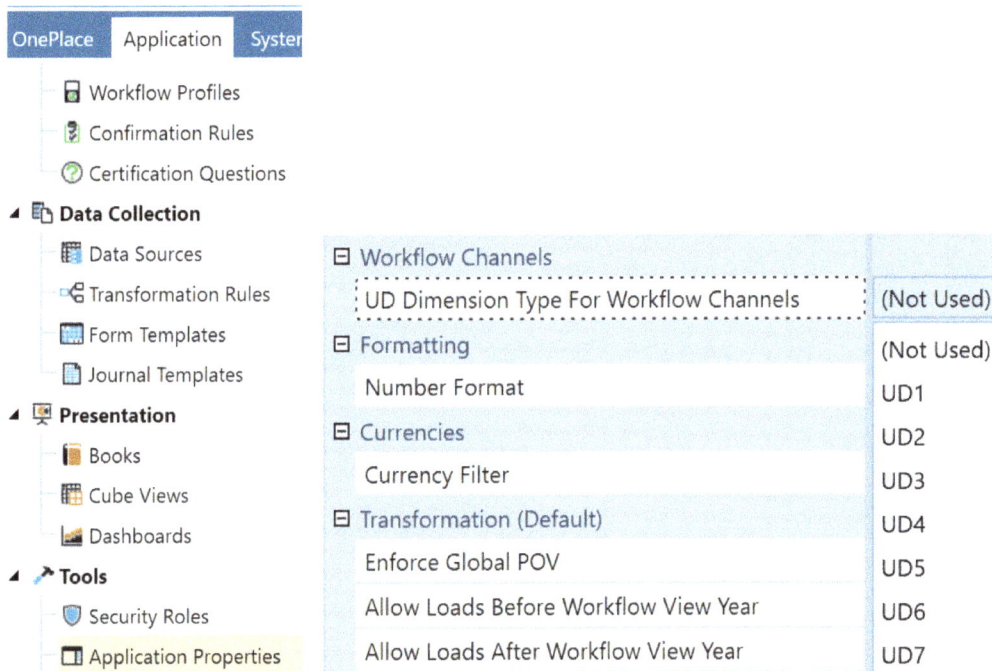

Figure 6.41

3. Apply the workflow channels to the relevant UD members.

4. Apply the NoDataLock workflow channel to the relevant account members.

5. Apply the workflow channels to the Workflow Profile steps.

> **Note:** Remember, if you opted for a UD workflow channel, you would need to ensure that all accounts have workflow channel set to `NoDataLock` and that your members in your UD have the relevant workflow channel assigned.

Workflow Channel Use Cases

This section covers various Workflow Profile organizations and settings with workflow channels. Each case covers an expected behavior depending on the given Workflow Profile setup for records sharing the same cube Data Unit and workflow Data Unit, or the same cube Data Unit but different workflow Data Unit:

1. When there are multiple import steps under the same base input.

   a. Cube Data Unit and workflow Data Unit are the same for these import steps with/without entity assignments.

   b. Cube Data Unit is the same for these import steps but the workflow Data Unit has different accounts.

   c. Cube Data Unit is the same for these import steps but the workflow Data Unit has the same accounts and a different Flow member.

2. When there are multiple base inputs.

   a. Cube Data Unit and workflow Data Unit combinations are the same for the import step that is under each of the base input Workflow Profiles.

   b. Cube Data Unit is the same but the workflow Data Unit has different accounts.

   c. Cube Data Unit is the same but the workflow Data Unit has the same accounts and a different Flow member.

Chapter 6

Depending on the setup related to the workflow step itself (e.g., Load Overlap Siblings = True, workflow channel setting, etc.), the creation of workflow channels, or the workflow channel setting on the relevant account or UD member, the result is to either keep records from all the imports, or to only keep the loaded records from the latest import.

Imports of the Same Base Input

If we have the following Workflow Profile setup, where we have multiple imports under the same base input, then:

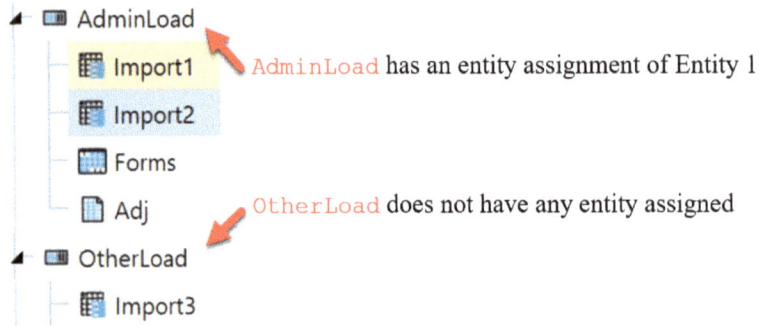

AdminLoad has an entity assignment of Entity 1

OtherLoad does not have any entity assigned

Figure 6.42

Cube Data Unit and Workflow Data Unit are the Same With or Without Entity Assignment

If the workflow channel is the same for WF1 (Import1) and WF2 (Import2), and the cube Data Unit and workflow Data Unit combinations are the same, the system will load both intersections into the cube, regardless of whether there are entity assignments.

Standard Workflow Channel							
WF1 (Import1)		WF2 (Import2)		End Result (Keep Both)			
Symbol	Member	Symbol	Member	Symbol	Member	Member
E#	Entity1	E#	Entity1	E#	Entity1	Entity1
C#	Local	C#	Local	C#	Local	Local
S#	Actual	S#	Actual	S#	Actual	Actual
T#	20XXM1	T#	20XXM1	T#	20XXM1	20XXM1
A#	100	A#	100	A#	100	100
F#	EndBalInput	F#	EndBalInput	F#	EndBalInput	EndBalInput
V#	YTD	V#	YTD	V#	YTD	YTD
O#	Import	O#	Import	O#	Import	Import
IC#	None	IC#	None	IC#	None	None
U1#	0000	U1#	0000	U1#	000	000
U2#	000	U2#	000	U2#	000	000
U3#	000	U3#	000	U3#	000	000
U4#	Data1	U4#	Data2	U4#	Data1	Data2
U5#	None	U5#	None	U5#	None	None
U6#	None	U6#	None	U6#	None	None
U7#	None	U7#	None	U7#	None	None

Standard Workflow Channel							
U8#	None	U8#	None	U8#	None	None	
Amount	10	Amount	15	Amount	10	15	

Figure 6.43

Using the same workflow structure presented in Figure 6.42, `Import1` will represent WF1. I load the WF1 record from Figure 6.43 into OneStream successfully, as presented in Figure 6.44.

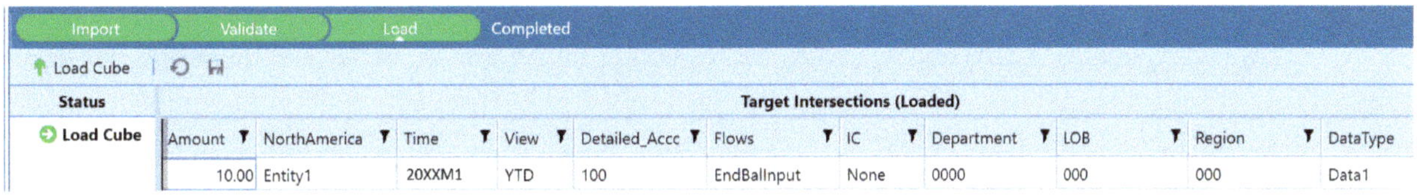

Figure 6.44

The Cube View shows WF1's intersections.

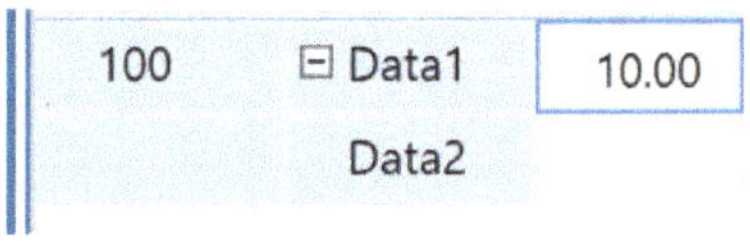

Figure 6.45

Using the same workflow structure presented in Figure 6.42, Import2 will represent WF2.

The WF2 record from Figure 6.43 is loaded into OneStream successfully, as presented in Figure 6.46.

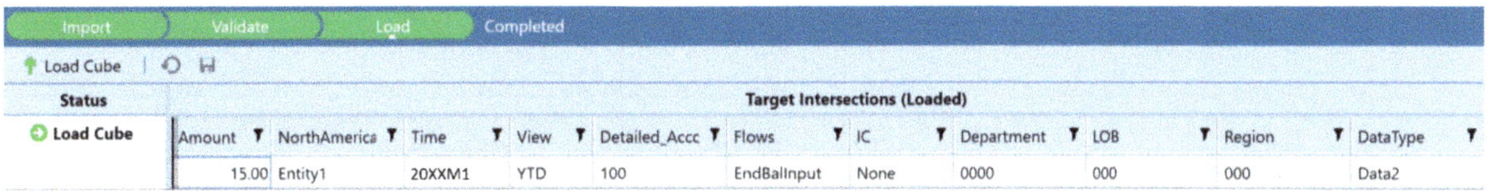

Figure 6.46

Notice that both loads appear successful.

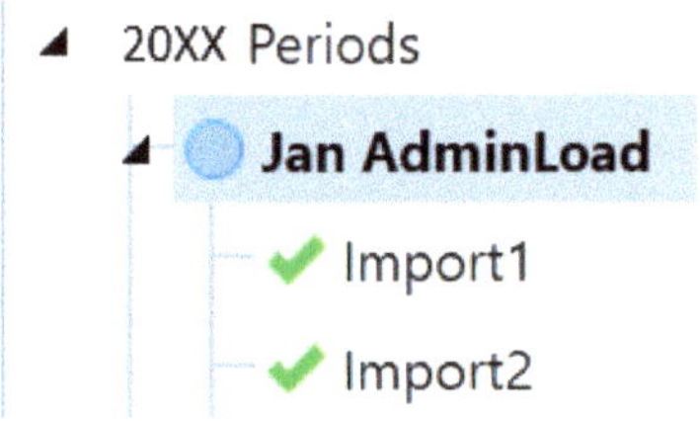

Figure 6.47

117

Notice that the Cube View retains the data.

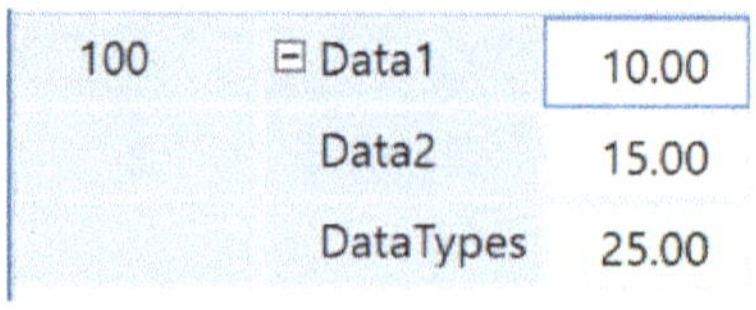

100	⊟ Data1	10.00
	Data2	15.00
	DataTypes	25.00

Figure 6.48

Cube Data Unit is the Same, but Workflow Data Unit Has Different Accounts

If both steps load to a different account, the system will not clear and will keep them both instead.

Standard Workflow Channel							
WF1 (Import1)		**WF2 (Import2)**		**End Result (Keep Both)**			
Symbol	**Member**	**Symbol**	**Member**	**Symbol**	**Member**	**Member**	
E#	Entity1	E#	Entity1	E#	Entity1	Entity1	
C#	Local	C#	Local	C#	Local	Local	
S#	Actual	S#	Actual	S#	Actual	Actual	
T#	20XXM1	T#	20XXM1	T#	20XXM1	20XXM1	
A#	110	A#	100	A#	110	100	
F#	EndBalInput	F#	EndBalInput	F#	EndBalInput	EndBalInput	
V#	YTD	V#	YTD	V#	YTD	YTD	
O#	Import	O#	Import	O#	Import	Import	
IC#	None	IC#	None	IC#	None	None	
U1#	0000	U1#	0000	U1#	000	000	
U2#	000	U2#	000	U2#	000	000	
U3#	000	U3#	000	U3#	000	000	
U4#	Data1	U4#	Data2	U4#	Data1	Data2	
U5#	None	U5#	None	U5#	None	None	
U6#	None	U6#	None	U6#	None	None	
U7#	None	U7#	None	U7#	None	None	
U8#	None	U8#	None	U8#	None	None	
Amount	10	Amount	15	Amount	10	15	

Figure 6.49

WF1 loaded successfully.

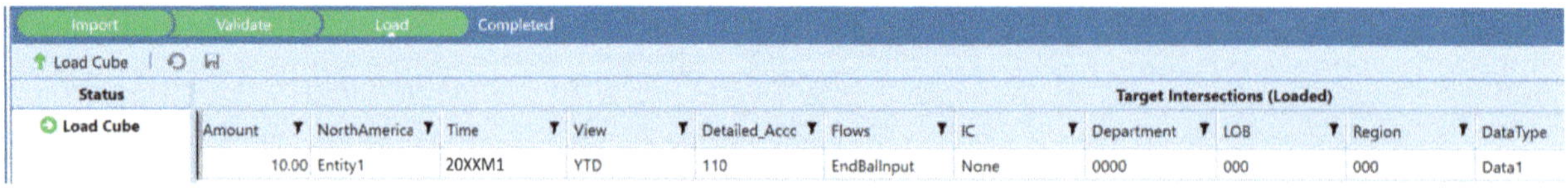

Figure 6.50

The Cube View shows WF1's intersections.

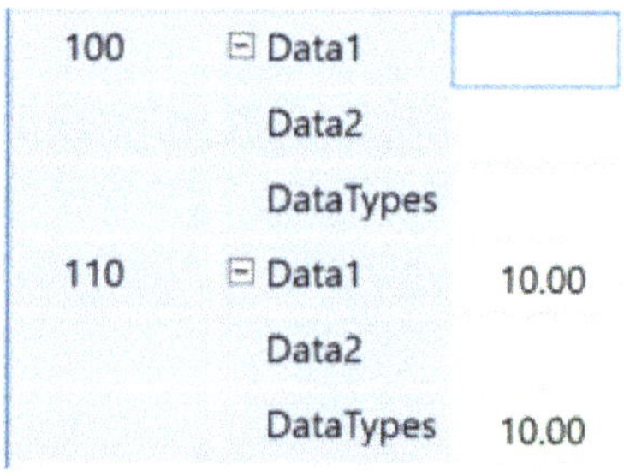

100	⊟ Data1	
	Data2	
	DataTypes	
110	⊟ Data1	10.00
	Data2	
	DataTypes	10.00

Figure 6.51

WF2 loaded successfully.

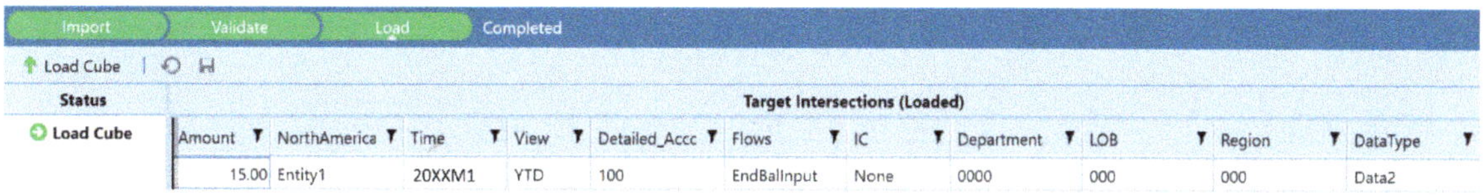

Import	Validate	Load	Completed										

Load Cube | ↻ | ⊟

Status				Target Intersections (Loaded)									
⊕ Load Cube	Amount ▼	NorthAmerica ▼	Time ▼	View ▼	Detailed_Accc ▼	Flows ▼	IC ▼	Department ▼	LOB ▼	Region ▼	DataType ▼
	15.00	Entity1	20XXM1	YTD	100	EndBalInput	None	0000	000	000	Data2

Figure 6.52

Notice that both loads appear successful.

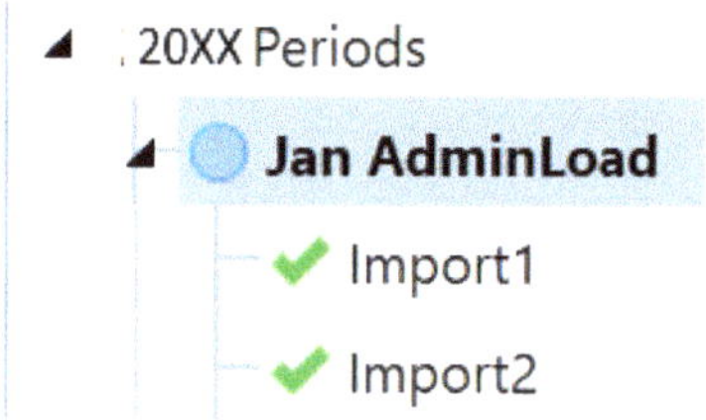

▲ 20XX Periods

  ▲ ◯ **Jan AdminLoad**

    ✔ Import1

    ✔ Import2

Figure 6.53

Notice that the Cube View retains the data.

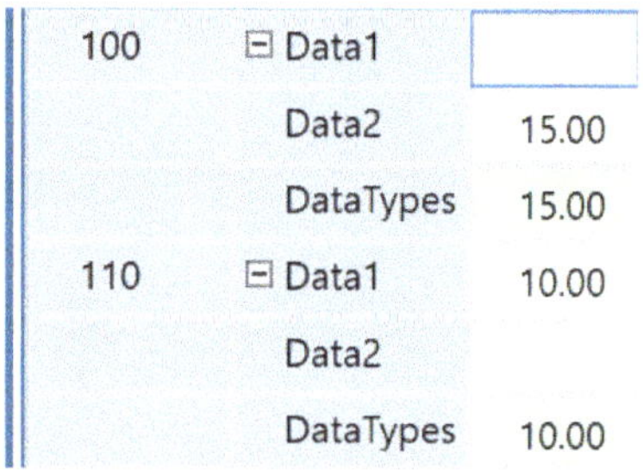

100	⊟ Data1	
	Data2	15.00
	DataTypes	15.00
110	⊟ Data1	10.00
	Data2	
	DataTypes	10.00

Figure 6.54

Cube Data Unit is the Same, but Workflow Data Unit has the Same Account and a Different Flow

If Load Overlapped Siblings = True on the parent (`AdminLoad`), then this will allow for accumulation based on the Entity and Origin members. In other words, we prevent a last-one-loaded-wins situation.

Chapter 6

If both steps load to a different Flow member but with the same accounts, and there is the standard workflow channel implemented, the system will keep both.

Standard Workflow Channel							
WF1 (Import1)		WF2 (Import2)		End Result (Keep Both)			
Symbol	Member	Symbol	Member	Symbol	Member	Member	
E#	Entity1	E#	Entity1	E#	Entity1	Entity1	
C#	Local	C#	Local	C#	Local	Local	
S#	Actual	S#	Actual	S#	Actual	Actual	
T#	20XXM1	T#	20XXM1	T#	20XXM1	20XXM1	
A#	110	A#	100	A#	110	100	
F#	EndBalInput	F#	Example2	F#	EndBalInput	Example2	
V#	YTD	V#	YTD	V#	YTD	YTD	
O#	Import	O#	Import	O#	Import	Import	
IC#	None	IC#	None	IC#	None	None	
U1#	0000	U1#	0000	U1#	000	000	
U2#	000	U2#	000	U2#	000	000	
U3#	000	U3#	000	U3#	000	000	
U4#	Data1	U4#	Data2	U4#	Data1	Data2	
U5#	None	U5#	None	U5#	None	None	
U6#	None	U6#	None	U6#	None	None	
U7#	None	U7#	None	U7#	None	None	
U8#	None	U8#	None	U8#	None	None	
Amount	10	Amount	15	Amount	10	15	

Figure 6.55

WF1 loaded successfully.

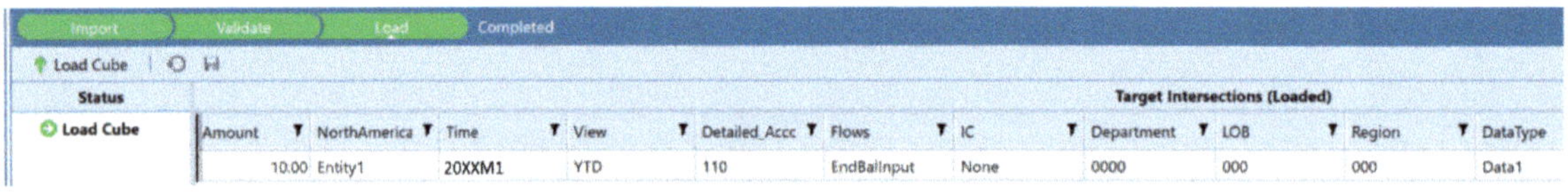

Figure 6.56

The Cube View shows WF1's intersections.

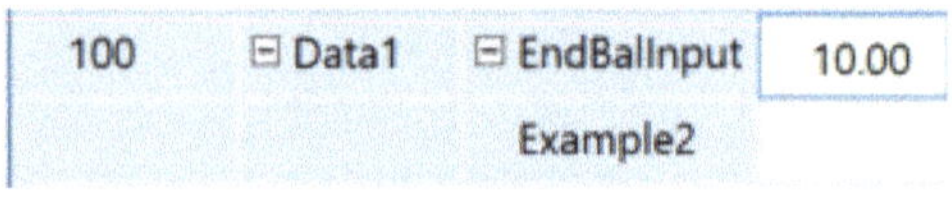

Figure 6.57

120

WF2 loaded successfully.

Figure 6.58

Notice that both loads appear successful.

Figure 6.59

Notice that the Cube View retains the data.

Figure 6.60

Imports of Different Base Inputs

From the examples above, we know that the sibling imports (Import1 and Import2) keep the intersections. Now, what happens if we add another import step that hits the same intersections?

This section covers the behavior between Import1 and Import3.

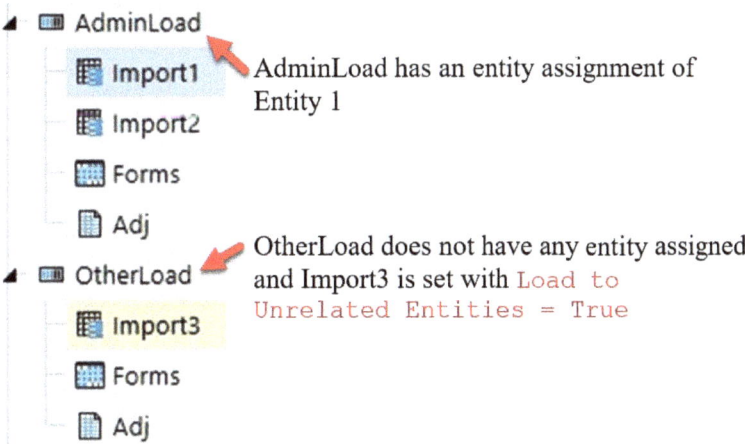

AdminLoad has an entity assignment of Entity 1

OtherLoad does not have any entity assigned and Import3 is set with Load to Unrelated Entities = True

Figure 6.61

Cube Data Unit and Workflow Data Unit Combinations are the Same

If there is a standard workflow channel for WF1 (Import1) and WF3 (Import3), and their cube Data Unit and workflow Data Unit combinations are the same, the system will replace and clear, and take the last one loaded.

Standard Workflow Channel								
WF1 (Import1)		WF3 (Import3)		End Result (Last Load Wins)				
Symbol	Member	Symbol	Member	Symbol	Member	Member		
E#	Entity1	E#	Entity1	E#	~~Entity1~~	Entity1		
C#	Local	C#	Local	C#	~~Local~~	Local		
S#	Actual	S#	Actual	S#	~~Actual~~	Actual		
T#	20XXM1	T#	20XXM1	T#	~~20XXM1~~	20XXM1		
A#	100	A#	100	A#	~~100~~	100		
F#	EndBalInput	F#	EndBalInput	F#	~~EndBalInput~~	EndBalInput		
V#	YTD	V#	YTD	V#	~~YTD~~	YTD		
O#	Import	O#	Import	O#	~~Import~~	Import		
IC#	None	IC#	None	IC#	~~None~~	None		
U1#	0000	U1#	0000	U1#	~~000~~	000		
U2#	000	U2#	000	U2#	~~000~~	000		
U3#	000	U3#	000	U3#	~~000~~	000		
U4#	Data1	U4#	Data2	U4#	~~Data1~~	Data2		
U5#	None	U5#	None	U5#	~~None~~	None		
U6#	None	U6#	None	U6#	~~None~~	None		
U7#	None	U7#	None	U7#	~~None~~	None		
U8#	None	U8#	None	U8#	~~None~~	None		
Amount	10	Amount	15	Amount	~~10~~	15		

Figure 6.62

WF1 loaded successfully.

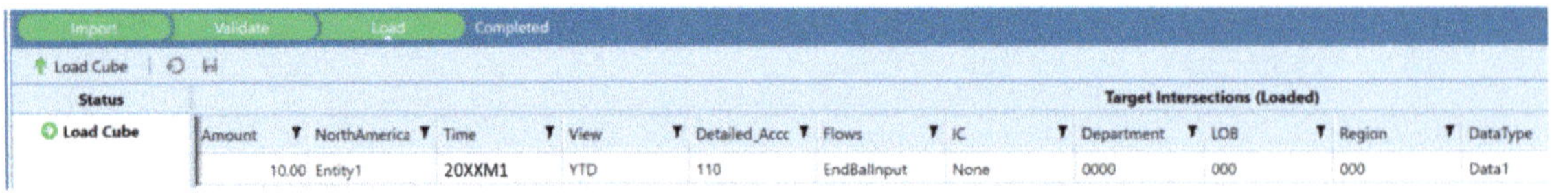

Figure 6.63

The Cube View shows WF1's intersections.

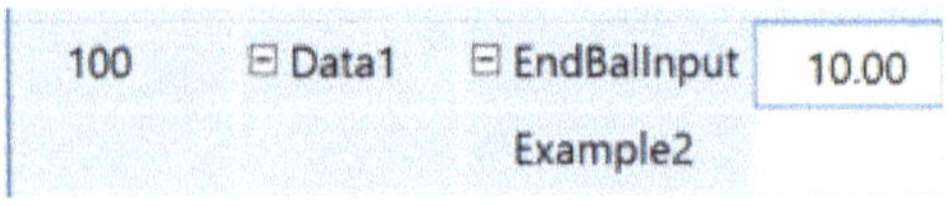

Figure 6.64

WF3 loaded successfully.

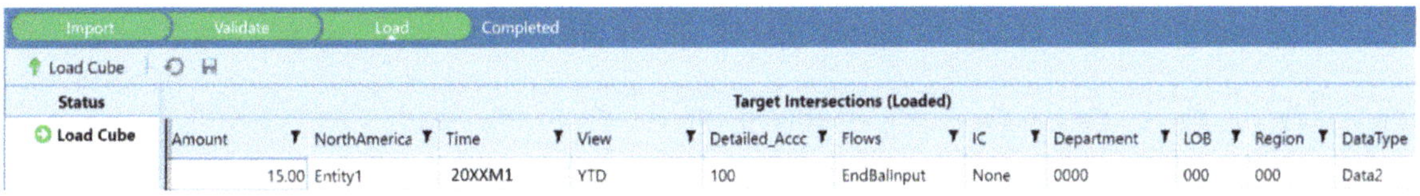

Status				Target Intersections (Loaded)								
Load Cube	Amount	NorthAmerica	Time	View	Detailed_Accc	Flows	IC	Department	LOB	Region	DataType
	15.00	Entity1	20XXM1	YTD	100	EndBalInput	None	0000	000	000	Data2

Figure 6.65

Notice that both loads appear successful.

Figure 6.66

Notice that the Cube View cleared the 10 and kept the last load of 15.

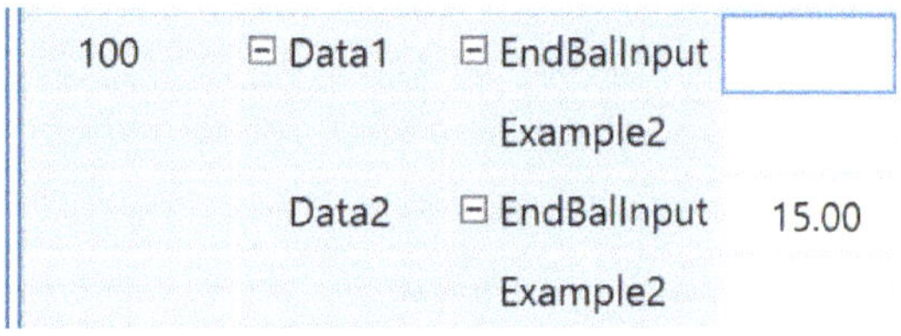

Figure 6.67

If we go back to Import1 and reload to the cube, the 10 amount appears and the 15 disappears.

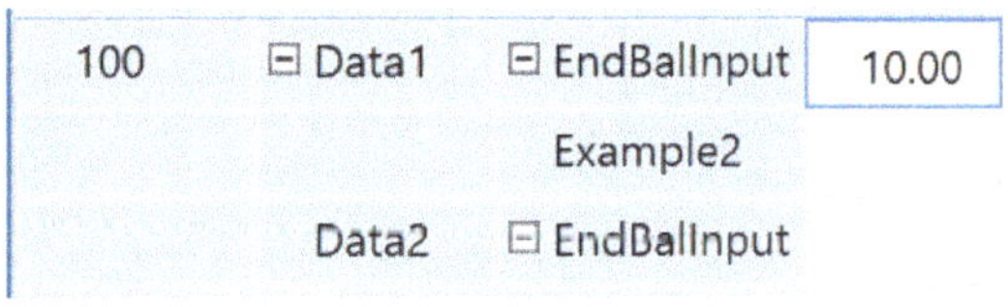

Figure 6.68

If we need both intersections, then we need to implement a UD workflow channel on UD4 in addition to possibly setting up a central import step – set to AllChannelInput – because of where the workflow steps are in this structure.

Let's go ahead and create two workflow channels – Data1 and Data2 – and enable UD4 as the workflow channel on Application Properties. Then, update the account member to NoDataLock and the UD4 members with Data1 and Data2 as the workflow channels. Then, apply the workflow channels to the Import1 and Import3 profiles.

Reload the data files, and the end result is now…

100	⊟ Data1	⊟ EndBalInput	10.00
		Example2	
	Data2	⊟ EndBalInput	15.00

Figure 6.69

Cube Data Unit is the Same, but Workflow Data Unit has Different Accounts

If both steps load to a different account and there is standard workflow channel, the system will not clear based on how the workflow structure is set up.

Standard Workflow Channel					
WF1 (Import1)		**WF3 (Import3)**		**End Result (Keep Both)**	
Symbol	**Member**	**Symbol**	**Member**	**Symbol**	**Member**	**Member**
E#	Entity1	E#	Entity1	E#	Entity1	Entity1
C#	Local	C#	Local	C#	Local	Local
S#	Actual	S#	Actual	S#	Actual	Actual
T#	20XXM1	T#	20XXM1	T#	20XXM1	20XXM1
A#	100	A#	110	A#	100	110
F#	EndBalInput	F#	EndBalInput	F#	EndBalInput	EndBalInput
V#	YTD	V#	YTD	V#	YTD	YTD
O#	Import	O#	Import	O#	Import	Import
IC#	None	IC#	None	IC#	None	None
U1#	0000	U1#	0000	U1#	000	000
U2#	000	U2#	000	U2#	000	000
U3#	000	U3#	000	U3#	000	000
U4#	Data1	U4#	Data2	U4#	Data1	Data2
U5#	None	U5#	None	U5#	None	None
U6#	None	U6#	None	U6#	None	None
U7#	None	U7#	None	U7#	None	None
U8#	None	U8#	None	U8#	None	None
Amount	10	Amount	15	Amount	10	15

Figure 6.70

WF1 Loaded successfully.

		Import	Validate	Load	Completed							
↑ Load Cube	⟳ ⊟											
Status					Target Intersections (Loaded)							
⊕ Load Cube	Amount	NorthAmerica	Time	View	Detailed_Accc	Flows	IC	Department	LOB	Region	DataType
	10.00	Entity1	20XXM1	YTD	100	EndBalInput	None	0000	000	000	Data1

Figure 6.71

For demonstration purposes, I simply clicked on Load Cube again on Import1. Because of my setup between Import1 and Import2, my Cube View will show both as loaded, as these intersections are contained in the same base input.

WF2 loaded intersections.

Import	Validate	Load	Completed										
⬆ Load Cube ⟳ ⊢													
Status						**Target Intersections (Loaded)**							
⊕ **Load Cube**	Amount	NorthAmerica	Time	View	Detailed_Accc	Flows	IC	Department	LOB	Region	DataType
	15.00	Entity1	20XXM1	YTD	100	EndBalInput	None	0000	000	000	Data2

Figure 6.72

100	⊟ Data1	⊟ EndBalInput	10.00
	Data2	⊟ EndBalInput	15.00

Figure 6.73

WF3 loaded successfully.

Import	Validate	Load	Completed										
⬆ Load Cube ⟳ ⊢													
Status						**Target Intersections (Loaded)**							
⊕ **Load Cube**	Amount	NorthAmerica	Time	View	Detailed_Accc	Flows	IC	Department	LOB	Regio	DataType
	15.00	Entity1	20XXM1	YTD	110	EndBalInput	None	0000	000	000	Data2

Figure 6.74

Notice that the Cube View kept all three loads.

100	⊟ Data1	⊟ EndBalInput	10.00
	Data2	⊟ EndBalInput	15.00
110	⊟ Data1	⊟ EndBalInput	
	Data2	⊟ EndBalInput	15.00

Figure 6.75

Cube Data Unit is the Same, but Workflow Data Unit has the Same Account and a Different Flow

If Load Overlapped Siblings = True on the parent (AdminLoad), then this will allow for accumulation based on the Entity and Origin members.

If both steps load to a different Flow member but with the same accounts, and there is just the standard workflow channel implemented, the system will clear and replace.

Standard Workflow Channel							
WF1 (Import1)		**WF3 (Import3)**		**End Result (Last Load Wins)**			
Symbol	**Member**	**Symbol**	**Member**	**Symbol**	**Member**	**Member**
E#	Entity1	E#	Entity1	E#	~~Entity1~~	Entity1
C#	Local	C#	Local	C#	~~Local~~	Local
S#	Actual	S#	Actual	S#	~~Actual~~	Actual
T#	20XXM1	T#	20XXM1	T#	~~20XXM1~~	20XXM1
A#	100	A#	100	A#	~~100~~	100
F#	EndBalInput	F#	Example2	F#	~~EndBalInput~~	Example2
V#	YTD	V#	YTD	V#	~~YTD~~	YTD
O#	Import	O#	Import	O#	~~Import~~	Import
IC#	None	IC#	None	IC#	~~None~~	None
U1#	0000	U1#	0000	U1#	~~000~~	000
U2#	000	U2#	000	U2#	~~000~~	000
U3#	000	U3#	000	U3#	~~000~~	000
U4#	Data1	U4#	Data2	U4#	~~Data1~~	Data2
U5#	None	U5#	None	U5#	~~None~~	None
U6#	None	U6#	None	U6#	~~None~~	None
U7#	None	U7#	None	U7#	~~None~~	None
U8#	None	U8#	None	U8#	~~None~~	None
Amount	10	Amount	15	Amount	~~10~~	15

Figure 6.76

WF1 and WF2 loaded successfully, and this is reflected in the Cube View.

100	⊟ Data1	⊟ EndBalInput	10.00
	Data2	⊟ EndBalInput	15.00

Figure 6.77

WF3 loaded successfully.

Import	Validate	Load	Completed									
⬆ Load Cube	↻ ⊟											
Status			**Target Intersections (Loaded)**									
⊕ Load Cube	Amount ▼	NorthAmerica ▼	Time ▼	View ▼	Detailed_Accc ▼	Flows ▼	IC ▼	Department ▼	LOE ▼	Region ▼	DataType
	15.00	Entity1	20XXM1	YTD	100	Example2	None	0000	000	000	Data2

Figure 6.78

Notice that the Cube View cleared what was loaded to EndBalInput.

100	⊟ Data1	⊟ EndBalInput	
		Example2	
	Data2	⊟ EndBalInput	
		Example2	15.00

Figure 6.79

If we need both intersections, then we need to implement a UD workflow channel on UD4 in addition to possibly setting up a central import step – set to `AllChannelInput` – because of where the workflow steps are in this structure.

Additional Use Cases for Workflow Channels

Workflow channels can be applied to forms and journals as well. Adding workflow channels to forms allows the individual workflow forms steps to be locked. Without the workflow channel, however, locking one form will inadvertently lock all form steps – especially if there are multiple form steps – under the given period and Workflow Profile. In the example below (Figure 6.80), the base input Workflow Profile has `Forms` and `Forms2` completed, representing the multiple form steps under a given Workflow Profile (base input). The moment I click Lock, both `Forms` and `Forms2` will be locked.

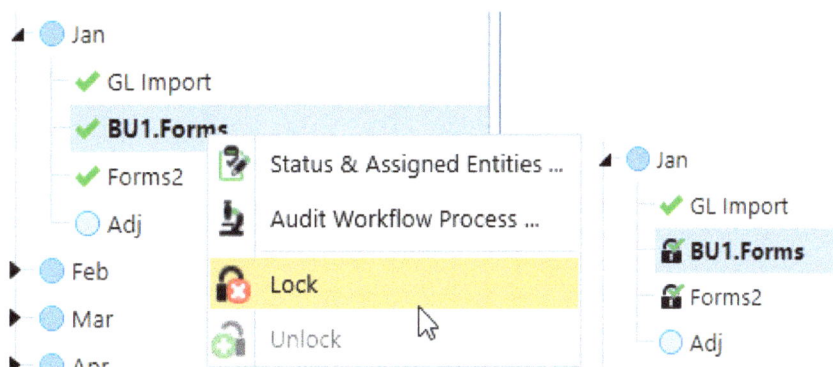

Figure 6.80

Common Troubleshooting on Workflow Channels

This section covers common errors when implementing workflow channels and steps to resolve them. Examples include not being able to update a workflow channel on a metadata member, and various validation error messages when importing to an import step with workflow channels.

Not Able to Update the Workflow Channel on my UD Base Member

Did you enable the UD dimension on your Application Properties?

By default, if you aren't explicitly assigning a UD for your workflow channel in Application Properties, the Workflow Channel row in your UD member will be greyed out.

Figure 6.81

Go to Application Properties > General > (Default) Scenario Type.

Figure 6.82

Here, (Not Used) is assigned to my UD Dimension Type for Workflow Channels. Thus, in this case, checking Application Properties allows the administrator to determine whether a UD dimension type is being used for workflow channels.

Validation Error Message #1: "The Data Cell is read-only…"

You may receive an error message along the lines of the following…

Error Message: "The Data Cell is read-only because the Parent Workflow Profile 'XXX' has no active Input Profiles for the Workflow Channels that are assigned to the Data Cell's Account and/or UD member. Entity=X,Account=Y,Origin=Import"

This error message might occur on your import step when trying to validate.

Checks to perform:

Check that the account is set to NoDataLock. Remember, NoDataLock takes the account member out of the workflow channel process and allows the account to be used across any Workflow Profile no matter what workflow channel is assigned *(must always be NoDataDock if using a UD workflow channel)*.

1. Check that the workflow channel is assigned to the profile import step (e.g., WF1 and WF3).

2. Check that the profile import step is active (e.g., WF1 and WF3).

Check that there is a "central import" that is active and set to AllChannelInput under the parent Workflow Profile (e.g., AdminLoad).

This profile needs to be AllChannelInput and set to Active to resolve the validation error. It does not matter that Can Load Unrelated Entities is set to False.

If additional workflow channels are created, ensure that the workflow channels are applied to the relevant metadata members and Workflow Profile steps.

> **Note:** After establishing the new workflow channels (e.g., AllChannelInput), the administrator may be required to re-import the data source for the changes to apply when going through the remaining validate and load steps.

Validation Error Message #2: "Cannot load data into …"

Error Message: "Cannot load data to account… because it is not assigned to Workflow Channel '…' or because the account is invalid for the specified Cube"

This error message might also occur on your import step when trying to validate.

Checks to perform, especially if a UD workflow channel is used:

1. Check that the account is set to NoDataLock on the specified Scenario Type.

2. Check for any new accounts that haven't been assigned the workflow channel NoDataLock.

Troubleshooting Inputs on Forms and Adj

1. If you get an error where you are unable to input through forms, even though you have an AllChannelInput set on the forms step, you may want to check that the default workflow has the AllChannelInput applied to the relevant step (e.g., AllChannelInput, AllChannelForms, AllChannelAdj) with the Profile Active = True.

As a general rule, we typically recommend not touching the default workflow except for changing the security groups (e.g., administrators) for a maintenance group. This section is a very specific exception and could occur if you have several complicated import, forms, and adj steps setup.

It may be useful to set the Workflow Name as Central Form Input or Central Import, as this is what the AllChannelInput will represent. Figure 6.83 offers an example of the default workflow set with AllChannel for Import.

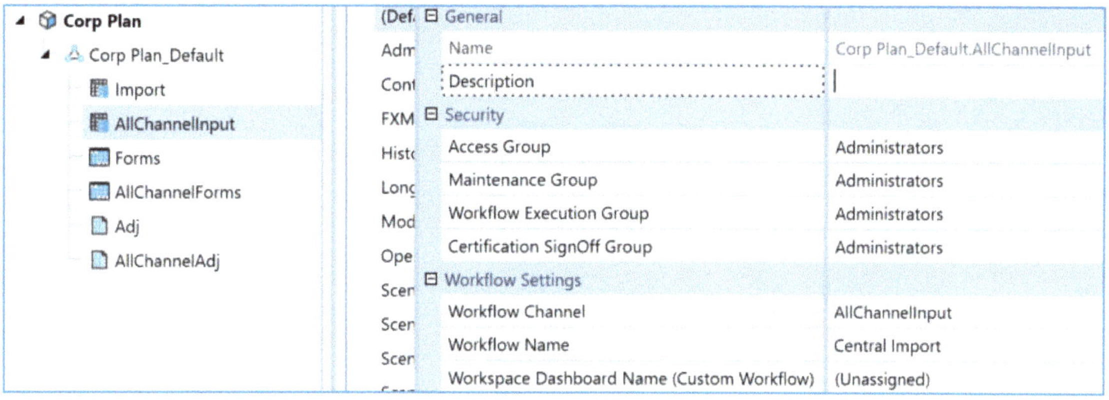

Figure 6.83

Remember that the default workflow is the one with the triangle icon next to it. Each workflow suffix created for a cube by Scenario Type will generate a default template by the suffix. Figure 6.84 is an example of the default workflow set with AllChannel for Forms.

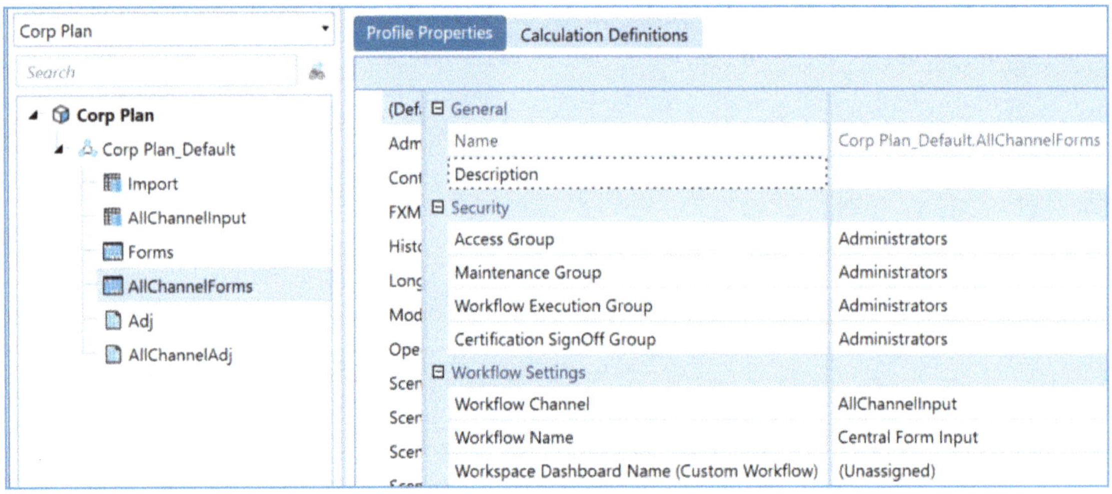

Figure 6.84

Meanwhile, Figure 6.85 is an example of the default workflow set with `AllChannel` for `Adj`.

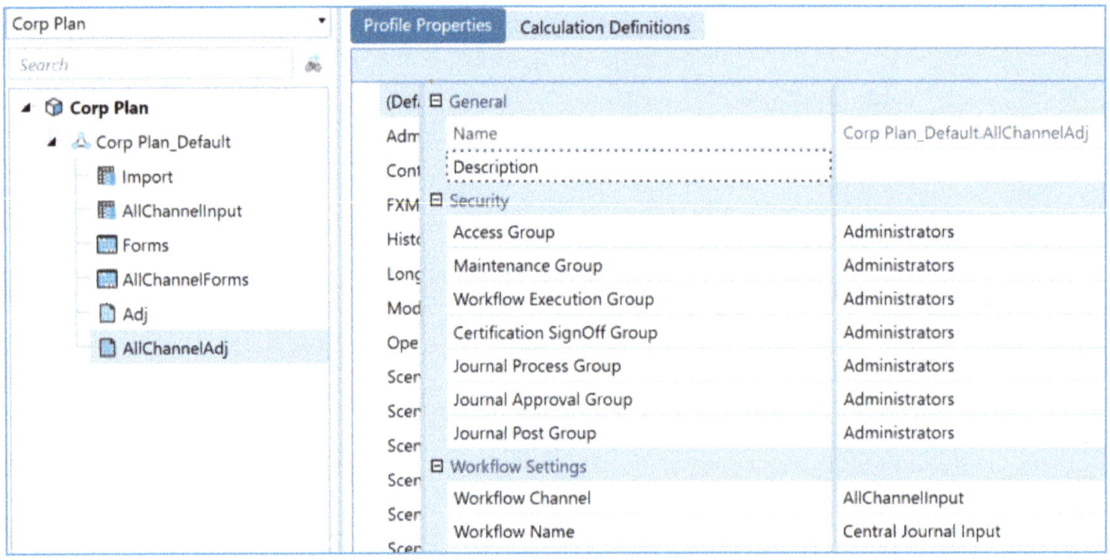

Figure 6.85

Locking and Unlocking Workflows

To ensure we are all on the same page, this section defines "locking" as "preventing users from importing or adjusting data via forms or journals into a given period". Since a lot of users access their tasks through OnePlace, via workflow, then locking the workflow accomplishes this.

When data is locked (explicitly or implicitly), the workflow engine will not allow any form of data input to the entities assigned to the Workflow Profile type.

- **Explicit Locks:** An explicit entity data lock is created when a workflow is locked, thereby locking its assigned entity(s) for the scenario and time associated with the Workflow Profile type.

- **Implicit Locks:** An implicit entity data lock is created when a workflow's parent workflow has been certified. Implicit locks are created to ensure that once a higher-level workflow is certified, the underlying entity data cannot be changed. Implicit locks can be cleared by un-certifying the Workflow Profile type.

- **Workflow Only Locks:** If a Workflow Profile type is locked and the Workflow Profile type does not have assigned entities, all workflow processing is blocked, even though there are no entity locks placed. However, this will not necessarily prevent users from entering inputs by other means (e.g., submit cells). If there are assigned entities to the workflow, then locking that workflow step will prevent users from further input. For the cases where there are no entity assignments, you can set up security in such a way that a user would not be able to enter data (I recommend thorough testing to see if slice security is sufficient before diving into other alternatives; for example, a custom conditional input rule).

Tip: Locking workflows can prove especially useful if there are assigned entities, because they prevent users from submitting through Excel to those entities.

Lock Workflow

This section covers a few options on how to lock a workflow, which you can do by right-clicking on the Workflow Profile or through workflow multi-period processing.

For the right-click and lock, navigate to the relevant Workflow Profile. Right-click on the selected month for the given Workflow Profile and click Lock.

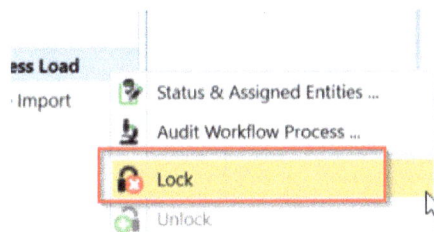

Figure 6.86

Tip: If you click on Status & Assigned Entities instead, you can view dependent workflow steps without navigating to each workflow. This allows you to see a summary of which steps are complete.

If you want to use workflow multi-period processing, you navigate to OnePlace. Click on the XXXX Periods. This will bring up Workflow Multi-Period Processing. Now you can batch process select workflow steps!

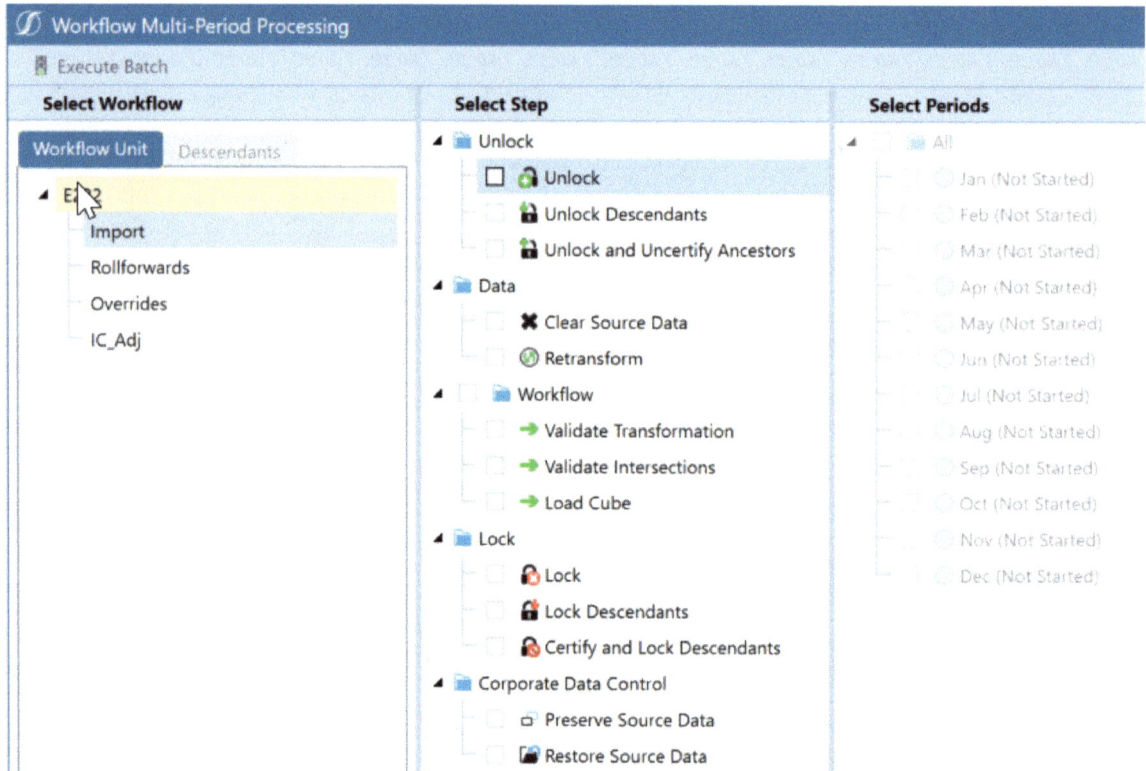

Figure 6.87

When locking, forms will gain a lock icon for relevant cells, as presented in Figure 6.88. Furthermore, you will also receive an error message when attempting to post or unpost a journal to a locked period.

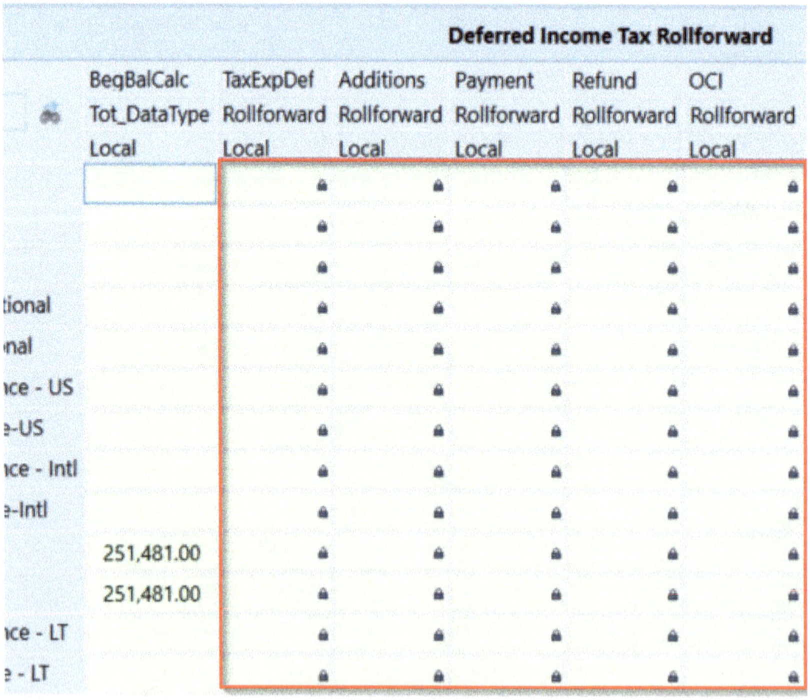

Figure 6.88

Unlock Workflow

This section covers methods to unlock a workflow, such as individually unlocking each workflow, leveraging Status & Assigned Entities to unlock descendants of a workflow, and the workflow multi-period processing.

To individually unlock each workflow, you can navigate to the specific workflow, right-click on the relevant month and select Unlock.

To unlock descendants of a workflow, navigate to the relevant Workflow Profile type. Right-click on the month and click on Status & Assigned Entities. Within the Workflow Status window, right-click on any of the steps to unlock. You can unlock the workflow and all descendants by right-clicking on the Workflow Parent > Unlock Descendants > All.

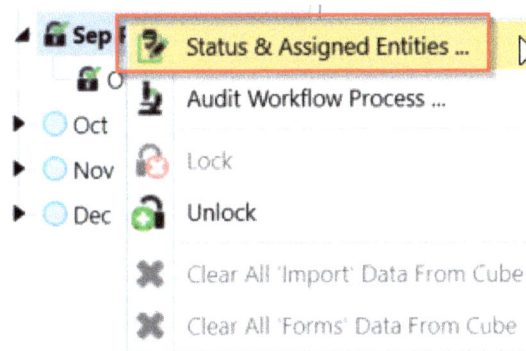

Figure 6.89

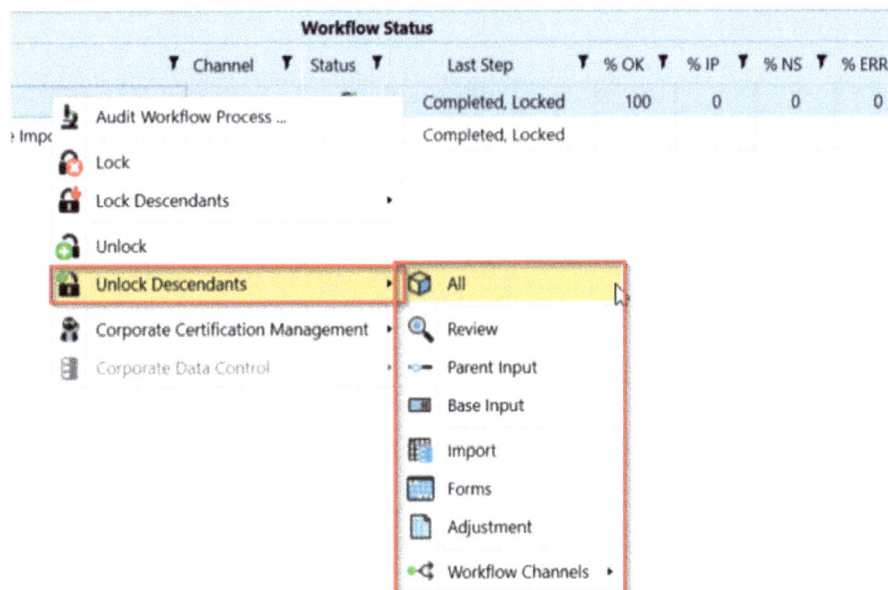

Figure 6.90

To use workflow multi-period processing, navigate to OnePlace. Click on the XXXX Periods. This will bring up Workflow Multi-Period Processing to batch the unlocking (Figure 6.87).

Consolidations and Rules Impact on Locked Periods

This section covers how running a consolidation or business rule can impact your locked periods.

Consolidation

When a User runs a consolidation, you cannot stop the process from impacting previously locked periods. The end result figures should not change, assuming you properly tested your Member Formulas and custom business rules. It is recommended that end-users should only consolidate data from their workflow process; this will ensure that when they sign-off on their workflow process, the relevant entities' status and numbers are up to date regardless of subsequent consolidations.

A **Force Consolidate** will consolidate all entities of the selected Data Unit being processed, irrespective of the calculation status. If a force consolidate runs and a business rule has been changed without following the above instructions (varying by time), the previous months in the current year could be impacted by the rule change. Keep this risk in mind; it can be avoided by always ensuring your rules are modified by time.

A **Consolidate** will consolidate up to the selected current period depending on the calculation status of the entities of the Data Unit being processed. It checks the calculation status on each entity and consolidates only what it needs to. In other words, any entities that have a calculation status of OK or OK, MC will not be calculated or translated during the consolidation.

Rules

Member Formula updates should leverage the use of Scenario Type and time. For example, you could have a Member Formula written to the default Scenario Type and time and then future updates can be applied to a particular Scenario Type and time. Text properties (often used when writing logic) can, and sometimes should, vary by Scenario Type and time.

Depending on the business rule, you can have specific Scenario Types and times used as conditions, or if the business rule is already associated with a data management step or sequence, you can have the business rule run off the scenario and time defined in the data management step or sequence.

Workflow Open and Closed State

The open and closed states of a Workflow Profile *should not* be used as a substitute for the locking/unlocking capability that we discussed in the earlier sections. The open and closed states are used to truly deprecate workflow hierarchy structures where you still want to retain the data used through those Workflow Profiles but no longer want users accessing them. When the workflow is set to close, the workflow engine will take a snapshot of the current workflow hierarchy structure and store it in a historical audit table for the scenario and time being closed. This also means the workflow hierarchy is not accessed from memory (cache), as would be the case with a workflow in an open state. A closed workflow must be read from the database rather than memory because it is considered a point-in-time snapshot stored in a historical table. This is a performance penalty, noticeable when reading the entire closed workflow hierarchy for a scenario and time.

Open State: The workflow is available, and locking is controlled at the individual Workflow Profile level. This also means the workflow hierarchy is accessed from memory (cache) rather than being read from the database, which provides very fast read performance.

Closed State: This triggers the workflow engine to place a high-level lock on the workflow. The closed state trumps individual Workflow Profile lock status values, and the workflow level will display a black circle to indicate a closed workflow.

If you ever wanted to access open and close functionality, you can access it through the cube root profile on the XXXX periods selection or by the selected period.

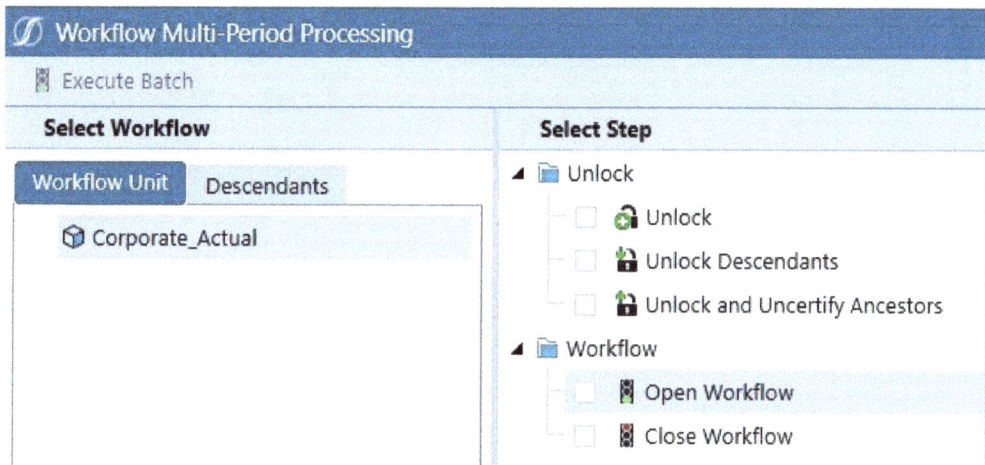

Figure 6.91

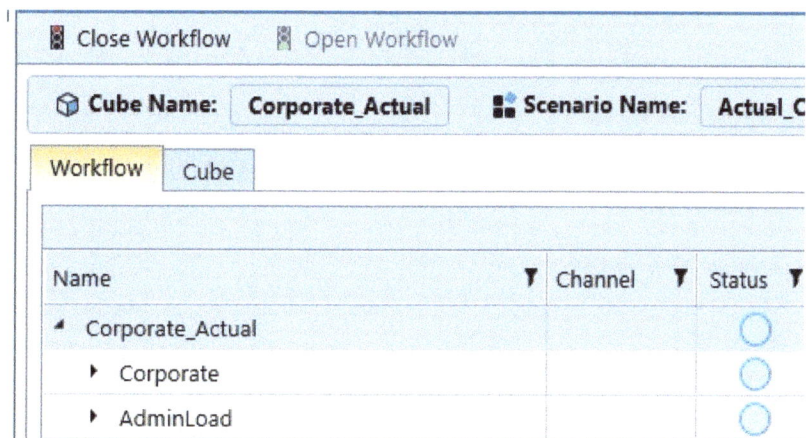

Figure 6.92

Workflow hierarchies should only be closed if major changes are being made to the workflow hierarchy and the structure of a cube and historical hierarchy relationships need to be preserved. Again, we recommend keeping workflows open due to the performance impact mentioned above.

Common Troubleshooting on Workflow Profiles

Many troubleshooting issues related to Workflow Profiles stem from implementing new processes on top of existing processes within OneStream. This section covers some of the common "issues" or considerations related to workflows and setup.

"Active" Profiles

Common issues regarding "active" profiles include, but are not limited to:

1. Creating the profile step, but users say they can't see this step through OnePlace. This issue may be due to security, or the profile not being set as active.

2. Attaching a form/journal/dashboard to a workflow step, but users don't see it on OnePlace. This may be due to security, or the profile not being set as active.

3. Users are unable to see certain Cube Views through OnePlace, but these same Cube Views are used as part of the forms channel, which is set to active. This could be due to security, or if you are using Cube Views, check that the Cube View is part of a Cube View profile and that the Cube View profile is set to be used in OnePlace.

135

4. Users cannot input to forms. Ensure that the forms step is set to active and – if assigned entities are used – ensure that they are properly assigned. Check that the Cube View used for the form is enabled for modifications (e.g., Can Modify Data set as True and check whether this setting is appropriate on the overall Cube View, its individual rows, or its individual columns).

Security

When someone asks me why a profile step isn't showing up through OnePlace, my immediate thought goes to security. Ensure that the user is active in the application, assigned to the relevant security group, and the security group is attached to the right profile. Ensure that the workflow step created has Profile Active set to True on the relevant Scenario Type.

Tips and Tricks on Workflow

General titbits an administrator should know about workflow:

1. Be mindful of how you name your workflows. Workflow Profile names must be unique across the application. If there are multiple cubes using the Scenario Type, consider adding a cube indicator (such as a letter or even the cube name) to the Workflow Profile name.

2. Once data is loaded into the given Workflow Profile type, you cannot delete the Workflow Profile type unless all the data that has been loaded via that given workflow for all time periods and Scenario Types has been cleared.

3. If you click on the ultimate top cube (the icon with the cube), there is a Grid View tab you can use to make mass updates. This assumes you don't want to use the template upload.

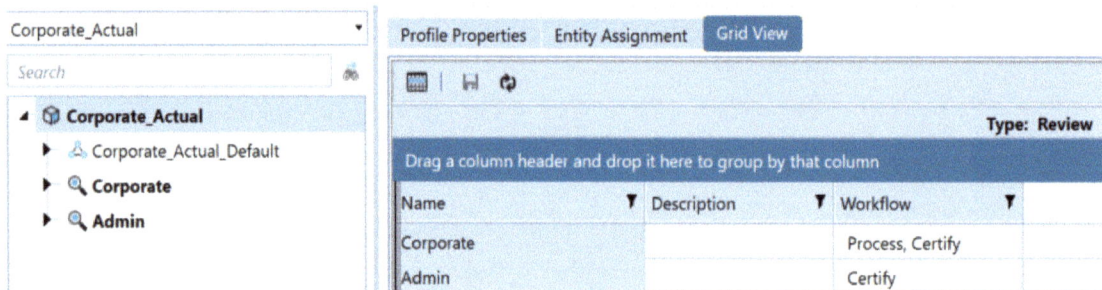

Figure 6.93

4. Mass processes through OnePlace. Click on the XXXX Periods. This will bring up workflow multi-period processing, which will allow you to batch locks/unlocks, clear source data, validate, and load data.

5. Mass processes through the cube root Workflow Profile. This is similar to the above workflow multi-period processing, but the difference is that you can see every workflow step under your cube root Workflow Profile. To access, all you have to do is click on your cube root profile, the one where the icon is a cube:

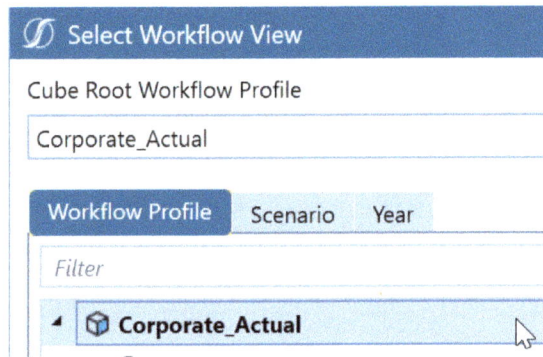

Figure 6.94

If you have a month selected, you will be brought to a Manage Workflow interface, which you can use to monitor workflow steps and status.

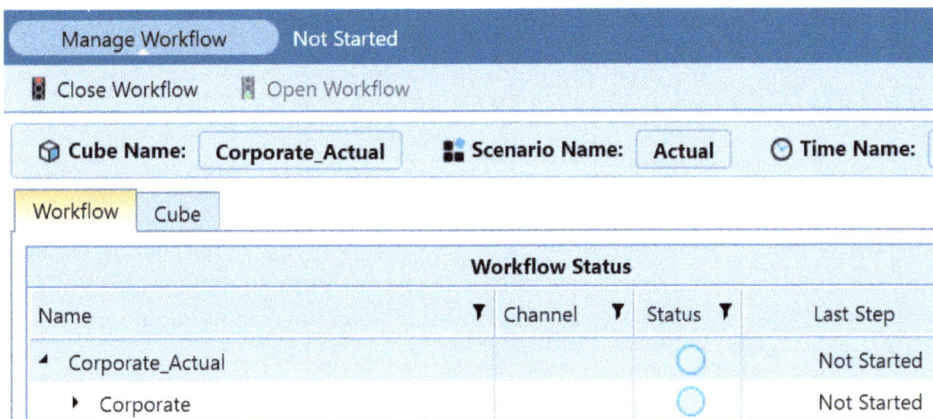

Figure 6.95

But what we care about is the XXXX periods (in my example, 2020 Periods).

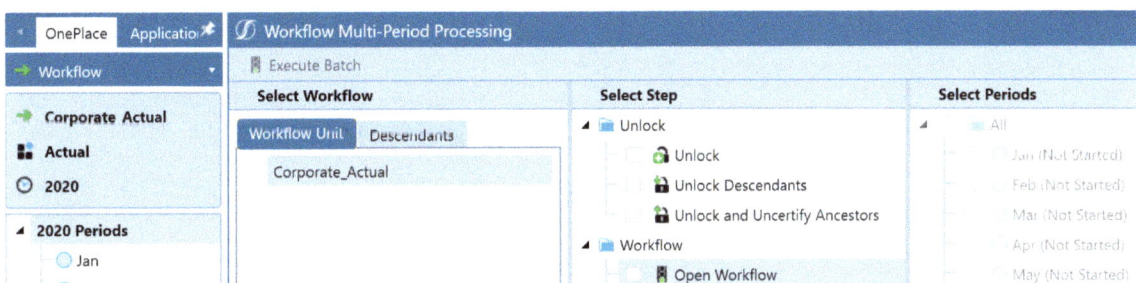

Figure 6.96

If you click on the Descendants tab, you are then able to filter on the profile type (e.g., Review, Base Input, Parent Input, Import, Adjustment, Forms).

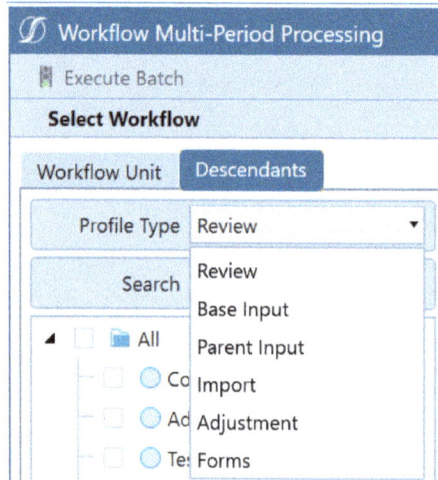

Figure 6.97

From here, you can multi-select steps to then run your batch processes.

Conclusion

This chapter covered the core components of Workflow Profiles, including the suffixes, hierarchies, and types of inputs we can create (e.g., base, parent, review).

It also showed examples of what happens if there are several import steps that could result in data clearing, as well as methods to resolve problems. Hopefully, this chapter will help you leverage workflow to your company's processes and responsibilities in the best possible way!

7

Data Troubleshooting

As an admin, probably the most dreaded message you can get from a user is some form of "My data looks off" or, even worse, "Where's my data?" Seeing this in your inbox usually means you're in for a headache. OneStream application builds can be complex, so finding the root cause of a data issue can be daunting (assuming there even is an issue in the first place).

The purpose of this chapter is to provide a framework for troubleshooting data issues. Fundamentally, there are three main ways to think about data in your application, each of which reflect a different cell status:

1. Input data refers to data that is loaded via workflows to O#Import or manually entered to O#Forms.

2. Calculated data refers to data that is calculated via business rules or Member Formulas.

3. Consolidated data at parent entities (as well as translated data at child entities).

Each section covers one of these categories, with issues being further categorized as either missing data or faulty data. We discuss troubleshooting techniques, as well as the most common causes of these issues and how to fix them. The hope is that this chapter can serve as a sort of decision tree, leading you down a series of yes/no questions to get you to the root cause of your data mysteries.

General Troubleshooting Tools

Before going into tactics for dealing with specific data issues, let's begin by covering some general tools that are invaluable when investigating and fixing data issues.

Drill Down

When you're investigating import, forms and adjustment cells, one of your best tools is the Drill Down window, which can be opened by right-clicking a cell and selecting Drill Down. From here, you can drill down to base intersections and see exactly where your data is coming from.

Amount	Cube	Entity	Parent	Consolidation	Scenario	Time	View	Account	Flow	Origin	IC	UD1	UD2	UD3	UD4	UD5	UD6
1,000.00	MainCube - Main entry	California - California		USD	Actual	2020M1	Periodic	10000	FndBal	BeforeAdj	None	Southropp	Ships	CC01	None	None	None
1,000.00	MainCube - Main entry	California - California		USD	Actual	2020M1	Periodic	10000	EndBal	BeforeAdj	None	Southropp	Ships	CC01	None	None	None

Amount	Cube	Entity	Parent	Consolidation	Scenario	Time	View	Account	Flow	Origin	IC	UD1	UD2	UD3	UD4	UD5	UD6	UI
1,000.00	MainCube - Main entry	California - California		USD	Actual	2020M1	Periodic	10000	EndBal	Forms	None	Southropp	Ships	CC01	None	None	None	N

Figure 7.1

Chapter 7

Drilling on Import Cells

If the base intersection is an O#Import cell, you can right-click the intersection and select Load Results for Imported Cell.

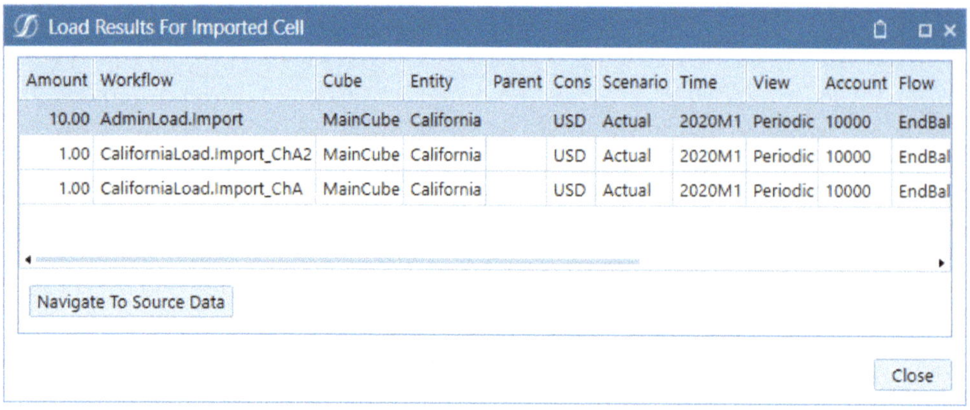

Figure 7.2

Clicking the Navigate to Source Data button will open the Source Data Drill Down window, as shown below, which gives you even more granular detail. From this window, you can right-click on a source intersection row to give you even more options:

1. Drill back to the source file that was loaded.

2. View what transformation rules the cell passed through from Stage to the cube.

3. Drill back to the source system (though this would require a connector rule and additional configuration on your data).

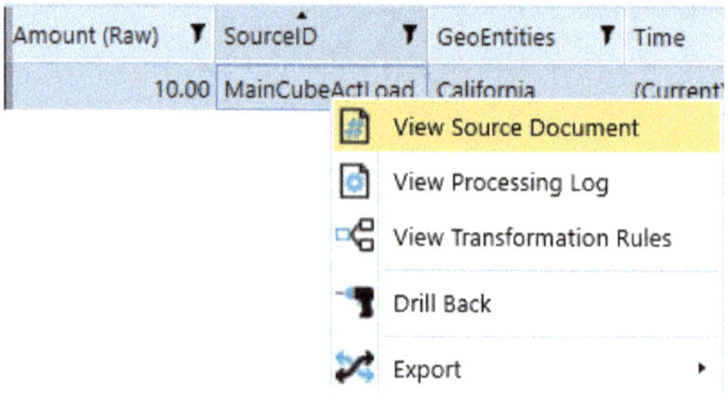

Figure 7.3

Drilling on Forms and Adjustment Cells

If the base intersection is a O#Forms or O#AdjInput cell, you can right-click the intersection and select Audit History for Forms or Adjustment Cell. This will show you the full history of who submitted data to this intersection, when they submitted it, and what method was used.

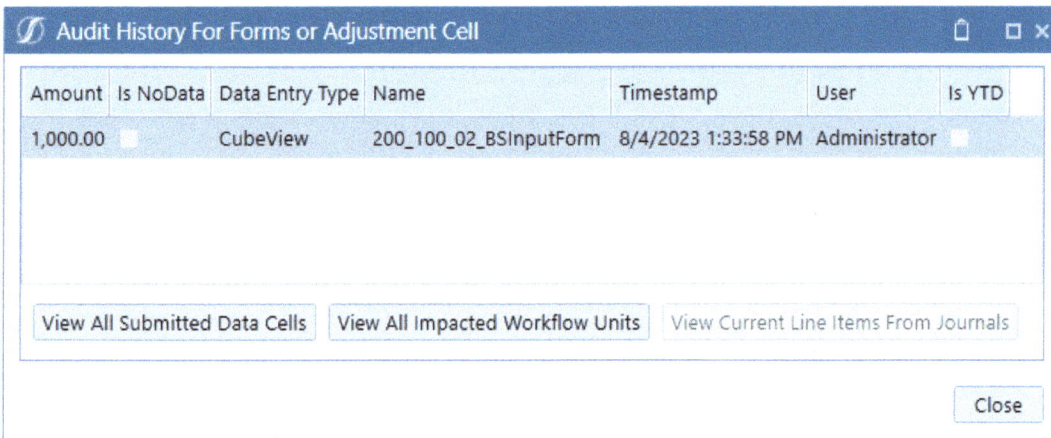

Figure 7.4

Quick Views

Quick Views in Excel spreadsheets are an excellent tool when investigating intersections in your cube. However, it is sometimes a bit of a pain to spin up Excel, create a Quick View, and fill in the entire Quick View POV. A nice tip is that you can swiftly create Quick Views with fully specified POVs by right clicking a cell and selecting Create Quick View Using POV From Select Cell.

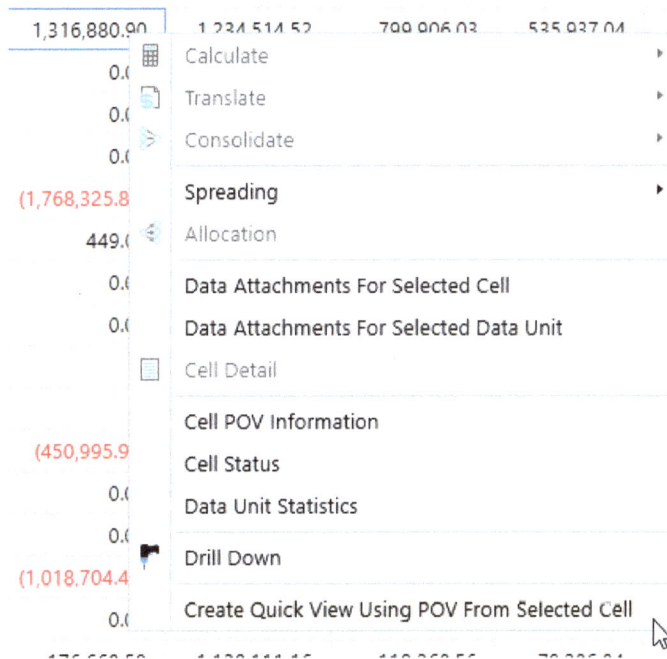

Figure 7.5

This will open up a new Spreadsheet tab in your OneStream window, and create a Quick View with the same POV as the selected cell already populated.

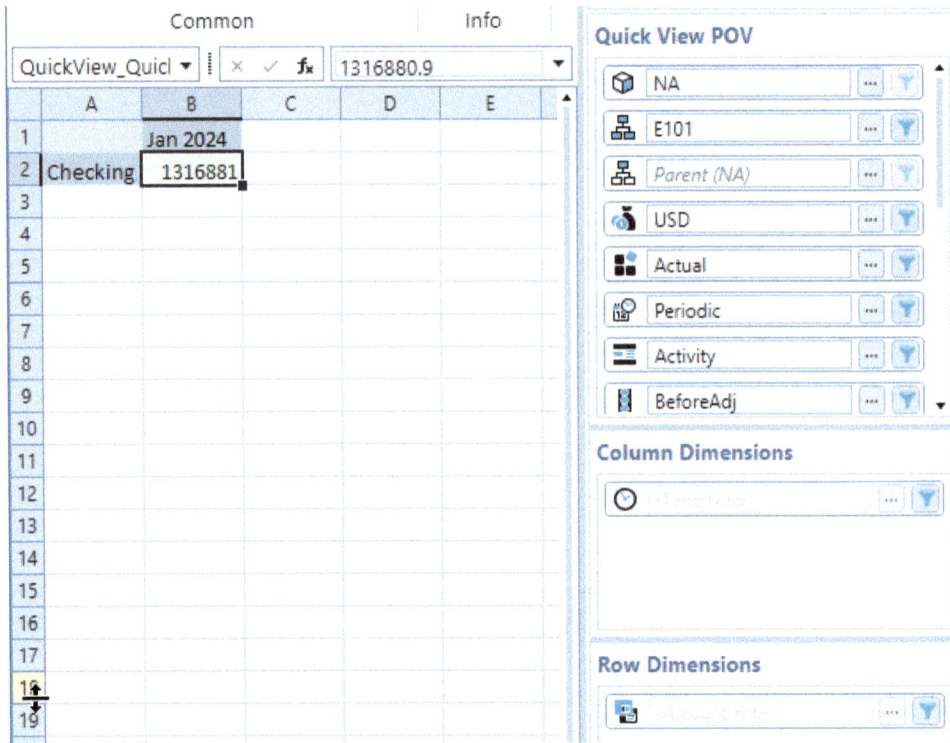

Figure 7.6

Clearing Inputted Data

Sometimes, you might have to clear data from your cube; for instance, if you suspect you have old data floating around in your cube. Here are a couple of options for handling this.

Clear Through Workflows

To clear loaded O#Import or O#Forms data, right-click the workflow step and select either Clear All 'Import' Data From Cube or Clear All 'Forms' Data From Cube, respectively. This will clear data that was previously loaded through this workflow, across all base input workflows.

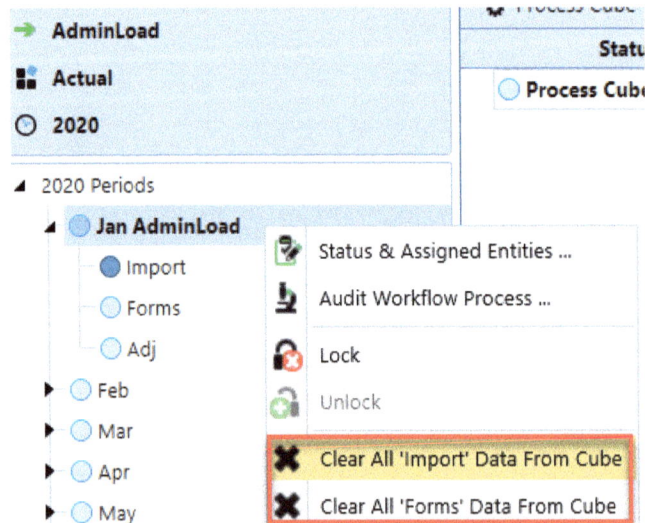

Figure 7.7

Clear Forms Data on Cube Views

Provided the Cube View settings are configured to allow for data modification, you can clear data directly from Cube Views by clearing out each cell. A nice trick is that you can shift-select multiple cells and hit ctrl+x to cut them all out!

Figure 7.8

Note: Something to be aware of is that if the cell POV is set to O#BeforeAdj, you can only clear out the O#Forms data and not the O#Import data. This is confusing when it occurs, since you can clear the cell but once you click save, the O#Import value will reappear.

DM Sequence

To clear import, forms, or adjustment data from an entire Data Unit, you can create a **clear data management step** and specify which origin members to clear.

General (Step)	
Name	MyClear
Description	
Data Management Group	100_PlanDM
Step Type	Clear Data
Use Detailed Logging	False
Data Units	
Cube	|PovCube|
Entity Filter	E#|PovEntity|
Scenario	|PovScenario|
Time Filter	T#|PovTime|
Origin	
Clear Imported Data	True
Clear Forms Data	True
Clear Adjustment Data And Delete Journals	True

Figure 7.9

ClearCalculatedData Method

The most common method for clearing calculated data is the `api.Data.ClearCalculatedData` method. When this method is called, the finance engine takes into account the active Data Unit; in other words, it will only clear data from the current Data Unit. Also, from a technical standpoint, this method will only clear cells that have their `StorageType` as "Calculation"; it won't clear loaded O#Import data or manually entered O#Forms data.

Another important note is that this method is overloaded. For the first version, there is no `clearDurableCalculatedData` parameter, so calling this method means durable data will not be cleared. If you do want to clear durable data, then you'll need to call the second version below, passing in `True` for `clearDurableCalculatedData`.

```
DataApi.ClearCalculatedData(clearCalculatedData As Boolean,
clearTranslatedData As Boolean, clearConsolidatedData As Boolean,
clearDurableCalculatedDataAsBoolean, Optional accountFilter As String,
Optional flowFilter As String, Optional originFilter As String,
Optional icFilter As String, Optional ud1Filter As String, Optional
ud2Filter As String, Optional ud3Filter As String, Optional ud4Filter
As String, Optional ud5Filter As String, Optional ud6Filter As String,
Optional ud7Filter As String, Optional ud8Filter As String)
```

You can restrict the clear by passing in Member Filters. If you don't pass in any arguments for these filters, then OneStream will clear all members in the current Data Unit. Here are some examples of how to call this method:

```
api.Data.ClearCalculatedData(True, True, True, "A#IncomeStatement.Base", "F#EndBal",,,"U1#Top.Base")        ' Don't clear durable data
api.Data.ClearCalculatedData(True, True, True, True, "A#IncomeStatement.Base", "F#EndBal",,,"U1#Top.Base")  ' Clear durable data
```

Figure 7.10

> **Note:** Do *not* use brackets when passing arguments into Member Filter arguments. OneStream will ignore any statement with brackets. It technically won't throw any runtime errors, but it just won't clear anything.
>
> For example, `[A#IncomeStatement.Base]` is invalid.

It's not common, but if you know exactly the base members you would like to clear, you can call another version of this method where you pass in a data buffer string (e.g., `A#10000:F#EndBal`).

```
DataApi.ClearCalculatedData(dataBufferScript As String,
clearCalculatedData As Boolean, clearTranslatedData As Boolean,
clearConsolidatedData As Boolean, clearDurableCalculatedDataAsBoolean)
```

> **Note:** You cannot use expansions or use the `FilterMember` function when passing in arguments to `dataBufferScript`. You would get runtime errors in both cases. Here are two examples of invalid uses:
>
> ```
> api.Data.ClearCalculatedData(True, True, True, True, "A#Cash.Base")
> api.Data.ClearCalculatedData("FilterMembers(A#10000, U3#TotalCC.Base)", True, True, True, True)
> ```
>
> Figure 7.11

SetDataBuffer Method

While the `api.Data.ClearCalculatedData` method allows you to clear calculated data, it does not allow you to clear inputted data. The `api.Data.SetDataBuffer` method is less common, but is more flexible in that it allows you to do just that – clear both inputted and calculated data.

The general idea with this technique is to pull the intersections you want to clear into a databuffer, then set all of the cell values to `0` along with the cell statuses to `NoData`. Let's cover a couple of examples.

Clear All Data

Here is an example that clears both inputted and calculated data (technically, it can clear consolidated data as well). There's a lot going on here, so let's go line by line.

```
Dim clearBuffer As DataBuffer = api.Data.GetDataBufferUsingFormula("
    FilterMembers(O#Import:F#EndBal, [A#IncomeStatement.Base]) * 0.0
")

For Each cell As DataBufferCell In clearBuffer.DataBufferCells.Values
    cell.CellStatus = DataCellStatus.CreateDataCellStatus(True, False)
Next

api.Data.SetDataBuffer(clearBuffer, api.Data.GetExpressionDestinationInfo(""))
```

Figure 7.12

We limit the clear by specifying specific intersections to pull into our `clearBuffer` databuffer using the `FilterMembers` function. Here, we are saying we only want to clear `O#Import` cells, the `EndBal` Flow member, and `Base` income statement accounts. Note that this data buffer will include both inputted and calculated cells, since O#Import only refers to the origin, and not the StorageType.

During the initial query stage, where we pull the data buffer, we set the values of all cells to 0 by multiplying the buffer by `0`. This is just a shortcut; we could also just pull the buffer as is, then manually set the cell values to 0 later, when we iterate through the cells.

In the loop, we set each cell as NoData by passing in `True` to the `isNoData` parameter for the `CreateDataCellStatus` method.

Finally, we call the `api.Data.SetDataBuffer` method to save the modified data buffer to the database. In this case, the modifications result in the data being cleared.

> **Note:** Technically, setting the cells to `NoData` is the only requirement for clearing the cell. Setting the cell values to `0` is redundant but is done as good practice to convey intent (it's more obvious that this code is clearing data when you can see cells are being set to 0).

Clear Only Calculated Data

Let's build on the previous example by restricting it further to only include calculated cells. The example is a bit more complicated, which we'll elaborate more on below.

```
Dim resultBuffer As New DataBuffer
Dim clearBuffer As DataBuffer = api.Data.GetDataBufferUsingFormula("
    FilterMembers(O#Import:F#EndBal, [A#IncomeStatement.Base]) * 0.0
")

For Each cell As DataBufferCell In clearBuffer.DataBufferCells.Values
    If cell.CellStatus.StorageType = DataCellStorageType.Calculation Then
        cell.CellStatus = DataCellStatus.CreateDataCellStatus(True, False)

        resultBuffer.SetCell(si, cell)
    End If
Next

api.Data.SetDataBuffer(resultBuffer, api.Data.GetExpressionDestinationInfo(""))
```

Figure 7.13

When we query intersections into clearBuffer, it contains both inputted and calculated data. However, we want to remove inputted cells from this buffer, since we only want to clear calculated data. Unfortunately, VB.NET does not allow you to remove objects from an iterable object (e.g., a collection) as you are iterating through it. Because of this, we must declare resultBuffer as an empty DataBuffer, and then use that as the container for the cells we want to clear.

In the loop, we now add a condition to check for whether the source cell has StorageType of Calculation. If it does, then we set the cell status to NoData, and then add it to our resultBuffer.

Finally, we pass the new resultBuffer to the SetDataBuffer method instead of passing clearBuffer as we did in the previous example.

> **Note:** While this technique does work to clear calculated data, in general, it's better to stick to api.Data.ClearCalculatedData – it's more efficient and less verbose. But it is important to be aware of this option, as it can give you some finer control in situations where you have very specific cells you need to clear.

Debugging Inputted Data

This section covers input data that is loaded via workflows or entered to forms. Data loaded this way will be tagged with either the O#Import or O#Forms Origin members, and will have cell status of Input. Journal entries can be treated similarly as input data, but note that journal data is tagged with the AdjInput Origin member and will have cell status of Journals.

> **Tip:** You can see whether data is inputted, calculated, translated, or consolidated by right clicking a cell in a report and selecting Cell Status. To use this feature, the cell must be comprised of base members only.

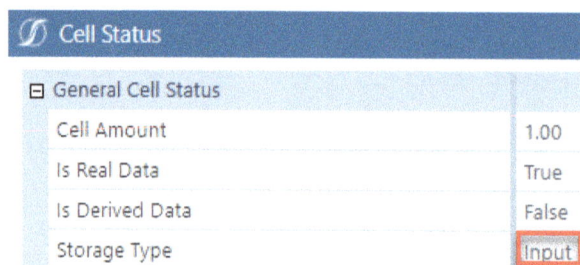

Figure 7.14

Inputted Data Clearing Unexpected

This section covers why data loaded through workflows can clear, as well as why data in your Stage tables aren't appearing in your cube as expected.

Data Cleared Manually

We start by covering an often-overlooked possibility – someone ran a clear without you realizing. Data loaded via workflows can be cleared directly from the workflow. To see if this occurred, you could view the Task Activity logs. To narrow down your searches, filter on Task Type to show only Clear Cube Data For Workflow. From here, you could filter further on Description to see if anyone cleared the data from your specific workflow.

Task Type	Description	Duration	Task Status	User	Application
Clear Cube Data For Workflow	WP#CaliforniaLoad:S#Actual:T#2020M1, Import	0.00:00:00.936	Completed	Administrator	Sandbox
Clear Cube Data For Workflow	WP#CaliforniaLoad:S#Actual:T#2020M1, Import	0.00:00:00.163	Completed	Administrator	Sandbox
Clear Cube Data For Workflow	WP#MainCube_Default:S#Actual:T#2019M1, Import	0.00:00:00.237	Completed	Administrator	Sandbox

Figure 7.15

In this example, someone has manually cleared all imported data loaded by the CaliforniaLoad workflow.

Overlapping Data Loads

It's possible for two workflow base import profiles to load to the same intersections. If this happens, OneStream looks at your workflow settings to decide how to handle conflicts. Depending on your setting, it's possible for the last processed workflow to overwrite previous data loads, throwing off your totals if you're expecting an aggregated result instead. There are several cases to consider, but this one is really the one you must be most careful of.

We'll cover this at a pretty high level, so if you'd like more details on this behavior and the available settings, refer to Chapter 6: Work the Workflow.

Base Input Profile with Sibling Import Children (Same WF Channel)

Let's consider the following case, where you have a single base input profile CaliforniaLoad with two sibling import child profiles that have the same WF channel assigned – in this case ChA.

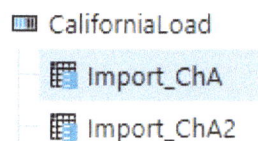

CaliforniaLoad
    Import_ChA
    Import_ChA2

Figure 7.16

By default, when you trigger an import step, OneStream will check to see if there are any sibling imports that have already been completed. If there are, then OneStream will clear the previously loaded data and then reload, aggregating data as necessary. This behavior is controlled by the Load Overlapped Siblings on your workflow, which is True by default.

However, if you set the Load Overlapped Siblings setting on your workflow to False, OneStream does not bother to check if there are any conflicts! If two workflows attempt to load to the same cells, the last processed workflow will overwrite the previous workflow's load (i.e., last one in wins).

For example, let's load $1 using Import_ChA, and then $1 using Import_ChA2 to the same intersection. If your Load Overlapped Siblings value is set to False, once both loads complete, the final value of the cell is $1. Instead of aggregating the two loads to get $2, as you might expect, the $1 from the Import_ChA2 overrides the initial load from Import_ChA. In fact, if you drill down on the cell details, you can even see that the audit history shows both loads from each workflow.

Figure 7.17

Base Input Profile with Sibling Import Children (Different WF Channels)

In the previous case, both import child profiles shared the same workflow channel. However, let's consider the case where a sibling import child profile is assigned AllChannelInput instead.

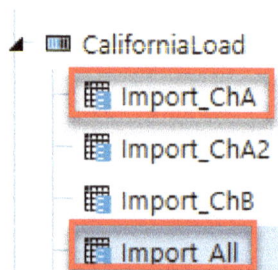

Figure 7.18

You might expect OneStream to flag that AllChannelInput means there could be potential overlaps. However, OneStream only checks for overlapping data intersections if the workflow channels are *exactly* the same, even if they are siblings. Since AllChannelInput and ChA are different, OneStream doesn't bother to check; instead, it will take the last processed workflow and overwrite previous loads.

Multiple Base Input Workflows

Let's now consider the final case, when there are multiple sibling base input workflows (CaliforniaLoad and AdminLoad) with import child profiles that load to the same intersections.

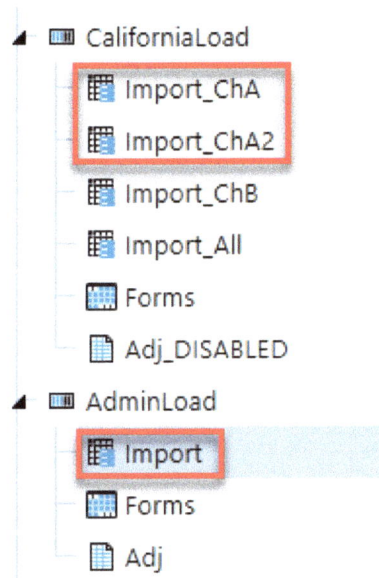

Figure 7.19

In this situation, the workflow channel assigned to import does not matter: it doesn't matter if `AdminLoad.Import` is assigned `AllChannelInput` or `ChA`. Because `AdminLoad.Import` is not a sibling of `Import_ChA` or `Import_ChA2`, the workflow engine does not check if there are any overlaps. In this case, the last processed workflow will overwrite any previous loads.

For example, say we load `$1` via `Import_ChA`, `$1` via `Import_ChA2`, and `$10` via `AdminLoad.Import` in that order. The audit history will display all three loads, but because `AdminLoad.Import` was loaded last, the cube will reflect `$10`.

Figure 7.20

Data in Stage Not Tying to Cube

Incorrect Transformation Rules

If you see your data in the Stage table, but can't find the data in the cube, this is a sign that you may need to investigate your transformation rules. There are really two main things to check here:

1. Check if the Stage member is mapped to the correct member in the cube. If your mappings are incorrect, the cube totals will reflect this.

2. Check that members are not mapped to (Bypass). Members that are mapped to (Bypass) are not loaded to the cube at all!

You can see what the Stage records have been mapped to after running through the transformation rules by going to the Validate step on your Import workflow.

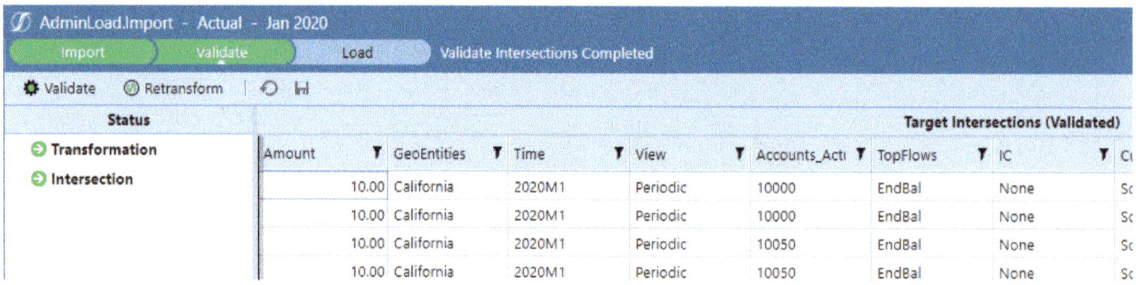

Figure 7.21

If you make any updates to your transformation rules, you will need to go back to the Validate step and click Retransform for the changes to apply.

Data Cleared From Stage

A common misconception is that the Clear button on the import step will clear data from the cube. However, it only clears data from the Stage table, and will leave previously imported cube data alone. This can be misleading since the empty Stage table makes it seem as if no data was loaded to the cube.

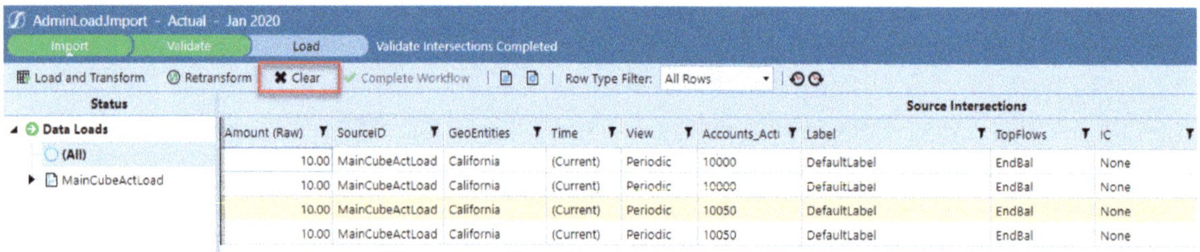

Figure 7.22

Derived Periodic/YTD Amount Incorrect

Incorrect NoDataView Settings

Let's begin by recalling that when you load data to a period, and the next period has no data, OneStream has logic that determines what that NoData means. To summarize, the No Data Zero View for Adjustments and No Data Zero View for NonAdjustments settings allow you to specify whether NoData means that the YTD value is 0, or the periodic value is 0 for a given account. This applies mainly to income statement accounts, where periodic and YTD amounts are treated differently.

Let's consider this example, where the NoDataZeroView settings for the scenario and account are YTD, and no data is loaded to revenue in February. Here, OneStream derives a 0 value for the YTD view, as shown below. However, to reconcile the YTD and periodic amounts, OneStream backs into a -$100 amount for the periodic view. If your user is expecting the YTD amount to carry forward, then you would need to change the NoDataZeroView settings to Periodic.

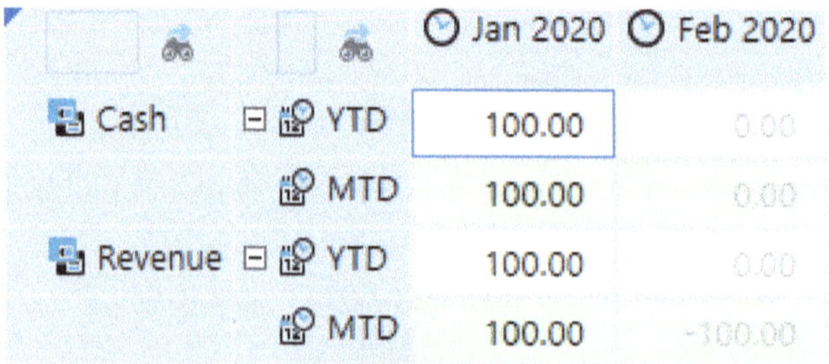

Figure 7.23

Something to consider is that because NoData is not necessarily the same as 0, you must be extremely careful when preparing your source files and configuring your data sources for loads. A common assumption is that if you leave income statement amounts as null, you will see 0 periodic activity in each month. However, as mentioned before, if the NoDataView setting is set to YTD, then OneStream will assume that null data means you want 0 YTD in each month, and derive a negative periodic amount in each month instead.

If this isn't the behavior you are expecting, you might have to load zeros, or change the NoDataZeroView settings. However, you'll have to be careful in deciding your approach as changing the NoDataZeroView settings will have many upstream and downstream effects.

Refer to Chapter 4's Scenario and Account NoDataView Settings for more details.

> **Note:** OneStream calculates and stores these derived values when the first real value is loaded to the database; it does not do it on the fly. What this means is that in the unlikely situation where you change NoDataZeroView settings on your scenario or account, you might need to reload your data or reconsolidate in order to get the derived values to update.

Incorrect View on Data Load

In general, the source files you load to Import workflows should match the same view (YTD / periodic) as your system settings. In other words, if your scenario is set as a YTD scenario, you would want to specify in your data source that the file contains YTD amounts.

For example, suppose we have the following file, and the data source is configured to load to periodic amounts.

Account	2020M1	2020M2	2020M3	2020M4	2020M5	2020M6
Revenue	10	20	30	40	50	60

General	
Name	Vw
⊞ Settings	
⊞ Position Settings	
⊟ Logical Expression And Override Settings	
Logical Operator	None
Logical Expression	(Unassigned)
Static Value	Periodic

Figure 7.24

With this configuration, the YTD amounts would be an accumulation of the loaded periodic activities, as shown below. This isn't necessarily wrong, but often the expectation is for the YTD amounts in reports to match the file exactly.

			Jan 2020	Feb 2020	Mar 2020	Apr 2020	May 2020	Jun 2020
Revenue	⊟	YTD	10.00	30.00	60.00	100.00	150.00	210.00
		Periodic	10.00	20.00	30.00	40.00	50.00	60.00

Figure 7.25

To get this behavior, you would have to change the data source to YTD, and then reload. This would result in the following values, where the YTD amounts match the file.

			Jan 2020	Feb 2020	Mar 2020	Apr 2020	May 2020	Jun 2020
Revenue	⊟	YTD	10.00	20.00	30.00	40.00	50.00	60.00
		Periodic	10.00	10.00	10.00	10.00	10.00	10.00

Figure 7.26

When loading though workflows, there are also three additional settings you must consider. This gives you additional control over how NoData is handled for specific accounts.

- Flow type no data zero view override (YTD/Periodic).

- Balance type no data zero view override (YTD/Periodic).

- Force balance accounts to YTD view (True/False).

> **Note:** Balance accounts, here, refers not to balance sheet accounts with an Account Type of Asset or Liability, but an Account Type of Balance specifically.

Stale Forms Data

When an import is triggered, the workflow engine will first clear previously imported data. This is critical for data integrity, as it clears old O#Import data from the system and ensures that all newly imported data is up to date.

However, there isn't an equivalent for inputted O#Forms data, which is either entered manually to forms, or loaded via Excel submission templates, and must therefore also be cleared manually. This becomes a problem when loaded or calculated data changes, but there is underlying O#Forms data that is now stale, which can throw off expected totals.

For example, suppose you loaded $100 to A#Cash and O#Import, and then subsequently entered a $50 adjustment to O#Forms to get to a final $150 at O#Top. If you then reload the O#Import data as $75, your new total at O#Top would be $125. To get back to the final amount of $150, you'll have to override the stale O#Forms adjustment to $75.

Debugging Calculated Data

This section covers calculated data that is calculated via business rules or Member Formulas. Before we continue, let's briefly cover some background on how OneStream handles calculated data. When any calculated data is generated, it is tagged with cell status of "Calculation" or "DurableCalculation".

Recall that when a calculation, translation, or consolidation is run, OneStream – as the first part of the Data Unit Calculation Sequence (DUCS) – will clear calculated data. However, it's important to note that OneStream will only clear regular, non-durable calculated data, and will *not* clear durable data as part of the DUCS.

Generally, data generated by Member Formulas as well as business rules attached to the cube, should be calculated as non-durable so that they clear and recalculate on the next consolidation. In contrast, data generated by custom calculate business rules triggered by events (e.g., on button presses) should be calculated as durable so that they don't clear unintentionally when consolidations are run.

With that said, many of the common situations and reasons for data not getting calculated correctly, or even worse – for clearing in inconsistent or unexpected ways – are due to a mix-up handling durable and non-durable data. While this list isn't exhaustive, it hopefully gives you a good starting point when troubleshooting.

Non-Durable Data Getting Cleared

One common scenario is data calculated in business rules clearing due to timing. If your users are seeing data in a report one day, and then not seeing it the next, the first thing you should check is whether that data is getting calculated as durable.

To calculate data as durable, you can either use the `api.Data.Calculate` or `api.Data.SetDataBuffer` methods, and pass `True` as the argument into `isDurableCalculatedData`. Here are the parameters for these methods:

1. DataApi.Calculate(formula As String, Optional accountFilter As String, Optional flowFilter As String, Optional originFilter As String, Optional icFilter As String, Optional ud1Filter As String, Optional ud2Filter As String, Optional ud3Filter As String, Optional ud4Filter As String, Optional ud5Filter As String, Optional ud6Filter As String, Optional ud7Filter As String, Optional ud8Filter As String, Optional onEvalDataBuffer As EvalDataBufferDelegate, Optional userState As Object, Optional isDurableCalculatedData As Boolean)

2. DataApi.SetDataBuffer(dataBuffer As DataBuffer, expressionDestinationInfo As ExpressionDestinationInfo, Optional accountFilter As String, Optional flowFilter As String, Optional originFilter As String, Optional icFilter As String, Optional ud1Filter As String, Optional ud2Filter As String, Optional ud3Filter As String, Optional ud4Filter As String, Optional ud5Filter As String, Optional ud6Filter As String, Optional ud7Filter As String, Optional ud8Filter As String, Optional isDurableCalculatedData As Boolean)

Unfortunately, both of these functions are overloaded (meaning that there are several versions of these methods), and it is possible to call versions where nothing is passed to `isDurableCalculatedData` (in which case it defaults to non-durable). It's also common to accidentally pass this as `False`, especially when copying and pasting lines from other business rules.

For example, both of these lines look fine and won't trip any runtime errors but will generate non-durable data! In both of these cases, after you run your calculation, you will see your calculated data in your reports initially, but if a user runs a consolidation in the future, that data will clear.

```
api.Data.Calculate("A#Revenue:O#Import:F#EndBal = A#Revenue:T#PovPrior1:F#EndBal:O#Top * 1.02")
api.Data.Calculate("A#Revenue:O#Import:F#EndBal = A#Revenue:T#PovPrior1:F#EndBal:O#Top * 1.02", False)
```

Figure 7.27

This is what you must check for when debugging. To correct this issue, simply pass in `True`! This is what the "durable" versions of the previous lines will look like. Of course, the same idea will apply to calls to `api.Data.SetDataBuffer`.

```
api.Data.Calculate("A#Revenue:O#Import:F#EndBal = A#Revenue:T#PovPrior1:F#EndBal:O#Top * 1.02",,,,,,,,,,,,,,,,True)
api.Data.Calculate("A#Revenue:O#Import:F#EndBal = A#Revenue:T#PovPrior1:F#EndBal:O#Top * 1.02", True)
```

Figure 7.28

> **Note:** Again, this mainly refers to data generated by custom calculate business rules, which generally are triggered on specific events like button presses and are not intended to clear on consolidation.

Stale Durable Calculated Data

The flip side to calculated data clearing unexpectedly is calculated data not clearing as expected. Because durable data never clears automatically as part of the DUCS, calculating data as durable and neglecting to clear it will result in stale data.

In order to avoid this issue, it's good practice to add logic at the beginning of rules to first clear the target intersections of previously calculated data. To clear calculated data, the most common way is to use the `api.Data.ClearCalculatedData` method. For more details, see the section: Clearing Calculated Data.

For example, suppose I have an allocation rule that spreads values to income statement accounts based on inputted drivers. The rule calculates data as durable, but doesn't have any logic to explicitly wipe allocated amounts.

The first time I run the calculation, I allocate $10 to AccountA, and $10 to AccountB. But let's say I want to allocate the full $20 to AccountA. I change my drivers, and then rerun the calculation. The second run will result in $20 in AccountA which is correct, but $10 in AccountB which was leftover from the last run.

If you're finding that durable data is not getting cleared on recalculation, there are three main things to check.

Clear Missing Completely

First, check if there is clear logic at the beginning of the rule. For example, to clear the stale data from the previous example, you can add this line:

```
api.Data.ClearCalculatedData(True, True, True, True, "A#IncomeStatement.Base")
```

Figure 7.29

Incorrect Filter Strings

If there is a clear statement at the beginning of the rule, then the next step would be to check if the filter strings look correct. It's fairly easy to place a filter string to the wrong parameter, make a typo in the parent, or even pass in the wrong parent.

For example, all of the following lines would clear no data, but also not throw any runtime errors!

```
api.Data.ClearCalculatedData(True, True, True, True, , "A#IncomeStatement.Base")   ' Extra comma. String is being passed to flowFilter parameter.
api.Data.ClearCalculatedData(True, True, True, True, "A#IncomeStatment.Base")       ' Typo
api.Data.ClearCalculatedData(True, True, True, True, "A#Expenses.Base")             ' Wrong parent
```

Figure 7.30

Calling Wrong Overloaded Version

Like `api.Data.Calculate`, the `api.Data.ClearCalculatedData` method is overloaded. It's possible to call the wrong version, and pass in nothing to the `clearDurableCalculatedData` parameter. This is one of the most commonly overlooked reasons for durable data not clearing.

For example, this code looks fine and will not throw any runtime errors, but will not clear durable data at all. Comparing it to the correct example from the section above, you can see that there are only three `True` arguments passed in.

```
api.Data.ClearCalculatedData(True, True, True, "A#IncomeStatement.Base")
```

Figure 7.31

Durable Data Getting Cleared

If durable data is clearing due to timing, then you should check whether there are business rules being triggered that explicitly clear data. It's common for these clears to not be sufficiently constrained, leading to them over-clearing intersections that were not supposed to be cleared.

Overclearing Data

Let's discuss what causes overclearing. To clear calculated data, the most common way is to use the `api.Data.ClearCalculatedData` method. However, if your Member Filters are not sufficiently constrained, you might clear more intersections than intended. For example, if I only want to clear income statement accounts, then I must pass in `A#IncomeStatement.Base` to the `accountFilter` parameter. If I pass in nothing, then the clear will apply to *all* accounts. These filter strings are what you'll have to check when troubleshooting.

How to Find Rogue Clears

Let's cover where to look for these rogue clears, so you aren't blindly combing through each business rule one-by-one. Typically, these clears are only added to custom calculate business rules that generate durable data. Explicit clears are redundant in regular calculations, where you typically calculate data as non-durable and allow the finance engine to clear that calculated data automatically as part of the DUCS.

The easiest approach is to figure out which button – when pressed – is causing data clearing issues. You can then trace which data management sequence is attached to that button, which will point you to the custom calculate business rule you'll need to debug. From there, you can search for calls to `api.Data.ClearCalculatedData` and evaluate whether the clears make sense.

> **Note:** It's also possible to clear data via the `api.Data.SetDataBuffer` method. If you don't see any `ClearCalculatedData` calls, then keep an eye out for this other clear pattern.

Business Rules Triggering in the Wrong Order

Almost inevitably, certain calculations will have dependencies on other calculations. Troubleshooting calculations with dependencies can be extremely hard to diagnose, especially if there is durable data involved, because your calculated values can change from run to run even when no data has changed. If you are suspicious that you have dependency issues, then there are two main reasons, which we'll cover now.

Incorrect Business Rule Order of Operation

If your calculations are contained in business rules attached to the cube, and spread across Member Formulas, then the Data Unit Calculation Sequence will apply. Refer to the Design and Reference Handbook for more details, but for convenience, here are the steps performed by the finance engine when a calculation is triggered:

1. Clear previously calculated data for the Data Unit.
2. Run the scenario's Member Formula.

3. Run reverse translations by calculating Flow members from other alternate currency input Flow members.

4. Execute Business Rules 1 and 2.

5. Run Formula Passes 1-4 for the cube's Account dimension members, then Flow members, and then User-Defined members.

6. Execute Business Rules 3 and 4.

7. Run Formula Passes 5-8.

8. Execute Business Rules 5 and 6.

9. Run Formula Passes 9-12.

10. Execute Business Rules 7 and 8.

11. Run Formula Passes 13-16.

The key idea here is that OneStream executes business rules and Member Formulas in a specific order that you can configure. This can get complex quickly, especially if there are many dependencies between rules.

For example, suppose we have a business rule called `CalcDepreciation` to calculate depreciation, which depends on my asset accounts having values. Here, the rule is attached to the cube as Business Rule 7.

Cube Properties	Cube Dimensions	Cube References	Data Access	Iı
□ General				
Name		MainCube		
Description		Main entry point for data		
Cube Type		Standard		
Time Dimension Profile		Standard		
⊞ Security				
⊞ Workflow				
⊞ Calculation				
□ Business Rules				
Business Rule 1		MainCube_NoInput		
Business Rule 2		(Not Used)		
Business Rule 3		ActCalcs		
Business Rule 4		(Not Used)		
Business Rule 5		(Not Used)		
Business Rule 6		(Not Used)		
Business Rule 7		CalcDepreciation		
Business Rule 8		(Not Used)		

Figure 7.32

Let's also say that asset accounts are calculated as Member Formulas, which are all configured as FormulaPass16.

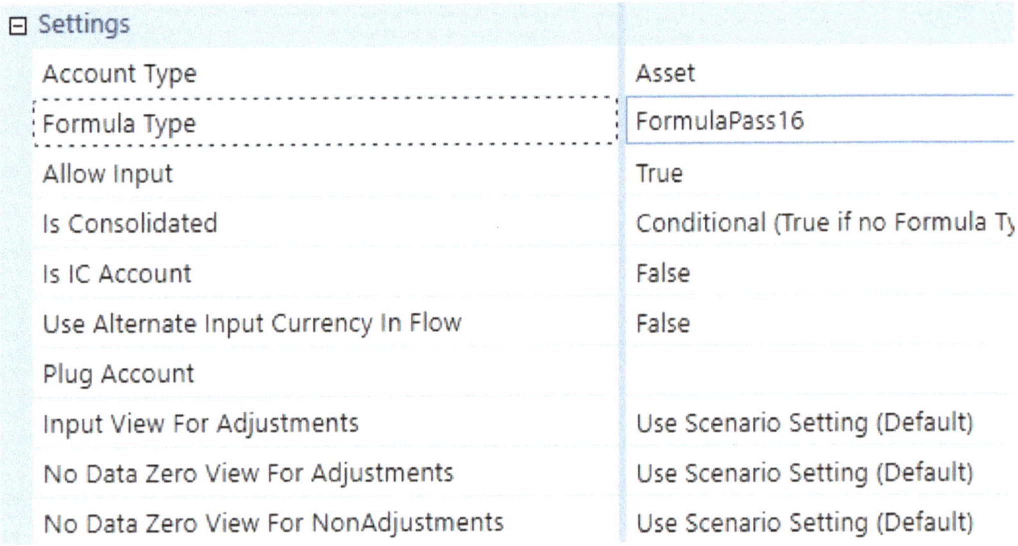

Figure 7.33

In this case, this configuration would mean that when we run a calculation on my cube, we would not see any depreciation amounts. Per the DUCS, `CalcDepreciation` would run first as Business Rule 7, and the Asset account as FormulaPass16 would run next. The fix, in this case, would be to set the Asset account as FormulaPass9 (or any formula pass that runs before Business Rules 7 and 8).

Incorrect DM Sequence Setup

If your calculations are custom calculations attached to data management steps, then you should check the data management sequence in question and confirm that 1. all of the calculations you expect are included in the sequence and 2. the steps are in the right order.

For example, say we have a set of plan calculations that are dependent on seeded data. Here, we can confirm that 1. the seed step with the seed business rule attached is assigned to my data management sequence, and 2. the seed step executes before my other plan calculations. This is a simplified example, but a more realistic example is a developer creating a new plan business rule, but neglecting to add the new rule to a data management sequence.

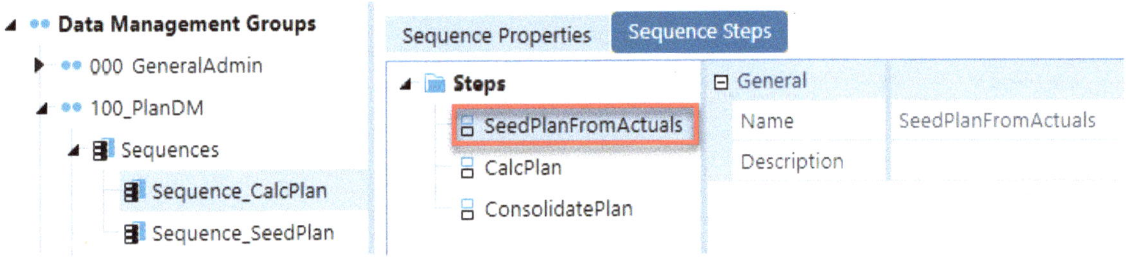

Figure 7.34

Let's now consider a more complex example that illustrates how dependency issues can cause apparently bizarre behavior. Suppose we have two custom calculate business rules to calculate planned assets and depreciation: `CalcAssets` and `CalcDepreciation`. Ideally, assets should be calculated first, based on some drivers, and then depreciation should be calculated as a percentage of those assets (let's say 20% for the sake of this example). However, let's say we accidentally configure depreciation to calculate before assets and walk through how our values would change from run to run:

1. **Run 1**

   `CalcDepreciation` executes. Depreciation amounts would be $0, since assets haven't been calculated yet.

   `CalcAssets` executes. Assets show as $100.

   Immediately, there is a variance, as the expected depreciation amount is $20.

2. **Run 2**

   `CalcDepreciation` executes. Depreciation is calculated as $20 off the $100 assets.

   `CalcAssets` executes. However, the drivers have changed, and assets now recalculate as $200.

   There is again a variance, since you would expect the depreciation to be $40.

3. **Run 3**

   `CalcDepreciation` executes. Depreciation is calculated as $40.

   `CalcAssets` executes. Drivers remain the same, and so assets remain as $200.

This is confusing since the values for assets and depreciation are changing from run to run, and it takes a minimum of two runs for the calculated amounts to look correct, even when no underlying data has changed. This is why debugging this sort of behavior can be a complete nightmare, but this example hopefully highlights what to look for if you notice strange cyclical behavior.

Inconsistent Calcs Over Scenarios

If your calculation is running correctly on one scenario but not another, here are three possible reasons.

Member Formulas Not Set On Scenario Type

A member can have different Member Formulas for each Scenario Type. A common mistake is to create a Member Formula on one Scenario Type, and neglect to copy the logic to other Scenario Types. For example, here, the member has a Member Formula for `Actual` scenarios, but nothing for `Plan` scenarios.

Figure 7.35

On the flip side, it's also common to place a Member Formula on `Default`, which would mean the calculation would run on every scenario, when really the formula should have been placed on a single Scenario Type.

Incorrect Order for Formula Passes

Because formula passes for Member Formulas are set directly on the members themselves, and cannot be assigned by Scenario Type, there is no way to have Member Formulas trigger in different orders depending on the scenario.

For example, if you wanted a driver Member Formula to run on Formula Pass 1 for Actual scenarios, but on Formula Pass 4 for Plan scenarios, you would need to find a different solution. One option would be to move the driver calculation to business rules attached to the cube instead, and add conditions to check for Scenario Type.

Business Rule Conditions

This is a bit harder to find, but another thing to check is control flow statements in business rules directly. Sometimes, conditions in your business rules are designed in a way where they might not trigger for your current Data Unit. An effective way to check is to add log messages in your code to confirm that your desired conditional branches are being reached.

For example, this business rule is constrained to only run on scenarios with the Actual Scenario Type.

```
Public Function Main(ByVal si As SessionInfo, ByVal globals As BRGlobals, ByVal api
    Try
        ' Only run these calcs for Actual type scenarios.
        If Not api.Pov.ScenarioType = ScenarioType.Actual Then Return Nothing
```

Figure 7.36

Cube Business Rules Not Triggering

If you are triggering a calculation or consolidation and finding that your business rule does not seem to be running, consider running a forced calculation instead. Calculations will only run on Data Units if the status of their base data has changed. If base data has not changed, even if you modified your business rule, OneStream will think that it does not need to recalculate that Data Unit. This specific issue usually only comes up when a new business rule is being written; once rules are stable, you can be confident that running regular calculations is sufficient.

Debugging Consolidated Data

This section covers consolidated data at parent entities. Data generated by the finance engine during the consolidation process will have cell status of "Consolidation".

If data looks correct at your base entities, but isn't consolidating up to parent entities, then here is a list of things to check. We also cover what happens if your base member amounts are not rolling up to parents correctly in reports. Many of these settings are referenced in the Dimension Member Management section of Chapter 4.

Consolidation Not Current

The first thing you should do if you see that your consolidated data at your parent entity does not match the data at your base entities is to check your cube's calculation status. This can be done by building a Cube View with entities in the rows, and the view member set to V#CS. See the Design And Reference Handbook section on Calculation Status for more details.

	Jan 2011	Feb 2011	Mar 2011
All Orgs	CN	CN	CN
Total GolfStream	CN	CN	CN
Clubs	CN	CN	CN
NA Clubs	CN	CN	CN
Canada Clubs	OK,MC	OK,MC	OK,MC
Montreal	OK,MC	OK,MC	OK,MC
Quebec City	OK,MC	OK,MC	OK,MC
US Clubs	CN	CN	CN
Augusta	OK,MC	OK,MC	OK,MC
Carlsbad	OK,MC	OK,MC	OK,MC
Houston	CN	CN	CN
Houston Heights	OK	OK	OK
South Houston	OK,MC	OK,MC	OK,MC
Europe Clubs	CN	CN	CN
Frankfurt	OK,MC	OK,MC	OK,MC
Golf Balls	OK,MC	OK,MC	OK,MC

Figure 7.37

If you see CN, that means descendant entity data has changed, and you'll need to reconsolidate. This is basically the OneStream equivalent of "Have you tried turning it off and on again?" It might seem overly simple, but we can't count the number of times a simple reconsolidation is all that's necessary to get numbers rolled up correctly.

Consolidating Wrong Hierarchy

Consider the following two dimensions. CorpEntities is assigned to the MainCube, while GeoEntities is assigned to the SubCube.

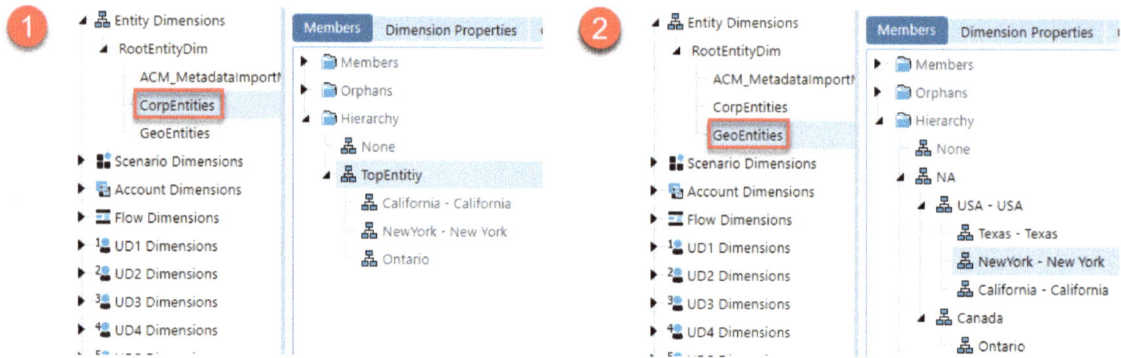

Figure 7.38

Here, if you were to consolidate the E#NA on the MainCube, then all of the base children under TopEntity will get recalculated. Reporting on California on both MainCube and SubCube would look correct. However, because you haven't explicitly consolidated E#NA on the SubCube, if you tried to report on NA, nothing would be there.

This is a subtle mistake because it's easy to assume that running a consolidation on the top entity of your main cube would mean that all of the base entities would get recalculated, and the top entity of your sub cube would be correct. However, the top entity of your main and sub cubes might not match, and recall that OneStream will only consolidate values up to the parent entity specified in the Data Unit.

To correct this, you would need to add a consolidation for NA to your data management sequence, after the consolidation for TopEntity, in order for all entities to have updated values.

> **Note:** In this case, you should use a regular consolidation rather than a force consolidation for the second consolidation step. Otherwise, you would be unnecessarily double calculating all of your base entities.

Entity Consolidation Settings

If you know that a consolidation was run recently, then the next thing you should check is the Is Consolidated setting on your entities. If your base and child entities are set to Is Consolidated as False, then you won't see their amounts roll up to parent entities, so confirm that they are set to True.

Figure 7.39

Next, check that your base and child entities have the correct Percent Consolidation percentage. It's common to accidentally set this as 0 for a use-case and forget, or to copy an entity's settings and neglect to update this value. Also, something to be careful of is that because an entity can belong to multiple hierarchies, it can actually have multiple Percent Consolidation values for each respective hierarchy.

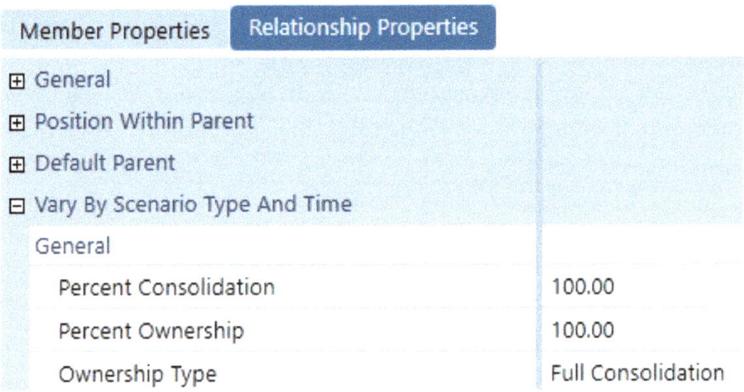

Figure 7.40

Note: This setting varies by Scenario Type and time, so if your consolidation is working for certain Scenario Types, but not for others, this is something to consider.

Finally, if you are finding that a base entity's data is consolidating up, but data for specific members is missing, then check the Is Consolidated setting on the members themselves.

A common "gotcha" here is that the default value for non-Data Unit dimension members is Conditional (True if no Formula Type (default)). This means if you add a Member Formula onto a member to calculate its own values, it won't consolidate up by default.

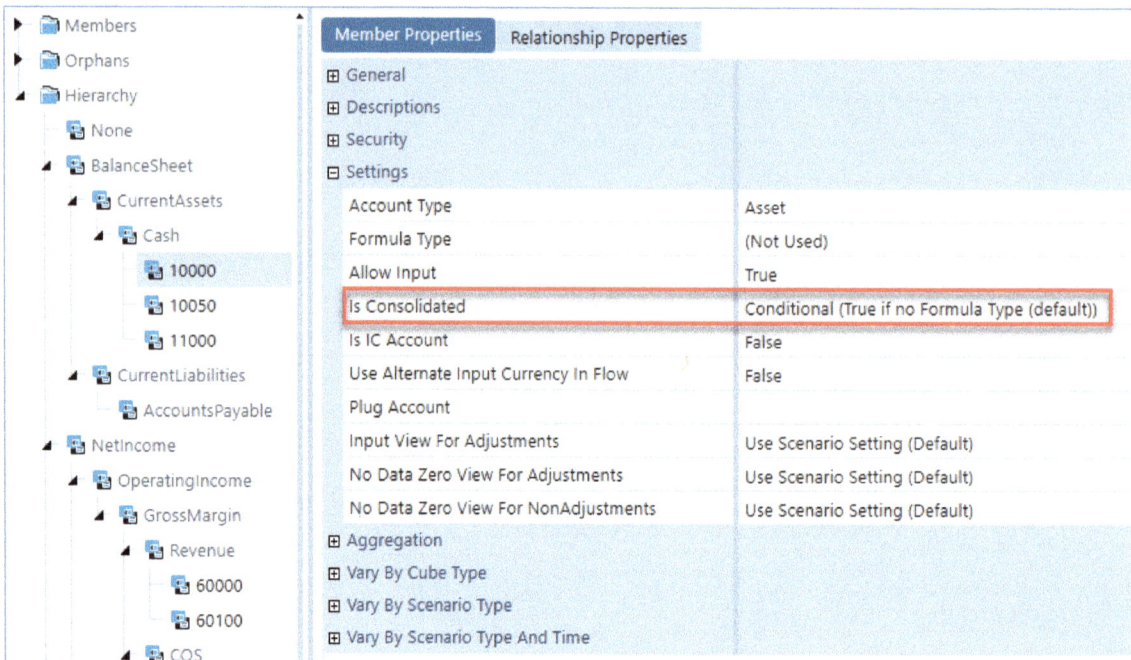

Figure 7.41

Aggregation Weights

Though this isn't technically a consolidation issue, it's similar enough, so we figured we would touch on it. If you are seeing that base members are not aggregating up to parent members, then check the base members' Aggregation Weight setting. This setting is analogous to the Entity Percent Consolidation setting, but is present on Account, Flow, and UD members. If these settings are not correct, you might see that your revenue total does not include all of the base revenue account amounts.

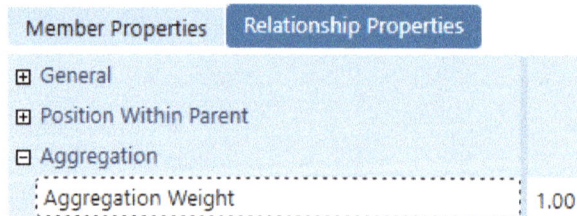

Figure 7.42

Translation Not Configured

If translation is not configured correctly, then base entities will have values at C#Local, but not at their parent entity currencies at C#Translated. Without these translated values, OneStream will have nothing to consolidate up to parent entities.

One reason translation might not be occurring is if your system is missing certain rates. If your Cube Translation Algorithm Type is set to Standard Using Business Rules for FX Rates or Custom, then you will need to open the corresponding business rule attached to the cube and see whether the correct rates are being returned or if the rule is not returning any rates at all.

For more details on translation configuration, see Chapter 5: Translation.

Conclusion

In this chapter, we covered a host of common data issues, explaining the several reasons underlying them as well as the approaches to solving them. We also covered some general troubleshooting techniques and pointed out common "gotchas" and strange idiosyncrasies that are confusing to new and experienced admins alike.

Troubleshooting data issues is one of the most frustrating and daunting tasks you will have to deal with regularly as an admin (trust us, we know). Hopefully, this chapter is structured intuitively so you don't have to read it front-to-back, and can instead use it as an as-needed reference when you're at your wit's end. For you nerds out there, "May It Be a Light to You in Dark Places, When All Other Lights Go Out."

8

Import and Validation Errors

Importing data into OneStream is a routine part of any admin's responsibilities. While this process is generally simple, the errors you can get when a data load fails can be somewhat cryptic. The purpose of this chapter is to cover the most common import and validation errors, explaining what might be causing them and hopefully giving you a better chance at resolving them.

Import Workflow Background

Executing Data Imports

Before listing errors, let's quickly cover the basics of Import workflows in OneStream. All inputted data in OneStream (including import data, form inputs, and journal entries) are handled by the workflow engine. In this chapter, we only deal with base Import workflows, which will generally have three steps: Import, Validate, and Load.

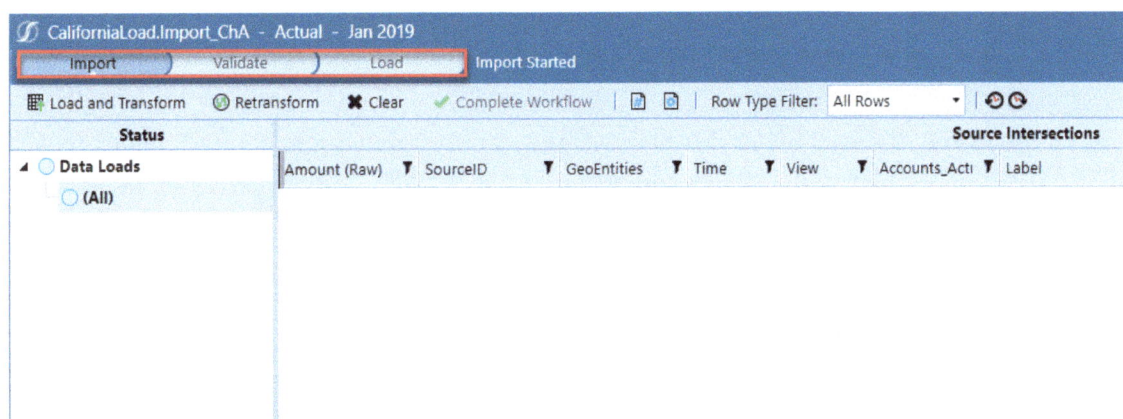

Figure 8.1

Each of these steps will give you access to various events. It's not obvious what is happening in the background, so let's cover what happens behind the scenes when each of these events is triggered. It's important to understand them, as you can generally infer where to look first, based on where you are getting your errors.

- **Load and Transform**: OneStream will import data into the source Stage table, using the data source configured on the current workflow step. Once complete, you can view the source cells that were successfully imported to Stage. *Typically, issues with your data source will manifest here.*

  Although the transformed cells aren't displayed here, OneStream will also transform the source cells into your cube dimensionality using the transformation rules configured on the same workflow step. The transformed data is stored on the target Stage table. Something to note is that because OneStream performs the transformation here, issues with your transformation rules can actually cause the entire import to fail.

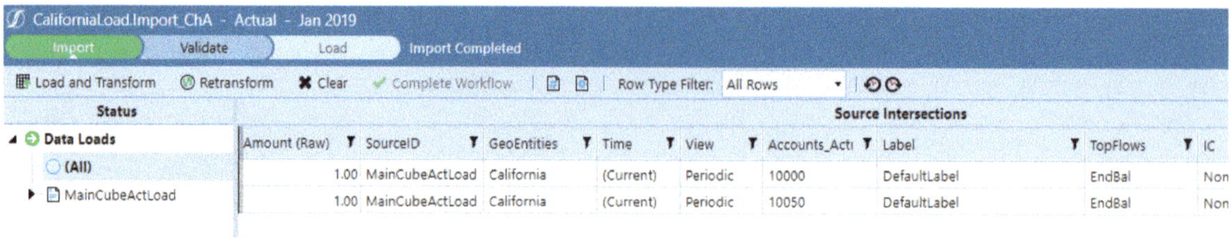

Figure 8.2

- **Validate**: OneStream will confirm that all source cells have a transformation rule, and also confirm that all transformed intersections are valid for the current cube. *If there are issues with your transformation rules, or with the entity or workflow channel assignment of your current workflow, they will appear here.*

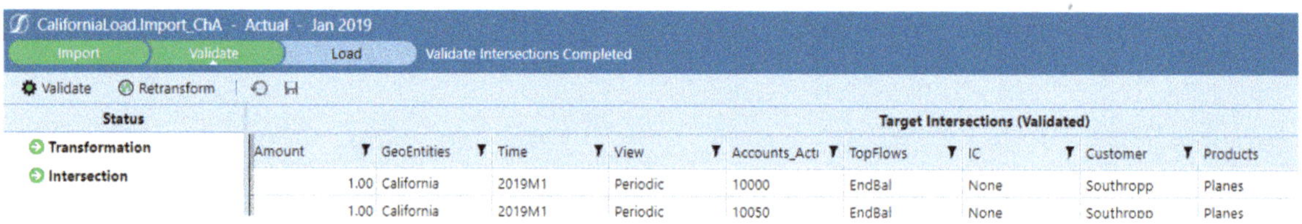

Figure 8.3

- **Retransform** (on the Validate step): OneStream will clear the previously generated target intersections and rerun the source cells through the transformation rules (same as it would in the Load and Transform steps) and then repeat the same validation steps from the Validate button.

- In general, it's safer to run Retransform over Validate, even if it might take slightly longer to process. If you only run Validate, and your transformation rules were recently changed, the target intersections will not reflect the changes.

- **Load Cube**: OneStream will load the transformed data to the cube. Typically, if you've made it this far, you're home free.

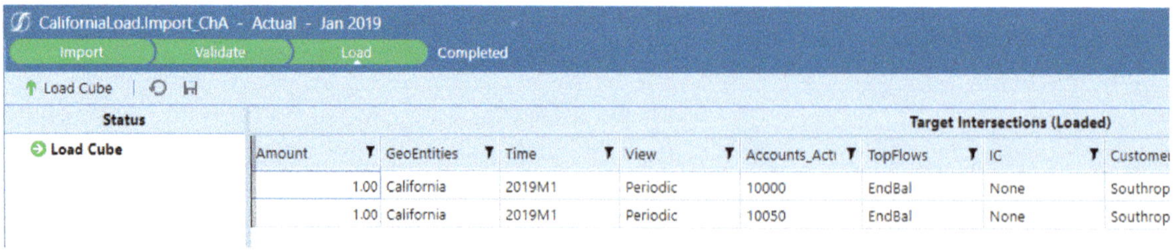

Figure 8.4

Configuring Imports

If there are issues with an import, you should first check the Workflow Profile properties of the offending workflow. Here, you can see what the attached Data Source and Transformation Profile are, making sure to check the properties for the correct Scenario Type. If you don't look at the correct Scenario Type, you might not realize that your import is using the default data source and transformation profile and causing invalid intersection errors.

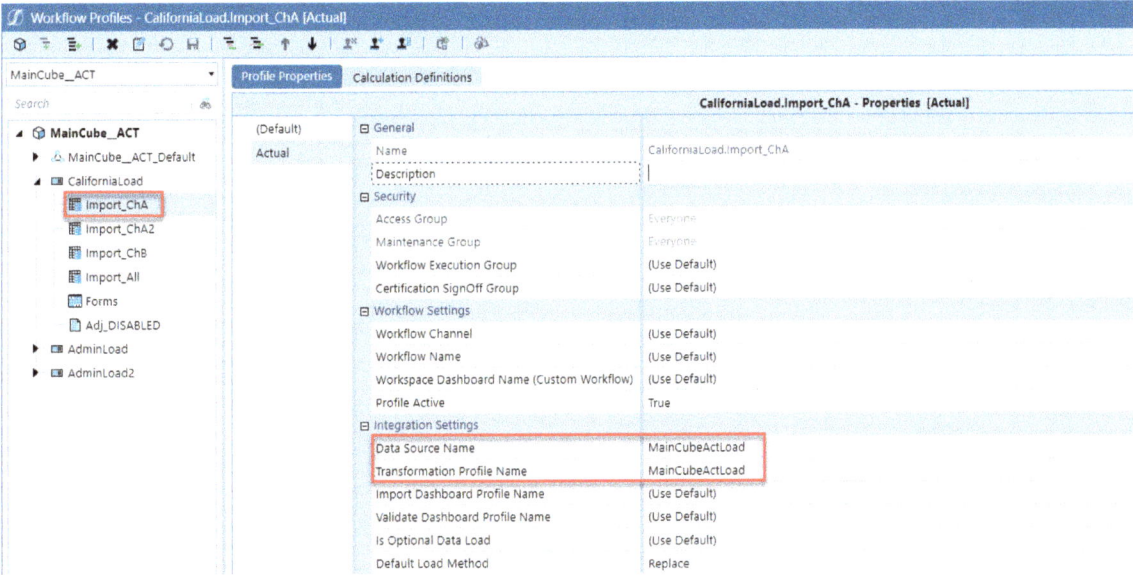

Figure 8.5

The vast majority of errors when importing data will stem from an issue with the workflow settings, the data source settings, or the transformation rule settings. In the following sections, we'll cover configuration mistakes that lead to common errors. For more details on workflow configuration in general, refer to Chapter 6: Work the Workflow.

Troubleshooting Tools

Task Activity Log

As always, the Task Activity log is a great tool for reviewing your error message and investigating what process is failing. You can access it by clicking the Task Activity Button on the top menu bar.

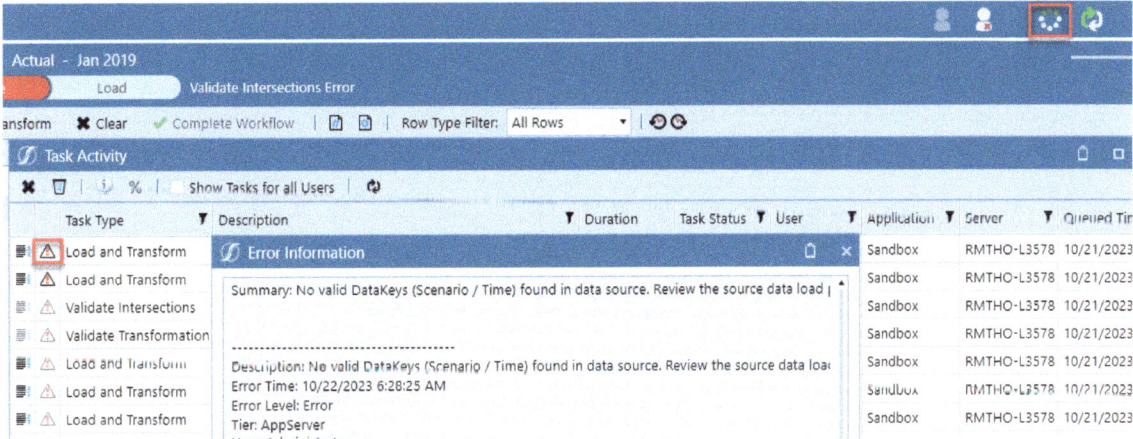

Figure 8.6

Processing Log

For detailed, row-by-row information on the processed source cells, you can access the processing log by clicking the View Last Log File Processed For Current Workflow Profile button. This functionality is typically included by default for most customers, but if you cannot access it, you will need to reach out to your cloud support team to configure the log server.

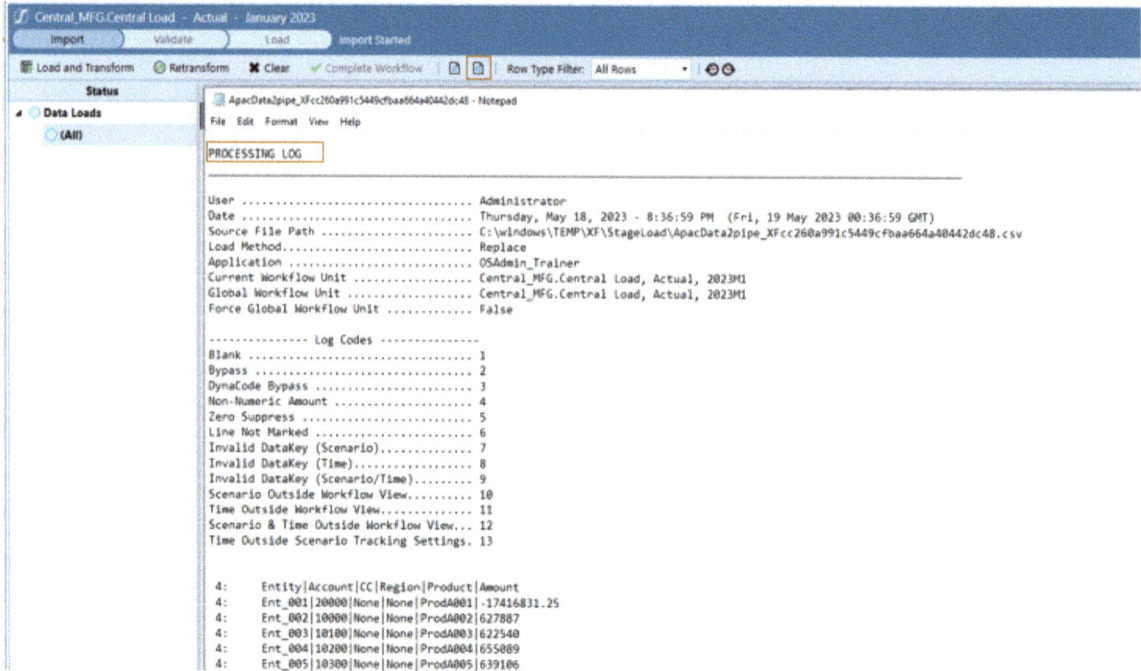

Figure 8.7

Import Errors

This section covers the common errors you can encounter on the import step.

No Assigned Data Source or Transformation Rule

These errors are self-explanatory: the current Workflow Profile doesn't have an assigned data source transformation rule.

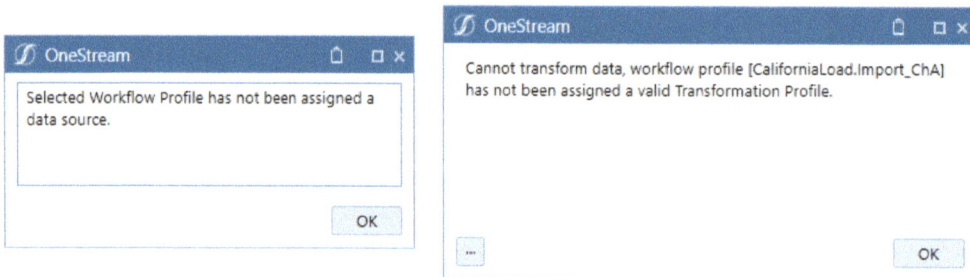

Figure 8.8

Usually, this error occurs when data sources are assigned to specific Scenario Types, but nothing is assigned to the `Default` Scenario Type. For example, suppose we create a new scenario with type Actual, and no data source is assigned to the Actual Scenario Type on the workflow. If there's nothing assigned to the `Default` Scenario Type, then OneStream throws these errors.

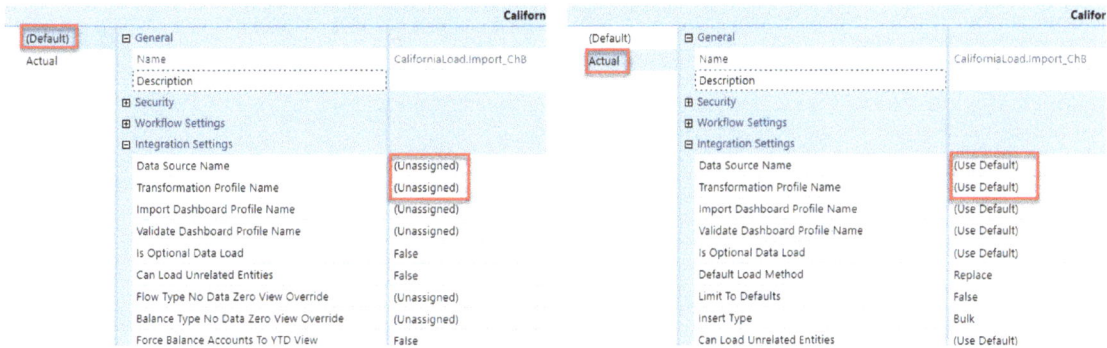

Figure 8.9

> **Note:** It's actually recommended to leave the Data Source and Transformation Profile unassigned for the `Default` Scenario Type. This gives you more flexibility in the future and prevents accidentally using the `Default` Scenario Type's settings when a new scenario is created. It's generally better to have OneStream throw an error rather than generate potentially faulty data.

Data Source is Missing Required Fields

This error is also fairly self-explanatory (and descriptive).

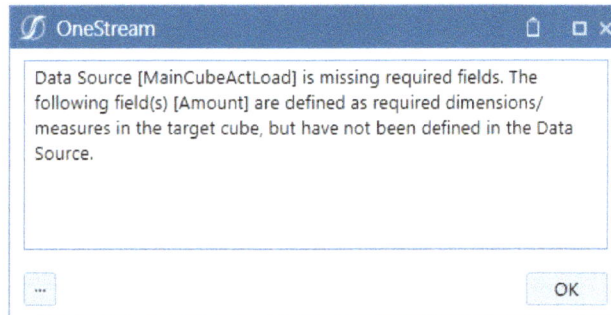

Figure 8.10

A common reason for this error to pop up is trying to reuse a data source for a new Scenario Type, where the dimensionality on the cube does not match. For example, Actual Type scenarios might have more or fewer dimensions assigned on the cube than Plan Type scenarios.

Regardless, resolving the error is simple. If you've attached the wrong data source, then you only need to assign the correct data source for your Scenario Type. If the data source is truly just incomplete, then go to the data source attached to the workflow and assign the missing dimensions in the Data Source tab.

No Valid DataKeys (Scenario/Time) Found in Data Source

The classic import error – getting this error is truly a rite of passage for every admin! We can safely say that there are few errors that generate as much hair-pulling as this single error. Luckily for you, we've suffered through the troubleshooting, so you don't have to!

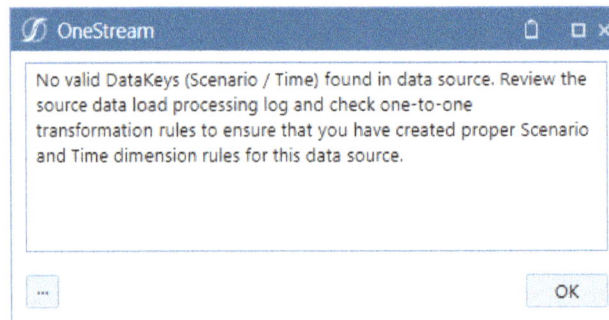

Chapter 8

Figure 8.11

To fully understand this error, we have to explain what OneStream means by valid DataKeys. In Chapter 6: Work the Workflow, we covered how the workflow engine is responsible for managing all incoming data entering the system. All incoming records are tagged with a **workflow cluster primary key**, which is comprised of three bits of information: the selected Workflow Profile, Scenario, and Time from your current Workflow POV.

The "key" here is that scenario and time are especially important dimensions because they are part of the **workflow cluster key**, and are therefore referred to as "DataKeys". The workflow engine will reject any incoming source data that is missing scenario and time information, with the error text notifying you that your transformed target intersections do not have a specified Scenario and Time member.

With that in mind, there are several possible reasons for scenario and time information to be missing, which we will cover now.

Case 1: No Source Records Found

If you are using a file data source, then an empty file would cause this error. The reason for this is that OneStream reads in zero rows, and then subsequently reports that there are zero rows tagged with the current workflow scenario and time. The error message, in this case, is not technically wrong but is a bit misleading. Additionally, configuring the data source incorrectly such that OneStream skips all source records would lead to the same behavior.

Similarly, if you are using a connector business rule in your data source, then having no data in your source system will cause the same error. Alternatively, if your connector runs successfully but returns no rows, then you will also get this error. In this case, the first thing you should check is the filter conditions in your query to confirm you aren't inadvertently filtering out all of your source records.

To see if this is the reason for your error, you can check the task log or processing log and see how many data rows were found in your source. If you see 0 rows, then that usually indicates that you'll need to check your source data system or your connector business rule.

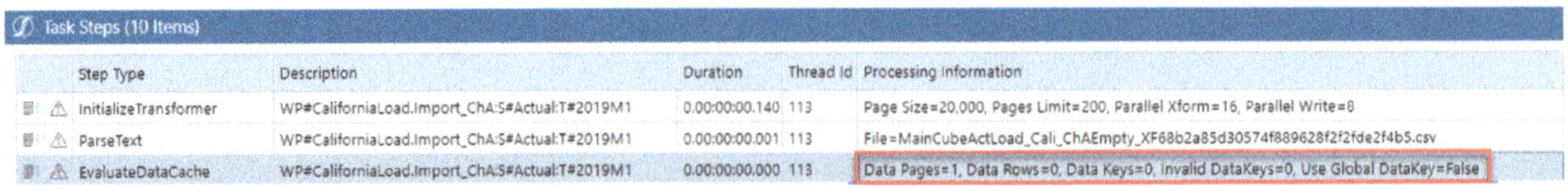

Figure 8.12

Case 2: Improper Data Source Scenario/Time Setup

If you are sure that your data source is returning records, the next step would be to check the configuration on the data source itself – specifically the Scenario and Time dimensions.

The most common setup is to set the Scenario Dimension Data Type as Current DataKey Scenario and the Time Dimension Data Type as Current DataKey Time. This ensures that – on import – all

170

records get tagged with the current Workflow's POV. However, when the data source is instead configured to pull other values for scenario and time, there is now a potential for the scenario and time on the source cells not to match the Workflow POV.

For example, suppose we are running an import for the Actual scenario on 2021M1. Here, because the Scenario's value for the data source is hardcoded to NotARealScenario, all source cells will be tagged with that value on import. However, since this does not match the expected value of "Actual" you will get an invalid DataKey error. The solution in this case would be to change the Static Value field to Actual.

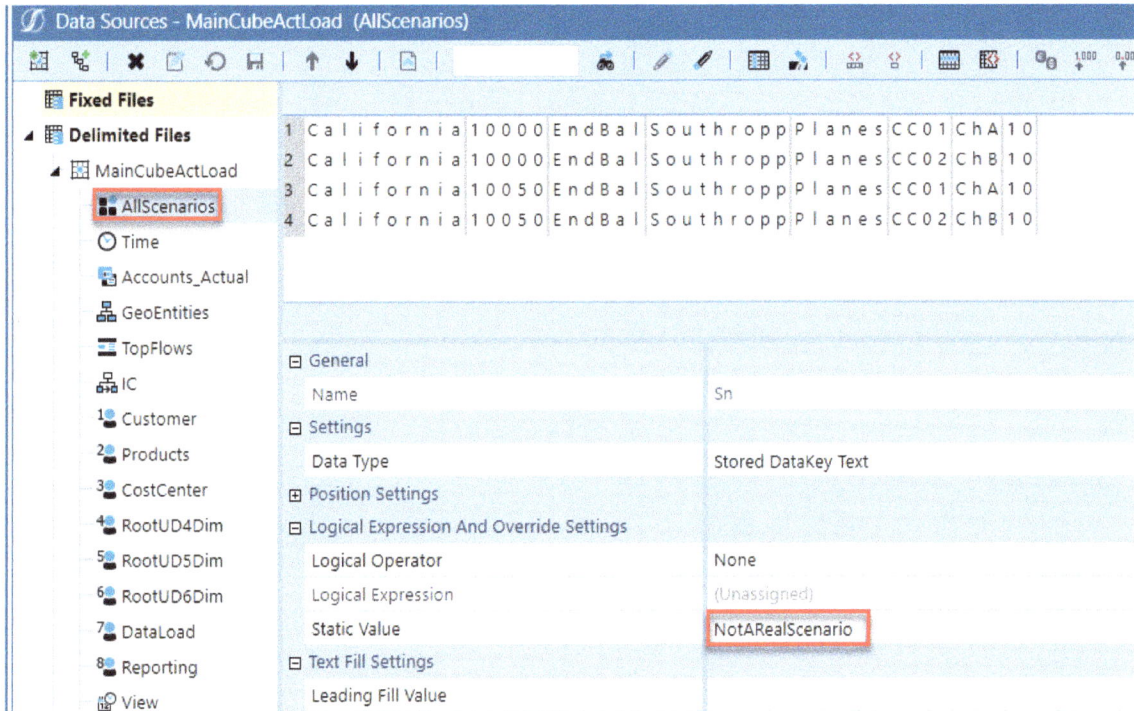

Figure 8.13

Note: Data sources are typically configured to use Current DataKey Scenario and Current DataKey Time for Actual scenarios where the workflow tracking frequency and input frequency are the same. For Plan scenarios where this might not be the case, you might have to use a different approach to guarantee the records to be imported match the Workflow POV.

Case 3: Missing Scenario or Time Transformation Rules

Recall that on the import step, clicking Load and Transform will both 1. import the source data into the source Stage table, and 2. transform the source data into the cube dimensionality using the assigned transformation rules.

Let's quickly discuss how OneStream determines the target scenario and time for transformed target cells. If the Scenario and Time dimensions on the data source are set to the Current DataKey Scenario/Time, OneStream knows to write the target cells to the current Workflow POV, and – in fact – doesn't look at the Scenario and Time transformation rules.

However, if you configure the Scenario and Time dimensions to take on custom values, OneStream will now attempt to run the scenario and time values through the assigned transformation rules.

For example, suppose we are loading data to the Actual scenario and have configured our data source to assign Actual as the scenario value for all source cells.

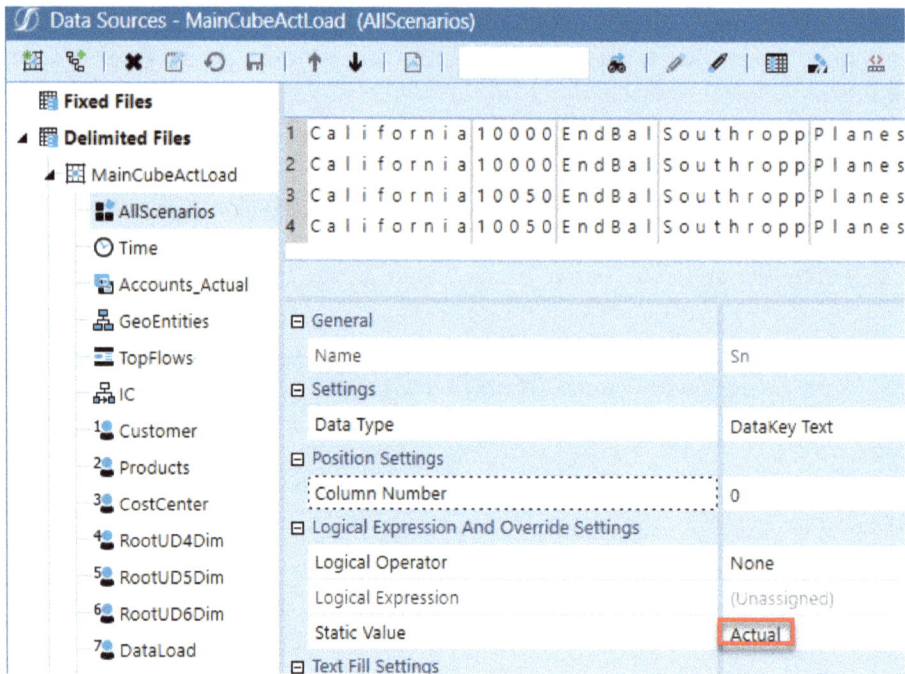

Figure 8.14

Because we have hardcoded the scenario value, OneStream will attempt to map Actual to a target value via the assigned transformation rules. It seems redundant, but for this import to succeed, there must be a pass-through mapping from Actual to Actual, as shown below. Without it, the target cells end up with null scenario values, leading to the infamous invalid DataKey error. Of course, the same logic would apply to the Time dimension.

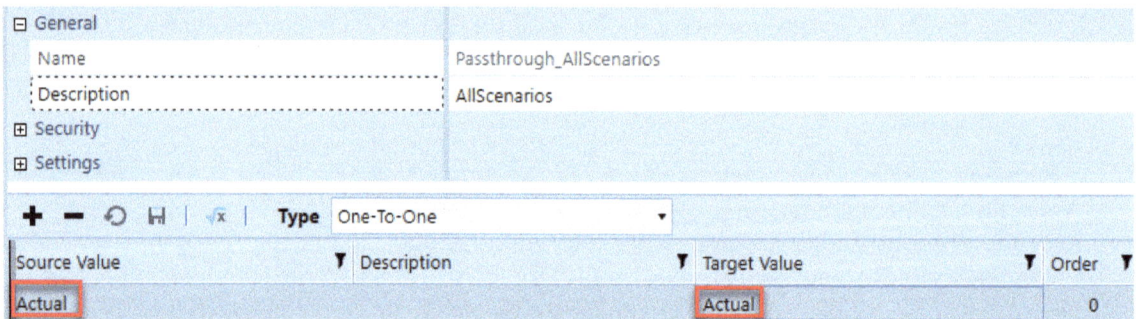

Figure 8.15

Setting the scenario and time values to the current DataKey values avoids this potential issue, which is why it is the recommended approach. If, instead, you've decided to live dangerously, it's common to have "pass through" transformation rules that simply map every Scenario and Time member one-to-one to itself, as shown below. Of course, this is extremely manual and error-prone: missing a few entries is usually the source of invalid DataKey errors.

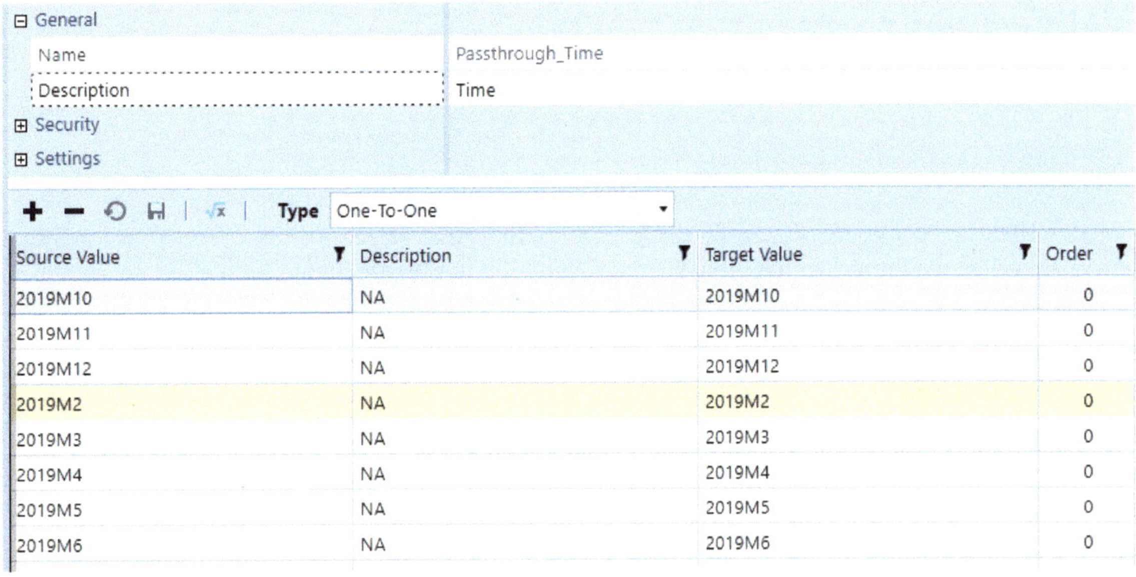

Figure 8.16

Case 4: Source File Missing Columns

Every target intersection must have a scenario, time, and amount value. If any of these values are missing, OneStream rejects the record. Going further, if the data source is configured incorrectly, such that *all* records have null values, then you end up with a similar situation to Case 1: No Source Records Found, where there are no records at all and OneStream informs you that none of your records have valid DataKeys.

For example, consider the following data source, which would result in the invalid DataKey error. The Amount field is configured to pull the value from column 20 of the source file. However, the source file only has 8 columns, which means – on import – all amount values would be null. This sort of situation can occur when source files change formats between loads, breaking Import workflows that worked in the past.

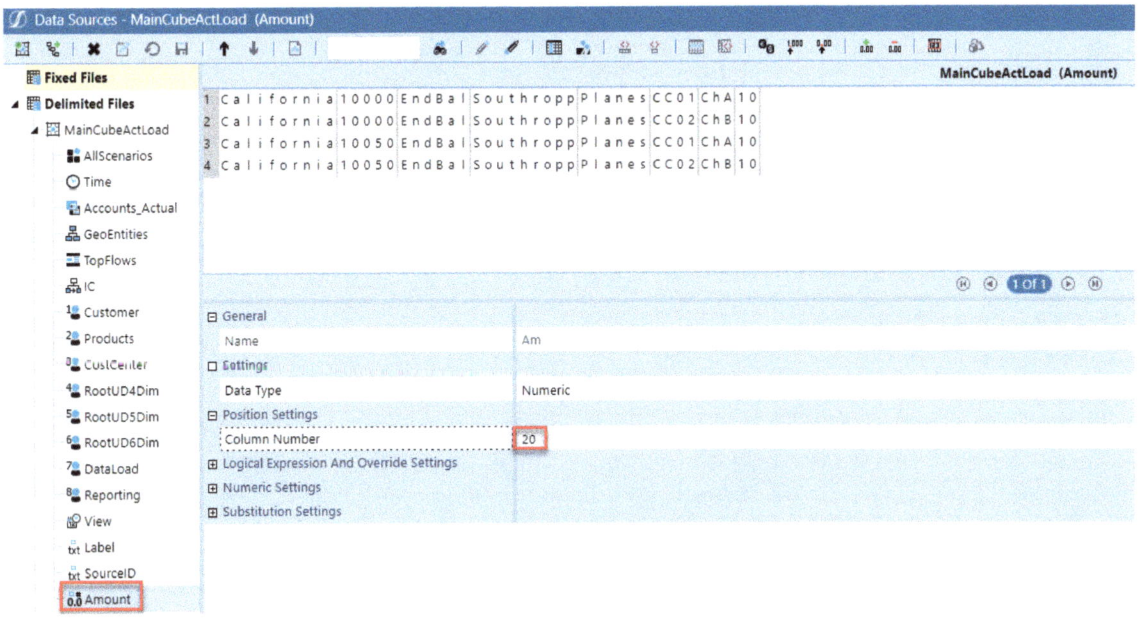

Figure 8.17

Validation Errors

This section covers the common errors you can encounter on the Validate step.

Transformation Errors

When you hit the Validate button, OneStream will attempt to map each field for each source record into a target dimension member using the transformation rules selected on the Workflow Profile. If there are fields with missing mappings, OneStream will list the offending records like so.

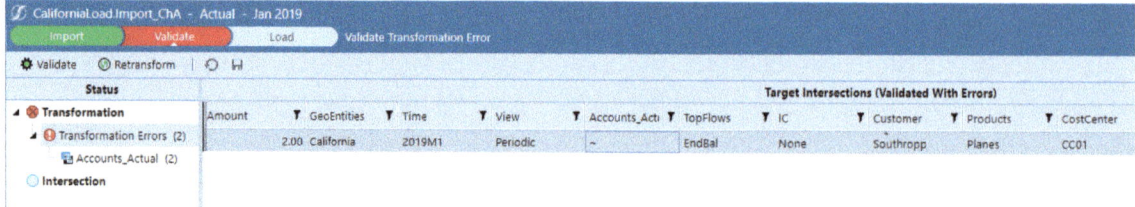

Figure 8.18

Fortunately, OneStream provides more detail on exactly which source values don't have mappings. For example, in Figure 8.19, the values 10000 and 10050 have no mappings in the Passthrough_Accounts transformation rule group.

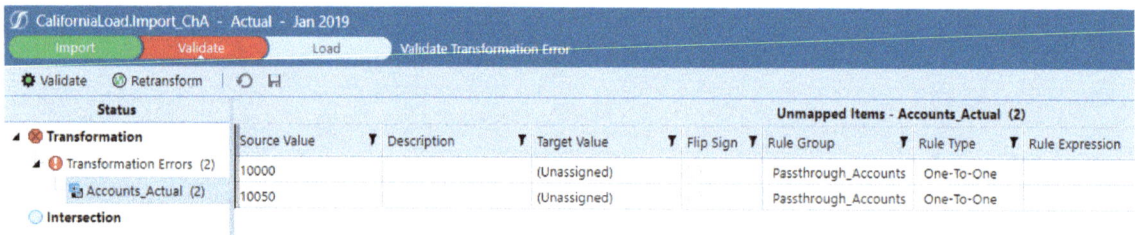

Figure 8.19

The solution here would be to map these values into their corresponding accounts, using any of the available transformation rule types (e.g., One-To-One).

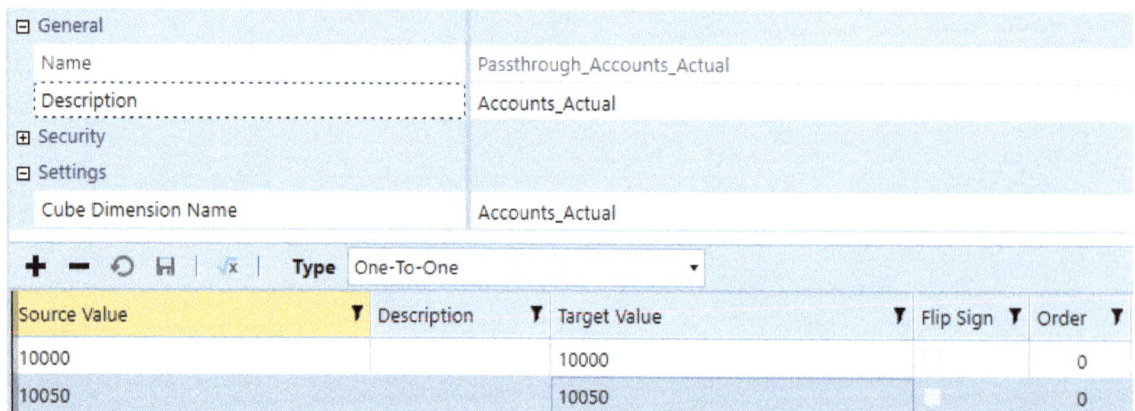

Figure 8.20

It's also common to implement "pass through" rules as a safeguard to capture unmapped records, to avoid missed one-to-one mappings from stalling imports entirely. To do this, you can create a "star-to-star" mask rule, which simply takes the source value and assigns it as the target value.

Rule Name	Description	Rule Expression	Target Value	Flip Sign	Logical Operator	Order
passthrough	passthrough	*	*	☐	None	0

Figure 8.21

Another option would be to create a general bypass mask rule, which takes any unmapped values and tells the system to simply ignore them. From a technical perspective, OneStream will not load any target intersection with (Bypass) to the cube. However, this is risky; by bypassing missing mappings, failing to review the bypassed target intersections might mean your cube ends up with missing data without you realizing. If you want to avoid this possibility, you could choose not to implement a bypass rule and instead reconcile any unmapped source records.

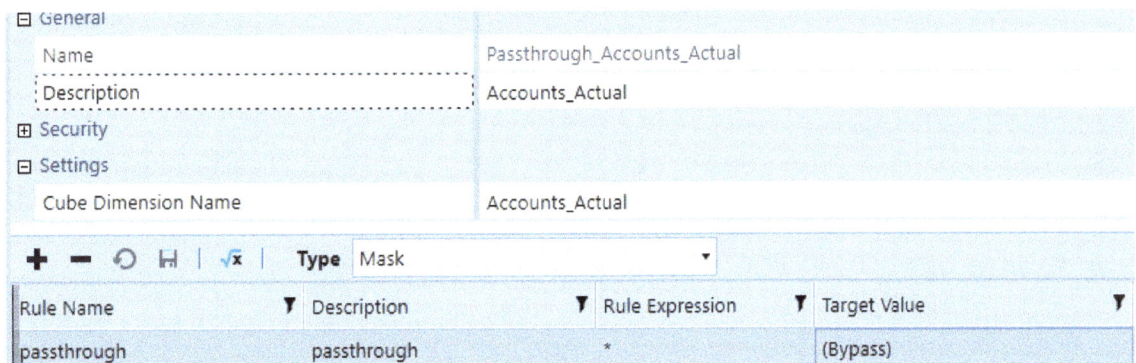

Rule Name	Description	Rule Expression	Target Value
passthrough	passthrough	*	(Bypass)

Figure 8.22

> **Note:** It's a minor detail, but mask rules run marginally slower compared to one-to-one rules. If you are seeing extremely slow transformation speeds, one option would be to convert all your rules into one-to-one mappings. The tradeoff, of course, is that the mappings now become a maintenance headache, so this isn't generally recommended as the increase in speed doesn't typically justify the increased chance of maintenance errors.

Invalid Intersection Errors

Once all source records are successfully transformed to the target values, OneStream performs various validation checks to confirm that the target intersections are valid for your target cube. Here are the most common errors during this step.

Invalid Member Name

When creating transformation rules, OneStream has safeguards to prevent you from assigning invalid member names in the target value field. However, if you have "star-to-star" mask rules in place, it's now possible for source values to get mapped to invalid targets. This will have to be addressed either at the data source level or through additional mappings to your transformation rules.

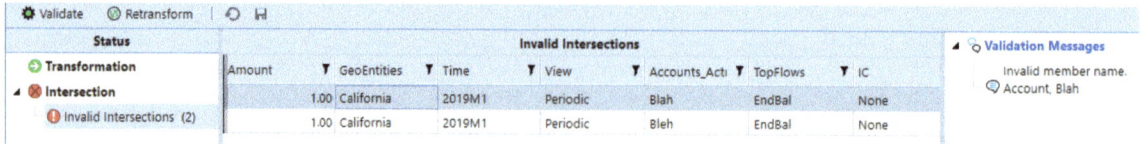

Figure 8.23

Loading to Parent Member

Recall that OneStream only allows you to load data to base members with respect to the current cube dimensions. If you attempt to load data to parent members, you'll get the following `Invalid Intersections` error.

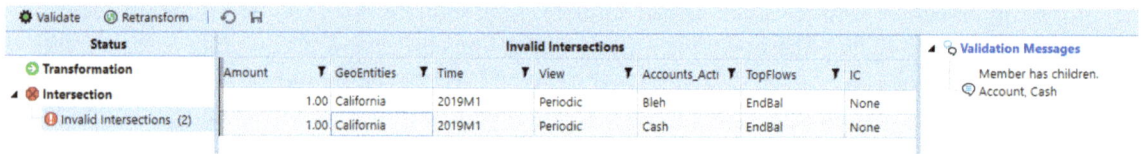

Figure 8.24

Constraint Violation

This error means that you've violated the **constraints** applied to your entity, account, or UD1. We discuss applying constraints in Chapter 9: Constraining and Locking Data. But for now, recall that constraints allow you to specify which intersection combinations are valid. In this case, account 10000 is restricted to only load to the "GolfStream" customer member.

In this situation, there's really no catch-all solution, since you'll have to evaluate if the constraint is legitimate for your business use case.

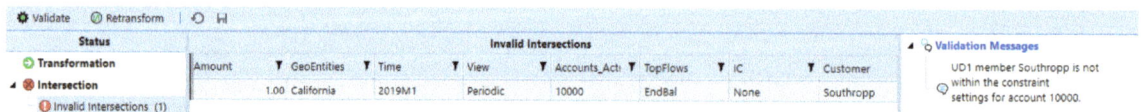

Figure 8.25

Entity Not Assigned to Workflow

OneStream throws this error if you are attempting to load a separate entity's records to the current workflow.

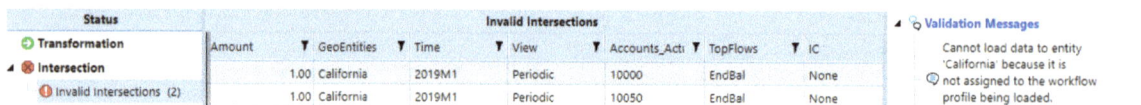

Figure 8.26

Depending on your situation, there are two possible solutions:

1. If this workflow should truly own this entity, and the assignment was just missed, then the entity can be assigned on the Workflow Profile pane on the Entity Assignment tab.

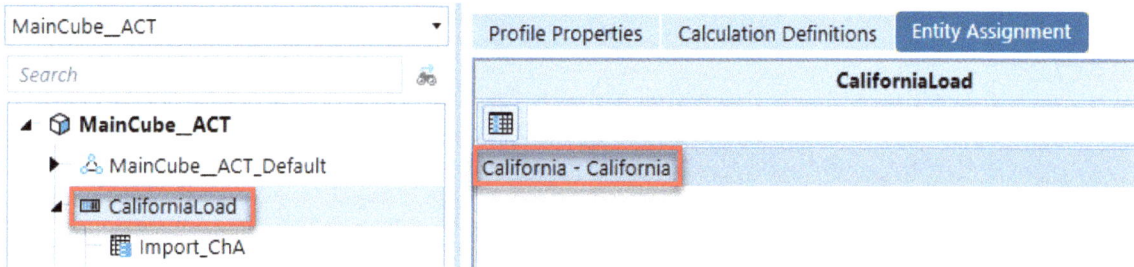

Figure 8.27

2. If the entity is assigned to another workflow, but the current workflow is a central input workflow that needs access to all entities, then you can set the Can Load Unrelated Entities field to True.

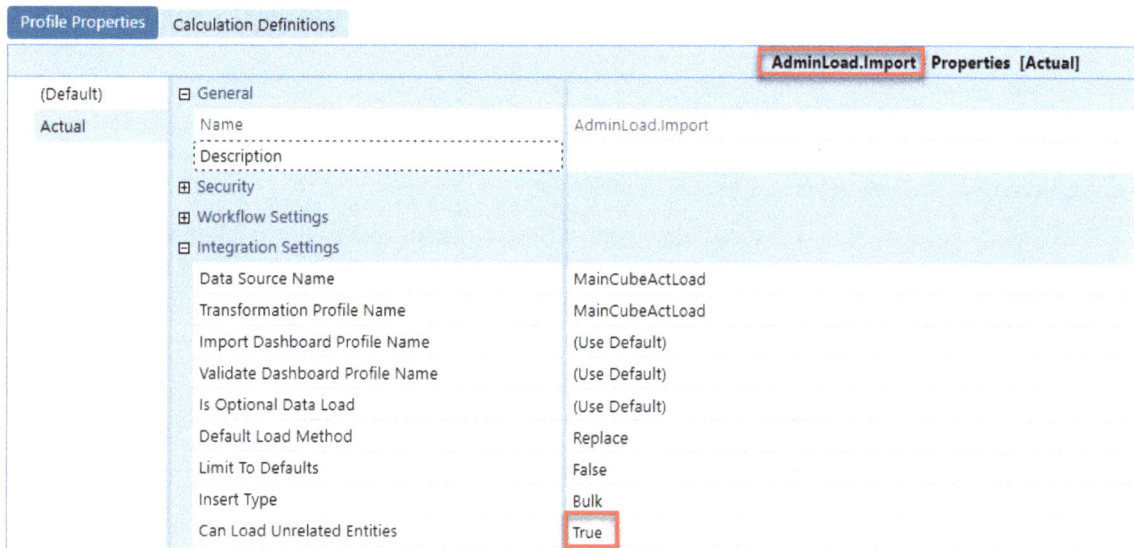

Figure 8.28

UD Member Not Assigned to WF Channel

If you have assigned a workflow channel to your base input workflow, OneStream will not allow you to load to target members that have a different workflow channel assigned to them.

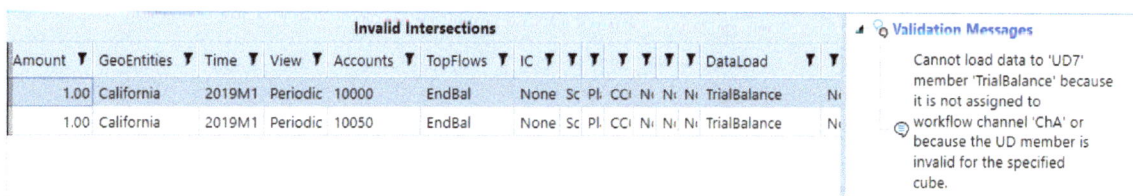

Figure 8.29

Here, for example, we've configured our application to apply workflow channels to the U7 dimension, and we've assigned Workflow Channel ChA to our workflow. However, since we have not yet assigned any workflow channels to the U7 `TrialBalance` member, OneStream throws the error above.

To fix this, we can navigate to the dimension library and set the Workflow Channel value of our `TrialBalance` member to ChA.

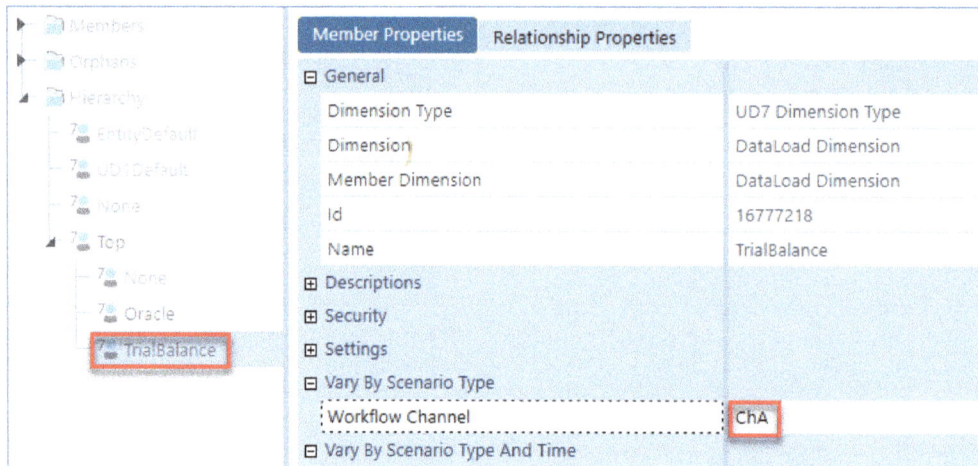

Figure 8.30

Account Not Assigned to WF Channel

Recall that even if you've configured your application to apply workflow channels to a different dimension, OneStream will still always apply workflow channels against the Account dimension as well. Unfortunately, this almost always leads to conflicts, as the old workflow channel assignments on your accounts will create errors on validation.

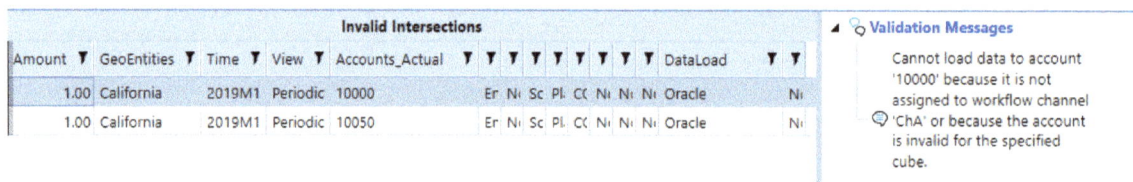

Figure 8.31

Let's consider the following configuration to see why this error occurs. Suppose our application was recently updated to apply workflow channels to the UD7 DataLoad dimension, and the current input workflow was also changed from ChB to ChA to allow us to write data to these DataLoad members.

This update will mean on the next data load, you will see the validation error from above. This is because our accounts were all initially assigned to Workflow Channel ChB, as shown below, to match the old workflow channel setting.

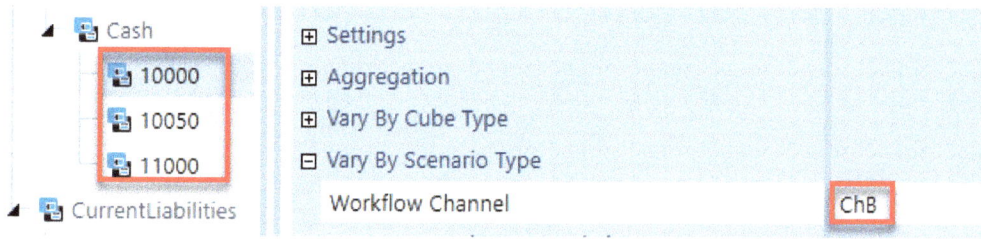

Figure 8.32

In this case, all accounts must have their workflow channel field updated to NoDataLock. By doing so, OneStream allows any workflow to load to these members, which bypasses the account WF channel errors.

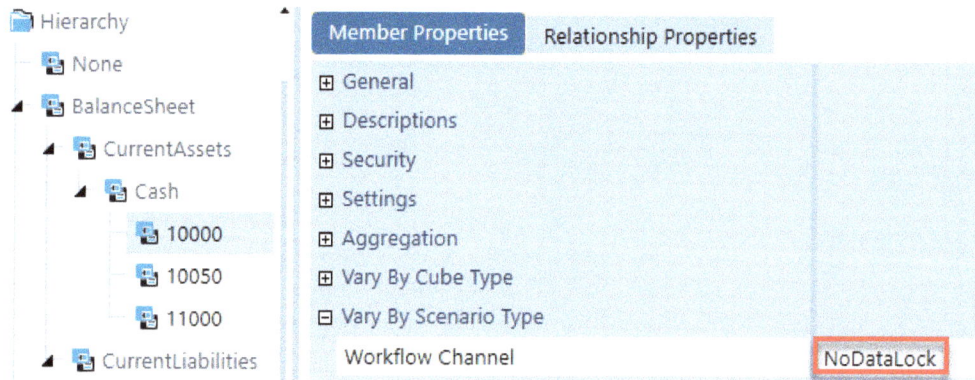

Figure 8.33

To understand more about how OneStream handles workflow channels during data loads, refer to Chapter 6: Work the Workflow.

Conditional Input Rule Locking

This error appears if you attempt to write to **read-only cells** that are locked due to conditional input business rules (i.e., NoInput rules).

Figure 8.34

To troubleshoot this error, check what business rules are attached to the cube, since all NoInput rules must be assigned to the cube and cannot trigger elsewhere. Once you've located the business rule, the first step would be to check the control flow conditions to make sure the rule is not triggering unexpectedly. For example, you might want to check that the rule is only triggering for specific entities, and not for all entities, depending on your requirements.

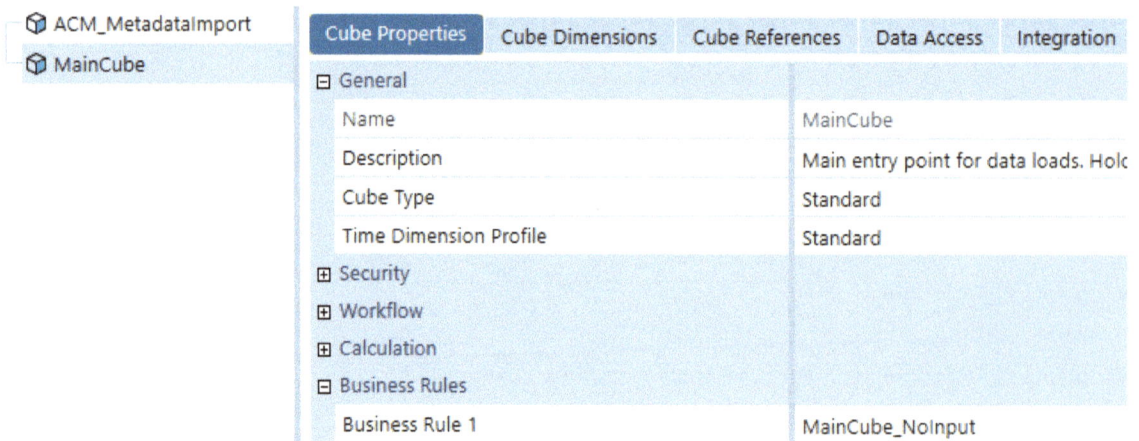

⬡ ACM_MetadataImport	Cube Properties	Cube Dimensions	Cube References	Data Access	Integration
⬡ MainCube	⊟ General				
	Name			MainCube	
	Description			Main entry point for data loads. Holɔ	
	Cube Type			Standard	
	Time Dimension Profile			Standard	
	⊞ Security				
	⊞ Workflow				
	⊞ Calculation				
	⊟ Business Rules				
	Business Rule 1			MainCube_NoInput	

Figure 8.35

For more details on NoInput rules, see Chapter 9: Constraining and Locking Data.

You can also get similar errors because of the settings applied on the Data Access tab on your cube. For more details on this type of security, refer to Chapter 12: Securing the Pieces.

Conclusion

In this chapter, we covered a number of common import and validation errors, explaining the various reasons why they might appear, and providing a framework for how to resolve them. It's also important to understand the background information on workflows and imports in order to develop a better intuition towards finding the root cause of data load issues; without it, there are simply too many possible errors to list. In closing, we know that data load errors are often panic inducing, so we hope that this chapter gives you some peace of mind for the times when that red flashing box inevitably pops onto your screen!

9
Constraining and Locking Data

There are a million reasons for implementing CPM systems like OneStream, but the core reason is really summed up by one phrase – *data integrity*.

Data integrity means having complete, accurate data (i.e., both correct and valid) that is consistent when accessed by different stakeholders. At the end of the day, it doesn't matter how nice your dashboards are, or how streamlined your workflows are, if your underlying data is unreliable. Of course, this is especially important when dealing with critical financial data and the threat of audits.

While one aspect of being an admin is ensuring your users have a seamless, pleasant experience, the other aspect is protecting users from themselves as they cause havoc, break your database, and email you at 5pm on Friday. To accommodate this need, OneStream provides a variety of methods for securing your data and guaranteeing data integrity. The purpose of this chapter is to cover these methods, which we have separated into two major categories: system-level controls and process-level controls.

As an added bonus, if you're here because you cannot figure out why a cell is flagged as invalid or read-only, then this chapter can also serve as a checklist for figuring out the root cause.

System-Level Controls

The system-levels control approach is to apply constraints directly onto your data by applying settings which enforce which intersections are valid. Since OneStream has so many related settings, the goal here is to collect the most common and useful options in one place. Something to note is that – while powerful – these options must be used judiciously since they can unexpectedly affect items beyond your initial scope.

Cube Settings

Dimension Settings

Cube dimension settings can be accessed on the Cube Dimensions tab of your cube. These are the most universal controls you can apply and should be the first level you consider when constraining your data.

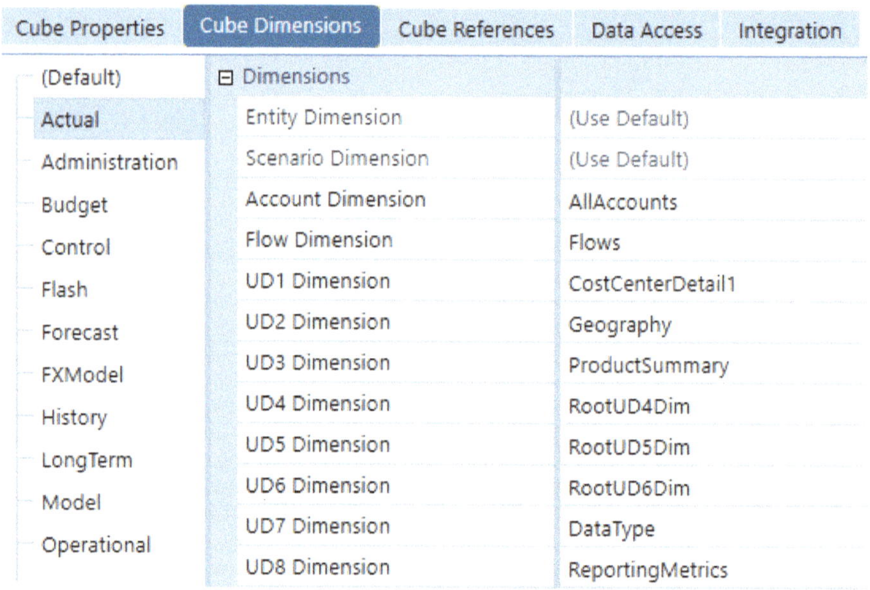

Figure 9.1

As an admin, there's a good chance the cubes in your application have already been configured. However, it's still critical for you to understand the implications of how dimensions are assigned. For the mechanics of modifying cube dimensions, refer to the Configuring Cubes section in Chapter 4: Metadata Management.

When you assign a dimension on the cube, OneStream will only allow you to write data to the members within that dimension; this means you've constrained your cube and effectively set which members are valid. This applies to all data, *regardless of the source* – data loads, manual inputs, calculated data, etc. This is useful because these settings guarantee you do not end up with incorrect or invalid data intersections.

This concept is closely tied to extensibility. By allowing you to assign different dimensions by cube and by Scenario Type, OneStream allows you to get extremely granular with how you constrain your data. For more details on extensibility and cube design, refer to the Foundation Handbook.

Use Case 1: Assigning Dimensions

Suppose you have two business entities, each with their own cube: NorthAmerica and Europe. Let's say you want to guarantee that NorthAmerica cube data only gets tagged with North American products, and European cube data with European products. To accommodate this, you could use UD3 as a product dimension and create two separate dimensions `Products_NA` and `Products_EU`. By assigning each of these product dimensions to their respective cubes, you have specified which products are valid for each cube.

With this setup, if an EU user tried to submit data to the European cube tagged with a North American product, they would get an error. Furthermore, if a power user tried to create a form to input data there, the cell would show up as an invalid cell, again preventing invalid inputs.

Use Case 2: Assigning Root

A special use case is that you can "disable" a dimension by assigning root to it (e.g., `RootUD1Dim`). By assigning root to a dimension, you are essentially constraining that dimension such that only the **None** member is valid: this is because None is the only member in each of the root dimensions.

> **Note:** Technically, the dimension is still enabled as far as the system is concerned, so you would still have to handle it when setting up data sources and transformation rules. It's only "disabled" in practice, since you'd never see values loaded to anything other than None.

Integration Settings

You can disable dimensions on the Integration tab of your cube by selecting a dimension and setting the Enabled field to False.

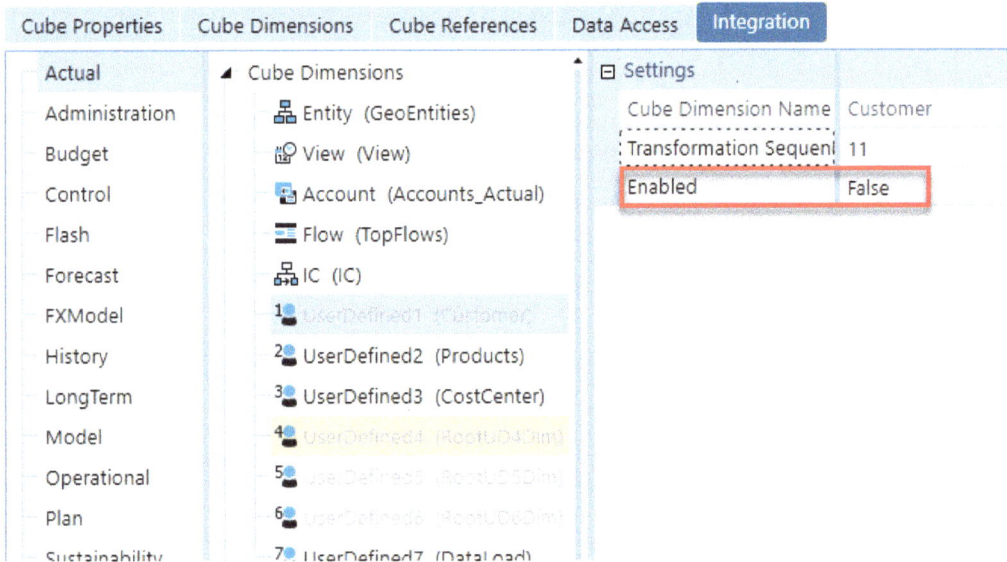

Figure 9.2

It's important to note, however, that the Integration tab only affects how data is loaded to this cube through workflows. While it's a common misconception, disabling a dimension on the Integration tab does *not* make this dimension invalid across your application. Pre-existing data tagged to disabled members does not get cleared, and users would still be able to write data to the "disabled" members.

When you disable a dimension through the Integration tab, three things happen:

1. When data is loaded through an Import workflow, OneStream will ignore whatever dimension is assigned to your data source, and will instead load all data to None for that dimension type.

2. Going forward, when you create data sources for your cube, configuration for the disabled dimension will not appear as an option.

3. When configuring transformation rules, you no longer have to specify mappings for the disabled dimension, as there will never be any member source data to transform in the first place.

To summarize, disabling a dimension in integration settings is the same as saying, "I don't want to load data to this dimension."

Entity and Member Constraints

Applying constraints to members is the most direct way of constraining your data. Like the dimension settings on your cube, these constraint settings apply to all sources of data. These settings are available for entity, account, and UD1 members. If you assign a parent member to a constraint field, only the base members under that parent are valid targets.

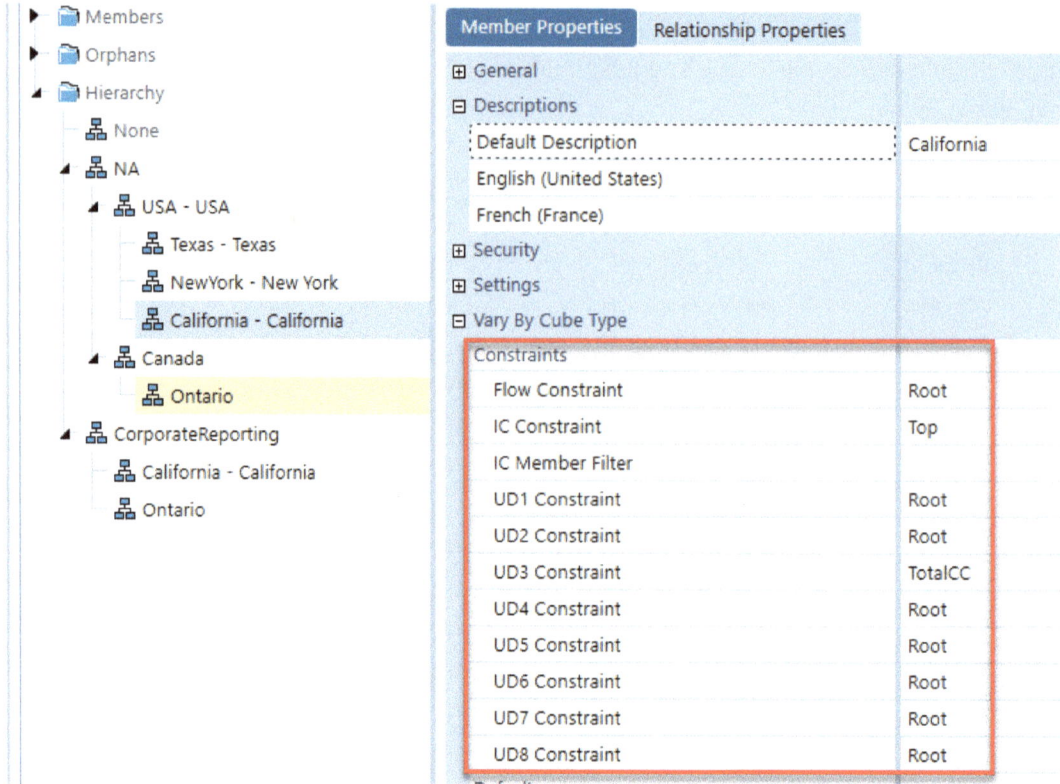

Figure 9.3

For example, here, we've assigned TotalCC to the UD3 constraint for the California entity. If you are writing data to California and attempt to tag data to a base cost center that isn't under TotalCC, you will get an error.

These are great when your constraint relationships are fairly simple but break down when you get to more complicated use cases. For example, if you wanted to apply "compound" constraints where you constrain UD4, based on the current UD2 and UD3, you would be unable to do this. One option would be to create conditional input business rules to accommodate this. Refer to the Conditional Input Business Rules Section for more details.

> **Note:** The UD1 dimension is special in that no other UD dimensions allow you to apply constraints.

Member Allow Input Settings

Accounts, flows, and UD members all have an Allow Input setting. When set to True, this setting allows users to enter data in the following ways:

1. Load to O#Import via Import workflows.

2. Manually enter to O#Forms via input forms.

3. Enter journal entries to O#AdjInput.

Note that this only applies to inputted and not calculated data: even when set to False, data can still be stored via formulas.

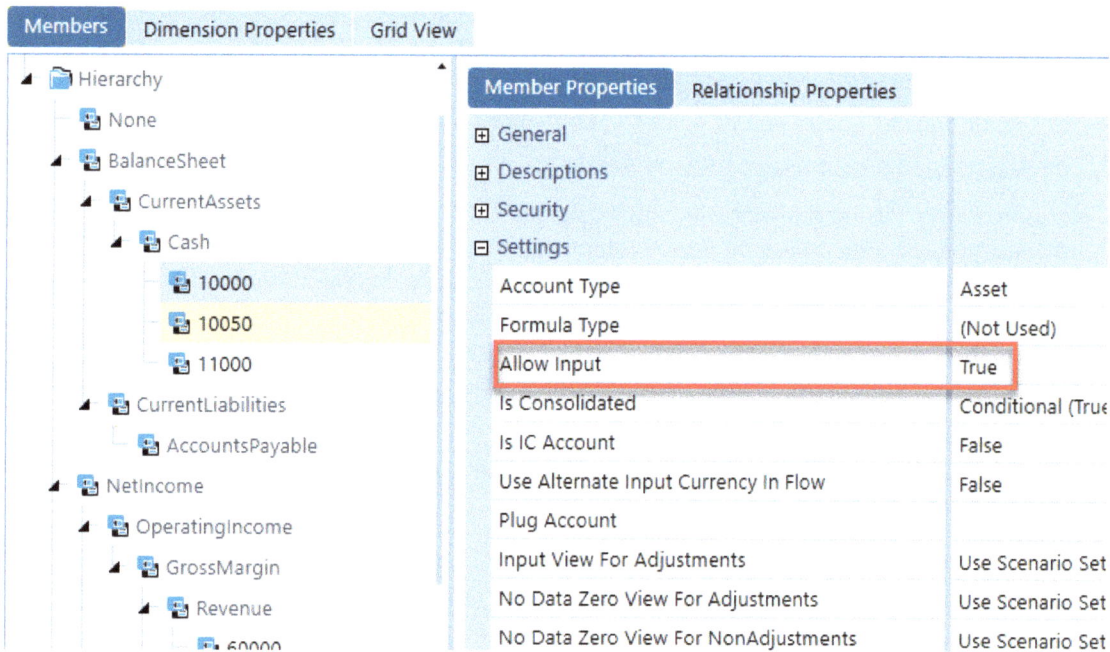

Figure 9.4

Scenario Input Settings

The Input Frequency and Workflow Tracking Frequency settings work together to control what time periods are valid for a given scenario member.

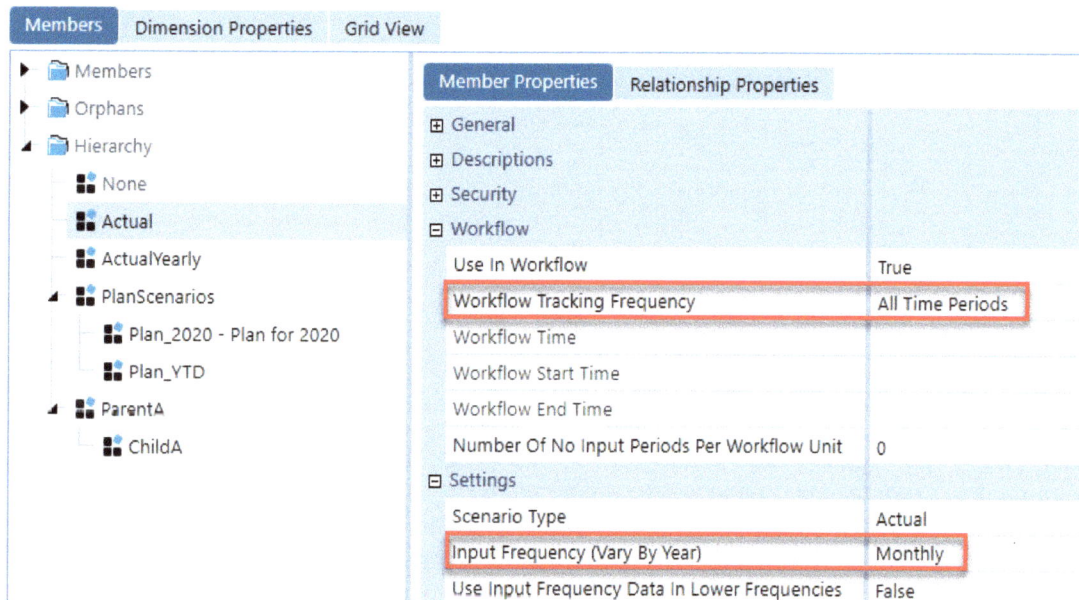

Figure 9.5

Here is a brief description of each setting and their possible values:

- **Input Frequency**: This setting determines which time periods are valid to write data to. If you set it as Monthly, then users may load data to any month. If you set it as Yearly, you would be able to load to 2019, but not to a month like 2019M3.

- **Workflow Tracking Frequency**: This setting controls what periods are displayed to users in workflows, but doesn't technically apply any constraints on what time periods are valid. For example, if you set the Workflow Tracking Frequency as Yearly, users can only see years in their Workflow POV. But if the Input Frequency is Monthly, and they had access to a form with monthly inputs, OneStream wouldn't prevent them from inputting monthly data.

Conditional Input Business Rules

Conditional input business rules (also called NoInput rules) are the most flexible types of constraints you can apply. At their core, NoInput rules are just regular finance business rules attached to your cube. Whenever data is being written to the cube, the business rule is run once – for each intersection – to determine if that intersection is read-only.

To create a NoInput rule, create a finance rule and add your logic under the `FinanceFunctionType.ConditionalInput` case block. When run against an intersection as data is being loaded, if the rule returns `ConditionalInputResultType.NoInput`, the intersection being processed will not be stored, and OneStream will instead throw an error saying the intersection is read-only.

```
Namespace OneStream.BusinessRule.Finance.MainCube_NoInput
    Public Class MainClass
        Const ENABLE_LOGGING As Boolean = True

        Public Function Main(ByVal si As SessionInfo, ByVal globals As BRGlobals, ByV
            Try
                Select Case api.FunctionType
                    Case Is = FinanceFunctionType.ConditionalInput
                        If Not api.Pov.Flow.Name.XFEqualsIgnoreCase("EndBal") Then
                            Return ConditionalInputResultType.NoInput
                        End If

                        Return ConditionalInputResultType.Default


                End Select

                Return Nothing
            Catch ex As Exception
                Throw ErrorHandler.LogWrite(si, New XFException(si, ex))
            End Try
        End Function
    End Class
End Namespace
```

Figure 9.6

Something to note is that, similar to member input settings, NoInput rules only prevent users from inputting data via data loads and manual data entry; *calculated data generated by business rule executions will bypass NoInput rules*. This is useful as it allows you to combine and layer NoInput rules on top of your calculations to prevent users from overwriting your calculated data.

For more details on creating NoInput rules, refer to the Design and Reference Guide as well as the OneStream Finance Rules and Calculations Handbook.

> **Note:** Because NoInput rules run against every intersection being stored or queried, it's critical that they are efficient. For example, if you add `BRApi.ErrorLog` calls or several database queries to your NoInput logic, you could potentially slow your system to a point where it's unusable.
>
> If you're seeing significant performance hits, you might want to consider caching data on a BRGlobals object, or even on a user session state, in order to avoid repeating expensive operations potentially millions of times.

Account Adjustment Type

The Adjustment Type setting can be found on Account Members and controls how data can be written to an account tagged with the O#AdjInput origin. There are three available values for this setting:

1. **Journals**: This is the default value as, traditionally, journals are used to write journal adjustments to O#AdjInput.

2. **Data Entry**: This is the setting to use if you want to input data to O#AdjInput via Cube View forms.

3. **Not Allowed**: Setting the Adjustment Type to Not Allowed fully disables inputs to O#AdjInput.

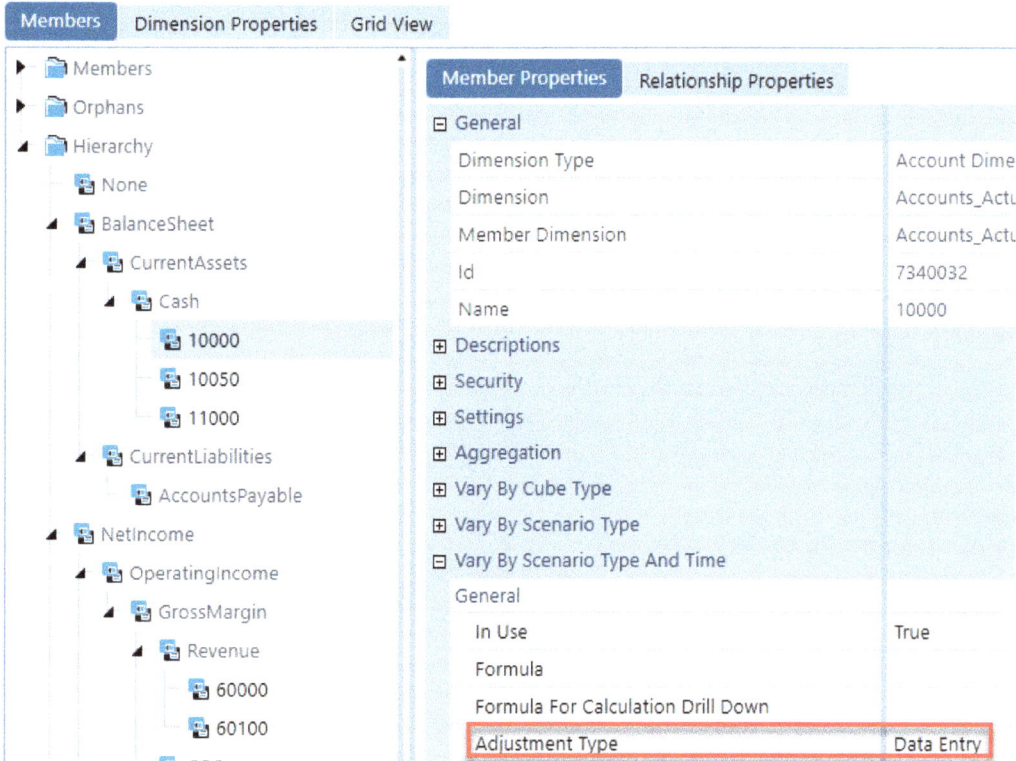

Figure 9.7

Process-Level Controls

While the system-level control approach is to apply hard constraints directly to data, the process-level control approach doesn't explicitly lock any data. Instead, the idea is to control the mechanisms to access and modify data (e.g., workflows and Cube Views). Put another way, this approach applies soft constraints to intersections by selectively giving users access to only the data they need to do their jobs – no more, no less.

To illustrate this approach, if we don't give a user access to income statement input forms, then there's no way for this user to accidentally see or mess up that data, even though – technically – nothing at a system level stops them from writing data there.

While not as holistic as system-level controls, process-level controls are a necessary tool and should be used hand-in-hand with system-level controls to enforce data integrity.

Background on Security

Before we discuss examples of process-level controls, we need to briefly discuss security, which is ultimately the backbone of process control.

Security settings allow you to control whether a user can access an artifact in OneStream. You could build the most sophisticated workflow processes in the world, but without the ability to selectively lock users out of workflows they shouldn't have access to, you're taking a huge risk with your data security and integrity.

In order to limit user access, there are really two settings on OneStream that you're looking for: 1. **Access Group** and 2. **Read and Write Data Group** (as well as **Read Data Group**). There are other settings, such as maintenance group and manage data group, but those deal with making sure other admins or consultants aren't modifying artifacts they shouldn't be (and aren't pertinent to this discussion).

The level at which you apply security will depend on your business processes; there is no "best practice" here. You might want to limit users at the cube level, dashboard level, or even at an extremely granular report level.

For a more detailed discussion of security, refer to Chapter 12: Securing the Pieces.

Direct Data Access

The following settings control which intersections are available to users. Note that the approach here is to prevent a subset of users from accessing a set of intersections; there is nothing technically making these intersections invalid. That said – from a practical standpoint – if no one has write-access to a set of data, that data is effectively completely locked!

Entity and Scenario Security

Entity and scenario members are part of the Data Unit dimensions, so it's not surprising that they have additional security settings compared to UD members. In particular, you can set read and write permissions using the Read Data Group and Read and Write Data Group fields.

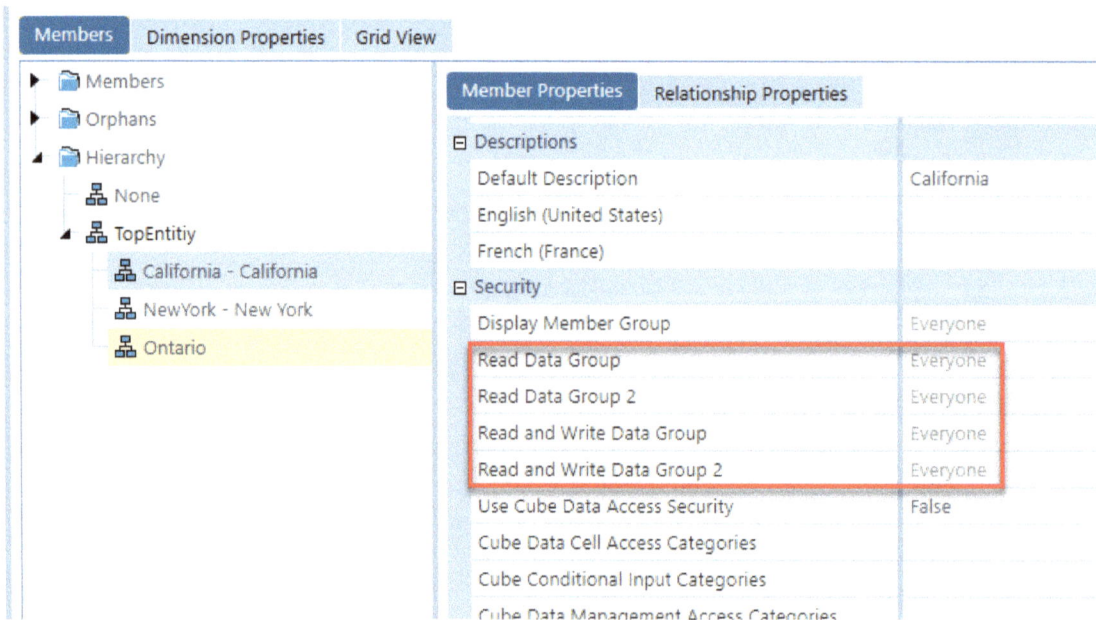

Figure 9.8

An example use-case for this setting would be to assign only California users with write access to the California entity. You haven't made the California entity invalid; you have just prevented a subset of users from reading data from and writing to the entity.

Cube Security Settings

Similar to the read/write settings on entities and scenarios, you can configure the Access Group setting on your cube directly to control which users can access the cube data as a whole.

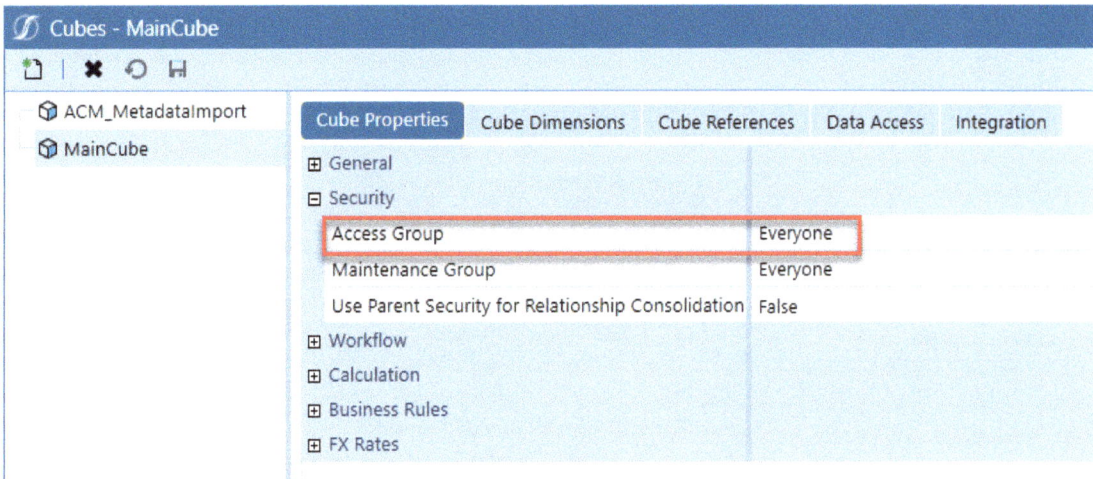

Figure 9.9

For even more granular control over intersections, you can implement slice security by going to the Data Access tab. Again, refer to Chapter 12 on security, for a more detailed discussion of slice security.

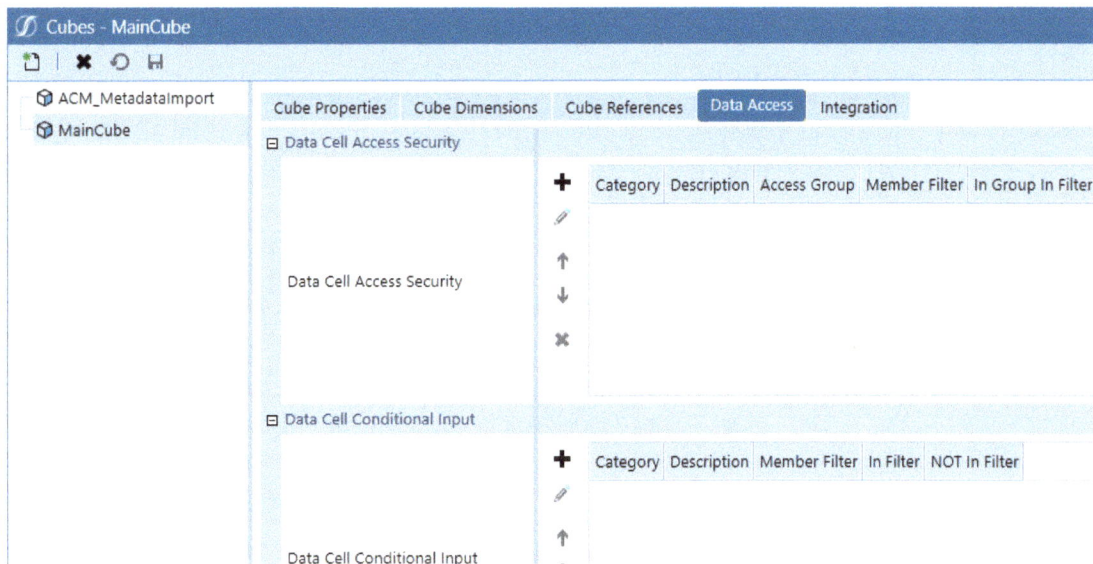

Figure 9.10

UI Access

In addition to limiting access to cubes and specific intersections, another approach would be to limit access to the UI elements that allow users to interact with data. The following sections outline the key UI elements that users typically interact with, and each serves as a different level for the application of access controls.

Workflow Design and Profile Settings

Process control in OneStream is primarily driven by workflow design. Ideally, your users would interact with their tasks and reporting almost entirely through workflows. You can then control user access to data by designing your workflows so that each workflow controls a different set of intersections, then assign the appropriate security group to each respective workflow.

For example, suppose you have a California business unit that should only have access to the California entity and a subset of income statement accounts. You can create a workflow called `CaliforniaLoad` and assign the California entity and appropriate workflow channel to it. By

Chapter 9

giving only California users access rights to this workflow and its children, and provided there are no other ways to access these intersections, you have limited these intersections only to the California business unit.

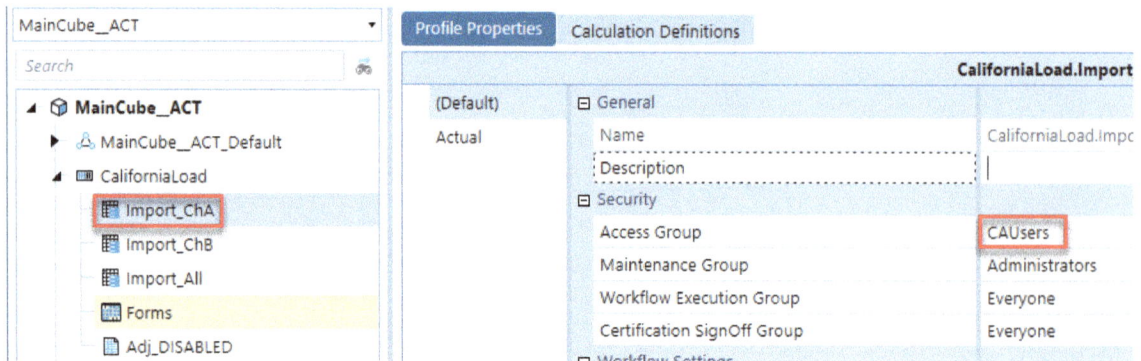

Figure 9.11

This is only one example, but the main idea is that your workflow design must always take security into account, as process flow and read/write access are closely interconnected concepts.

For more details on workflow design and workflow channels, refer to Chapter 6: Work the Workflow.

Dashboard Restrictions

Dashboards are typically embedded into workflow Workspaces, although they can also be accessed directly through OnePlace. With that in mind, you can restrict access to dashboards that have responsibility for set intersections to limit users' access to that data.

It's subtle, but you might want to apply security access at this level – over workflows – in the event that dashboards are shared between different workflows. For example, suppose you have two workflows: CaliforniaLoad and NewYorkLoad, that both share several dashboards, one of which is PNLAdjustments. If you wanted to lock only the California users out of the PNLAdjustments form, then you could change the Access Group of the dashboard to match the Access Group of the NewYorkLoad workflow. By applying these settings, California users would be able to access all other dashboards except for California Load, while New York users retain all of their access.

Cube View Restrictions

Cube Views are typically embedded into dashboards but can also be accessed directly through OnePlace. With this in mind, you can restrict Cube Views at the lowest level by applying security settings directly on the Cube View Groups.

Additionally, Cube Views have the Can Modify Data setting, which allows you to control whether data can be entered via this Cube View or if the Cube View is read-only. This setting exists even more granularly on individual columns and rows, although these settings are ignored if the overall Cube View is set as read-only.

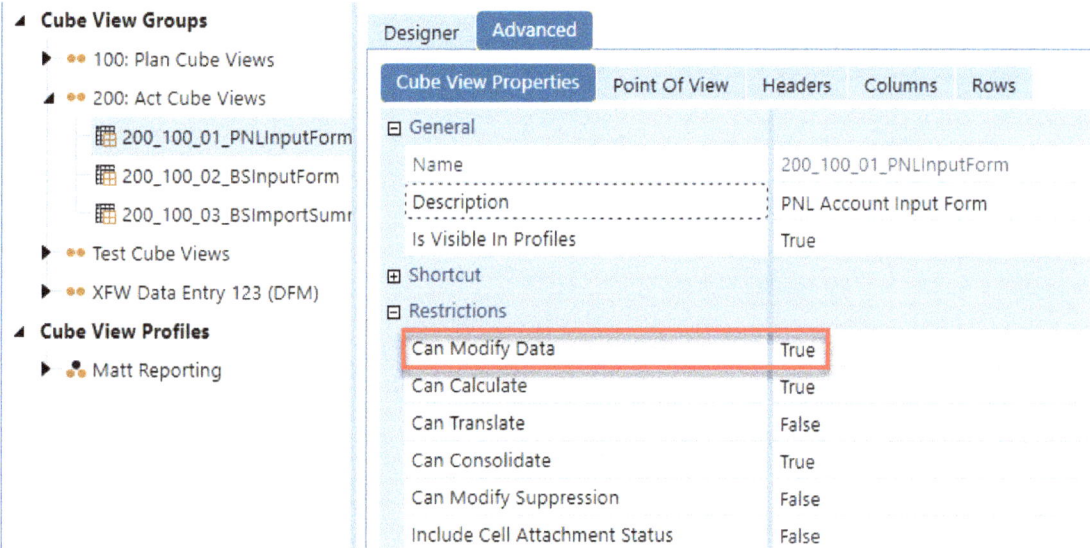

Figure 9.12

Conclusion

In this chapter, we covered the two main approaches for constraining your data in OneStream: system-level controls and process-level controls. There are many ways to enforce data integrity in OneStream, so we hope this chapter gives you a framework for thinking about the best way to secure your data. We also hope that it gives you a solid starting point for things to consider when a user is unable to load data to locked intersections, or even worse when they are!

10
Business Rules

For many admins, business rules are the most intimidating part of maintaining an application, particularly for those who don't already have a coding background. Business rules, when written poorly (and sometimes even when written well), can be cryptic maintenance nightmares. Honestly, we doubt there is anyone that enjoys getting an email saying a calculation isn't working properly.

If you're reading this chapter, it's likely that you have business rules that you are maintaining or debugging and, if so, then you've come to the right place. This book is written with your needs as an admin in mind, and focuses mainly on maintenance and troubleshooting techniques. We also cover some best practices for business rules, to help you write and refactor maintainable code for the sake of *future you*.

However, we don't go into detail on writing calculations and the various use-cases that business rules can solve, which is covered in the OneStream Finance Rules and Calculations Handbook. Also, we assume that you have at least some basic exposure to C# or VB.NET, and finance rules through the Admin Training Course: it's enough that you are able to read basic syntax.

This chapter will cover a lot of fairly technical topics, but we assure you that – as intimidating as business rules can be – everyone can learn to write and maintain good code! With that, let's strap in and get started.

Finance Engine

While the concepts in this chapter technically apply to all types of business rules, we will focus mainly on finance rules as that is where you will likely spend the majority of your time in your OneStream career. With that in mind, we first provide some context around the finance engine before delving into the nitty gritty of business rules.

The **finance engine** is an in-memory financial analytic engine that is responsible for consolidating data up to parent entities and executing complex calculations through business rules and Member Formulas. We realize that's a bit abstract, and you might be wondering what *is* the finance engine really and, more importantly, how do I interact with it?

Well, the finance engine performs work when triggered by certain events, like running a calculation, translation, or a custom calculation. Depending on the event triggered, the finance engine will also execute the business rules attached to your cube to check if you've applied any custom logic. When these business rules are executed, the finance engine as the overall controller will pass in several arguments to the `Main` function call. To understand what these arguments represent, let's continue by breaking down the anatomy of a finance business rule.

Finance Rule Structure

General Template

All finance rules must contain a `Main` function, which is the main entry point for the rule and is the function that is executed by the finance engine when various events are triggered. From the function declaration, we can see that a finance rule expects four objects to get passed in:

1. `SessionInfo`

2. `BRGlobals`

3. `FinanceRulesApi`

4. `FinanceRulesArgs`

```vb
Namespace OneStream.BusinessRule.Finance.Test
    Public Class MainClass
        Public Function Main(ByVal si As SessionInfo, ByVal globals As BRGlobals, ByVal api As FinanceRulesApi, ByVal args As FinanceRulesArgs) As Object
            Try
                Select Case api.FunctionType

                    Case Is = FinanceFunctionType.MemberList
                        'Example: E#Root.CustomMemberList(BRName=MyBusinessRuleName, MemberListName=[Sample Member List], Name1=Value1)
                        'If args.MemberListArgs.MemberListName.XFEqualsIgnoreCase("Sample Member List") Then
                            'Dim objMemberListHeader As New MemberListHeader(args.MemberListArgs.MemberListName)
                            'Dim objMemberInfos As List(Of MemberInfo) = api.Members.GetMembersUsingFilter(args.MemberListArgs.DimPk, "E#Root.Base", Nothir
                            'Dim objMemberList As New MemberList(objMemberListHeader, objMemberInfos)
                            'Return objMemberList
                        'End If

                    Case Is = FinanceFunctionType.DataCell
                        'If args.DataCellArgs.FunctionName.XFEqualsIgnoreCase("Profit") Then
                            'Return api.Data.GetDataCell("A#Sales * 0.9")
                        'End If

                    Case Is = FinanceFunctionType.FxRate
                        'Try to get the FxRateType from the account's Text1 field.
                        'Dim fxRateTypeForAccount As String = api.Account.Text(api.Pov.Account.MemberId, 1)
                        'If Not String.IsNullOrEmpty(fxRateTypeForAccount) Then
                            'Dim rate as Decimal = api.FxRates.GetCalculatedFxRate(fxRateTypeForAccount, args.FxRateArgs.SourceCurrencyId, args.FxRateArgs.
                            'Return new FxRateResult(rate)
                        'End If

                    Case Is = FinanceFunctionType.Calculate
                        'api.Data.Calculate("A#Profit = A#Sales - A#Costs")

                    Case Is = FinanceFunctionType.ConditionalInput
                        'If api.Pov.Account.Name.XFEqualsIgnoreCase("ReadOnlyAccount") Then
                            'Return ConditionalInputResultType.NoInput
                        'End If
                        Return ConditionalInputResultType.Default

                    Case Is = FinanceFunctionType.CustomCalculate
                        'If args.CustomCalculateArgs.FunctionName.XFEqualsIgnoreCase("Test") Then
                        'api.Data.Calculate("A#Profit = A#Sales - A#Costs")
                        'End If

                End Select

                Return Nothing
            Catch ex As Exception
```

Figure 10.1

Whenever you create a finance rule from scratch, OneStream will automatically populate the `Main` function with several empty case statements, where you can add your logic depending on the type of event you want to configure.

Finance Rules API

The key object here – the secret sauce – is the `FinanceRulesApi` object, which is assigned to the `api` variable. The `FinanceRulesApi` class gives you access to all the functions you might need to calculate and store financial data – i.e., everything the finance engine is responsible for! So, for our earlier question of how we interact with the finance engine, the `FinanceRulesApi` object is the answer.

This becomes even clearer when we dig into the class properties, which essentially categorize the finance engine's responsibilities into sub-APIs. The following table lists the key properties of the `FinanceRulesApi`. At the end of the day, getting "experienced" coding in OneStream really means developing an intuition on where the function you need is.

Property	Description
FunctionType	Contains information on the triggering event. This is discussed in more detail below.
Pov	Contains information on the active Data Unit (cube, scenario, time). Depending on the triggering event, it might contain additional member info (e.g., if we are checking whether a fully-defined data cell is read-only, then this will include account, UDs, etc.). As a nice tip, this API has all of the dimensions on the active cube baked-in (e.g., `api.Pov.AccountDim`).
Data	Contains all functions related to querying data buffers and cells, and saving calculated data to the database. The most famous function is, of course, `api.Data.Calculate`
Dimensions	Contains functions related to getting dimension information. Most often, you'll be using the `api.Dimensions.GetDim` function to grab a dimension for its primary key.
Member	Contains functions to pull member information and traverse member hierarchies within a dimension.
Entity	Contains functions to get entity-specific member info, in particular consolidation and aggregation setting values.
Time	Contains useful helper functions to get time periods, and get other time periods relative to a given time period (e.g., get the period two months prior to the current period).
Account, Flow, ..., UD1, ..., UD8	Functions to get member info for each of the specific dimension types.
LogMessage	A quick shortcut to write log messages to the Error Log.

Figure 10.2

> **Note:** For a more detailed list of the functions in each of these classes, you can refer to the OneStream API Details and Documentation. Refer to the Technical References Section to see how to access this.

FinanceFunctionType

Let's cover the final piece of the puzzle, the `api.FunctionType` property. Whenever the finance engine triggers a business rule on the cube, it sets this property on the `api` object before passing it to the rule's `Main` Function. Let's take a look at a few of the `api.FunctionType` values:

- **FinanceFunctionType.Calculate**: This is what the finance engine passes as an argument when you trigger a calculation manually, or if a calculation is triggered as part of a translation or consolidation.

- **FinanceFunctionType.FXRate**: This is what the finance engine passes when you trigger a translation.

- **FinanceFunctionType.ConditionalInput**: This is what the finance engine passes when it checks the read-only status of each intersection on data loads.

- **FinanceFunctionType.MemberList**: This is what the finance engine passes when you call a member list expansion in a Member Filter (e.g., triggered in a Cube View).

195

The takeaway here is that the available values for `api.FunctionType` represent the list of events that can trigger a `Finance Business Rule`, and more importantly, are events that you can customize with code.

For example, by adding code to the `FinanceFunctionType.FXRate` case block and disabling the default translation algorithm on the cube, you can add custom logic for what FX rates to use instead of the system default FX rates.

Cube Data Unit

Recall that when the finance engine performs any task – whether it is loading data, clearing data, or calculating data – it operates on the cube Data Unit (also known as the Level 1 Data Unit). A cube Data Unit is the largest unit of work in OneStream and is comprised of the six Data Unit dimensions: Cube, Entity, Parent, Consolidation, Scenario, and Time.

When we say, "operates on", what we mean technically is that when the finance engine performs any work on a specified Data Unit, it will first query and cache all records from the database contained within the specified Data Unit in-memory. By caching these records, when you call functions like `api.Data.GetDataBuffer`, OneStream does not need to repeat expensive operations and re-query records directly from the database.

In the context of finance rules, these six Data Unit dimensions will always be appended by default to any `api.Data` method call. For example, when you call `api.Data.Calculate` you do not need to specify your target cube or entity; the finance engine already knows because you have specified it in your active Data Unit. Furthermore, the six members making up your Data Unit are loaded into the `api.Pov` object so they are available without you having to manually query them.

Data Unit Calculation Sequence (DUCS)

When a calculation is triggered, after pulling the cube Data Unit into memory, the finance engine will perform a series of steps, defined as the Data Unit Calculation Sequence.

1. Clear previously calculated data for the Data Unit.
2. Run the scenario's Member Formula.
3. Run reverse translations by calculating Flow members from other Alternate Currency Input Flow members.
4. Execute Business Rules 1 and 2.
5. Run Formula Passes 1-4 for the cube's Account dimension members, then Flow members, and then User-Defined members.
6. Execute Business Rules 3 and 4.
7. Run Formula Passes 5-8.
8. Execute Business Rules 5 and 6.
9. Run Formula Passes 9-12.
10. Execute Business Rules 7 and 8.
11. Run Formula Passes 13-16.

Business Rule Best Practices

Writing clean, easy-to-read code is essential for scalability and maintainability, especially when the responsibility for maintaining code falls on you as the admin. Debugging messy code has massive time costs: if you have ever spent weeks deciphering jumbled, messy business rules thousands of lines long, you understand what we mean. In the worst case, sometimes technical debt becomes so great that the only option is to jettison the code and start from scratch, starting a new development and testing cycle that might not have been budgeted for.

But what is "clean code"? This phrase is often thrown around like a magic spell, but very rarely explained. To us, clean code is code that *clearly conveys meaning*. Remember that code is meant to be read by humans, not machines. So, your goal should always be to write code that a stranger would be able to read without guidance and still parse your intent. You'll know you've failed if that stranger instead asks themselves "What is this code even doing?" The funny thing about messy code is that, oftentimes, the stranger asking that question might just be the *future you*.

Writing clean code boils down to a few key concepts:

1. Following agreed-upon standards.

2. Leveraging the correct data structures and code patterns.

3. Organizing code through careful naming and abstraction.

In this chapter, we focus mainly on VB.NET, but the concepts discussed will apply to C# and, indeed, every programming language in general, though there might be some minor variations in conventions and syntax.

.NET Coding Standards

In this section, we cover the recommended Microsoft .NET coding standards for VB.NET, and provide context on why these standards exist. We'll also show examples of how to apply these standards in OneStream-specific business rules.

Naming Conventions

While it seems like such a trivial thing, it's extremely important to always use meaningful, descriptive names for all the objects in your program, especially variables and functions; we are all guilty of being lazy sometimes and using generic names like `objStr` or `buffer1` (I certainly am).

However, naming accounts for 80% of the readability of your code, so it's always worth taking a little extra time to be thoughtful when choosing names. That said, proper naming is actually quite difficult, as it requires you to understand the structure and intent of your code ahead of time, and is often more of an art than an exact science.

Variables

Use camelCase notation for local variables. Avoid single-letter variable names, except for loop counters.

```
Dim customerName As String
Dim orderTotal As Decimal
```

Figure 10.3

Again, *always use meaningful, descriptive names for variables*. For example, I always make sure to name my `DataBuffer` variables to describe the data they represent. Compare the following two examples.

- The first example (while shorter) is harder to understand, because I *must* parse each argument in the calculation one by one, and it is unclear what intersections I'm affecting.

- The second is better because I can understand at a glance what the intent of the calculation is (multiply prior asset amounts by growth rates), and I can guess what the source intersections are (asset accounts) without having to refer to the dimension library.

```
' Example 1: Ambiguous
Dim resultBuffer As DataBuffer = api.Data.GetDataBufferUsingFormula("FilterMembers(U8#GrowthRates * T#POVPrior1:U8#None, [A#100000.Base])")

' Example 2: Clear
Dim assetGrowthRates As DataBuffer = api.Data.GetDataBufferUsingFormula("FilterMembers(U8#GrowthRates, [A#100000.Base])")
Dim priorYearAssets As DataBuffer = api.Data.GetDataBufferUsingFormula("FilterMembers(T#POVPrior1:U8#None, [A#100000.Base])")

api.Data.FormulaVariables.SetDataBufferVariable("assetGrowthRates", assetGrowthRates, False)
api.Data.FormulaVariables.SetDataBufferVariable("priorYearAssets", priorYearAssets, False)

Dim plannedAssets As DataBuffer = api.Data.GetDataBufferUsingFormula("$assetGrowthRates * $priorYearAssets")
```

Figure 10.4

Also, avoid adding the types of variables to their names; this is redundant since you should be declaring the type of your variable anyway, and IntelliSense will allow you to quickly hover over a variable to get the same information. This habit is a carryover from out-of-date, weakly-typed programming languages and is universally discouraged today.

```
' Don't do this
Dim accountString As String
Dim strFlow As String
Dim intValue As Integer
Dim doubleAmount As Double

' Here, option 2 is cleaner, though it is arguably personal preference
Dim parentList As List(Of String)
Dim parents As List(Of String)
```

Figure 10.5

Constants

Named constants should use PascalCase and should convey the meaning of the constant.

```
Public Const MaxItems As Integer = 100
Public Const SalesTaxRate As Double = 0.08
```

Figure 10.6

Methods

Use PascalCase for method names. Also, remember that methods always *do* something, and so method names should always start with a verb, to indicate an action. For example, for event handlers, a common convention is to prefix the name with Handle.

```
Public Function CalculateTotal() As Decimal
    ' ...
End Function

Private Sub HandleButtonClick(sender As Object, e As EventArgs)
    ' ...
End Sub
```

Figure 10.7

The same logic when naming variable names comes into play here; always take the time to create simple, meaningful function names. Also, be equally careful when naming your function parameters! If a function is well-named, you can often guess what it does based on its name and its parameters alone, without needing to scroll to the function to read its header or pull out the documentation.

Consider these two examples in the screenshot below.

- The first example shows a very common coding pattern: creating a function to check if a variable meets a condition. Here, it's easy to reason-out – from its name – that the function is checking whether the active Data Unit time is a planned period. Because we named the function in a meaningful way, the code almost reads like English: "If we're in a planned period, run our plan calcs."

- The second example is also self-explanatory. Take a logger object, and write its contents to a file called `PlanCalcLOG.txt` in the `Groups/Administrator/TestLogs` directory in the `FileShare`. If the function writes to the application database instead, I would have instead named the function `WriteLoggerToAppDB`.

```
Public Function SampleMethodCalls(ByVal si As SessionInfo, ByVal globals As BRGlobals, _
    ByVal api As FinanceRulesApi, ByVal args As FinanceRulesArgs) As Object

    ' Example 1: State checker function
    If isPlannedPeriod(api, api.Pov.Time.Name) Then
        Me.ExecutePlanCalcs(si, api)
    End If

    ' Example 2: Log writing function
    WriteLoggerToFileShare(si, api, logger, "PlanCalcLOG.txt", "Groups/Administrator/TestLogs")

End Function
```

Figure 10.8

Hopefully, this example demonstrates that if you are deliberate about naming your variables and methods, your code will read like English and require fewer comments and documentation to understand.

Classes

`Class` names should be nouns, indicating the object that the class represents.

Use PascalCase for `Class` names.

```
Public Class Customer
    ' ...
End Class
```

Figure 10.9

Properties

`Property` names should be nouns, indicating the data that the property represents.

Use PascalCase for `Property` names.

```
Public Class Customer
    Public Property FirstName As String
    Public Property LastName As String
End Class
```

Figure 10.10

Enums

Enum type names should be singular. Enum members should be PascalCase.

```
Public Enum Day
    Sunday
    Monday
    Tuesday
    Wednesday
    Thursday
    Friday
    Saturday
End Enum
```

Figure 10.11

Indentation Conventions

Indentation is crucial to understanding the hierarchical relationship between different code blocks; without it, it becomes extremely difficult to follow the flow of control through your code. This is especially true when your code is long enough that the beginning and end of control blocks don't fit on the same page, and when there are lots of nested control blocks. Let's compare an example of poorly indented code with the same code indented well to illustrate how much indentation affects readability.

This first example is extremely difficult to parse for a multitude of reasons. For one, it is difficult to determine which End If belongs to which starting If, so you have to manually scan line by line to find a match. For another, you cannot even tell how many case blocks there are without scanning the entire rule. Obviously, the example is a bit contrived but not wholly unrealistic.

```vb
Public Class MainClass
Public Function Main(ByVal si As SessionInfo, ByVal globals As BRGlobals, ByVal api As FinanceRulesApi, ByVal args As FinanceRulesArgs) As Object
Try
Select Case api.FunctionType

    Case Is = FinanceFunctionType.Calculate
    If isPlannedPeriod(api, api.Pov.Time.Name) Then
Me.ExecutePlanCalcs(si, api)
    End If

    Case Is = FinanceFunctionType.CustomCalculate
    If args.CustomCalculateArgs.FunctionName.XFEqualsIgnoreCase("ExecuteAllocation") Then
    Dim productsToAllocate As New List(Of String) From {"Frisbees","Golfballs","Basketballs"}
    For Each product In productsToAllocate
    Me.AllocateProduct(si, api, product)
    Next

    Else If args.CustomCalculateArgs.FunctionName.XFEqualsIgnoreCase("SeedActuals") Then
Me.SeedActuals(si, api)

    End If
End Select

Return Nothing

Catch ex As Exception
    Throw ErrorHandler.LogWrite(si, New XFException(si, ex))
End Try

End Function
End Class
```

Figure 10.12

This next example is much better. You can clearly see where each control structure begins and ends, and only look at the blocks that you care about. For example, if I know I am debugging within the Calculate case block, I can ignore anything in the CustomCalculate case block.

```
Public Class MainClass
    Public Function Main(ByVal si As SessionInfo, ByVal globals As BRGlobals, ByVal api As FinanceRulesApi, ByVal args As FinanceRulesArgs) As Object
        Try
            Select Case api.FunctionType

                Case Is = FinanceFunctionType.Calculate
                    If isPlannedPeriod(api, api.Pov.Time.Name) Then
                        Me.ExecutePlanCalcs(si, api)
                    End If

                Case Is = FinanceFunctionType.CustomCalculate
                    If args.CustomCalculateArgs.FunctionName.XFEqualsIgnoreCase("ExecuteAllocation") Then
                        Dim productsToAllocate As New List(Of String) From {"Frisbees","Golfballs","Basketballs"}

                        For Each product In productsToAllocate
                            Me.AllocateProduct(si, api, product)
                        Next

                    Else If args.CustomCalculateArgs.FunctionName.XFEqualsIgnoreCase("SeedActuals") Then
                        Me.SeedActuals(si, api)

                    End If
            End Select

            Return Nothing

        Catch ex As Exception
            Throw ErrorHandler.LogWrite(si, New XFException(si, ex))
        End Try

    End Function
End Class
```

Figure 10.13

Use Tabs/Spaces

Use four spaces or a tab for each level of indentation. It doesn't matter which you choose as long as you stay consistent with the rest of your code base.

```
Sub Main()
    Dim num As Integer = 10
    If num > 5 Then
        Console.WriteLine("Number is greater than 5")
    End If
End Sub
```

Figure 10.14

Indent Control Structures

The following control structures must all be indented. Keep the beginning and end of each control structure at the same indent level, and indent all statements in between with an additional level of indentation.

- If…Then…Else

- Select…Case: This block is special because it really is made up of a combination of the Select…End Select block, with additional Case expressions, both of which should be indented.

- Try Catch…Finally

- While…End While

- Do…Loop

- For…Next loops, For Each…Next loops

- Using…End Using

- With…End With

- Classes within Namespaces

- Functions and Subs within Classes

- Regions

Here, for example, the `If`, `Else`, and `End If` keywords are all on the same level; the console statements between them are all indented one additional level.

```
If num > 0 Then
    Console.WriteLine("Positive number")
Else
    Console.WriteLine("Non-positive number")
End If
```

Figure 10.15

Indent Long Lines

When a line of code is too long to fit on a single line, break it up and indent the continued line with an additional level of indentation.

```
Dim result As Integer = FunctionWithLongNameAndLotsOfParameters(
    parameter1, parameter2, parameter3, parameter4, parameter5,
    parameter6, parameter7, parameter8)
```

Figure 10.16

This happens very frequently with `api.Data.GetDataBuffer` statements when you have a lot of complicated arguments and filters. As a tip, I personally like breaking up the initial script and the filters into separate rows for better readability.

```
' Instead of letting this line shoot off into the void...
Dim assets As DataBuffer = api.Data.GetDataBufferUsingFormula("RemoveZeros(FilterMembers(Cb#MainCube:E#California:V#Periodic:S#Actual:F#EndBal:O#Import:I#None:U7#Top

' Indent!
Dim assets As DataBuffer = api.Data.GetDataBufferUsingFormula("
    RemoveZeros(FilterMembers(Cb#MainCube:E#California:V#Periodic:S#Actual:F#EndBal:O#Import:I#None:U7#Top:U8#None,
    [A#Cash.Base], [U1#TotalCust.Base], [U2#TotalProd.Base.Where(Text1 = NA)], [U3#TotalCC.Base]))
")
```

Figure 10.17

> **Note:** When indenting strings like this, be careful where you place your whitespace, as it might cause an error at runtime. If we had placed a space before the `E#` for example, OneStream would have thrown an error when executing the script.

Spacing Conventions

Good spacing improves code readability. These are some common guidelines, but note that there is some room for flexibility: for example, you might want to add additional blank lines to separate groups of related code, like local variables from the business logic.

1. Add spaces around both sides of all operators (`=`, `<>`, `<`, `>`, `<=`, `>=`, `And`, `Or`, `+`, `-`, `*`, `/`, etc.)

```
Dim sum As Integer = num1 + num2
Dim result As Boolean = (num1 > num2) And (num1 < num3)
```

Figure 10.18

2. An exception to the previous rule is that you should not add spaces around the `.` operator used for member access.

```
Dim name As String = customer.Name
```

Figure 10.19

3. Use a single space between function arguments and array elements.

```
Dim result As Integer = AddNumbers(num1, num2, num3)
Dim numbers As Integer() = {1, 2, 3, 4, 5}
```

Figure 10.20

4. Do not use spaces immediately inside parentheses.

```
Dim result As Boolean = (num > 10) And (num < 20)
```

Figure 10.21

5. Add blank lines between `Property` and method declarations.

```
Public Property Name As String

Public Function CalculateTotal() As Decimal
    ' ...
End Function
```

Figure 10.22

Organization

Order of Class Elements

Elements should generally be in the following order, from top to bottom:

1. Fields
2. Constructors
3. Properties
4. Methods

```vbnet
Public Class Customer
    ' Fields
    Private Shared nextId As Integer
    Private id As Integer

    ' Constructors
    Public Sub New()
        id = System.Threading.Interlocked.Increment(nextId)
    End Sub

    ' Properties
    Public Property Name As String
    Public ReadOnly Property Id As Integer
        Get
            Return id
        End Get
    End Property

    ' Methods
    Public Function GetNameAndId() As String
        Return $"{Name}, {Id}"
    End Function
End Class
```

Figure 10.23

Imports

Imports should always be placed at the top of the file, sorted alphabetically.

```vbnet
Imports System
Imports System.Collections.Generic
Imports System.Linq
Imports System.Text
```

Figure 10.24

Regions

Region(s) are useful for grouping related members together. For example, a common use is to group fields and properties together, or to group certain functions together. A neat benefit of using regions is that, like functions, most editors will allow you to collapse and expand regions. OneStream's built-in editor will have all regions collapsed by default, which is nice if your business rule is large and you have a lot of helper classes and functions.

```vb.net
#Region "Plan Calculation Routines"

    Public Sub CalculatePlanMain()
        #Region "Time variables"

            Dim currPeriod As String
            Dim priorPeriod As String

        #End Region

        "Member Filters"

            ' Execute plan subroutines
            Me.CalcPlannedAssets()
            Me.CalcPlannedLiabilities

    End Sub

    Public Sub CalcPlannedAssets...

    Public Sub CalcPlannedLiabilities...

#End Region

#Region "Time Helper Functions"

    Public Function IsPlannedPeriod() As Boolean...

    Public Function GetPrior3Periods() As List(Of String)...

#End Region

"Logging Helper Functions"
```

Figure 10.25

However, while the judicious use of regions can help code organization and readability, overuse of regions can become a crutch and potentially make code harder to read. No number of regions will make up for poor abstraction – separating responsibilities into different namespaces, classes, and functions. If you find that your class or function is too long, and you're depending on regions to keep things readable, that's a good sign that you should refactor and break it up into smaller pieces.

Comments

Comments can greatly improve code readability and maintainability because they're the most direct way to describe the context around your code. You should try to make your code as self-explanatory as possible through meaningful naming and careful abstraction using functions and classes, and add comments to provide context or detail that is not obvious in the code. Comments should explain the 'why' of your code; the reasons you approached the requirements a certain way.

Overall, the purpose of comments is to help other developers – including *future you* – understand your code. If you have the choice between over-commenting or under-commenting, it is better to err on the side of over-commenting (within reason, of course).

Conventions

Here are the standard conventions for commenting within VB.NET:

1. Put comments on a separate line instead of on the same line as a line of code.

2. Start comment text with an uppercase letter, and end comment text with a period.

3. Insert one space between the comment delimiter (') and the comment text.

```vb.net
    ' I am a well formated comment.
    BRApi.ErrorLog.LogMessage(si, "Blah blah")
```

Figure 10.26

Chapter 10

Examples of Useful Comments

Use inline comments to explain *why* certain decisions were made in your code. Here are several examples:

1. Add the business rationale to your code!

```
' San Diego Office was sold in 2021, so don't include in allocation calculation after 2021
If currYear > 2021 And api.Pov.Entity.Name.XFEqualsIgnoreCase("SanDiego") Then
    Return Nothing
End If

Me.CalculateAllocation(api.Pov.Entity.Name)
```

Figure 10.27

2. Include technical details from the overall application build.

```
' Flow in Cube A is pivoted into U6 in Cube B, so we must map
' the source flows into target u6s before seeding
Dim sourceBuffer As DataBuffer = api.Data.GetDataBufferUsingFormula("FilterMembers(Cb#CubeA:E#California, [A#Cash.Base])")
Dim transformedBuffer As DataBuffer = Me.MapFlowToU6(sourceBuffer)

api.Data.FormulaVariables.SetDataBufferVariable("transformedBuffer", transformedBuffer, False)

api.Data.Calculate("Cb#CubeB:E#NewYork = $transformedBuffer")
```

Figure 10.28

3. Provide alternatives to the code that you tried.

```
' Do not use the WinZIP API unzip file method; it's been deprecated and will throw
' a runtime exception. Had to use the 7Z API unzip file method instead.
SevenZip.UnzipFile(userFile)
```

Figure 10.29

4. Explain why certain parameters were passed.

```
' We have to pass in False here to avoid changing IDs to common
' Otherwise we we'll lose the member names for logging purposes.
Dim bufferToLog As DataBuffer = api.Data.GetDataBufferUsingFormula("A#Cash", DataApiScriptMethodType.Calculate, False)
```

Figure 10.30

5. Use comments to quickly summarize complex blocks of code.

```
' Source data lies at different levels based on scenario:
' If scenario is actual, source data resides at a base entity level.
' Otherwise for plan, pull source from summarized top entity.
Dim sourceBuffer As DataBuffer

If api.Pov.ScenarioType = ScenarioType.Actual Then
    sourceBuffer = Me.GetBaseEntityData()

Else
    sourceBuffer = Me.GetTopEntityData()

End If
```

Figure 10.31

Avoid Redundant Comments

Avoid comments that simply restate one-for-one what the code is doing or, in other words, comments that provide the same level of detail as the code. These comments add no value and – in fact – subtract value by cluttering your code. Here are some examples of comments to avoid:

1. Commenting declarations.

```
Dim account As String = "blah"                  ' Initialize string variable
Dim currTime As String = api.Pov.Time.Name  ' Initialize time variable

' Initialize list
Dim myList As New List(Of String) From {"Foo", "bar"}
```

Figure 10.32

2. Commenting the end of control blocks.

```
Namespace OneStream.BusinessRule.Finance.Bleh
    Public Class MainClass
        Public Function Main(ByVal si As SessionI
            If (num > 0):
                api.LogMessage(num)

            Else
                For i As Integer = 1 To 5
                    api.LogMessage(i)
                Next ' End For
            End If ' End If

        End Function 'End Function
    End Class 'End Class
End Namespace 'End Namespace
```

Figure 10.33

If you are doing this because your control blocks are so large that you cannot trace their beginnings and ends visually, that is usually a sign you need to refactor your code.

> **Note:** I am not sure where or when this pattern originated, but it is very common and a tiny, personal pet peeve of mine.

3. Repeating or restating code

```
' Get data buffer
Dim myBuffer As DataBuffer = api.Data.GetDataBufferUsingFormula("A#Cash")

' Query data from database
BRApi.Database.ExecuteSql(dbConn, sqlQuery, True)
```

Figure 10.34

Note that the main idea is to avoid *meaningless* comments, not all comments in general. The examples above are all examples of comments that do not add any detail or context to the code.

Purge Commented Code

As you develop and maintain business rules in OneStream, you'll often comment out large chunks of code temporarily for testing. Once you're done testing, and you're ready to commit to your new code, it's often extremely tempting to just leave that old code be: it's not hurting anybody, and better safe than sorry, right? Unfortunately, the answer here is no. [Figure 10.35 – is this supposed to return "Bork"?]

```vbnet
Public Shared Function WriteLogger(
    ByVal si As SessionInfo, ByVal api As Object, ByRef logger As System.Text.StringBuilder,
    Optional ByVal fileName As String = "LOG", Optional ByVal folderName As String = "TestLogs",
    Optional ByVal fileSuffix As String = Nothing, Optional ByVal fileExtension As String = "txt") As String

    ' Saves log to text file on application database
    '
    ' Parameters
    '   logger: string builder object with contents of log file
    '   fileName: optional log file name. defaults to LOG
    '   folderName: optional log folder destination. defaults to TestLogs
    '   fileSuffix: optional log file suffix. defaults to system time
    ' Returns
    '   filepath of log file

    If fileSuffix Is Nothing Then
        fileSuffix = DateTime.Now.ToString("yyyy-MM-dd_HHmmss")
    End If

    Dim logFileName As String = $"{fileName}_{fileSuffix}.{fileExtension}"
    Dim targetFolder As String = folderName
    Dim targetPath As String = "Documents/Public"

    'Create folder if it does not exist
    Dim folderPath As XFFolderEx = BRApi.FileSystem.GetFolder(si, FileSystemLocation.ApplicationDatabase, targe
    If folderPath Is Nothing Then
        BRApi.FileSystem.CreateFullFolderPathIfNecessary(si, FileSystemLocation.ApplicationDatabase, targetPath,
    End If

    'Create File with logger contents and save in folder
    Dim targetDir As String = BRApi.FileSystem.GetFolder(si, FileSystemLocation.ApplicationDatabase, targetPath
    Dim dbFileInfo As New XFFileInfo(FileSystemLocation.ApplicationDatabase, logFileName, targetDir, XFFileType
    dbFileInfo.ContentFileContainsData = True
    dbFileInfo.ContentFileExtension = dbFileInfo.Extension
    Dim dbFile As New XFFile(dbFileInfo, String.Empty, System.Text.Encoding.UTF8.GetBytes(logger.ToString))
    BRApi.FileSystem.InsertOrUpdateFile(si, dbFile)

    Return dbFile.FileInfo.FullName

    Return "Bork"
End Function
```

Figure 10.35

There are several reasons why you should always purge your commented-out code once you're done with it:

1. At best, the commented-out code gets ignored, creating clutter and hiding the relevant, important code.

2. At worst, the commented-out code creates doubt and confusion around the existing code. Future developers (potentially *future you*) will always wonder if that old code is important; or they may even wonder if the commented-out code is actually correct, and if the active code is test code that never got commented-out and then forgotten. This is a waste of their time and potentially additional people's time if they stop development to hunt down the original developer to confirm their doubts.

3. If you're worried about preserving old versions of your code, let's emphasize that *commenting code is never an appropriate form of version control*. Ideally, you would use a version control like Git. Alternatively, you can save a backup locally, though this is a tad archaic. Finally, in the worst-case scenario, OneStream retains every version of each business rule in the audit tables, which you can access manually or via the business rule utility.

Leaving commented-out code is a bad habit stemming from a lack of confidence. You would be better served being confident in your code and confident in your ability to revert if your testing turns out to be flawed – believe in yourself!

Finally, we'll extend this concept by suggesting that not only should you purge out your own commented-out code, but you should also purge *any* block of commented-out code that you stumble across as you refactor. Chances are that it was an artifact left by another developer, while testing, that they've since forgotten about and will never access again. In fact, even if they did stumble upon it, they probably wouldn't remember what they were doing in the first place (I can speak from personal experience).

> **Note:** This section isn't to say that comments themselves are bad, only that blocking out large amounts of deprecated code is bad.

Update Comments

Remember that code is a living document, and its comments should always be kept up to date. Whenever you update code, make sure to read and update any corresponding comments. Failing to do so will lead to confusion and misinformation.

Just as many developers are afraid to delete old commented code, they are also afraid of incorrectly updating other developers' comments. However, as soon as you've made updates, the context of that code has already changed. In this case, leaving out-of-date comments is arguably worse than being a bit off with your new description.

Function Headers

There are different formats for these types of comments, but the idea is the same. Public functions and methods should all have header comments that describe what the method does, its parameters, and its return value.

```vbnet
Public Shared Sub AppendDBToLogger(ByVal api As FinanceRulesApi,
    ByRef buffer As DataBuffer, ByRef logger As System.Text.StringBuilder, Optional ByVal maxRows As Integer = 1000)

    ' Appends every row of databuffer to logger in place

    ' Parameters
    '   buffer: Data buffer to write to logger
    '   logger: string builder object with contents of log file
    '   maxRows: max number of rows to write from data buffer to log

    If buffer Is Nothing Then
        logger.AppendLine("Buffer is empty.")
        Exit Sub
    End If

    logger.AppendLine("Common Members: " & buffer.CommonDataBufferCellPk.CreateMemberScriptBuilder(api).GetMemberScript)

    For i = 0 To Math.Min(maxRows, buffer.DataBufferCells.Values.Count - 1)
        Dim cell As DataBufferCell = buffer.DataBufferCells.Values(i)

        Dim cellScript As String = cell.DataBufferCellPk.CreateMemberScriptBuilder(api).GetMemberScript

        logger.AppendLine($"{cellScript}, {cell.CellAmount}, {cell.CellStatus.ExistenceType.ToString}, {cell.CellStatus.StorageType.ToString}")
    Next

    If (buffer.DataBufferCells.Values.Count > maxRows) Then
        logger.AppendLine("... Maximum row display limit reached. Increase maxRows in AppendDBToLogger call.")
    End If

End Sub
```

Figure 10.36

In particular, in OneStream, a commonly recommended practice is to create a header for the `Main` function to list a couple of key pieces of information: the overall purpose of the business rule, what events trigger the business rule, metadata on who created the rule and when it was last updated, and finally a change log.

```vb
Public Class MainClass
    Dim logger As New Text.StringBuilder
    Const ENABLE_LOGGING As Boolean = True

    Public Function Main(ByVal si As SessionInfo, ByVal globals As BRGlobals, ByVal api As FinanceRulesApi, ByV
        ' Contains calculations for Actuals, specifically Cash Flow Calculations
        ' and reporting metrics.
        '
        ' Triggered by: Cash Flow Calculations triggered by Calculate Cash Flow button on Cash Flow dashboard.
        '               Reporting Calculations triggered on consolidation.
        '
        '
        ' Author:       Matthew Ha
        '
        ' Last Updated: 2023-12-15
        '
        ' Change Log
        ' 20220724:     Created business rule
        ' 20220815:     Fixed issue with cash flow calculation where certain rollforwards were not
        '               getting calculated.
        '
```

Figure 10.37

It should be noted that this function header isn't strictly the best practice. In an ideal world, change logs and metadata – like author and last updated date – would be handled in a version control system like Git. However, we realize that customers often lack a version control system, or have them but do not have the security controls in place to accommodate storing financially sensitive financial calculations in them. In lieu of this, storing this information here in the function header can act as a compromise. That said, it is important to keep these headers up to date, as discussed in the Update Comments section.

Code Smells and Heuristics

In programming, code smells are signs that there are deeper problems with your program. Often, these code smells are subjective since they're not strictly 'wrong' in the sense your code isn't compiling and because there are many ways to approach a problem when coding. They might be subtle or glaring. Regardless, code smells are still a good set of heuristics for you to evaluate if your code needs to be optimized or refactored. You should train yourself to always look for them, so that you can quickly pivot and refactor your code into better patterns.

Nested If Statements

If you have large numbers of nested `If` statements, following the logic flow becomes extremely difficult because – at each level – you have to remember the current state of the conditions leading to the current branch. The code is harder to parse visually as well due to the additional indentation levels. With that in mind, high nesting is a sign there is a logic flaw that needs to be addressed or simplified. Let's cover a couple of heuristics you can use to combat this issue.

Early Returns

This is an extremely common and effective pattern, and you should look to implement it wherever it makes sense. The Early Return pattern entails checking for exit conditions early, and not executing any code following the exit condition once it is met.

Oftentimes, this involves inverting some logic statement. So instead of saying "If X, do Y", you flip the logic to say, "If not X, do nothing. Otherwise, do Y."

For example, consider the following code:

```
' Only run calculation if current entity is a US entity
' Also only run for planned periods
If IsUSEntity(currEntity) Then
    If IsPlannedPeriod(currTime) Then
        CalculateStuff()

    End If
End If
```

Figure 10.38

We bracket `CalculateStuff()` in an `If` block for no real reason; since there is no `Else` statement, if the entity isn't a US entity we just do nothing. This code should really be refactored as follows:

```
' Only run calculation if current entity is a US entity and we're in a planned period
If Not (IsUSEntity(currEntity) And IsPlannedPeriod(currTime)) Then
    Return Nothing
End If

CalculateStuff()
```

Figure 10.39

This is better for two reasons.

1. Reading from top to bottom, the logic is easier to follow since I do not need to mentally keep track of the states of `currEntity` and `currTime`. I check for their states once at the beginning, and either end the execution or continue.

2. The meat of the code is no longer indented two additional levels!

Default Branches

Many `Else` statements are redundant and can be eliminated outright. For example, consider the following code. The `Else` really doesn't add any semantic or logical value.

```
If bonus <> 0 Then
    Return basePay + bonus

Else
    Return basePay

End If
```

Figure 10.40

Instead, it can be refactored without the `Else` entirely. The new code now reads like, "If you have a bonus, return the total comp as the sum of base pay and bonus; otherwise return only the base pay by default."

```
If bonus <> 0
    Return basePay + bonus

End If

Return basePay
```

Figure 10.41

211

Simplify and Abstract Conditions

Oftentimes, nested `If` statements are used in place of proper logical operators (AND, OR, NOT). The resulting code is messy and often results in duplicated code. Let's take a look at this case study in what not to do, and show how we might refactor it to be more readable.

```
' Nesting
If api.Pov.Scenario.Name.XFContainsIgnoreCase("Plan") Then
    If api.Pov.Time.Name.EndsWith("M3") Then
        If api.Time.GetPeriodNumFromId(api.Pov.Time.MemberId) < 6 Then
            Me.SeedActualsToPlan()
        End If

    Else If api.Pov.Time.Name.EndsWith("M6") Then
        If api.Time.GetPeriodNumFromId(api.Pov.Time.MemberId) < 6 Then
            Me.SeedActualsToPlan()
        End If

    Else If api.Pov.Time.Name.EndsWith("M9") Then
        If api.Time.GetPeriodNumFromId(api.Pov.Time.MemberId) < 6 Then
            Me.SeedActualsToPlan()
        End If

    Else If api.Pov.Time.Name.EndsWith("M12") Then
        If api.Time.GetPeriodNumFromId(api.Pov.Time.MemberId) < 6 Then
            Me.SeedActualsToPlan()
        End If

    End If
End If
```

Figure 10.42

Here are a few things we could do to improve this code.

1. First, we can abstract the conditional expressions into functions that express their intent better.

    a. Checking if the period is before M6 is really checking whether we are in a planned period or not.

    b. Checking the string to see if we end in 3, 6, 9, or 12 is really checking whether the active time is a quarter month.

    c. Checking if the active scenario contains Plan in the name is really checking whether we are in a planned scenario.

2. We can combine conditions using logical operators, to reduce nesting.

3. As a cherry on top, we can implement the Early Return pattern to reduce nesting further.

Let's see what the code looks like now! The logic is much easier to parse, and we now only need to reference SeedActualsToPlan once.

```
' Only execute rule for plan scenarios
If Not IsPlanScenario() Then
    Return Nothing
End If

' Execute seed for seeded quarter months
If IsQuarterMonth() And IsSeededPeriod() Then
    Me.SeedActualsToPlan()
End If
```

Figure 10.43

Duplicate Code

This is one of the most common code smells I see when maintaining and debugging code in OneStream. Often, duplicate code gets created when code is copied from one section to another, with only slight variations. If you see what looks like duplicate or repeating code, that is almost always a sign that you should be refactoring.

Iterate Using Data Structures

If you see the same pattern repeat multiple times, consider using some sort of loop structure instead. For example, let's look at this example:

```
' Email completed log file to users
EmailFile("john@gmail.com")
EmailFile("jane@gmail.com")
EmailFile("doe@gmail.com")
```

Figure 10.44

Notice that there is nothing different between these calls to `EmailFile` other than the passed email address. This would be better written like so:

```
' Email completed log file to users
Dim emailRecipients As New List(Of String) From {"john@gmail.com", "jane@gmail.com", "doe@gmail.com"}

For Each recipient As String In emailRecipients
    EmailFile(recipient)
Next
```

Figure 10.45

This conveys the intent of the code better, as it is more obvious that we're just calling the same code block, with the only thing changing between calls being the recipient. Also, the code is more scalable, as it's easier to modify the list of recipients.

Abstract Using Functions

In OneStream, calculations are often duplicated due to thoughtless copy/pasting. Rather than taking the time to generalize or extend the calculation, it's often tempting to take preexisting code, copy it, and modify variables as needed to replicate functionality. The solution here, instead, is to abstract the code into a function so it can be reused, and then reference that function. In the world of software engineering, this concept is known as "DRY", which stands for Don't Repeat Yourself.

For example, let's consider this example of an allocation calculation, which allocates to the base `U3` Products under `NAProducts`. The code was copied to extend the allocation to `EUProducts` as well.

```vb
Public Function CalcPlan(ByVal si As SessionInfo, ByVal globals As BRGlobals, ByVal api As FinanceRulesApi, ByVal args
    ' Spread corporate target across products based on their % of total revenue
    Dim resultBuffer As New DataBuffer()

    Dim parentMember As Member = api.Members.GetMember(DimTypeId.Account, "NAProducts")
    Dim baseMembers As List(Of Member) = api.Members.GetBaseMembers(api.Pov.UD3Dim.DimPk, parentMember.MemberId)

    Dim corpTarget As Decimal = api.Data.GetDataCell("A#CorporateTarget:U3#NAProducts").CellAmount
    Dim parentRevenue As Decimal = api.Data.GetDataCell("A#Revenue:U3#{parentMember.Name}").CellAmount

    For Each baseMember As Member In baseMembers
        Dim resultCell As New DataBufferCell
        resultCell.DataBufferCellPk.UD3Id = baseMember.MemberId

        Dim baseRevenue As Decimal = api.Data.GetDataCell("A#Revenue:U3#{baseMember.Name}").CellAmount

        Dim allocationPercent As Decimal = baseRevenue / parentRevenue

        resultCell.CellAmount = allocationPercent * corpTarget
        resultCell.CellStatus = New DataCellStatus(DataCellExistenceType.IsRealData, DataCellStorageType.Calculation)

        resultBuffer.SetCell(si, resultCell)
    Next

    Dim parentMember2 As Member = api.Members.GetMember(DimTypeId.Account, "EUProducts")
    Dim baseMembers2 As List(Of Member) = api.Members.GetBaseMembers(api.Pov.UD3Dim.DimPk, parentMember2.MemberId)

    Dim corpTarget2 As Decimal = api.Data.GetDataCell("A#CorporateTarget:U3#EUProducts").CellAmount
    Dim parentRevenue2 As Decimal = api.Data.GetDataCell($"A#Revenue:U3#{parentMember2.Name}").CellAmount

    For Each baseMember As Member In baseMembers2
        Dim resultCell As New DataBufferCell
        resultCell.DataBufferCellPk.UD3Id = baseMember.MemberId

        Dim baseRevenue As Decimal = api.Data.GetDataCell("A#Revenue:U3#{baseMember.Name}").CellAmount

        Dim allocationPercent As Decimal = baseRevenue / parentRevenue2

        resultCell.CellAmount = allocationPercent * corpTarget2
        resultCell.CellStatus = New DataCellStatus(DataCellExistenceType.IsRealData, DataCellStorageType.Calculation)

        resultBuffer.SetCell(si, resultCell)
    Next

    api.Data.SetDataBuffer(resultBuffer, api.Data.GetExpressionDestinationInfo(""))
End Function
```

Figure 10.46

The code is verbose and difficult to follow. Without reading line by line, it would be difficult to notice that the only real difference between the two blocks is that the U3 parent referenced is NAProducts in the first calculation, and EUProducts in the second calculation. Let's refactor this code so that the calculation is contained in a subroutine instead.

```
Public Function CalcPlan(ByVal si As SessionInfo, ByVal api As FinanceRulesApi) As Object
    ' Spread corporate target across products based on their % of total revenue
    Dim allocationBuffer As New DataBuffer

    Dim allocationProducts As New List(Of String) From {"NAProducts", "EUProducts"}

    For Each allocationProduct In allocationProducts
        AllocateProducts(si, api, allocationProduct, allocationBuffer)
    Next

    api.Data.SetDataBuffer(allocationBuffer, api.Data.GetExpressionDestinationInfo(""))
End Function

Private Function AllocateProducts(ByVal si As SessionInfo, ByRef api As FinanceRulesApi,
    ByVal allocationTarget As String, ByRef allocationBuffer As DataBuffer)

    ' First pull allocation amount which is planned corporate target
    Dim corpTarget As Decimal = api.Data.GetDataCell($"A#CorporateTarget:U3#{allocationTarget}").CellAmount

    ' Get parent product revenue
    Dim parentProduct As Member = api.Members.GetMember(DimTypeId.UD3, allocationTarget)
    Dim parentRevenue As Decimal = api.Data.GetDataCell($"A#Revenue:U3#{allocationTarget}").CellAmount

    ' Loop over base products, calculating allocation for each product
    Dim baseProducts As List(Of Member) = api.Members.GetBaseMembers(api.Pov.UD3Dim.DimPk, parentProduct.MemberId)

    For Each baseProduct As Member In baseProducts
        Dim allocationCell As New DataBufferCell
        allocationCell.DataBufferCellPk.UD3Id = baseProduct.MemberId

        Dim baseRevenue As Decimal = api.Data.GetDataCell("A#Revenue:U3#{baseMember.Name}").CellAmount

        Dim allocationPercent As Decimal = baseRevenue / parentRevenue

        allocationCell.CellAmount = allocationPercent * corpTarget
        allocationCell.CellStatus = New DataCellStatus(DataCellExistenceType.IsRealData, DataCellStorageType.Calculation)

        allocationBuffer.SetCell(si, allocationCell)
    Next
End Function
```

Figure 10.47

This is much better, let's cover what was changed:

1. The calculation logic is abstracted into the `AllocateProducts` function, so that you only need to pass in the product hierarchy which needs to be allocated. Arguably, this function still does a bit too much and should be broken down further, but this is sufficient for now.

2. The variable names in the `AllocateProducts` function have been given more meaningful names, so the logic is easier to track.

3. Finally, we loop over a list of products which contains both `NAProducts` and `EUProducts` and call `AllocateProducts` once for each. This conveys that the logic for the allocation is the same for both products.

Functions Should Do One Thing

If your function or sub is getting extremely long and doing too much, that's usually a sign that you need to refactor. In the words of Robert C. Martin in Clean Code, functions should "Do One Thing." Though the whole idea of "one" thing is a bit subjective and shouldn't be taken too literally, the idea is that you want to break up your functions so they each have a single responsibility.

Here are a couple of signs that your function is too complicated:

1. Too many lines: at a couple of dozen lines, I would start getting suspicious (though raw line number isn't always the best metric).

2. Complicated conditions: once your conditions start getting complicated and you have nesting three levels deep, or you notice three+ code branches, I would start looking into breaking up the function into sub-functions that each handle different groups of conditions.

3. Lots of paragraph breaks or regions: these usually indicate a logical grouping of code, and if you find that you are depending on them to break up your code, I will argue that these groupings should instead be broken out into separate functions.

Let's cover an example of a function that, while not overly long, is doing too many things.

```
Public Function PayEmployees() As Object
    For Each emp As Employee In employees
        If emp.IsPayday() Then
            Dim pay As Double = emp.CalculatePay()
            emp.DeliverPay(pay)
        End If
    Next
End Function
```

Figure 10.48

Really, this function is doing three things: it loops over all the employees, checks whether each employee should be paid, and then actually pays the employee. We can refactor this code by breaking it up like so:

```
Public Function PayEmployees() As Object
    For Each emp As Employee In employees
        PayIfNecessary(emp)
    Next
End Function

Private Function PayIfNecessary(ByRef emp As Employee) As Object
    If emp.IsPayDay() Then
        CalculateAndDeliverPay(emp)
    End If
End Function

Private Function CalculateAndDeliverPay(ByRef emp As Employee) As Object
    Dim pay As Double = emp.CalculatePay()
    emp.DeliverPay(pay)
End Function
```

Figure 10.49

In OneStream, it's common to have massive finance rule files with thousands of lines of calculations and business logic. These should be broken up into sub-calculation routines so that when updates must be made, they can be made into small manageable chunks; this applies to debugging as well.

Vertical Separation

As a general rule of thumb, variables and functions should be declared as close to where they are used as possible.

A common example of extreme vertical separation is the convention where all variables are declared at the top of a code block. This isn't strictly 'wrong' and comes from the desire to group things together (they are all variables, after all). However, it's more useful to group objects together that share a purpose, so you do not have to scroll around to figure out what a variable is or refactor if necessary.

```
        Public Function Main(ByVal si As SessionInfo, ByVal globals As BRGlobals, ByVal api As FinanceRule
            #Region "Declare all variables"
                Dim currTime As String = api.Pov.Time.Name
                Dim noInputAccountFilter As String = "A#NonCash.Base"
                Dim calcAccountFilter As String = "Cash.Base"
            #End Region

            Try
                Select Case api.FunctionType
                    Case Is = FinanceFunctionType.ConditionalInput
                        ' Prevent loads to non cash accounts
                        Dim noInputAccounts As List(Of Member) = api.Members.GetMembersUsingFilter(
                            api.Pov.AccountDim.DimPk, noInputAccountFilter)

                        If noInputAccounts.Contains(api.Pov.Account.Name) Then
                            Return ConditionalInputResultType.NoInput
                        End If

                        Return ConditionalInputResultType.Default

                    Case Is = FinanceFunctionType.Calculate
                        ' Calculate end balances
                        api.Data.Calculate("F#EndBal = F#BegBal + F#Activity", calcAccountFilter)

                End Select

                Return Nothing

            Catch ex As Exception
                Throw ErrorHandler.LogWrite(si, New XFException(si, ex))
            End Try

        End Function
```

Figure 10.50

It would be better to move the account filter declarations into the appropriate case blocks so that they live next to the code that references them. Also, while we're at it, we might as well refactor the code and create subfunctions so that the main function does not contain low-level implementation detail.

```
    Public Function Main(ByVal si As SessionInfo, ByVal globals As BRGlobals, ByVal api As FinanceRulesApi, ByVal args As Fi
        ' Declare shared variables
        Dim currTime As String = api.Pov.Time.Name

        Select Case api.FunctionType
            Case Is = FinanceFunctionType.ConditionalInput
                Return GetLockStatus(api, api.Pov.Account)

            Case Is = FinanceFunctionType.Calculate
                Me.CalcEndBal(api)

        End Select

        Return Nothing

    End Function

    Private Function GetLockStatus(ByVal api As FinanceRulesApi, ByVal account As Member) As ConditionalInputResultType
        ' Prevent loads to non cash accounts
        Dim noInputAccountFilter As String = "A#NonCash.Base"

        Dim noInputAccounts As List(Of Member) = api.Members.GetMembersUsingFilter(
            api.Pov.AccountDim.DimPk, noInputAccountFilter).Select(Function(x) x.Member)

        If noInputAccounts.Contains(api.Pov.Account) Then
            Return ConditionalInputResultType.NoInput
        End If

        Return ConditionalInputResultType.Default
    End Function

    Private Sub CalcEndBal(ByVal api As FinanceRulesApi)
        ' Calculate end balances
        Dim calcAccountFilter As String = "Cash.Base"

        api.Data.Calculate("F#EndBal = F#BegBal + F#Activity", calcAccountFilter)
    End Sub
```

Figure 10.51

Dead Code

Dead code is code that never gets reached or never gets called. There are many forms of this, but here are a couple of examples:

1. Deprecated variables that are no longer referenced. OneStream and most IDEs will warn you when compiling a rule with unreferenced variables.

2. Functions that are never called.

3. Code in conditional blocks where the condition is impossible.

   A common example of this is checking against some conditional variable, but there is nowhere in the code where that variable is ever modified. The code in the conditional block is not only pointless, it's misleading because it implies there are situations where you should do something when the state flag is tripped.

   Here, if nothing ever modifies the value of state, then we never get to the block of code with 'do something'. It's always dead code.

```
' Initialize state as true, and set as false
' when we find a product that shouldn't exist
Dim state As Boolean = True

' Add code here...

If Not state Then
    ' Do something

End If
```

Figure 10.52

Dead code should almost always be removed. Just like with commented-out code, they create clutter at best; at worst, they create confusion and slow development time.

Luckily, the first two examples are easy to address.

- When you compile a business rule and see warnings that variables are not referenced, simply go to those lines and jettison them!

- As for dead functions, when parsing through new business rules, the first thing I do is use an IDE or a simple find-all to see whether functions are being called at least once in the code. If not, then I will delete those unreferenced functions.

Over-abstraction

While under-abstraction and duplicate code are code smells that should be addressed, over-abstraction is also an issue. This is where coding becomes more of an art than a science, as the definition of "over-abstraction" is a hotly debated topic.

Over-abstraction can lead to complex and tightly coupled code, which means that making changes in one place requires you to make changes in many other places. As a general rule, if you are finding that when you are troubleshooting, you must constantly navigate through multiple layers of abstraction to get to the code to debug, that is usually a sign that you should refactor your code to reduce unnecessary abstraction.

Remember that abstraction should make code simpler and easier to read—you should strive to be deliberate about when you apply abstraction, as abstraction for abstraction's sake isn't necessarily good.

Syntax Tips

While there are many ways to get to the same result in VB.NET, there are certain patterns that you should seek to implement as they are easier to read and maintain; conversely, there are patterns that you should avoid as they create confusion and clutter.

String Interpolation

String interpolation is a feature in VB.NET (and many other programs) that lets you embed expressions into strings using the string interpolation operator ($). Overall, string interpolation is usually better than complex string concatenation with the concatenation character (&). Technically, you can also insert expressions into strings using the `String.Format()` method, but string interpolation is easier, faster, and nicer to read.

Here are two use cases for string interpolation:

1. Building file paths.

```
Dim fileName As String = "CaliforniaImport.csv"
Dim fileDirectory As String = "Groups/Everyone/ImportTemplates"

Dim filePath As String = $"{fileDirectory}/{fileName}"

' filePath resolves to
' ---> Groups/Everyone/ImportTemplates/CaliforniaImport.csv
```

Figure 10.53

2. Building member scripts in-line.

```
' This sample could be refactored to be cleaner using string interpolation
Dim priorYearAssets As DataBuffer = api.Data.GetDataBufferUsingFormula("" & _
    "FilterMembers(T#" & priorTime & ":V#YTD:" & sourceUDs & ", " & _
    accFilter & ", " & flowFilter & ")")

' Here's the nicer version, which is also less typo-prone
Dim priorYearAssets As DataBuffer = api.Data.GetDataBufferUsingFormula($"
    FilterMembers(T#{priorTime}:V#YTD:{sourceUDs},
    {accFilter}, {flowFilter})
")
```

Figure 10.54

> **Note:** Be extremely careful not to miss the string interpolation character! Without it, VB.NET won't perform the expression replacements, and just resolves the string literally 'as-is'. This is particularly important with Member Filters, like `A#{topAccount}.Base`. Without the $, OneStream will search for an account named `{topAccount}` and find nothing.

Multi-line Strings

VB.NET can support multi-line string literals as of 2015, so abuse it! This lets you avoid using large numbers of line continuation characters (_) just to make your string readable, or using workarounds like `Text.StringBuilder` objects, both of which create code that is hard to read and update.

A common use case for multi-line strings is dealing with large, embedded SQL queries. Let's first look at what *not* to do, and then follow it with why the multi-line approach is cleaner.

```vb
' Don't do this
Dim sql As String = "SELECT Employees.Id, Employees.FirstName, Employees.LastName, Salaries.Amount" & _
    " FROM Employees" & _
    " INNER JOIN Salaries ON Employees.Id = Salaries.EmployeeId " & _
    " WHERE Salaries.Amount > 50000 " & _
    " AND Employees.LastName LIKE 'j%'"

' Don't do this
Dim sql As Text.StringBuilder
sql.Append("SELECT Employees.Id, Employees.FirstName, Employees.LastName, Salaries.Amount")
sql.AppendLine(" FROM Employees")
sql.AppendLine(" INNER JOIN Salaries ON Employees.Id = Salaries.EmployeeId")
sql.AppendLine(" WHERE Salaries.Amount > 50000")
sql.AppendLine(" AND Employees.LastName LIKE 'j%'")
```

Figure 10.55

By using multi-line strings, you now have the ability to indent your query as you normally would in SQL, and even copy and paste it between editors without having to reformat every time. Much better!

```vb
' Do this!
Dim sql As String = "
    SELECT Employees.Id, Employees.FirstName, Employees.LastName, Salaries.Amount
    FROM Employees
    INNER Join Salaries On Employees.Id = Salaries.EmployeeId
    WHERE Salaries.Amount > 50000
      AND Employees.LastName Like 'j%'
"
```

Figure 10.56

Collection Initializers

You can create and populate collections using the `From` keyword followed by braces (`{ }`). This is easier to implement and read compared to initializing an empty collection and calling the `Add` method repeatedly. Let's look at two examples.

Initialize Lists

Let's look at this list:

```vb
Dim names As List(Of String)
names.Add("Kevin")
names.Add("Tom")
names.Add("Bob")
```

Figure 10.57

This code can be refactored like so. Both of these versions are acceptable, but the second version is better when the list of strings is extremely long and won't fit on a single line.

```vb
' Both of these are valid
Dim names As New List(Of String) From {"Kevin", "Tom", "Bob"}

Dim names As New List(Of String) From {
    "Kevin",
    "Tom",
    "Bob"
}
```

Figure 10.58

Initialize Dictionaries

Let's look at this dictionary, which can also be refactored using collection initializers:

```vb
Dim days As Dictionary(Of Integer, String)
days.Add(0, "Sunday")
days.Add(1, "Monday")
days.Add(2, "Tuesday")
days.Add(3, "Wednesday")
```

Figure 10.59

Again, we can refactor the code as follows. The syntax is slightly different than with the lists, as each element itself is a collection with its own brackets.

```vb
Dim days As New Dictionary(Of Integer, String) From {
    {0, "Sunday"}, {1, "Monday"},
    {2, "Tuesday"}, {3, "Wednesday"}
}
```

Figure 10.60

LINQ

LINQ stands for Language-Integrated Query; it is a feature that allows you to query from SQL Server databases or even local collections. You can think of LINQ as having the same sort of query capabilities as SQL, with similar syntax. For example, here we perform a full LINQ query on a list of customers.

```vb
' Obtain a list of customers.
Dim customers As List(Of Customer) = GetCustomers()

' Return customers that are grouped based on country.
Dim countries = From cust In customers
                Order By cust.Country, cust.City
                Group By CountryName = cust.Country
                Into CustomersInCountry = Group, Count()
                Order By CountryName

' Output the results.
For Each country In countries
    Debug.WriteLine(country.CountryName & " count=" & country.Count)

    For Each customer In country.CustomersInCountry
        Debug.WriteLine("    " & customer.CompanyName & "    " & customer.City)
    Next
Next

' Output:
'   Canada count=2
'       Contoso, Ltd  Halifax
'       Fabrikam, Inc.  Vancouver
'   United States count=1
'       Margie's Travel  Redmond
```

Figure 10.61

Something interesting, though, is that all enumerable objects in VB.NET – by default – have access to the **System.Linq enumerable static methods**, which include things like `Select()` and `Where()`. These methods behave as you would expect them to in SQL, which is useful when you want to either filter a set of objects by some condition, or grab only certain properties of a set of objects. These are just shorter, in-line alternatives to executing a 'full' LINQ query as shown in the example above.

LINQ Select

Let's cover an example of what a LINQ `Select` statement looks like:

```
Dim accountNames As List(Of String) = api.Members.GetBaseMembers(
    accDimPK, currAccID).Select(Function(item) item.Name).ToList()
```

Figure 10.62

There are a lot of elements here, so let's break them down one by one.

1. First, we grab the base members under our current account using `GetBaseMembers()`. This returns a `List(Of Member)`, which is an enumerable object. This means it has access to the `Select()` method.

2. We call the `Select()` method, and pass it a transform function which we use to map each item in the member list to the property we want. In this case, each item will be of type member, and we want the name of each member in our final list, so we extract it with `item.Name`.

3. The `Select` method returns an **IEnumerable** Collection, so we must cast the output to a list manually, otherwise we will get a runtime error because VB.NET will attempt and fail to cast the output to a `List(Of String)`.

After all of this, `accountNames` should consist of a list of the names of each member we got from the `GetBaseMembers()` call.

> **Note:** For the transfer function, `item` could be anything; we could have named it arbitrarily "x" and it would have been valid. Whatever we specify is just used as the variable pointing to each element of the collection you're looping through, similar to a `For...Each` loop.

LINQ Where

Let's cover an example of a LINQ `Where` statement, which is similar to a LINQ `Select` statement.

```
Dim baseAccs As List(Of Member) = api.Members.GetBaseMembers(
    accDimPK, currAccID).Where(Function(item) item.Name <> "Cash").ToList()
```

Figure 10.63

The difference here is that rather than passing in a transform function into the `Where()` method, we pass in what is known as a **predicate function**. This is a function that we use to test the condition we are filtering for. In this case, we want to keep only the members whose `Name` value does not equal `"Cash"`.

> **Note:** For more details on LINQ and the built-in enumerable query methods, refer to the Microsoft VB.NET Documentation pages.

Troubleshooting Business Rules

Common Business Rule Errors

Compilation Errors

Compilation errors are generated by the compiler before the code is executed, and generally refer to syntax errors. Here are the most common compilation errors and how to resolve them.

Casting Errors

VB.NET is generally surprisingly good about implicitly casting values upon assignment. In particular, most objects in VB.NET have robust ToString methods, so almost everything can be cast to a string object. For example, here, the integer `1234` is automatically cast to a string as it is assigned to the `str` variable.

```
Dim str As String = 1234
BRApi.ErrorLog.LogMessage(si, $"Str = {str}")
```

Description	Error Time
Str = 1234	12/15/2023

Figure 10.64

However, you will get a casting error when VB.NET does not have a built-in way to cast between objects of one class to another. This will typically happen when you are using custom classes. For example, here we get an error because our function expects the `inputArgs` parameter to be of type `FinanceRulesArgs`, but we pass in `args` which is declared as `ExtenderArgs`.

```
Public Function Main(ByVal si As SessionInfo, ByVal globals As BRGlobals, ByVal api As Object, ByVal args As ExtenderArgs) As Object
    PrintNVPairs(si, args)
    Function MainClass.PrintNVPairs(si As SessionInfo, inputArgs As FinanceRulesArgs) As Object

End Function
```

1) Error at line 24: Value of type 'ExtenderArgs' cannot be converted to 'FinanceRulesArgs'.

Figure 10.65

In this specific case, we can fix the error by updating the function definition so `inputArgs` is of type `ExtenderArgs`.

Scoping Errors

Without going into too much detail, scoping is the concept that variables are only accessible in the enclosing block they are declared in. If you try to access a variable outside the scope they exist in, VB.NET will throw an error and tell you that the variable has not been declared, which might seem confusing because you can see the declaration 'right there!' But really what it means is that the variable hasn't been declared within your current scope.

Consider the example below. Because we declare `amount` within the `If` block, as soon as the `If` block ends, the variable is no longer accessible.

```
If IsPrintEnabled Then
    Dim amount As Integer = 50
End If

BRApi.ErrorLog.LogMessage(si, amount)
```

→ 1) Error at line 121: 'amount' is not declared. It may be inaccessible due to its protection level.

Figure 10.66

To fix this, simply declare amount outside and right before the If block and initialize it with a default value. This way, amount is accessible from the outer block, and will always have a value even if the If block is never entered.

```
Dim amount As Integer = 0

If IsPrintEnabled Then
    amount = 50
End If

BRApi.ErrorLog.LogMessage(si, amount)
```

Figure 10.67

> **Note:** If you'd like to read up more on scoping as a concept, refer to the Microsoft VB.NET documentation.

Missing End Statement

Every control flow structure (e.g., If...Then...Else, For...Next, While...End While, etc.) is marked by starting and ending keywords. If you are missing an ending expression, you will receive a compilation error detailing which opening condition you need to close.

Error compiling Business Rule 'AdminGuideExamples'.

1) Error at line 129: 'If' must end with a matching 'End If'.

Figure 10.68

This is where, hopefully, you've been disciplined with your indentation; if you were, then finding the matching End If is as simple as going to line 129, hovering your cursor over the starting indentation of the If expression, and scrolling down until you find where the code jumps indentation incorrectly.

Runtime Errors

Object Reference Not Found

This error occurs at runtime when you attempt to access a property or method of a variable that is null. Typically, this happens when you assign a variable the output of a function, and the function on runtime returns nothing.

A common example of this in OneStream is in connectors when a SQL query returns no records. Here, if the ExecuteSql function returns no records, the queryRecords objects remain empty. If you then attempt to loop over the records, you will get the infamous "Object Reference Not Found" error.

```
' Execute query to pull records from database
Dim queryRecords As New DataTable

Using dbConn As DBConnInfo = BRApi.Database.CreateApplicationDbConnInfo(si)
    queryRecords = BRApi.Database.ExecuteSql(dbConn, sqlQuery.ToString, False)
End Using
```

Figure 10.69

To protect against situations like this, it's usually a good idea to implement checks to prevent the code from progressing unnecessarily on certain conditions. For example, here we can add a check to end the program execution if the query returns no records.

```
' Execute query to pull records from database
Dim queryRecords As New DataTable

Using dbConn As DBConnInfo = BRApi.Database.CreateApplicationDbConnInfo(si)
    queryRecords = BRApi.Database.ExecuteSql(dbConn, sqlQuery.ToString, False)

    If queryRecords Is Nothing OrElse queryRecords.Rows.Count = 0 Then
        Return Nothing
    End If
End Using
```

Figure 10.70

If you are already too late and you are troubleshooting this error, then your only option is to build out a logger to see at what point your program is failing, to narrow down which variable is coming back as null.

Invalid Script

This error occurs when you have specified an invalid member in a member script in an `api.Data.Calculate` call.

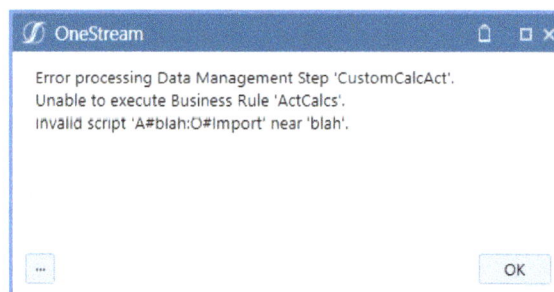

Figure 10.71

Usually, this means one of a couple of things:

1. The member does not exist.

2. You have a typo.

3. The member truly is invalid, which means you should check your cube dimensionality to see if you're choosing a member that exists at the wrong extensibility level.

Logging Techniques

The main method of troubleshooting and debugging business rules is building logs, especially since OneStream does not have a built-in debugger. Logs can then be displayed directly in the error logs, written to files in the FileShare, or even emailed to yourself.

This section will cover the syntax to build and create robust log files.

Building Your Log

Appending to Loggers

Generally, the traditional approach of logging in OneStream is to sprinkle in `BRApi.ErrorLog.LogMessage()` calls as needed. This is typically what is covered in business rules courses, and is what is shown in the admin training course.

```
Dim varA As String = "HELLO"
brapi.ErrorLog.LogMessage(Si, "Log Message Here = " & varA)
Dim varB As String = "World"
brapi.ErrorLog.LogMessage(Si, "Log Message Here = " & varB)
Dim varC As String = "Testing Writing Logs"
brapi.ErrorLog.LogMessage(Si, "Log Message Here = " & varC)
Dim varD As String = "Final Variable"
brapi.ErrorLog.LogMessage(Si, "Log Message Here = " & varD)
```

Figure 10.72

While this is fine for quick one-off logging, it quickly falls apart for any sort of complicated troubleshooting as you try to add log messages to different code branches. This is because each LogMessage call appears as a separate entry in the error log tables. If you add logging in loops, you could even flood your logs completely; finding any one specific log entry becomes almost impossible.

Description	Error Time	Error Level	User	Application	Tier	App Server
Log Message Here = Final Variable	11/16/2023 6:34:43 AM	Information	Admin	GolfStreamDemo_2022	App Server	RMTHO-D5172
Log Message Here = Testing Writing Logs	11/16/2023 6:34:43 AM	Information	Admin	GolfStreamDemo_2022	App Server	RMTHO-D5172
Log Message Here = World	11/16/2023 6:34:43 AM	Information	Admin	GolfStreamDemo_2022	App Server	RMTHO-D5172
Log Message Here = HELLO	11/16/2023 6:34:43 AM	Information	Admin	GolfStreamDemo_2022	App Server	RMTHO-D5172

Figure 10.73

The problem becomes even worse when you begin running data management sequences on multiple entities at once, as OneStream will create threads in parallel. Now, your logs will intertwine with each other in no guaranteed order – first thread in wins.

To solve these issues, a much better way to log is by creating a single `Text.StringBuilder` logger object; build your log by appending to that instead. Then, you write the contents of this logger to the error log a single time at the end of your code.

```
Dim logger As New System.Text.StringBuilder


Dim varA As String = "HELLO"
logger.AppendLine("Variable = " & varA)

Dim varB As String = "World"
logger.AppendLine("Variable = " & varB)

Dim varC As String = "Testing Writing Logs"
logger.AppendLine("Variable = " & varC)
logger.AppendLine("Aare we making it to this section of the rule???")
logger.AppendLine("Line 35")

Dim varD As String = "Final Variable"
logger.AppendLine("Variable = " & varD)

brapi.ErrorLog.LogMessage(si, logger.ToString)
```

Figure 10.74

As you can see, every time you would normally call LogMessage, you instead call the logger objects AppendLine() method and pass in your text as a string argument. Doing this gives you a log file that is much more user-friendly!

Description	Error Time	Error Level	User	Application	Tier	App Server
Variable = HELLO Variable = World Variable = Testing Writing Logs Aare we making it to this section of the rule??? Line 35 Variable = Final Variable	11/16/2023 6:47:54 AM	Information	Admin	GolfStreamDemo_2022	App Server	RMTHO-D5172
Log Message Here = Final Variable	11/16/2023 6:34:43 AM	Information	Admin	GolfStreamDemo_2022	App Server	RMTHO-D5172
Log Message Here = Testing Writing Logs	11/16/2023 6:34:43 AM	Information	Admin	GolfStreamDemo_2022	App Server	RMTHO-D5172
Log Message Here = World	11/16/2023 6:34:43 AM	Information	Admin	GolfStreamDemo_2022	App Server	RMTHO-D5172
Log Message Here = HELLO	11/16/2023 6:34:43 AM	Information	Admin	GolfStreamDemo_2022	App Server	RMTHO-D5172

Figure 10.75

If you were expecting to debug multiple entities, you could even start each log by adding details on the active entity, scenario, and time, so you can differentiate between each thread's execution in the error log later.

> **Note:** You must convert the logger object explicitly to a string using the ToString function when passing it into the LogMessage function, otherwise you will receive a casting error.

Logging List Contents

This section really defines how to log a list within your string of code. Let's create an example list of fruit and log out that list.

```
Dim myList As New List(Of String)({"Apple", "Banana", "Orange", "Kiwi", "Cherry", "Other"})
```

Figure 10.76

If you tried to log this list variable – as you normally would using the `LogMessage()` function – you would receive a compilation error.

```
brapi.ErrorLog.LogMessage("My List = "& mylist)
```

Figure 10.77

To resolve this, you can use the built-in `String.Join` function, which concatenates each element of a list together into a single string.

```
Brapi.Errorlog.Logmessage(Si, "List: " & String.Join("|",mylist))
```

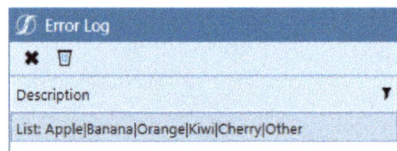

Figure 10.78

> **Tip:** Notice that the first argument into the `String.Join()` function is a delimiter. This could be any character we choose. In the example above, we chose a | character, but we could just as easily have chosen a comma.

Logging Dictionary Contents

Logging a dictionary is very similar to logging a list. However, while lists consist of items that are single objects, dictionaries consist of key-value pairs. Let's initialize a dictionary and cover how you would log both the keys and the values in a readable format.

```
Dim mydict As New Dictionary(Of String, String)
    Mydict.Add("Apple", "Green")
    Mydict.Add("Banana", "Yellow")
    Mydict.Add("Cherry", "Red")
```

Figure 10.79

The main idea here is that you can log the dictionary values and keys separately by using the values and keys properties of a dictionary object. Both of these properties return enumerable objects, which can be passed to the `String.Join()` method just like lists.

```
Brapi.Errorlog.LogMessage(si, "DictValues: " & String.join("|", mydict.Values))
Brapi.Errorlog.LogMessage(si, "DictKeys: " & String.join("|", mydict.Keys))
```

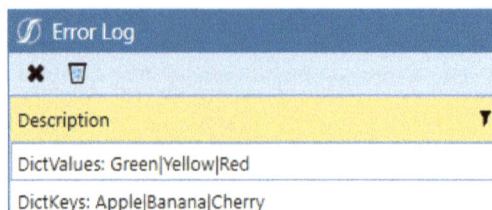

Figure 10.80

Serializing Objects

Oftentimes, you'll have objects that contain many properties. Instead of individually logging each property one by one, which would be incredibly tedious, you can instead "serialize" the object, converting the object to a string in JSON format.

To do this, you can import the `Newtonsoft.Json` and `Newtonsoft.Json.Linq` namespaces, and use the `JsonConvert.SerializeObject()` function.

```vb
Imports Newtonsoft.Json
Imports Newtonsoft.Json.Linq

Namespace OneStream.BusinessRule.Extender.z_Test_MH
    Public Class MainClass
        Public Function Main(ByVal si As SessionInfo, ByVal globals As BRGlobals, ByVal api As Object, ByVal args As ExtenderArgs) As Object

            Dim wfInitInfo As WorkflowInitInfo = BRApi.Workflow.General.GetUserWorkflowInitInfo(si)
            Dim stringifiedObj As String = JsonConvert.SerializeObject(wfInitInfo, Formatting.Indented)

            BRApi.ErrorLog.LogMessage(si, stringifiedObj)
```

Figure 10.81

The resulting string is where each property is listed next to its value. This is particularly useful when debugging when you are trying to figure out what an object contains.

```json
"WorkflowViewItems": [
  {
    "WorkflowUnitInfo": {
      "ProfileName": "Corporate Cash Flow",
      "ScenarioName": "BSCFCAPEXTest_ProfitPlan2023Q2",
      "TimeName": "2023Q2",
      "WorkflowName": "Process, Certify",
      "WfUnitPk": {
        "ProfileKey": "86ffd77b-6ea9-4ac4-b4c1-4991eca874bb",
        "ScenarioKey": 1048878,
        "TimeKey": 2023006000,
        "WorkflowKey": "cc70bb7b-844e-486e-a67a-3c22c1584a0f"
      }
    },
    "WorkflowUnitTimeInfo": {
      "InputFrequenciesByYear": {
        "-1": 0,
```

Figure 10.82

Writing Logs to ErrorLog

To write logs to the `ErrorLog`, use the `BRApi.ErrorLog.LogMessage()` function. This will create an Information entry in the error log.

```vb
Public Function PrintLog(ByVal si As SessionInfo) As Object
    BRApi.ErrorLog.LogMessage(si, "Hello world!")

    Return Nothing
End Function
```

Description	Error Time	Error Level	User	Application
Hello world!	12/16/2023 3:4	Information	Administrator	Sandbox

Figure 10.83

If you are in a finance rule, the finance API provides you with a nice shortcut via the `api.LogMessage()`.

In fact, this is actually recommended whenever possible, as the `api.LogMessage` function is slightly more performant than `BRApi.ErrorLog.LogMessage()`; this is because the BRApi version creates a new connection to the log database on every execution.

```
api.LogMessage("Hello world!")
```

Figure 10.84

Writing Logs to FileShare

This code will allow you to write logs to the FileShare as a file. Here are a couple of notes about the current implementation:

- It assumes that you are building a `Text.String` builder logger as recommended in the previous sections.

- If an execution tries to write to a file that already exists, it will append the logger to the end of the file.

```vb
Public Shared Function WriteLoggerToFileShare(
    ByVal si As SessionInfo, ByVal api As Object,
    ByRef logger As System.Text.StringBuilder,
    Optional ByVal fileName As String = "LOG",
    Optional ByVal fileSuffix As String = Nothing,
    Optional ByVal targetFolder As String = "TestLogs") As String

    ' Append logger to text file in Groups\Administrators directory
    '
    ' Parameters
    '    logger: string builder object with contents of log file
    '    fileName: optional log file name. defaults to LOG
    '    fileSuffix: optional log file suffix. defaults to system time
    '    targetFolder: optional log folder destination. defaults to TestLogs
    '
    ' Returns
    '    filepath of log file

    If fileSuffix Is Nothing Then
        fileSuffix = DateTime.Now.ToString("yyyy-MM-dd-HH")
    End If

    Dim logFileName As String = fileName & "_" & fileSuffix & ".txt"
    Dim folderPath As String = BRApi.Utilities.GetFileShareFolder(si,
FileShareFolderTypes.ApplicationRoot, Nothing) & "\" & si.AppName.ToString &
"\Groups\Administrators\" & targetFolder

    Dim targetPath As String = $"{folderPath}\{logFileName}"

    If Not system.IO.File.Exists(targetPath) Then
        'Create network file
        System.IO.File.Create(targetPath).Close
    End If

    'Write logger to file
    File.AppendAllText(targetPath, logger.ToString)

    Return targetPath
End Function
```

Figure 10.85

Calling this code will result in a file being placed in the Groups/Administrators FileShare directory in the TestLogs folder by default, or the passed target Folder.

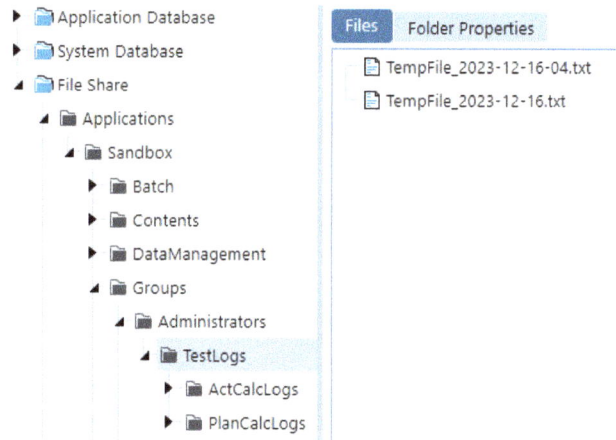

Figure 10.86

Muti-threaded Logging

This is a fairly advanced concept, but recall that when you run data management sequences on multiple entities at once, OneStream will create multiple threads in parallel. In this situation, the code for writing logs to the FileShare in the previous section will fail, as multiple threads won't be able to access the same file simultaneously.

To address this issue, here is a slightly more complicated version of the logging code that accounts for multi-threaded execution. Otherwise, the function can be used in exactly the same way. Here are a couple of important notes:

- You must import the System.Threading library at the top of whatever file contains this function.

- You must declare the shared locker variable in the same scope as the AsyncAppendToFile function.

As one final recommendation, because we've discussed so much on abstraction, rather than copying the code directly into every business rule, instead copy the code to a shared global business rule. Then, that global rule can be imported into each finance rule as necessary, and the AsyncAppendToFile function called from that context.

```vb
Imports System.Threading

...

Shared Dim locker As New ReaderWriterLock()

Public Shared Function AsyncAppendToFile(
    ByVal si As SessionInfo, ByVal api As Object,
    ByRef logger As System.Text.StringBuilder,
    Optional ByVal fileName As String = "LOG",
    Optional ByVal fileSuffix As String = Nothing,
    Optional ByVal targetFolder As String = "TestLogs",
    Optional ByVal timeoutInMS As Integer = 30000) As String

    ' Append logger to text file in Groups\Administrators directory using
multi-threading.
    ' Note: this logger handles multi-threading for a given user. if two users
attempt to write to
    ' the same file simultaneously, then the function errors.
    '
    ' Parameters
    '   logger: string builder object with contents of log file
    '   fileName: optional log file name. defaults to LOG
    '   fileSuffix: optional log file suffix. defaults to system time in yyyy-
MM-dd_HH format
    '   targetFolder: optional log folder destination. defaults to TestLogs
    '   timeoutInMS: how long to wait for previous thread to release file
before continuing
    '
    ' Returns
    '   filepath of log file

    If fileSuffix Is Nothing Then
        Dim logTime As String = DateTime.Now.ToString("yyyy-MM-dd-HH")
        Dim logUser As String = si.UserName.Split(" ")(0)

        fileSuffix = $"{logTime}_{logUser}"
    End If

    Dim logFileName As String = $"{fileName}_{fileSuffix}.txt"

    Dim folderPath As String = BRApi.Utilities.GetFileShareFolder(si,
FileShareFolderTypes.ApplicationRoot, Nothing) & "\" & si.AppName.ToString &
"\Groups\Administrators\" & targetFolder
    Dim targetPath As String = $"{folderPath}\{logFileName}"

    ' Obtain lock, then append text to file (creating file if it doesn't
exist)
    ' Then release lock for next thread
    Try
        locker.AcquireWriterLock(timeoutInMS)

        If locker.IsWriterLockHeld Then
            If Not System.IO.Directory.Exists(folderPath) Then
                System.IO.Directory.CreateDirectory(folderPath)
            End If

            If Not System.IO.File.Exists(targetPath) Then
                System.IO.File.Create(targetPath).Close
            End If

            System.IO.File.AppendAllText(targetPath, logger.ToString)
        End If
    Catch ex As ApplicationException
        Throw New Exception($"Error in AsyncAppendToFile: Thread timed out as
previous thread took too long to write to file. Increase method timeout.")

    Finally
        If locker.IsWriterLockHeld Then
            locker.ReleaseWriterLock()
        End If
    End Try

    Return targetPath
End Function
```

Figure 10.87

Emailing Logs

Here is a function I wrote that allows you to email a log file on the FileShare to yourself or your fellow admins. To use this file, there are a few pre-requisite configuration steps:

- You must import the `System.IO.Compression` library at the top of the file containing this function.

- The following `dll`s must be added to the Referenced Assemblies field of the business rule:
  `C:\Windows\Microsoft.NET\Framework64\v4.0.30319\System.IO.Compression.dll`;
  `C:\Windows\Microsoft.NET\Framework64\v4.0.30319\System.IO.Compression.FileSystem.dll`

	Properties	Formula	
⊟ General			
	Name		MattGlobalHelperLibrary
	Type		Finance
	Language Type		Visual Basic
	Contains Global Functions For Formulas		False
	Referenced Assemblies		C:\Windows\Microsoft.NET\Framework64\v4.0.30319\System.IO.Compression.dll; C:\Windows\Micrc
	Is Encrypted		False

Figure 10.88

Here is the code itself:

```vb
Imports System.IO.Compression

...

Public Shared Function EmailLogFile(ByVal si As SessionInfo, ByVal recipientList As
List(Of String), ByVal logFileName As String, ByVal logFolder As String)
    ' Parameters:
    ' recipientList:    list of email address (e.g., bob@onestream.com)
    ' logFileName:      use as header
    ' logFolder:        folder path with respect to Groups\Administrators (e.g.,
'TestLogs\CalcLogs')

    ' First zip log file
    Dim zipFolderPath As String = $"{BRApi.Utilities.GetFileShareFolder(si,
FileShareFolderTypes.ApplicationRoot,
Nothing)}\{si.AppName.ToString}\Groups\Administrators\{logFolder}"

    Dim originalFilePath As String = $"{zipFolderPath}\{logFileName}"
    Dim zipFilePath As String =
originalFilePath.Replace(Path.GetExtension(logFileName), ".zip")

    Using fs As New FileStream(zipFilePath, FileMode.Create)
        Using arch As New ZipArchive(fs, ZipArchiveMode.Create)
            arch.CreateEntryFromFile(originalFilePath, logFileName)
        End Using
    End Using

    ' Then send email with zipped log file attached
    Dim attachments As New List(Of String) From {zipFilePath}
    BRApi.Utilities.SendMail(si, "OneStreamEmail", recipientList, logFileName, "Log
file attached here.", attachments)

    Return Nothing
End Function
```

Technical References

Member Filter Syntax

Member Filter syntax in OneStream is sometimes hard to remember. In particular, you must be very careful with whitespace and the use of brackets. To save you the trouble, we've tested every permutation for Member Filters and compiled our results in this section.

Member Filters as Arguments

Many finance API functions such as `api.Data.ClearCalculatedData`, `api.Data.Calculate`, and `api.Members.GetMembersUsingFilter` all allow you to pass Member Filters as arguments.

```
⊕ Sub DataApi.Calculate(formula As String, Optional accountFilter As String, Optional flowFilter As String, Optional originFilter As String,
  Optional icFilter As String, Optional ud1Filter As String, Optional ud2Filter As String, Optional ud3Filter As String, Optional ud4Filter As String,
  Optional ud5Filter As String, Optional ud6Filter As String, Optional ud7Filter As String, Optional ud8Filter As String, Optional onEvalDataBuffer As
  EvalDataBufferDelegate, Optional userState As Object, Optional isDurableCalculatedData As Boolean)
```

Figure 10.89

Here are the rules when passing in filter strings as arguments:

- OneStream will ignore any statement surrounded by brackets, and any subsequent statement is guaranteed to also fail.

- It is counterintuitive, but if the first statement has no brackets, that filter will succeed. Subsequent filters that are surrounded by brackets will fail as usual.

- Brackets must be used to surround string literals with spaces.
  For example, (Text1 StartsWith [Corporate Account]).

For your convenience, here are some sample examples:

Example	Result
`api.Data.Calculate("A#Revenue = A#Revenue:T#PovPrior1",,,,,, "U2#TotalProd.Base.Where(Text1 = CatA), U2#TotalProd.Base, ,,,,,,,,,True)`	Succeeds
`api.Data.Calculate("A#Revenue = A#Revenue:T#PovPrior1",,,,,, "U2#Vehicles.Base, [U2#TotalProd.Base.Where(Text1 = CatB)]", ,,,,,,,,,True)`	OneStream will successfully process Vehicles.Base, but the second filter will fail
`api.Data.Calculate("A#Revenue = A#Revenue:T#PovPrior1",,,,,, "[U2#TotalProd.Base], [U2#TotalProd.Base.Where(Text1 = CatB)]", ,,,,,,,,,True)`	Fails quietly

Figure 10.90

> **Note:** Technically, OneStream will not throw an error when the bracket syntax is incorrect. What is happening is that OneStream applies the filter and returns no records, and just continues quietly. This makes it seem as if OneStream has done nothing.

Member Filters in FilterMembers Function

Functions that process data buffers in the background, such as `api.Data.Calculate` and `api.Data.GetDataBufferUsingFormula`, will allow you to use the `FilterMembers` function to filter the source data buffers. The syntax when doing this is slightly different compared to passing arguments directly in the overall function call.

Here are the rules when passing filters as arguments in the `FilterMembers` function:

- OneStream will evaluate any statement surrounded by brackets, but it is not technically necessary if the statement does not have a member expansion function.

- If a statement has a member expansion function (e.g., `Where`), this statement must be surrounded by brackets or OneStream will throw an error saying it is expecting a comma.

- When passing UD Member Filters, you can wrap each item in a bracket individually or together; it doesn't matter which.

  For example, `[U3#CC01, U3#CC02]` and `[U3#CC01], [U3#CC02]` are both valid.

For your convenience, here are some sample examples:

Example	Result

`api.Data.GetDataBufferUsingFormula("FilterMembers(`
`    A#Revenue:T#PovPrior1:O#Top:F#EndBal:U1#Northropp,`
`    [U2#TotalProd.Base.Where(Text1 = 'CatA')],`
`[U2#TotalProd.Base])")`
	Succeeds

`api.Data.GetDataBufferUsingFormula("FilterMembers(`
`    A#Revenue:T#PovPrior1:O#Top:F#EndBal:U1#Northropp,`
`    U2#Vehicles.Base, [U2#TotalProd.Base.Where(Text1 = 'CatB')])")`
	Succeeds

`api.Data.GetDataBufferUsingFormula("FilterMembers(`
`    A#Revenue:T#PovPrior1:O#Top:F#EndBal:U1#Northropp,`
`    U2#Vehicles.Base, U2#TotalProd.Base.Where(Text1 = 'CatB'))")`
	Fails at runtime with invalid script error

Figure 10.91

Business Rule Shared Constants

Many functions in OneStream will require you to pass some sort of integer ID as an argument, but when you're just starting out in OneStream, it's often unclear where to get these values. For example, consider the following method – even knowing that you are looking for a member with the Account DimType, where would you even begin to look for that pesky ID?

`api.Members.GetMember(dimTypeID As Integer, dimName As String, memberName As String)`

Fortunately, the majority of these commonly accessed constants are contained within classes and enumerations under the `OneStream.Shared` namespace, which itself is divided into four sub-namespaces. These will always be imported for you by default at the top of every business rule, and so you can use IntelliSense (ctrl + space) to open up a dialog box and scan through the constants available to you.

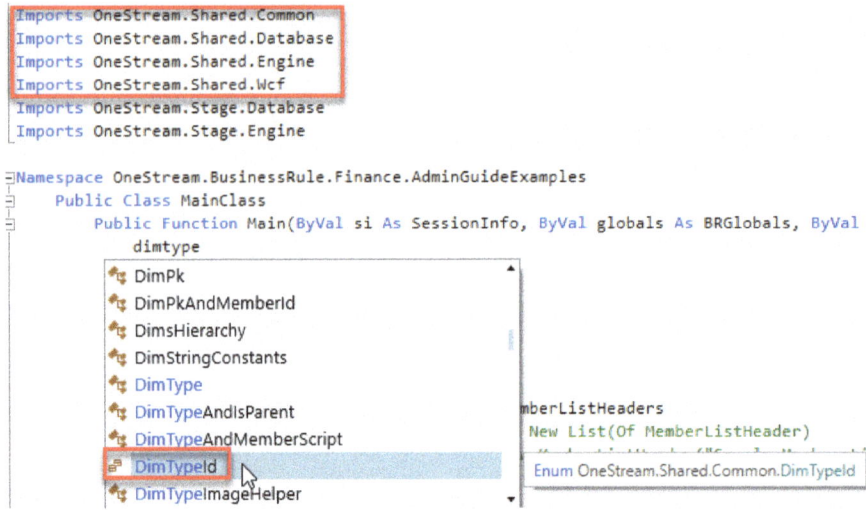

Figure 10.92

Common Constants

For your convenience, here is a table listing the most commonly used constants:

Enum/Class	Members	
AccountTypeId	Member	Value
	Asset	3
	Balance	6
	BalanceRecurring	7
	DynamicCalc	9
	Expense	2
	Flow	5
	Group	0
	Liability	4
	NonFinancial	8
	Revenue	1
	Unknown	-1
CalcStatusId	Member	Value
	NeedsCalcAndConsol	7
	NeedsCalcAndTrans	6
	NeedsCalcTransAndConsol	9
	NeedsCalculation	3
	NeedsConsolidation	5
	NeedsTransAndConsol	8
	NeedsTranslation	4
	NoActivity	0
	OK	1
	OKButMetadataChanged	2
	Unknown	-1

Enum/Class	Members
ConsMemberId	**Member** / **Value** **Currencies** -10 **Elimination** -12 **Local** -16 **OwnerPostAdj** -11 **OwnerPreAdj** -14 **Share** -13 **Top** -100 **Translated** -15 **Unknown** -1
CurrencyId	**Member** Value **AED** 0 **AFN** 1 **ALL** 2 **AMD** 3
ScenarioTypeId	**Member** Value **Actual** 0 **Administration** 10 **All** -5 **Budget** 1 **Control** 11 **Flash** 2 **Forecast** 3 **FXModel** 4
SharedConstants.Work flowProfileAttribute Indexes	JournalTemplateProfile LimitToDefaults NamedDependents ProcessCubeDashboardProfile ProfileDescription Text1 Text2 Text3 Text4 TransformationProfile UseDetailedLogging ValidateDashboardProfile Workflow WorkflowChannel WorkflowExecutionGroup WorkspaceDashboardWorkflow

Enum/Class	Members
DimTypeId	<table><tr><th>Member</th><th>Value</th></tr><tr><td>Account</td><td>5</td></tr><tr><td>Consolidation</td><td>1</td></tr><tr><td>Entity</td><td>0</td></tr><tr><td>Flow</td><td>6</td></tr><tr><td>IC</td><td>8</td></tr><tr><td>Origin</td><td>7</td></tr><tr><td>Scenario</td><td>2</td></tr><tr><td>Time</td><td>3</td></tr><tr><td>UD1</td><td>9</td></tr><tr><td>UD2</td><td>10</td></tr></table>
DimConstants	☐ AdjConsolidated ☐ AdjInput ☐ Adjustments ☐ Aggregated ☐ All ☐ Analysis ☐ BeforeAdj ☐ BeforeElim ☐ Common

Figure 10.93

These are just a few of the enumerations available to you; for a full list, refer to the OneStream API Details and Documentation.

Use Case 1: Function Arguments

In general, whenever a method calls for some sort of ID as a parameter, it's a good first step to see if there is an Enum that exactly matches the name of the parameter (e.g., DimTypeId from our earlier example). Surprisingly, the majority of the time you'll find that there is a constant that will exactly fit the bill!

```
' Get Member requires an integer DimTypeID as its first parameter
Return api.Members.GetMember(DimTypeID.Account, "Accounts_Actual", "Cash")
    ⊕  Function IMembersApi.GetMember(dimTypeId As Integer, dimName As String, memberName As String) As Member
```

Figure 10.94

Use Case 2: Comparisons using Constants

Whenever possible, it's better to write comparison expressions using these constants. The resulting code is less error prone and is more readable.

```
' Don't do this.
If api.Pov.ScenarioType.Name = "Actual" Then
    Return Nothing
End If


' Do this instead!
If api.Pov.ScenarioType = ScenarioType.Actual Then
    Return Nothing
End If
```

Figure 10.95

> **Tip:** In general, it's good practice to avoid hardcoding strings and doing string comparisons. A really common example of this is looking for string patterns in scenario names, which almost always ends up causing problems down the road when someone makes a typo or renames a scenario. Doing type comparisons with enumerations is much more robust.

Use Case 3: Joining to Database Tables

In the backend tables, OneStream typically stores the IDs of objects. However, some of these IDs are not stored in any tables, so you cannot perform any SQL joins to get the names of these members. The consolidation ID field (`ConsID`) is an example of this.

PartitionId	CubeId	EntityId	ParentId	ConsId	ScenarioId	YearId	AccountId	FlowId	OriginId	ICId	UD1Id	UD2Id	UD34Id	UD56Id	UD78Id	UD3Id
2	0	4194306	-1	176	5242880	2019	7340032	-999	-999	-999	8388608	9437184	-4290660794367	-4286377362407	-4290655551487	115343
2	0	4194306	-1	176	5242880	2019	7340032	10485760	-999	-999	8388608	9437184	-4290660794367	-4286377362407	-4286377362407	115343
2	0	4194306	-1	176	5242880	2019	7340033	-999	-999	-999	8388608	9437184	-4290660794367	-4286377362407	-4290655551487	115343
2	0	4194306	-1	176	5242880	2019	7340033	10485760	-999	-999	8388608	9437184	-4290660794367	-4286377362407	-4286377362407	115343

Figure 10.96

If you wanted to format this in a report that shows the actual currency names, you would have to query the database using a business rule and then map the currency IDs to their respective names via the `CurrencyID` enumeration.

Cell Status Table

Each data record in the application database has 12 YTD values, one for each month, and corresponding cell status codes. This is the same information that is shown to you when you right-click a cell to view its cell status.

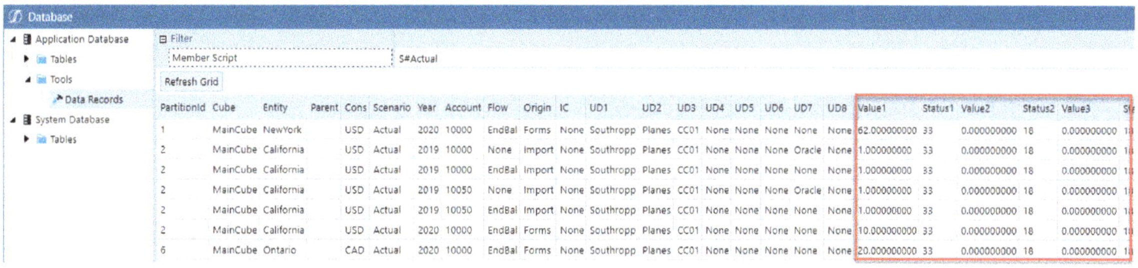

PartitionId	Cube	Entity	Parent	Cons	Scenario	Year	Account	Flow	Origin	IC	UD1	UD2	UD3	UD4	UD5	UD6	UD7	UD8	Value1	Status1	Value2	Status2	Value3
1	MainCube	NewYork		USD	Actual	2020	10000	EndBal	Forms	None	Southropp	Planes	CC01	None	None	None	None	None	62.000000000	33	0.000000000	18	0.000000000
2	MainCube	California		USD	Actual	2019	10000	None	Import	None	Southropp	Planes	CC01	None	None	None	Oracle	None	1.000000000	33	0.000000000	18	0.000000000
2	MainCube	California		USD	Actual	2019	10000	EndBal	Import	None	Southropp	Planes	CC01	None	None	None	None	None	1.000000000	33	0.000000000	18	0.000000000
2	MainCube	California		USD	Actual	2019	10050	None	Import	None	Southropp	Planes	CC01	None	None	None	Oracle	None	1.000000000	33	0.000000000	18	0.000000000
2	MainCube	California		USD	Actual	2019	10050	EndBal	Import	None	Southropp	Planes	CC01	None	None	None	None	None	1.000000000	33	0.000000000	18	0.000000000
2	MainCube	California		USD	Actual	2020	10000	EndBal	Forms	None	Southropp	Planes	CC01	None	None	None	None	None	10.000000000	33	0.000000000	18	0.000000000
6	MainCube	Ontario		CAD	Actual	2020	10000	EndBal	Forms	None	Southropp	Planes	CC01	None	None	None	None	None	20.000000000	33	0.000000000	18	0.000000000

Figure 10.97

For your reference, here is a chart listing what each of these status codes represent.

Data Record Status Fields		
Status (Stored Int)	**Existence Type**	**Storage Type**
16	NoData	StoredButNoActivity
18	IsDerivedData	StoredButNoActivity
32	NoData	Input
33	IsRealData	Input
34	IsDerivedData	Input
37	IsDerivedData	StoredButNoActivity
48	NoData	Journals
49	IsRealData	Journals
50	IsDerivedData	Journals
64	NoData	Calculation
65	IsRealData	Calculation
66	IsDerivedData	Calculation
80	NoData	Translation
81	IsRealData	Translation
82	IsDerivedData	Translation
96	NoData	Consolidation
97	IsRealData	Consolidation
98	IsDerivedData	Consolidation
113	IsRealData	DataCellDetail
144	NoData	DurableCalculation
145	IsRealData	DurableCalculation
146	IsDerivedData	DurableCalculation

Figure 10.98

Derived Cell Status

Let's discuss what the default cell status is, and how cell status changes when data is written. If you load data to period N (where N is an int from 1-12), two things will happen:

1. Prior periods <N will get updated with cell amount = 0 and cell status = 16 (NoData and storage type = StoredButNoActivity)

2. Future periods >N will get updated with derived cell amount = 0 and with cell status = 18 (IsDerivedData and storage type = StoredButNoActivity).

These derived values are actually calculated and stored in the database for quick retrieval during reporting.

A subtle detail is that the derived 0 amount might be placed in either the YTD or the periodic view, based on the No Data Zero View for NonAdjustments setting on your scenario. If you put YTD, the system will assume the next period's YTD amount is 0. If you put periodic, the system assumes the next period's MTD amount is 0. This mainly affects PNL accounts which are handled as periodic, since BS accounts treat MTD and YTD as the same.

Filtering by Cell Status

Understanding how OneStream uses cell status is important because it helps you understand how OneStream filters when performing various operations. Here are two examples of this:

- When you call api.Data.ClearCalculatedData, what the finance engine is really doing behind the scenes is filtering for all data in your Data Unit that has storage type Calculation (and DurableCalculation if you've specified to also clear Durable).

- When you grab a data buffer using api.Data.GetDataBufferUsingFormula, the finance engine will actually include NoData cells with the status of StoredButNoActivity by default. You'd have to use the Member Filter function RemoveNoData to get rid of these.

Microsoft VB.NET Documentation

If you are new to VB.NET, it can be intimidating sorting through the swathe of available resources via Google. These are the official Microsoft VB.NET documentation sites, which I often refer to myself when writing business rules.

Use the .NET API to look at available modules and methods. The Language Reference offers explanations on VB.NET syntax. Finally, the Language Features pages explain core concepts of the language.

- Home page: https://docs.microsoft.com/en-us/dotnet/
- Language Reference: https://docs.microsoft.com/en-us/dotnet/visual-basic/language-reference/
- Language Features: https://docs.microsoft.com/en-us/dotnet/visual-basic/programming-guide/language-features/
- .NET Standard Guide: https://docs.microsoft.com/en-us/dotnet/standard/
- .NET Framework Guide: https://docs.microsoft.com/en-us/dotnet/framework/
- .NET API: https://docs.microsoft.com/en-us/dotnet/api/?view=netframework-4.8

OneStream API Details and Documentation

This provides documentation on the namespaces of the OneStream API. This is useful for figuring out the methods available for each engine, and also for seeing the available enumerations you can reference in business rules.

You can find the API in the `Documentation` directory of any OneStream installation package (though you do have to dig a bit). For example, for version 6.6.0, the API can be found at:
`OneStream_6.6.0/OneStream_Doc_On_Prem_6.6.0/Documentation/OneStreamAPIDetails`
`AndDocumentation_6.6.0.zip`

Recommended Reading

These are not OneStream official endorsements, but two books that are well-regarded in the programming space that I also personally recommend to everyone, regardless of whether you are new to your programming journey or already a seasoned veteran.

- Clean Code: A Handbook of Agile Software Craftmanship by Robert C. Martin
- The Art of Clean Code by C. Mayer

Of course, some of the rules proposed are subjective, just as some of the rules in this chapter are subjective. The key is to focus not on following each rule to the extreme, but keeping in mind the general principles of writing clean code, which is to make code as readable as possible.

Useful Tools

Snippets

The **Snippets Marketplace Solution** contains sample code for many common business rule patterns in OneStream. For example, there are snippets for querying databases, creating files in the FileShare, and automating workflows. It's a good idea to skim through the available snippets, as they'll save you a lot of time in the long run – no need to reinvent the wheel!

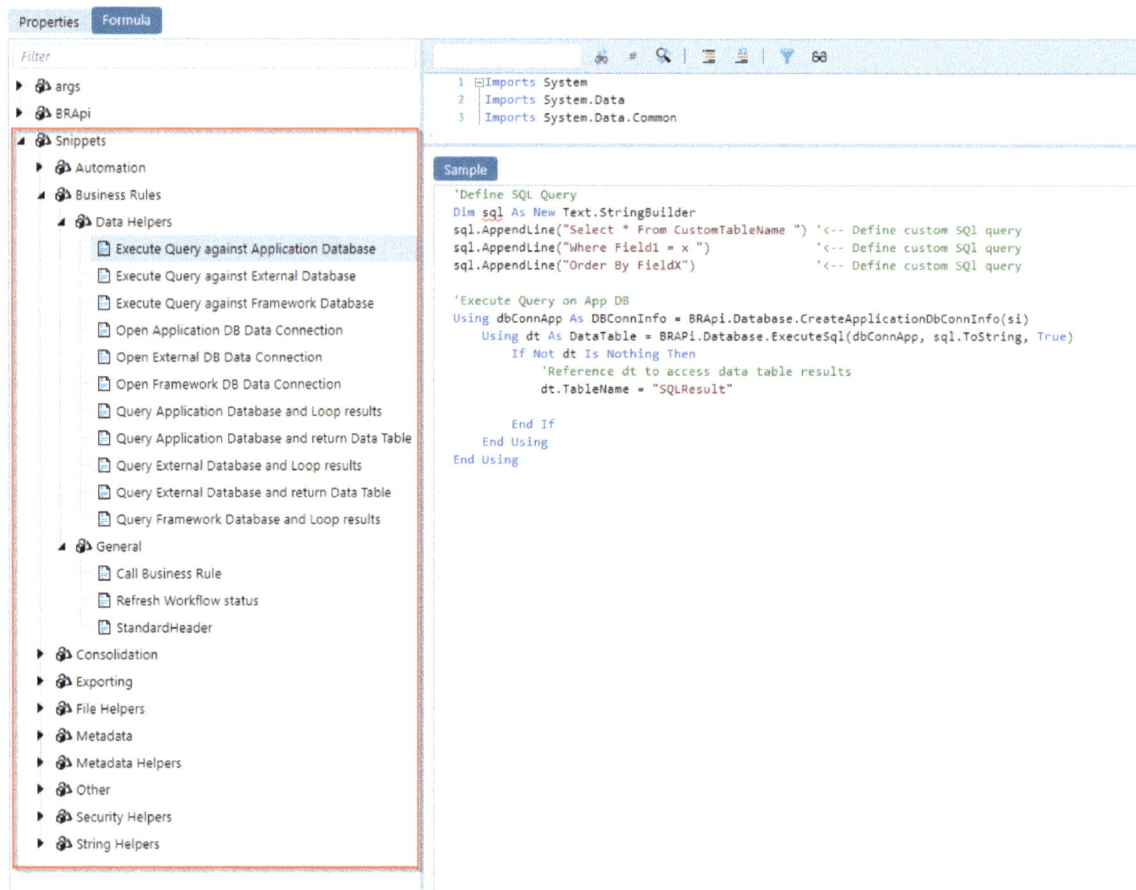

Figure 10.99

IDEs and Text Editors

There are a lot of great options for code development in VB.NET. In particular, Visual Studio is really tailor-made by Microsoft for VB.NET and C# development, allowing you to easily download the correct .NET framework for your application. Notepad++ is also a nice lightweight option.

These editors have a couple of great advantages over the built-in editor in OneStream:

1. Auto-indentation and formatting.

2. Comparison tools that allow you to quickly highlight differences between files and versions.

3. Refactoring tools, enabling you to quickly refactor variable and function names or reorganize code.

However, there is a trade-off to using these IDEs. Typically, it is not possible to access the OneStream DLLs, meaning that you cannot import the standard OneStream libraries and leverage IntelliSense. Also, even if the dlls were available, you would not be able to debug business rules in the IDE out of context. You would still have to copy your code into your development environment to test.

Generally, my workflow is to do my initial pass of my business rule and most of my development in general in the OneStream code editor but then migrate code over to Visual Studio or Notepad++ when I need to do heavy refactoring or formatting, especially when updating old code.

Business Rule Viewer

The **Administrator Solution Tools Marketplace Solution** contains a business rule viewer, which allows you to view all previous versions of business rules. We would always recommend downloading it as it allows you to have confidence you can always roll back your code or review old code in the context that it was run in.

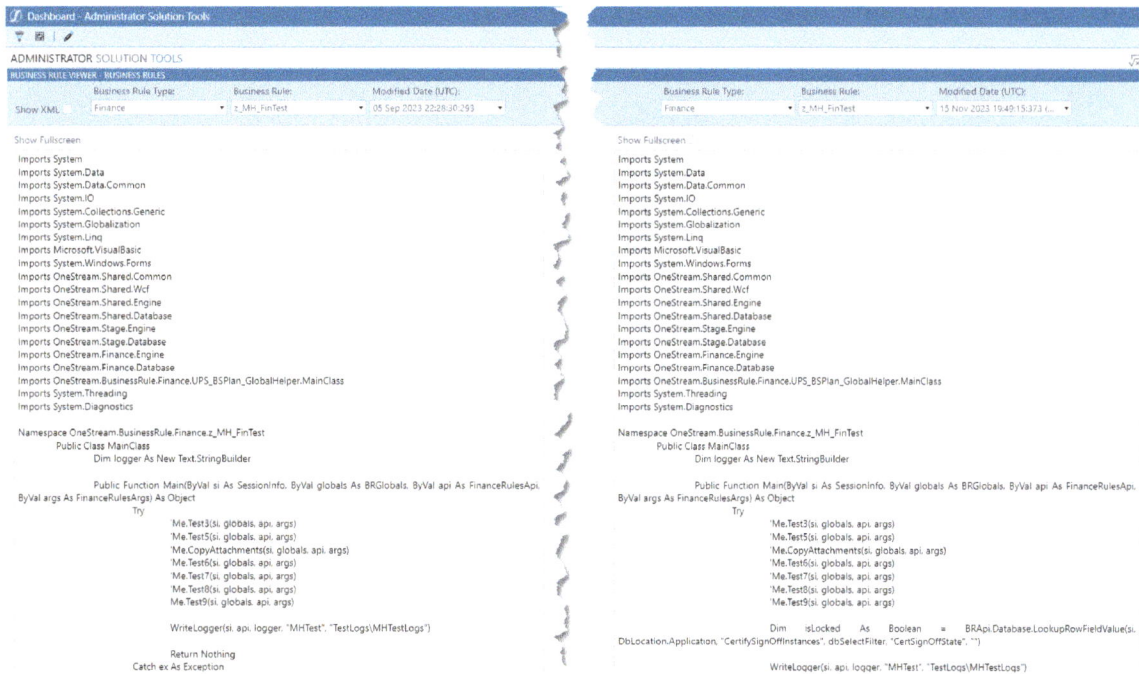

Figure 10.100

Conclusion

In this chapter, we covered a large number of technical topics. We covered the basics and context around the finance engine and how to interact with it in finance rules using the finance API. We listed best practices around business rules, focusing on accepted coding standards as well as heuristics to identify if there are flaws in your code that need to be addressed. Finally, we provided a guide to troubleshooting rules, focusing heavily on advanced logging techniques.

Again, we know that business rules are a complicated topic, so we hope that this chapter is a helpful supplement to all of the other resources available to you, which typically teach you the rote levers of how to code but very rarely the *why*.

11
Cube Views

Cube Views are synonymous with the term report. When a customer asks, "Can you put this in a report for me?" they are asking, "Can you build a Cube View?" A Cube View is quite literally the view of data that exists inside the cube, hence the appellation Cube View.

A Cube View is a view of the cube through an x and y axis. The axes, in this case, are better known as the row and column sets, respectively. However, the OneStream Cube View is unique in that it can do math against specific data points and – even better – it can do math against its own rows and columns. If this wasn't somehow expansive enough, you can apply business rules and other unique logic against your Cube View. To say that the Cube View is the backbone of OneStream reporting would be an understatement.

Cube View knowledge will also be needed if your company has any OneStream forms. Forms are built based on the rows and columns in a Cube View. Forms then can have some specific properties assigned to the Cube View. Then, these forms can be assigned to the Workflow Profile properties.

This unique reporting capability offers so many expansive features that it would be nearly impossible to put them all in one chapter. In this chapter, we will cover an array of topics around easily maintaining your Cube View, Cube View math versus the GetDataCell expression, and finally some common troubleshooting cases. One of the more commonly read sections of this chapter will likely be *Cells are Red, Invalid or Blank*. May you find this chapter beneficial on your Cube View journey!

Maintaining the Cube View

Cube Views can be easy to maintain unless there is a large, fundamental company shift in reporting strategy. Cube Views can be time-consuming to build, format or validate, but the go-forward of maintenance is typically easy as minimal updates should be required following the initial build. This section covers tips on making maintenance easier.

Cube View Templates

Cube View templates are Cube Views built to allow the rows or columns to be shared to another Cube View. OneStream typically recommends using a row or column template if said row or column will be replicated more than once. Using a row or column template is a very simple process. Create a standard Cube View using either the rows or columns (or both) with the desired intersection. Then, apply those to another empty Cube View.

Chapter 11

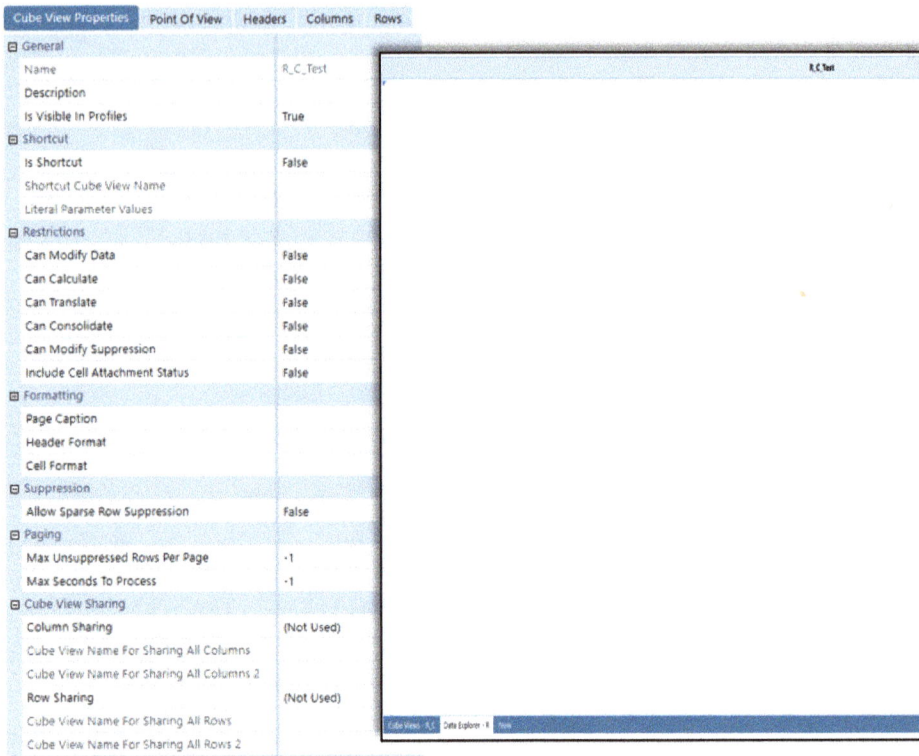

Figure 11.1

Figure 11.1 shows the created Cube View with no rows or columns assigned. Once we assign either a row or column template for sharing, then those specific sections will be greyed out on the inheriting Cube View.

Figure 11.2 shows the assignment of the row and column templates. Although it's not recommended to override any of the templates, if the row or columns ever needed to be altered, the row or column override section of a Cube View would still be available to change the specific row or column as necessary.

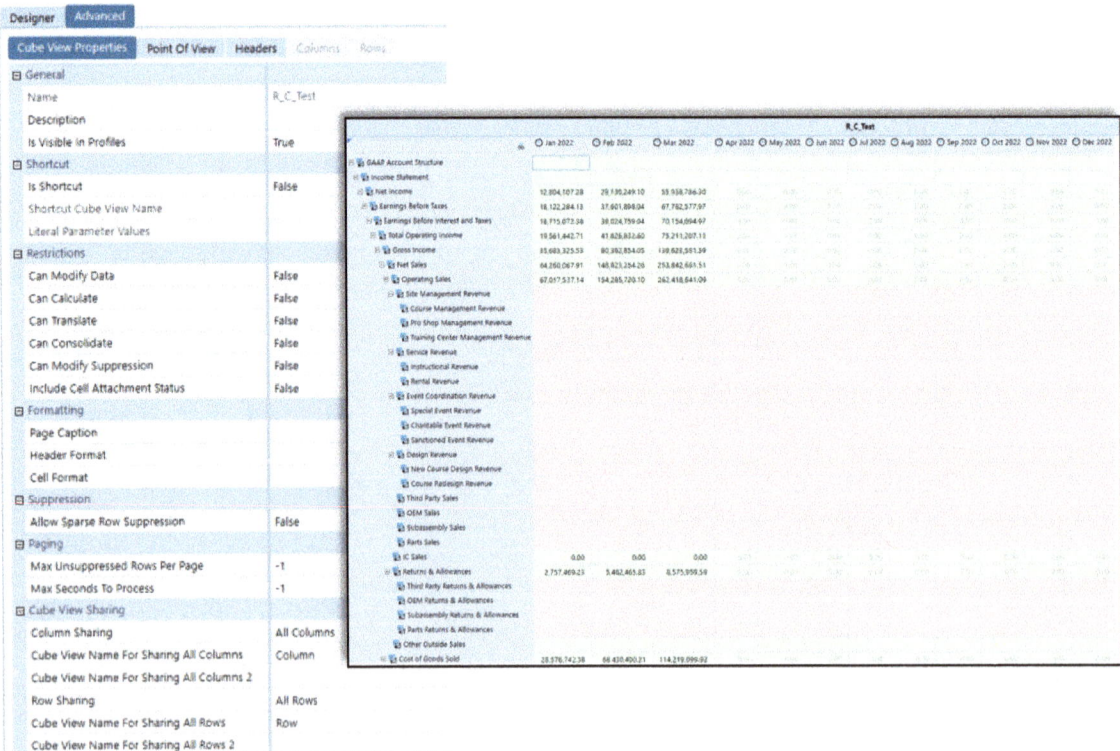

Figure 11.2

Note: If someone were to render just the row or column template independently, no data would be rendered. Applying the row and column templates together allows the inheriting Cube View to retrieve those intersections together and render the data properly.

We sometimes see the misuse of row or column templates. For instance, you wouldn't necessarily need to create a row or column template for every possible Cube View. Some Cube Views are unique or specific to a report and it wouldn't make sense to create a row or column template. Cash flow matrix or proof is one example of this type of report that wouldn't necessarily need a row or column template.

Some examples of the most common templates to build for a column set are **time templates** and **scenario templates** (Figure 11.3). The most common row sets are specific accounts for either balance sheets or income statements in a tree format (Figure 11.4). However, there is no limitation on row or column usage for templates.

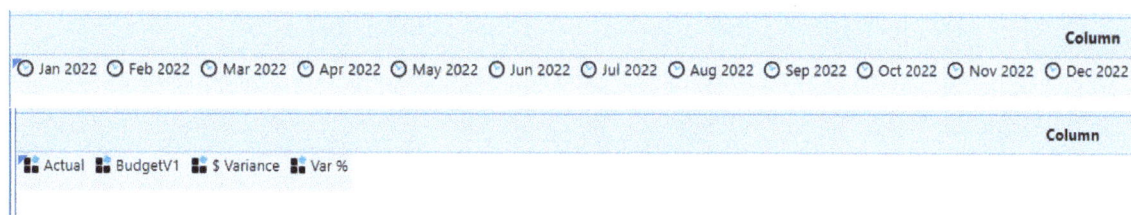

Figure 11.3

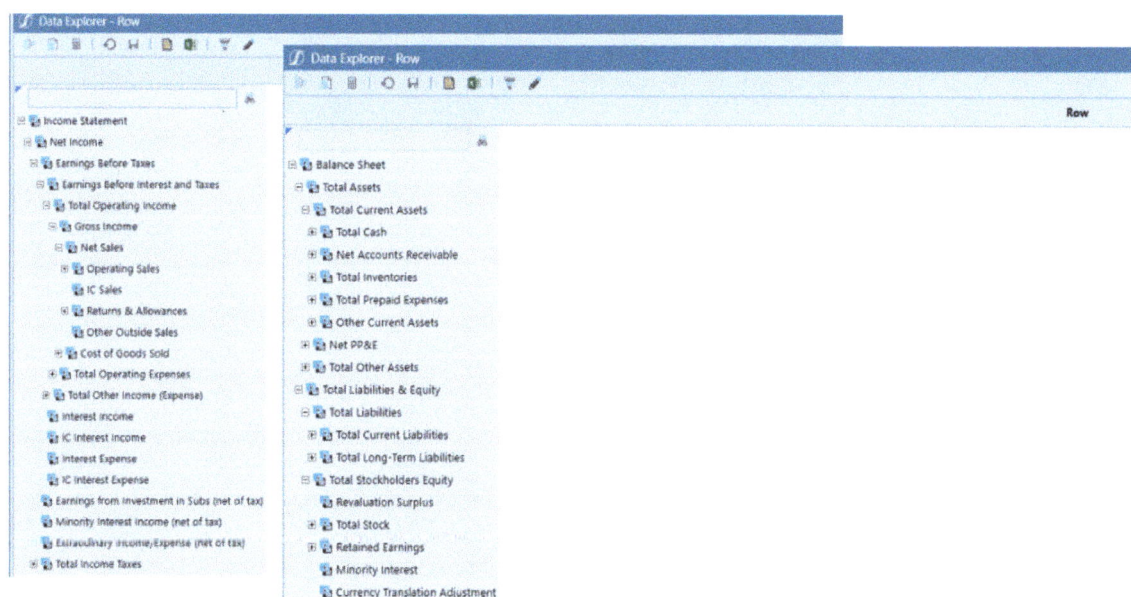

Figure 11.4

One of the great benefits of using row and column templates is that if you update the template, it will be applied to *all* the Cube Views that use that template. This makes any change to an organization's reporting structure easy for an administrator; they can update all the impacted Cube Views by modifying just one (or many) template(s).

Note: Should an administrator find the need to impact only a specific column or row within the template, they could simply use **Copy Cube View** functionality and create a new template that applies to just that Cube View. Another option would be to use the column or row override. Although using column or row overrides on the column or row template diminishes their value, we recognize that there could be one-off scenarios where this solution is needed.

Parameters

Parameters can make a Cube View very dynamic and allow one report to become multiple reports. Parameters also offer the ability to standardize report formatting or easily pass in information through a linked Cube View.

An example of a formatting parameter might see a company opt only to use one decimal in a percentage, then – a year later – change its mind to display two decimals. Instead of an administrator updating hundreds of reports, they would only need to update the one parameter to accommodate this change. This section should help identify the use of parameters in a Cube View in the most common ways – standardizing the report building process during the implementation of OneStream. This section will not cover what each type of parameter does, as this is extensively covered in the OneStream Reference Guide.

Format Parameters

OneStream recommends finding a common format that all departments can agree upon and placing it into a parameter. To accomplish this feat, the Report Designer can simply set all the requested format(s) for the Cube View, and then copy and paste it into a literal parameter.

One example of parameter formatting is setting the cell or header format within a Cube View (Figure 11.5).

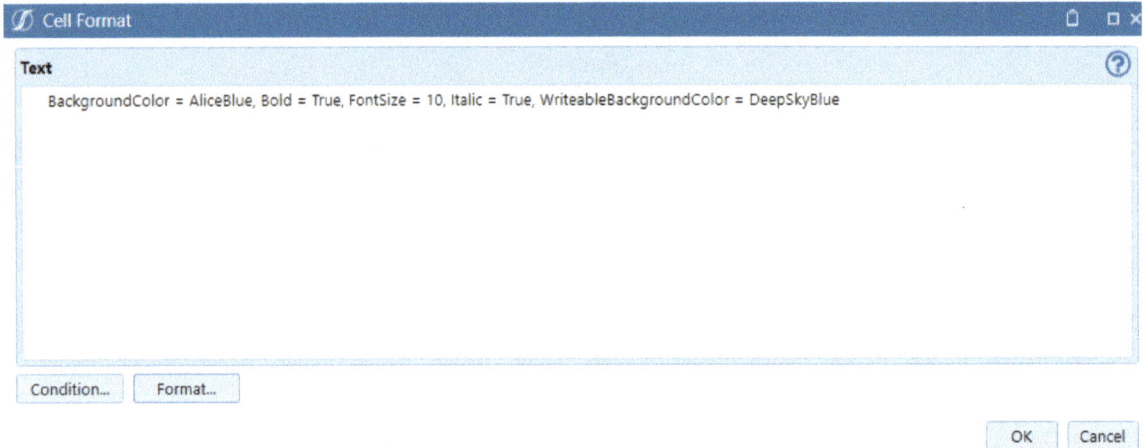

Figure 11.5

Copy this cell format from a Cube View into a parameter with the type set to Literal Value to standardize the formatting of any Cube View.

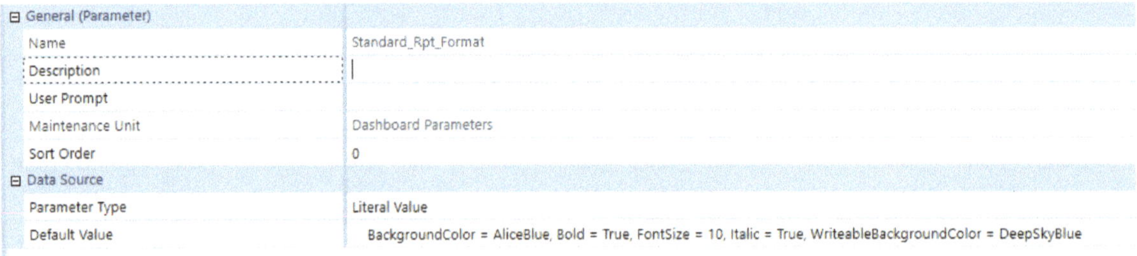

Figure 11.6

> **Note:** Nomenclature is important when locating this parameter and understanding how it is used for your future Cube Views. Usually, it would be a delineation between the cell format and the header format. As an example, the company could use `Standard_Cell_Format` or `Standard_Header_Format`.

This formatting parameter is then pasted into the cell or header formatting using the standard Parameter call `|!Parameter Name!|` on the Cube View Properties tab. A company might think they are bound to this report formatting forever, and unable to change it, but this is far from the truth. By pasting this parameter to the Cube View Properties tab, the report creator can still overwrite the specific row or column with different formatting.

> **Note:** An important thing to remember – when determining when and where to place the parameter – is the order of precedence for Cube Views. This applies to data interaction on a Cube View as well.
>
> 1. Cube POV
>
> 2. Cube View POV
>
> 3. Column POV
>
> 4. Row POV
>
> 5. Row override on the column page
>
> 6. Column override on the row page
>
> The numbers should make this easier to remember. A higher number means it will win the formatting or intersection.

Member Selection Parameters

Cube Views can also have selectable parameters. OneStream has the ability to alter a POV in the Cube View POV section or applied in the member expansion section of the Cube View. This applies to both the row and column member expansion section. These types of parameters are typically either member lists or delimited lists. These are not the only types of parameters that can appear in these sections, just the two most common types.

These parameters are used to further the cause of making Cube Views dynamic. A common use case for this type of parameter is to have actuals in the first column alongside (in the second column) the ability to select a scenario for some type of comparison.

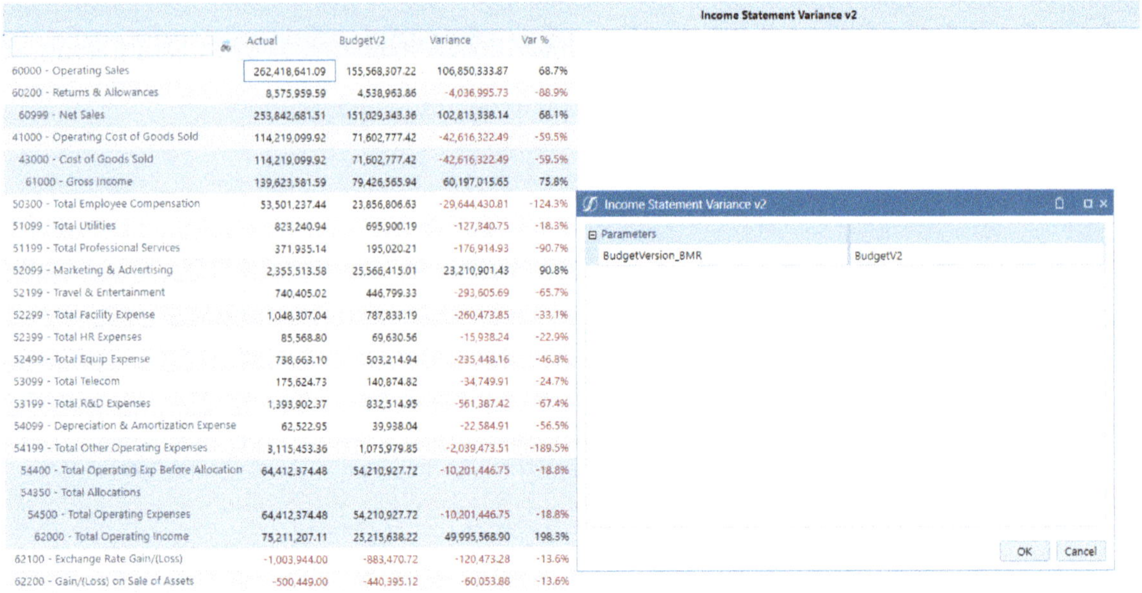

Income Statement Variance v2

	Actual	BudgetV2	Variance	Var %
60000 - Operating Sales	262,418,641.09	155,568,307.22	106,850,333.87	68.7%
60200 - Returns & Allowances	8,575,959.59	4,538,963.86	-4,036,995.73	-88.9%
60999 - Net Sales	253,842,681.51	151,029,343.36	102,813,338.14	68.1%
41000 - Operating Cost of Goods Sold	114,219,099.92	71,602,777.42	-42,616,322.49	-59.5%
43000 - Cost of Goods Sold	114,219,099.92	71,602,777.42	-42,616,322.49	-59.5%
61000 - Gross Income	139,623,581.59	79,426,565.94	60,197,015.65	75.8%
50300 - Total Employee Compensation	53,501,237.44	23,856,806.63	-29,644,430.81	-124.3%
51099 - Total Utilities	823,240.94	695,900.19	-127,340.75	-18.3%
51199 - Total Professional Services	371,935.14	195,020.21	-176,914.93	-90.7%
52099 - Marketing & Advertising	2,355,513.58	25,566,415.01	23,210,901.43	90.8%
52199 - Travel & Entertainment	740,405.02	446,799.33	-293,605.69	-65.7%
52299 - Total Facility Expense	1,048,307.04	787,833.19	-260,473.85	-33.1%
52399 - Total HR Expenses	85,568.80	69,630.56	-15,938.24	-22.9%
52499 - Total Equip Expense	738,663.10	503,214.94	-235,448.16	-46.8%
53099 - Total Telecom	175,624.73	140,874.82	-34,749.91	-24.7%
53199 - Total R&D Expenses	1,393,902.37	832,514.95	-561,387.42	-67.4%
54099 - Depreciation & Amortization Expense	62,522.95	39,938.04	-22,584.91	-56.5%
54199 - Total Other Operating Expenses	3,115,453.36	1,075,979.85	-2,039,473.51	-189.5%
54400 - Total Operating Exp Before Allocation	64,412,374.48	54,210,927.72	-10,201,446.75	-18.8%
54850 - Total Allocations				
54500 - Total Operating Expenses	64,412,374.48	54,210,927.72	-10,201,446.75	-18.8%
62000 - Total Operating Income	75,211,207.11	25,215,638.22	49,995,568.90	198.3%
62100 - Exchange Rate Gain/(Loss)	-1,003,944.00	-883,470.72	-120,473.28	-13.6%
62200 - Gain/(Loss) on Sale of Assets	-500,449.00	-440,395.12	-60,053.88	-13.6%

Income Statement Variance v2

Parameters

BudgetVersion_BMR — BudgetV2

OK   Cancel

Figure 11.7

The setup for this particular parameter usage is easy to accomplish; have the parameter in the column to be selected.

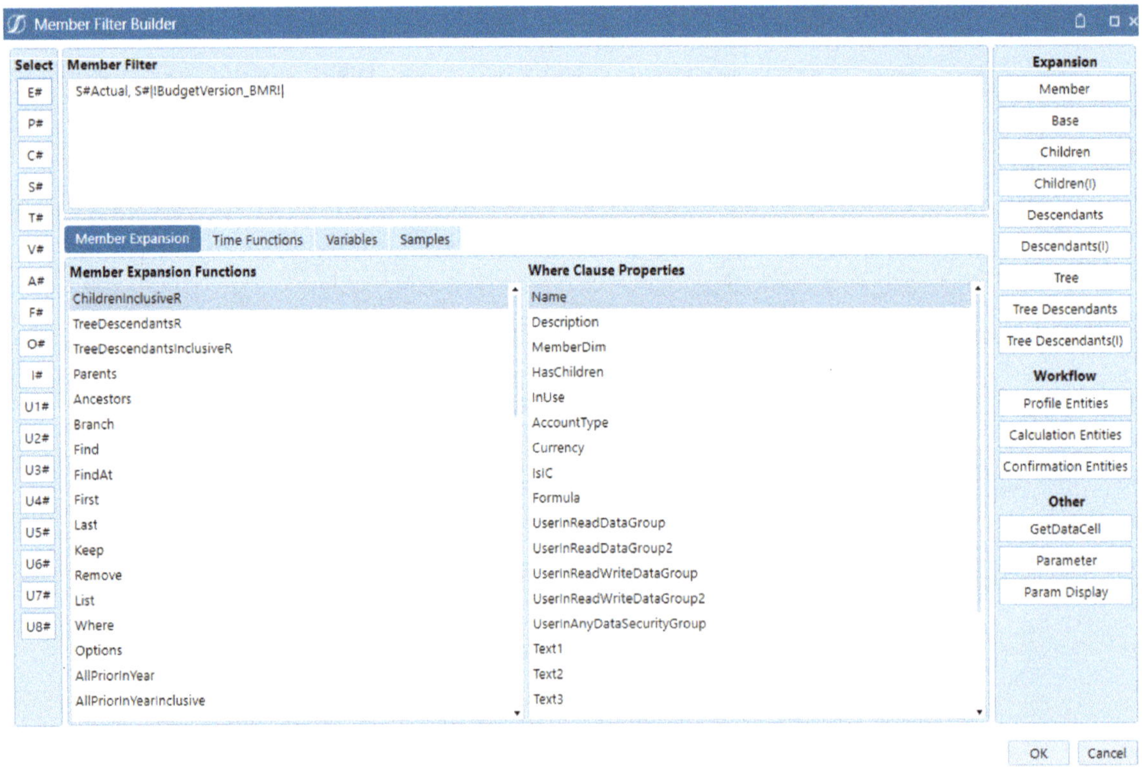

Member Filter Builder

Member Filter

S#Actual, S#!BudgetVersion_BMR!|

Select: E#, P#, C#, S#, T#, V#, A#, F#, O#, I#, U1#, U2#, U3#, U4#, U5#, U6#, U7#, U8#

Member Expansion | Time Functions | Variables | Samples

Member Expansion Functions
- ChildrenInclusiveR
- TreeDescendantsR
- TreeDescendantsInclusiveR
- Parents
- Ancestors
- Branch
- Find
- FindAt
- First
- Last
- Keep
- Remove
- List
- Where
- Options
- AllPriorInYear
- AllPriorInYearInclusive

Where Clause Properties
- Name
- Description
- MemberDim
- HasChildren
- InUse
- AccountType
- Currency
- IsIC
- Formula
- UserInReadDataGroup
- UserInReadDataGroup2
- UserInReadWriteDataGroup
- UserInReadWriteDataGroup2
- UserInAnyDataSecurityGroup
- Text1
- Text2
- Text3

Expansion
- Member
- Base
- Children
- Children(I)
- Descendants
- Descendants(I)
- Tree
- Tree Descendants
- Tree Descendants(I)

Workflow
- Profile Entities
- Calculation Entities
- Confirmation Entities

Other
- GetDataCell
- Parameter
- Param Display

OK   Cancel

Figure 11.8

This same concept for parameters can be used throughout the Cube View build in both rows and columns, as well as the Cube View POV. This type of parameter concept makes the company Cube View build dynamic and easy to use, as well as providing a great end-user experience.

Member Filter Substitution Variables

Member variables are commonly used, predefined parameters that are stored to be used in the **Member Filter Builder**. These are used in a variety of ways, and one common use case might be to plug a substitution variable like `|POVUD1|` into the intersection on the report. This allows end-users to utilize the report based on their own POV selection, eliminating the need to create several custom parameters. This also makes the report completely dynamic in this aspect. The OneStream Reference Guide does an excellent job of detailing each of these variables and the *where* and *when* of their use in a Cube View.

GetDataCell or Cube View Math

The header of this section could possibly be misleading as both the GetDataCell expression and Cube View math start with the nomenclature of GetDataCell. The reference to GetDataCell is typically some type of math function using a dimension (Example: `GetDataCell(A#10000 - A#20000)`). Cube View math is meant to be some type of either row math or column math, performing the same math functions but using row or column names instead of members. An example of this type of math is `GetDataCell(CVR(Row1) - CVR(Row2))`.

When using a `GetDataCell` expression either for the dimensional tagged math or Cube View math, the existing Cube View must render in cache, and then the `GetDataCell` expression is triggered to perform the math functions.

Use Cases

Imagine a company report that uses derived numbers, which are not stored accounts, and where the company does not want to have the values calculated or stored within the system. The requirement is to perform a math function off these accounts, and build some type of check column. For example, a use case for using Cube View math would be where you need to cherry pick accounts in a hierarchy, but the customer doesn't want to create an alternate hierarchy. As an example, let's say you have the following hierarchy of cash accounts:

10000 – Total Cash

    10010 – Cash California

    10020 – Cash Texas

    10030 – Cash Canada

    10040 – Cash Florida

Perhaps you do not want to alter the structure of `Total Cash` but you want to report out both US-based cash and total cash. To accomplish this feat, you could create a row with Cube View Math of `GetDataCell(A#10010 + A#10020 + A#10040)`. This would eliminate the need for an alternate hierarchy but still satisfy the reporting requirement.

Row/Column Override Considerations

A column or row override simply overrides a specific row, column, or intersection on a Cube View that already has an applied value. Member Filters in overrides must be used consistently in Cube Views. As an example, if you have a column name `Col1` with a Member Filter of `A#10000`, then the override in the row referencing `Col1` should use a query for the Member Filter (e.g., `A#AR`). This will allow the column or row with the original value to be overwritten with the new updated value.

Likewise, if a column name `Col1` uses a `GetDataCell` for the Member Filter, then the override in the row referencing `Col1` should also use a Member Filter of `GetDataCell`. If `Col1` uses a Member Filter of `A#10000`, but you have a row override of `GetDataCell(A#10000 + A#10001)`, then the amount will not appear to be overwritten. This is another example of being consistent with the row or column overrides. If you have a GetDataCell in a specific row or column, you must use the same GetDataCell syntax in the override as well.

If an administrator is attempting to use a list in a row or column override, this will cause an issue with the override. The override will ignore the other members and only apply to the first member. As an example, in Figure 11.9, only the member of T#2021 will be applied to the override. The other T# members will be ignored.

Figure 11.9

If a list is needed or multiple members need to be applied to the Cube View, the administrator may want to consider using a UD8 member. If that isn't an option, then the Cube View may need to be restricted in a way to accommodate the required listing.

XFBR vs UD8

An XFBR (Extensible Finance Business Rule) is a OneStream business rule that allows for the ability to pass along data types of string in the programming languages of either VB.NET or C# throughout specific sections of the application. Those sections are through dashboard parameters, Cube Views, and alternate business rules.

Most commonly, OneStream will use XFBRs for specific formatting purposes on a Cube View. However, that is not the only reason to use an XFBR. XFBRs can return specific intersections based on clearly defined criteria. As an example, should you need to change an intersection based on scenario, an XFBR can accomplish this feat.

OneStream typically recommends using the UD8 dimension as some type of reporting dimension. This allows for the ability to create dynamic calculations to replace common Cube View math functions. One common example is variance analysis from current year to prior year. One of the key benefits of using a UD8 member is the ability to create a custom drill down. This will allow end-users to see how the number is derived in the dynamic calculation.

Troubleshooting

Troubleshooting is a common topic of conversation throughout the lifecycle of any project and even following implementation. Troubleshooting issues will be a recurring theme no matter how mature the application is. This section isn't intended to be a catch-all for every possible problem or scenario that could arise with your Cube Views; however, it is intended to look at the common problems that have been found alongside common solutions. Are these the only problems that can be found with Cube Views? No. Are these the only solutions to the problems listed below? No. OneStream is so robust that there could be so many solutions that it would be difficult to list them all!

OneStream is an expansive platform that offers many different features and functionalities. However, most problems tend to be very customer-centric and often unable to be 100% troubleshot. These nuanced cases can take a great amount of time to find and fix issues. The cases listed below are intended to be helpful pointers on where to start troubleshooting if you are facing similar issues.

This section is mainly meant to be Cube View-related, however Cube Views and dashboards play a hand-in-hand role. Therefore, we have listed a few troubleshooting cases that are synonymous with Cube View issues in dashboards, but which could apply to a lot of dashboard issues.

What Happens If I Want to Change My Cube View Name?

Typically, name changes will have a minimal impact within OneStream other than a name update. However, if you have a Cube View attached to a dashboard (Cube View component) – and the name changes – the Cube View component will not automatically update to the new name, and the dashboard will render as an invalid name.

To correct this function, update the name in the dashboard Cube View component to the newly updated name. All other name changes regarding Cube Views will automatically update, and the end-user will experience minimal disruption.

A Dashboard No Longer Renders or Errors Appear While Using a Cube View

This will occur when a Cube View is either deleted or renamed. To correct this, validate that the Cube View exists and correct the name within the Cube View dashboard component.

Dashboard Migration

This section isn't specific to Cube Views or the dashboard Cube View component, but it is worth mentioning as a troubleshooting exercise. When migrating dashboard components, you must take all the components that exist in any given maintenance unit. If the migration fails to have every component and a dashboard is migrated, it will drop all the components not brought over from the existing dashboard. This isn't typically a problem for a new dashboard, but a bigger problem for existing dashboards.

In the example below, there is a basic dashboard setup with two components in a Cube View and a button. The scope has changed for this dashboard, and now the company wants to add a combo box. It's a simple update to add the new component.

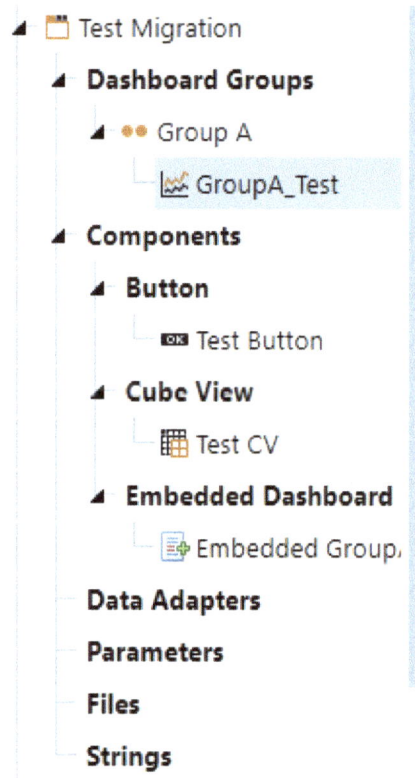

```
▲ ▤ Test Migration
    ▲ Dashboard Groups
        ▲ •• Group A
            └ ⤬ GroupA_Test
    ▲ Components
        ▲ Button
            └ ⊡ Test Button
        ▲ Cube View
            └ ⊞ Test CV
        ▲ Embedded Dashboard
            └ ⊞⊕ Embedded Group,
    Data Adapters
    Parameters
    Files
    Strings
```

Figure 11.10

253

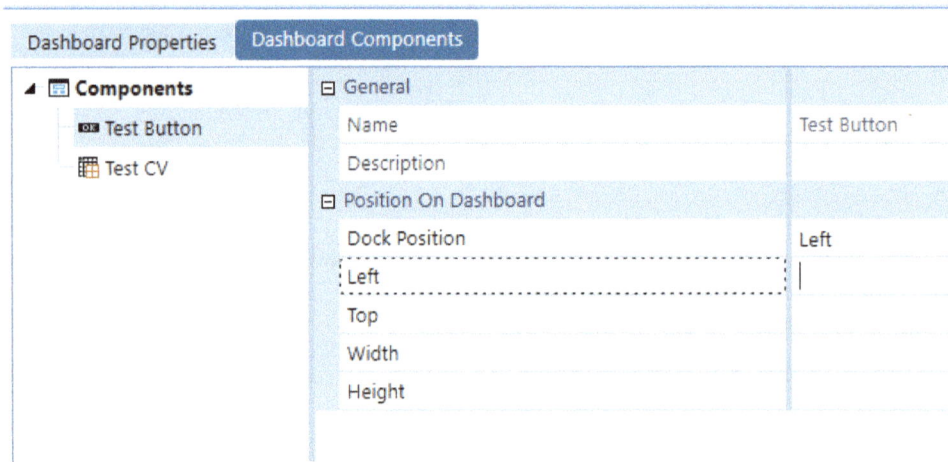

Figure 11.11

When the administrator just adds the combo box and doesn't bring all the components over, it will remove the button and Cube View.

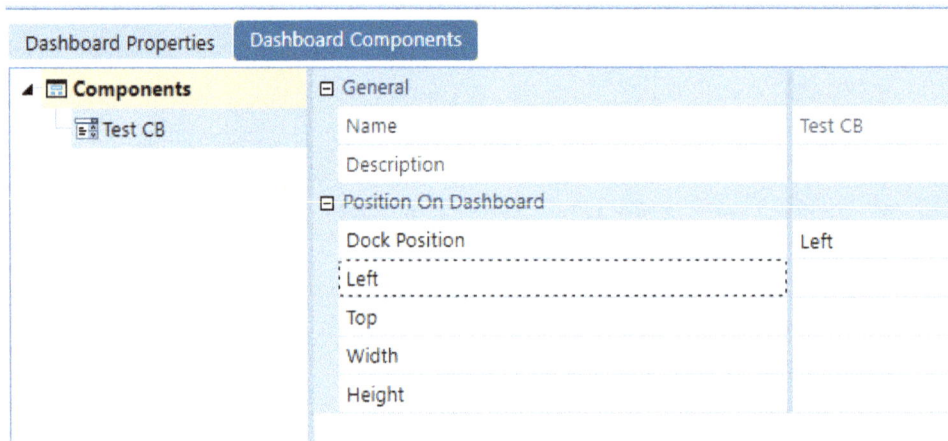

Figure 11.12

> **Note:** Figure 11.12 shows what the dashboard looks like after migrating just the combo box and not all the dashboard components at one time.

This is an important piece of information when you are migrating dashboard components between environments. It's the common reason a dashboard fails when you migrate between development, QA, and production environments. To help mitigate this risk, ensure that you are only keeping necessary dashboard components in your desired dashboard maintenance unit and then select the *full* maintenance unit to migrate, rather than attempting to select individual components.

Why Can I Scroll on My Cube View but Not When It's in a Dashboard?

This is a common dashboard or Cube View problem with first-time build components. The problem here typically tends to be that someone added a Cube View that worked with no issues and now the scope has changed, or additional components were added to the dashboard, and someone is unable to scroll on the report or Cube View.

When you first start building the dashboard, you just add the Cube View component and it is usually set to uniform. This will allow the Cube View on the dashboard to scroll without issue. However, if you start layering additional components into the dashboard and adjust sizes or hard code pixels, this is when you typically see a Cube View that is unable to scroll.

It is recommended to go back to the initial dashboard – where the Cube View component is attached – and run just that dashboard first. If you can scroll, then you keep moving along all the dashboards until you find the dashboard where the Cube View is unable to be scrolled or paged.

One of the main things to look out for is a grid layout in the Layout Type setting for the dashboard. Then, you need to look for hard-coded values for pixels. If possible, try using either the * ("Star") or Auto setting for the height or width of any row or column.

Cells are Red, Invalid or Blank

If you have skipped ahead, welcome to the party of Cube View building and troubleshooting. When it comes to troubleshooting Cube Views, the most common issue encountered is **invalid data cells**, indicated by red cells. The first thing a user should always check, in this case, is the Point of View in the data cells. This can be done by right-clicking on any cell in the Cube View and opening Cell POV Information.

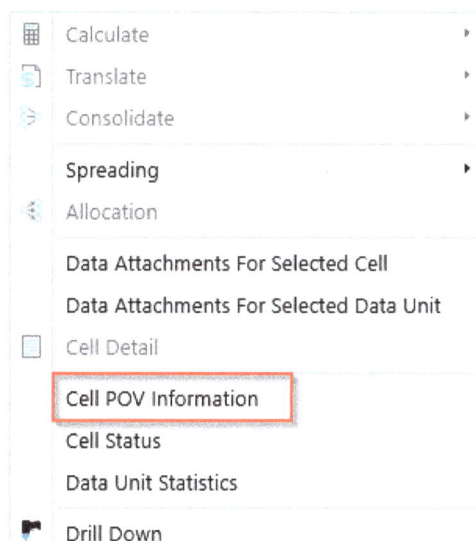

Figure 11.13

A red/invalid cell can be the product of either of the following two issues:

One of the dimensions is not defined. We would identify this courtesy of a question mark next to one of the dimensions in the cell POV window. To fix this, we want to go back into the Cube View editor, go to our Point of View tab, and ensure all dimensions are defined here or in the Rows and Columns tab.

> **Note:** There may be a question mark next to the 'parent' dimension. This is okay depending on what you are trying to query. For example, if you are looking at a particular consolidation audit trail, you may need to define the Parent.

If no dimensions have question marks next to them (or only the parent dimension has a question mark), then the issue is an **invalid intersection**.

In some cases, with Cube Views, there may be a mix of valid and invalid cells. This is usually okay; it just means we need to turn on our suppression setting to suppress invalid cells in order to only show valid cells on the report.

When a Cube View comes up blank with no cells that are either valid or invalid, it typically means there are suppression settings on that are not displaying invalid cells, or NoData cells that would normally be displaying. Turn off the suppression settings one by one to determine what kind of cells they are, and solve the problem appropriately by either changing the dimensions or by referring to the section above. Also, you may accidentally be running a report that only has columns or rows defined (such as a template). Check to make sure you are running the correct report.

Depending on how the Cube View is built, there is a chance that not all dimensions are defined in the rows/columns/cube POV. Any dimensions not referenced explicitly in the Cube View will default to the user's POV, and there is a chance that the user's POV is not set up (missing dimensions will be denoted with ?).

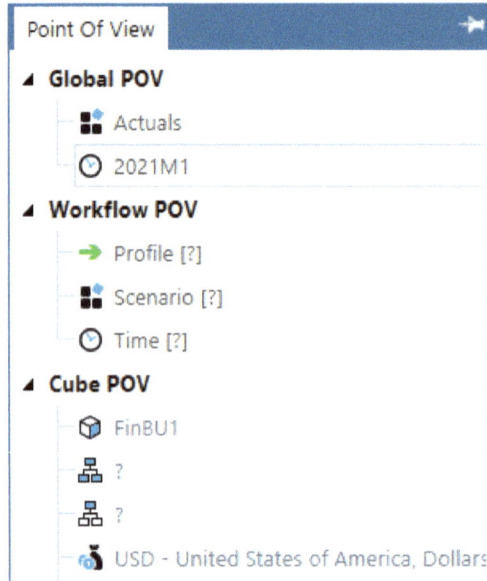

Figure 11.14

Why Does My Cube View Take a Long Time to Render?

When a Cube View takes a long time to run, it is typically a sign that the system is generating a lot of data or that a Level 1 Data Unit has been assigned to a row. This may be encountered when we have multiple dimensions nested, as demonstrated below.

> **Note:** The Level 1 Data Unit consists of the Cube, Entity, Parent, Consolidation, Scenario, and Time dimensions.

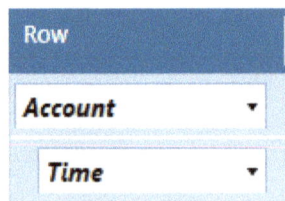

Figure 11.15

Figure 11.15 would show each account at each time period. This is purely hypothetical, but you can see how a situation like this would exponentially multiply the amount of data being generated. If any reports need multiple nested dimensions, like this, it's important to make sure we are doing two things:

1. Turning on all row/column suppression, including spare row suppression. We don't want the system to generate any more rows/columns than it needs to.

2. Avoiding calling all members in the dimension. By this, we mean making sure not to call all members from the 'top' level (e.g., U1#Top.Tree).

If a Cube View has all row/column suppression settings turned on, and it is calling all necessary levels of data and still taking a long time to render, it may be that there is a Level 1 Data Unit in the rows or that other processes are running in the system in the background that are slowing things down momentarily. If that isn't the case, our final option would be to restructure the report.

Should I Put My Entities in the Row Set?

Can you put your entities in your Cube View row set? Yes, you can. The real question that is being asked is, *should you*? No, you shouldn't put entities in the row set.

One entity in the row set is really no issue. However, if the organization has several entities, then this could cause a significant performance problem as each entity is now attempting to pull a new Data Unit for every reporting line with the entity. By building this type of report, an administrator could potentially hold the entire application RAM in-memory for the one report. If this does happen, clear the server IIS and remove the entities from the report.

Cube View Data Says No Access

When the end-user's Cube View renders with "No Access" in the cells, this is a sign that they have restricted access to view the data being displayed in the Cube View. If they should have access, then it means the security settings need to be re-evaluated (see Chapter 12 – Securing the Pieces). If they should not be allowed to see the data, then this is working as intended.

Cube View Says #Error or The Data Is Completely Wrong

A calculated row/column is one that is doing math on-the-fly, such as GetDataCells. When doing GetDataCell calculations in rows or columns, a GetDataCell row must not intersect a GetDataCell column. The system does not have an order of operations when it encounters two GetDataCells and will either show #Error in the cell, or it will simply do the wrong math (e.g., 1 + 2 = 5).

To solve this issue and avoid it in the future, create a new member in a dimension for the impacted dimension that is being calculated in OneStream. This prevents doing the math on the Cube View.

Tips and Tricks

Whether you're a seasoned administrator or new to OneStream, everyone loves some helpful tips and tricks to support any report building. This section will cover some common tips and tricks that support building and maintaining Cube Views.

How Can I Use the Same Point of View (POV) for Multiple Cube Views?

An administrator can copy a specific Cube View POV and paste it into another Cube View. On the Cube View Point Of View tab, the administrator can right-click on a specific section (see Figure 11.16) and select copy and then paste (Figure 11.17).

If you right-click on the section that is not highlighted in red, the administrator will receive the option to cut, copy, or paste. These options do not pertain to the POV but the text in the specific row.

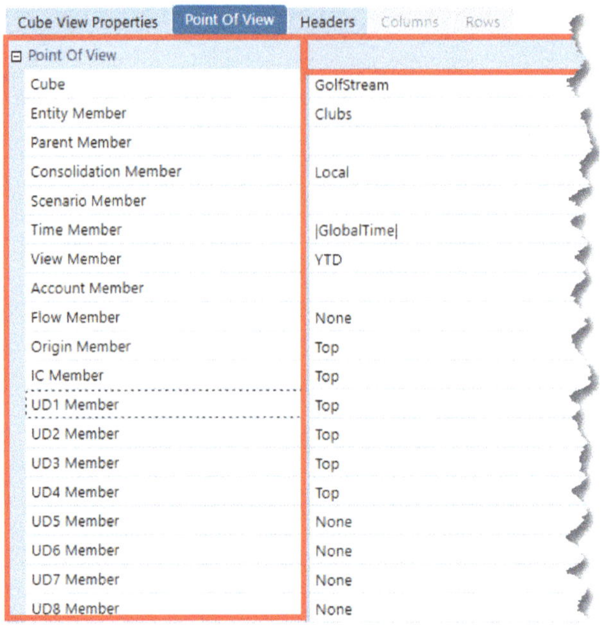

Figure 11.16

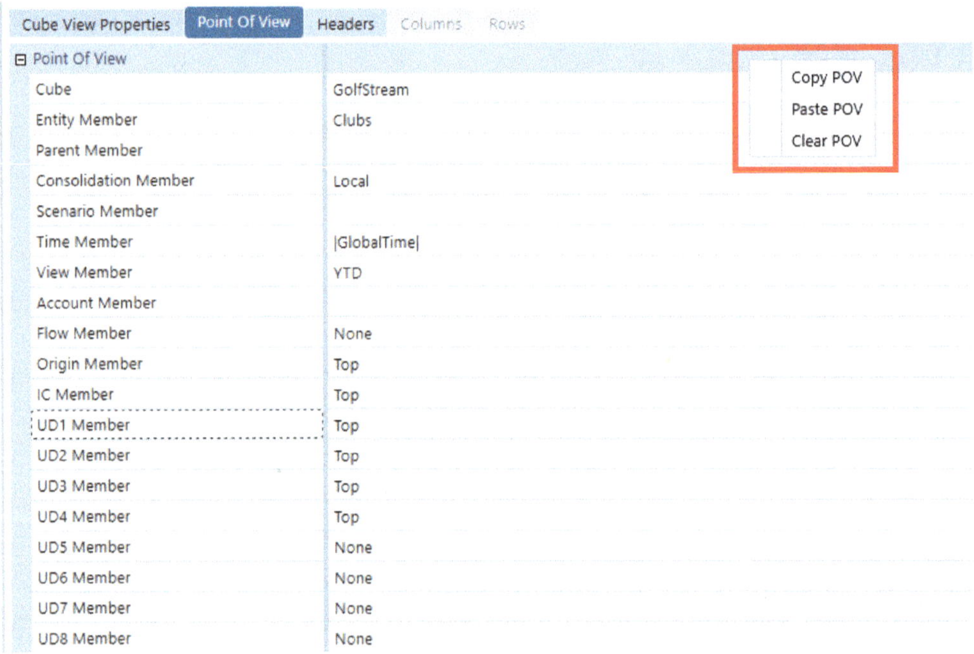

Figure 11.17

Who Can or Should Build New Cube Views?

The answer here might surprise some people. In other systems, the answer would be that building is limited to special access for administrators. However, with OneStream's custom security model builds, literally anyone can build a Cube View if there is a desire for that to be the case. Indeed, the customer may determine it's best for a group of end-users to build reports and lighten the administrative burden. For further explanation on how to achieve this feat, see Chapter 12: Securing the Pieces.

How Do I Email a Report to Someone That Doesn't Have OneStream?

This answer here is intuitive for some administrators; however, this question has been asked enough that we decided to include it in the book! An end-user can simply export the report using the Show Report or Export to Excel buttons (Figure 11.18). The end-user can then save the report and simply email it.

Figure 11.18

OneStream also offers the Parcel Service Marketplace Solution, which allows for the ability to set up report packages and email them to customizable distribution groups of users that may or may not have OneStream access. For additional information regarding the Parcel Service Marketplace Solution, see the installation instructions and guides.

Conclusion

All setup, configuration, and data imports lead to the point of reporting. Every OneStream end-user wants the data to be correct and as expected. Will you encounter issues outside of this chapter? Probably. But this chapter hopefully provides a thoughtful view of how troubleshooting reporting/Cube View builds can help the administrator in the future.

We have addressed the most common problems asked by customers and administrators, and as mentioned, this isn't intended to be a definitive list of problems with the Cube View or data inside the Cube View. However, this chapter should guide the administrator into thinking about troubleshooting differently… facilitating the path to a clean report.

If you need additional or more detailed information, take a look at the OneStream Advanced Reporting and Dashboards book.

12
Securing the Pieces

OneStream has been implemented, and your application is ready for security assignment. In most cases, OneStream recommends starting with minimal security and layering additional security as the need arises. The main reason is that it is easier to layer additional security than unwind an existing complex security model to a less complex security model.

Why is it easier? Well, if your application starts with extensive layered security, it will be difficult and more cumbersome to apply very specific intersection security. Additionally, organizational leadership changes can alter fundamental beliefs regarding security access, and it's important to keep this in mind when designing your security model. The OneStream Foundation Handbook (Chapter 9: Security) does an excellent job of detailing security. This chapter supplements that content by helping the administrator to recognize where security exists throughout the application, best security practices, and basic administrator security tasks.

Introduction to Security

Security is commonly defined as the state of being free from danger. Although there is no physical harm should there be a lack of OneStream security, there could be severe business consequences if application security is not applied.

This section will cover security within the OneStream application and where it exists. Why is this fundamental information important? Knowing the fundamentals of security will help make the use cases (later in the chapter) more relevant. Securing your application will make auditing partners happy and the life of the administrator for **Information Technology Governance Controls** (ITGC) testing (mentioned in Chapter 2: Testing) easier.

What is Security within OneStream?

When end-users think of security, they often think of the parts of the application they are not allowed to visit, or chunks of data they are not allowed to view. When admins think of security, they look at security as another tool (or possible guide) to help send the end-user to the correct location of the application, or to help the end-user perform the correct task.

There is some merit that security is attempting to limit end-user interaction with parts of data or the application. A company would not want to give view access to everyone's salary, or compensation details for every employee. This is a liability for the company – for multiple reasons – and will not be broached in this chapter.

Security in OneStream, though, can be thought of as two sections. Application security is often the one discussed most frequently and probably the most important. This is the ability to limit an end-user's interaction within the application or data. This type of security exists in many locations within the application.

The unsung hero of security, however, is **System Security Roles** under the System tab, and the Security listing within the Administration section (Figure 12.1).

System Security Roles can grant additional administration duties to alternate parts of an organization, and offer the ability for an organization to assign security to the artifacts that reside under the System tab. This could alleviate some of the administrative burden of the finance administrator and assign some responsibility to another department.

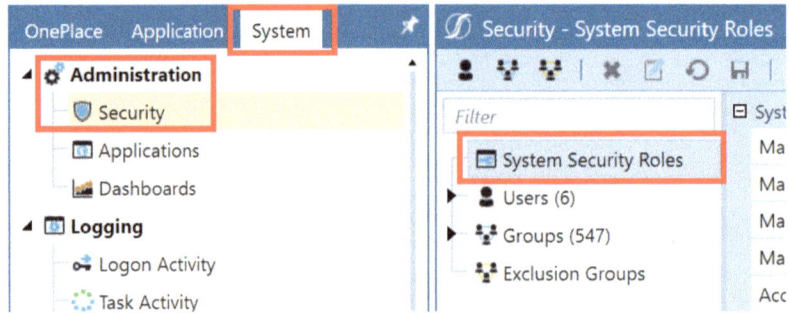

Figure 12.1

Where Does Security Exist?

Though security feels like it exists anywhere and everywhere in the system (which it does), there is a method to OneStream's security practices. As stated in this chapter, and in the security chapter in the OneStream Foundation Handbook, security should start as a basic model and work its way to become a detailed and complex security model. Again, it is easier to start basic and work up to complex, versus unwinding a detailed and complex security model. This point will be driven home over and over in this chapter!

This chapter is not a definitive overview of security; the Reference Guide in every application will cover those terms. Instead, this chapter will attempt to list all the places that security can be found (with maybe a quick comment or two), whilst deeper and more common security artifacts can be found in later sections of the chapter. Figure 12.2 shows an exhaustive table of all security within the OneStream Application, and if it can restrict data or access to the artifact.

Component	Explicit Read/ Read and Write	Explicit Access/Maintenance
Security Groups	N	N
Cubes > Cube Properties	N	Y
Cubes > Data Access	Y	Y
Metadata (Entity, Scenario)	Y	Y
Metadata (Account, Flow, UD1-UD8)	N	Y*
Workflow Profiles	N	Y
Confirmation Rules	N	Y
Certification Questions	N	Y
Data Sources	N	Y
Transformation Rules > Groups and Profiles	N	Y
Form Templates > Groups and Profiles	N	Y
Journal Templates > Groups and Profiles	N	Y
Cube Views > Groups and Profiles	N	Y
Workspaces > Maintenance Units	N	Y
Dashboards** > Dashboard Groups	N	Access Group (Pre 8.0)
Workspaces ** > Dashboard Profiles	N	Y
Application > Tools > Security Roles	N	Y
Business Rules	N	Y
Data Management > Groups and Profiles	N	Y
File Explorer	N	Y

Component	Explicit Read/ Read and Write	Explicit Access/Maintenance
System Security	N	Y
System Dashboards	N	Y
System Business Rules	N	Y

*Account, Flow, and the custom UD members only have the Display Member Group as a security option. This option controls who can view the selected Account dimension member.

** For versions older than 8.0, you will find "Dashboards" as a valid selection, whereas in 8.0+, the Dashboard label is no longer applicable and is replaced by "Workspaces" security that can be applied interchangeably between dashboards and Workspaces.

Figure 12.2

As you can see, this is an exhaustive amount of security to apply. Are all or even most of the security filters/features used? No, that would be security overkill for your application. However, there are unique circumstances where some of these would be used or needed. This chapter will cover more of the common security applications.

> **Note: Slice security** is a term used to describe specific cell or intersection security. Slice security is also named **data cell access security**. This is where slice security is built and managed. The OneStream Foundation Handbook does a great job of providing additional slice security detail.

Figure 12.3

Nomenclature

Though each organization might have its own naming convention standards, OneStream has tried its best to state clearly what each security group is attempting to secure within the name of the group. For example, if the company is applying entity-based security, it might have `E_Read` or `E_Write` to assign entity read or entity write rights. As a further example, `E_Write_Austin` or `E_Read_Austin` would assume that the end-user has either the right to read data or write data to the Austin entity.

OneStream recommends using this same nomenclature for other security groups as well. E for Entity, WF for Workflow, J for Journal, S for Scenario, SSR for System Security Roles, ASR for Application Security Roles, and AUIR for Application User Interface Roles. Use identifiers in the name. Examples of identifiers would be the source of data (JDE, Oracle, Excel, PeopleSoft), geography/region, and the business unit or department that uses that data source (Corp, BUx, LOB).

This is meant to be a guide, not a hard and fast rule, of course. It is recommended to thoroughly document the naming conventions for an existing implementation, plus future security uses as well. People often change roles or leave a company, and no company would want mixed naming conventions due to a change of administrators.

Chapter 12

Common Security Practices

Each company will have its own unique security model, and this section just reflects common practices – used by many different organizations – and should be treated as such. The question of why we are not covering slice security will be asked, and we hope to address that here. Slice security is unique to specific use cases and is dependent on how stringent your company is with data.

OneStream security model implementations can be "mostly" covered by either limiting access to data or limiting access to artifacts. Limiting access to the data is probably the more critical security element to focus on first during (or post) implementation.

Security Roles versus System Security Roles

Security Roles, found on the Application tab, provide the security to truly administer the application, and allows access to control or manage the application and grant or limit access as the company sees fit.

System Security Roles, found under Security on the System tab, allows *specific users* to control or manage the security found on the System tab.

> **Note:** Additional security is unable to be applied to roles until security groups are created.

Metadata Security

Metadata security can be thought of in terms of three security elements. The first security element is the ability to view the member within the hierarchy of the dimension. The Display Member Group setting restricts who can see the member in a hierarchy. However, if the user knows the member name, they could type this into the Spreadsheet or Excel add-in tool to view the data associated with that member. This Display Member Group security setting applies to all dimensions except the Scenario dimension.

The second security element limits the access of data. This can be accomplished on both the entity and the Scenario dimension members. Both Entity and Scenario members have the ability to bifurcate specific security settings to read only the data and read and write the data as defined by the implementing company. If entity and scenario security are not restrictive enough, then applying cube data access security (aka "slice security") will be the next course of action.

The third and final metadata security element is related to the Dimension Properties tab. The Access Group and Maintenance Group control who can access this specific dimension. It can also facilitate access to a specific hierarchy for maintenance purposes. Utilizing this security setting can reduce the burden on an administrator in terms of maintaining a hierarchy. If someone other than the administrator will be performing dimension maintenance, security on the application Security Roles page will need to be adjusted. As an example, Figure 12.4 shows how the DimensionLibraryPage setting can be adjusted to the correct corresponding role.

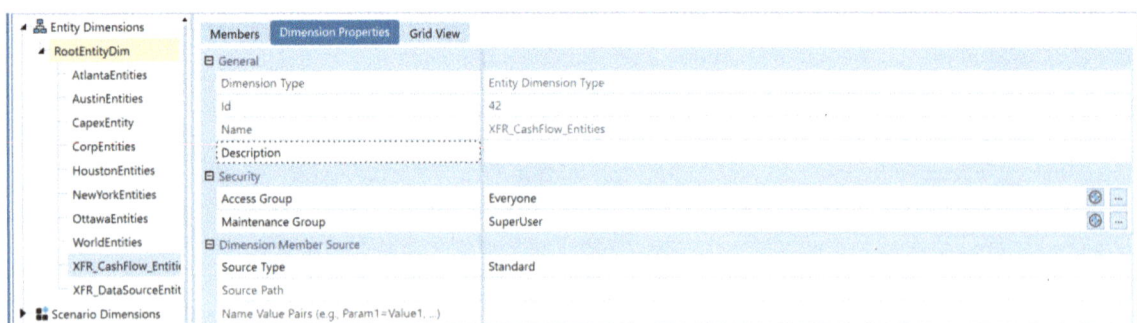

Figure 12.4

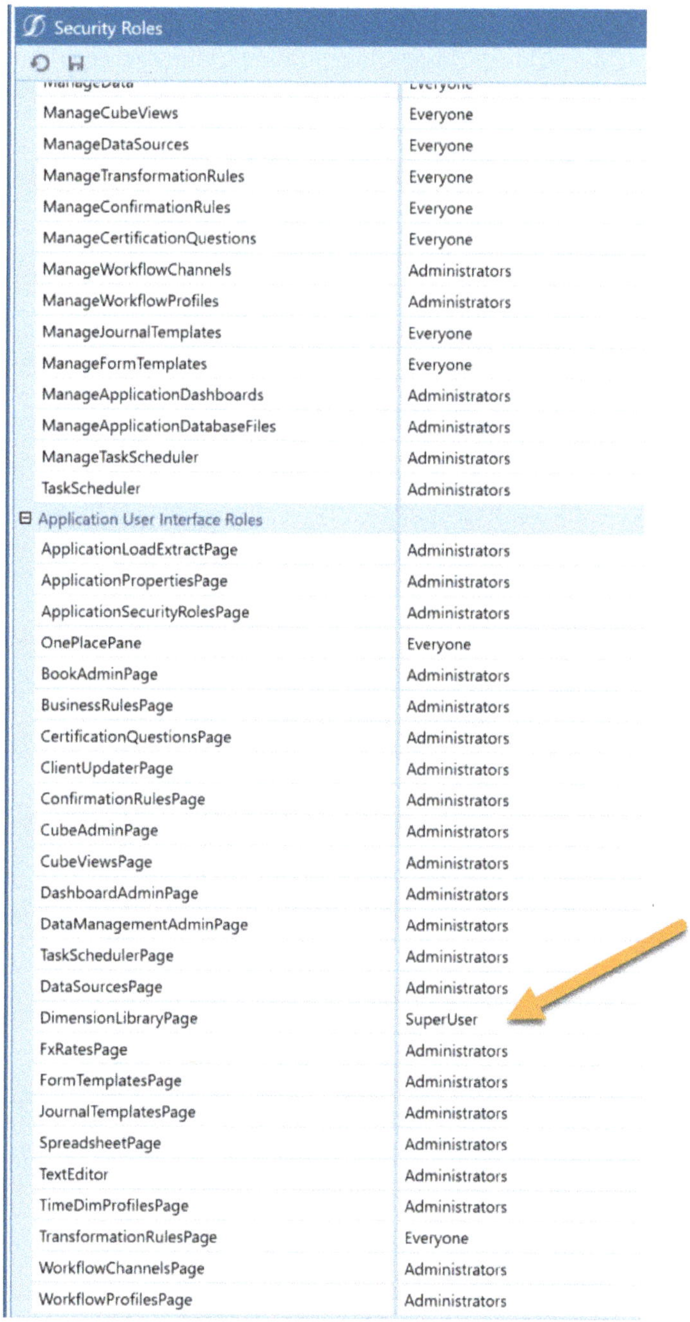

Figure 12.5

If the correct security access is applied, the newly created role will be able to edit a selected dimension but receive an error when attempting to edit other dimensions (i.e., where the role is not applied).

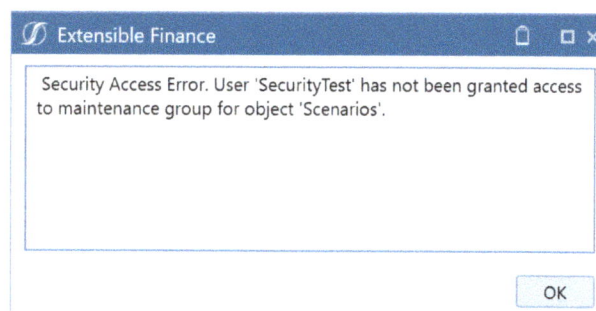

Figure 12.6

When applying security to metadata members, it's best to think about what needs to be accomplished by applying the security. Do you want to limit who can view the member? Do you want to limit who can view the data? Or do you want to provide more access to whomever can perform maintenance? Knowing the answers to these questions will help provide a better security model for metadata.

Artifact Security

Let's say a hypothetical company has decided to only employ one or two administrators. In such cases, requests for ad hoc or one-off reports will typically be overwhelming. These administrators may spend all day doing nothing but building reports or Cube Views that may only be used once. There are myriad reasons why a company would refrain from building reports using the Excel add-in. The company may not have Microsoft Excel, they may have made an organizational decision not to use Microsoft Excel, they may want reports printed to PDF from the application, or leadership may want specific formatting.

The point here is that the administrator shouldn't always be the one creating these ad-hoc reports. A select group of end-users can create them. This can be accomplished by applying the same desired security group to the Maintenance Group setting and CubeViewsPage on the Security Roles page. In the examples below, SuperUser as a security group is intended to be generically used and can be replaced with any security group a company desires in its place.

General (Cube View Group)	
Name	aSuperUser
Description	
Security	
Access Group	SuperUser
Maintenance Group	SuperUser

Figure 12.7

Security Roles	
BookAdminPage	Administrators
BusinessRulesPage	Administrators
CertificationQuestionsPage	Administrators
ClientUpdaterPage	Administrators
ConfirmationRulesPage	Administrators
CubeAdminPage	Administrators
CubeViewsPage	SuperUser
DashboardAdminPage	SuperUser
DataManagementAdminPage	Administrators
TaskSchedulerPage	Administrators
DataSourcesPage	Administrators
DimensionLibraryPage	Administrators
FxRatesPage	Administrators
FormTemplatesPage	Administrators
JournalTemplatesPage	Administrators
SpreadsheetPage	Administrators
TextEditor	Administrators
TimeDimProfilesPage	Administrators
TransformationRulesPage	Administrators
WorkflowChannelsPage	Administrators
WorkflowProfilesPage	Administrators

Figure 12.8

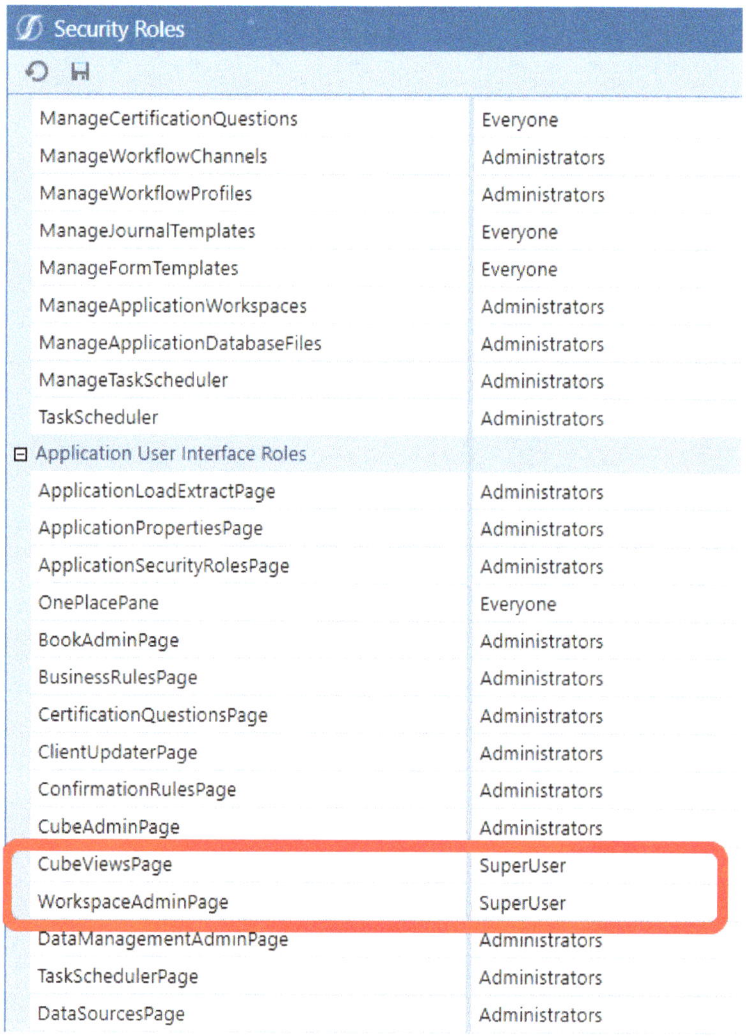

Figure 12.9

If your organization decides to allow end-users to have access to build reports, it is recommended to change the security on the Cube View Group of Maintenance Group from Everyone to Administrator. Security can't be applied to individual Cube Views, and only applied to a specific Cube View group. This setup will allow the end-users to view the Cube Views as necessary, and not allow non-administrator security groups to edit or alter any key reports.

Often, there will be an organizational decision that select people are able to create ad-hoc reports. They are not, however, allowed to view each other's work. To accomplish this, you can set the Access Group and Maintenance Group to have different access levels. Figure 12.10 is an example of three different security groups for end-users to alter the Cube Views that reside in those groups. This limits each group from seeing the work performed in the other reporting groups.

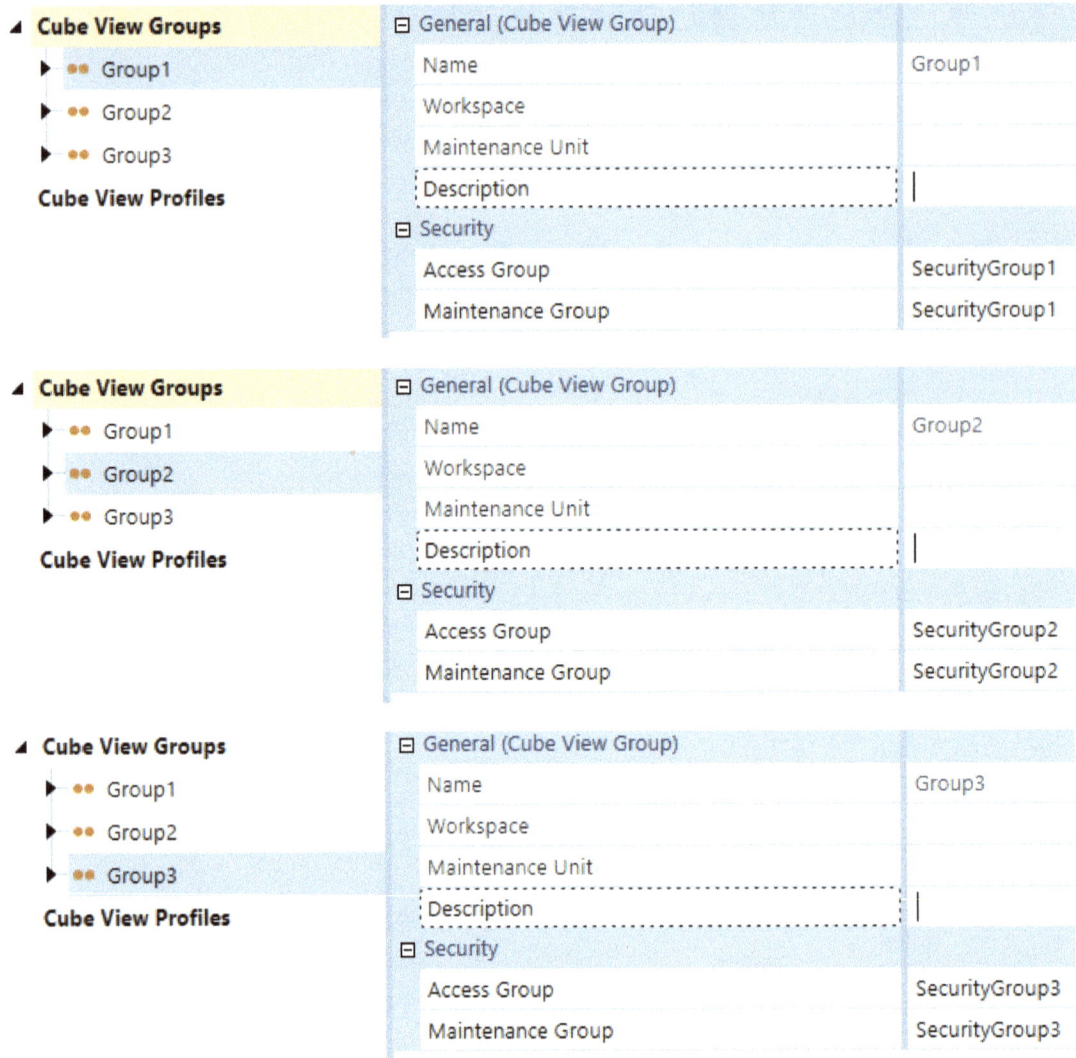

Figure 12.10

This type of setup will limit the ability of end-users to view or modify other end-users' Cube Views/reports, if the company chooses to permit this limitation.

This section has mostly discussed Cube Views, but the same type of access can be performed against Workspaces as well. Workspaces and maintenance units have the same access and maintenance group assignment structure as Cube Views. In Figure 12.11, we accomplish the same setup for Workspaces by assigning the SuperUser security group to the WorkspaceAdminPage.

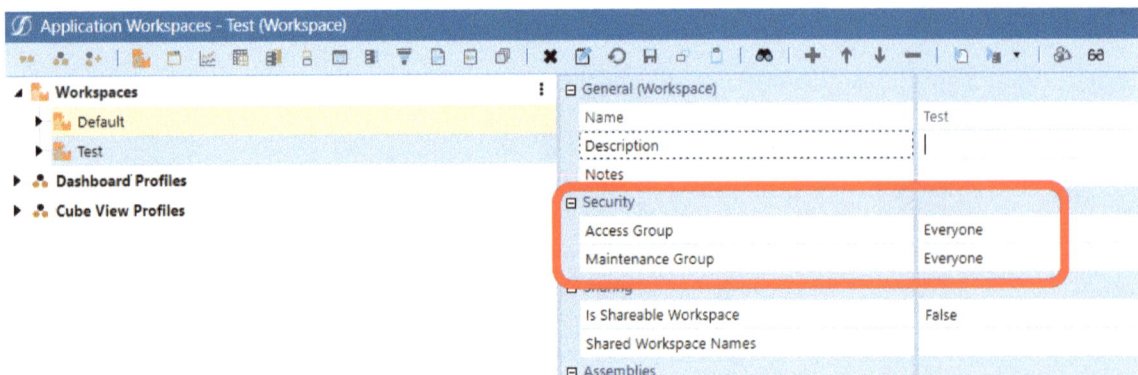

Figure 12.11

> **Note:** The default Workspace within the Dashboard page can't alter security. Maintenance units within the default Workspace can still have security adjusted.

FX Security

Companies will sometimes delegate FX maintenance to someone from Treasury or corporate accounting. To perform this activity, change the desired security on the Security Roles page. The security settings to change here are for both ManageFXRates under Application Security Roles; and FXRatesPage under Application User Interface Roles (Figure 12.12 & Figure 12.13).

If you only have ManageFXRates assigned, then that end-user will have the ability to change rates but will not be able to access the page. If you only have FXRatesPage access assigned, then that end-user can access the page but will be unable to alter any of the rates. Both are needed to access and alter any of the rates.

This end-user also has the ability to lock and unlock the FX rates if the same security group is assigned to LockFXRates and UnlockFXRates. Business requirements will determine how your security should or will be assigned for FX rates.

Figures 12.12 and 12.13 highlight that corresponding roles work together to allow someone other than the administrator to perform admin tasks on the FX page. Figure 12.12 shows that ManageFXRates grants the ability to actually change the FX Rates; Figure 12.13 shows the security setting that will grant access to the page.

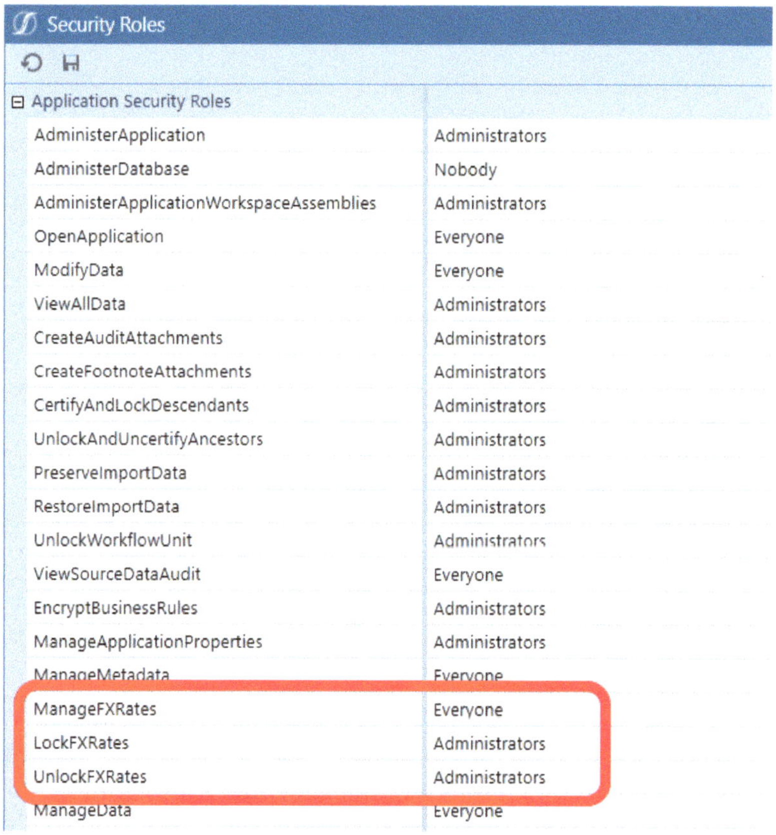

Figure 12.12

Application User Interface Roles	
ApplicationLoadExtractPage	Administrators
ApplicationPropertiesPage	Administrators
ApplicationSecurityRolesPage	Administrators
OnePlacePane	Everyone
BookAdminPage	Administrators
BusinessRulesPage	Administrators
CertificationQuestionsPage	Administrators
ClientUpdaterPage	Administrators
ConfirmationRulesPage	Administrators
CubeAdminPage	Administrators
CubeViewsPage	SuperUser
WorkspaceAdminPage	SuperUser
DataManagementAdminPage	Administrators
TaskSchedulerPage	Administrators
DataSourcesPage	Administrators
DimensionLibraryPage	Administrators
FxRatesPage	Treasury
FormTemplatesPage	Administrators
JournalTemplatesPage	Administrators
SpreadsheetPage	Everyone
TextEditor	Administrators
TimeDimProfilesPage	Administrators
TransformationRulesPage	Everyone
WorkflowChannelsPage	Administrators

Figure 12.13

Workflow Security

Workflow security can be the essential building block of security. By applying the correct workflow security, a company can control data loads, form adjustments, and journal entries all through different security groups or different end-users. Workflow security should drive your consolidation end-users versus your plan or budget end-users.

Each section of workflow security has the same standard four pieces of security:

- Access Group
- Maintenance Group
- Workflow Execution Group
- Certification SignOff Group

> **Note:** Adjustment Workflow Profile types offer three additional security groups. Journal Process Group, Journal Approval Group, and Journal Post Group. The three groups are discussed in detail further into the section.

The access group security feature allows physical access to this section of the workflow. The access group can also act as a view-only security setting. The access group will allow access to the section of the workflow, but the end-user must have the security assigned to them that also has security assigned to the **Workflow Execution Group**. If they do not, then they can only access and view the workflow.

If the company wanted to prevent budget end-users from accessing the actual workflow processes, then they could apply a security group to prevent the budget end-users from entering this workflow using the access group.

Maintenance groups should generally be administrators. There are rare cases (which will be discussed later in this chapter) when permission might be given to super users.

The Workflow Execution Group allows a set of end-users to have the ability to complete a workflow step. This becomes important as it enables *multiple* end-users to complete workflow steps. The Certification SignOff Group allows individuals (assigned to the group) to sign off on processes, signaling that everything in the workflow has been completed.

> **Note:** The Certification Signoff Group is only applicable if "certify" is part of the workflow name. Also, if the company has Lock After Certify set to True, then manually locking a workflow is not applicable as every time an end-user certifies the workflow, each level of the workflow will automatically lock. This setting is found in the Application Properties section. Additional detail can be found in Chapter 3: Application Properties.

One of the more common security requests received by OneStream is the assurance that the same end-user cannot create and post a journal. The settings to accomplish this feat for workflow security are found under the Security section for the Workflow Profile. The three extra groups relate specifically to the journaling process. The Journal Process Group can create an actual journal, whilst the Journal Approval Group (as the name suggests) can approve newly created journals. Finally, the Journal Post Group (anyone have a guess?) will post created and approved journals.

Preventing an end-user from creating *and* posting a journal will be a common security request from both your internal and external auditing partners. The report can be viewed under the Application Reports Dashboard by running the report "Workflow Profile Rights by User". This report will allow someone to know what security each user has for a specific Workflow Profile. If you are unfamiliar with workflow structures or setups, refer to Chapter 6 in this book (Work the Workflow), or refer to the Foundation Handbook.

Organizational decisions will need to be made regarding the security around journals. Some companies will want the bifurcation of all three, which will mean three different sets of end-users to create, approve, and post a single journal. Some companies will say it is okay for the creator of the journal to also be the approver, but a poster needs to be a different end-user.

In versions 8.0 and greater, OneStream now offers two new segregation of duties settings related to journals. These new settings are **Prevent Self-Post** and **Prevent Self-Approval**. This second one prevents users from approving journals if the user has created or submitted the journal. Enabling the settings will disable **Quick Post** functionality within the adjustment workflow. These settings eliminate the need for a journal event handler rule to handle this functionality for them, as was the case in the past. For versions older than 8.0, a journal event handler rule will need to be created to accomplish the same segregation of duties as the settings below.

General	
Name	Houston.Journals
Description	Adjusting entries for Houston
Security	
Access Group	Houston Combined Access
Maintenance Group	Houston Maintenance
Workflow Execution Group	Houston Workflow
Certification SignOff Group	Houston Workflow
Journal Process Group	Houston Workflow
Journal Approval Group	Houston Journal Post
Journal Post Group	Houston Journal Post
Prevent Self-Post	False
Prevent Self-Approval	False
Require Journal Template	False
Workflow Settings	
Workflow Channel	Standard
Workflow Name	Journal Input
Workspace Dashboard Name (Custom Workflow)	(Unassigned)

Figure 12.14

> **Note:** No matter what the security setup here, no notifications will be systemically sent to notify an approver or poster that the journal is ready for review and is actionable. If this is a requirement or request, a journal event handler business rule will be required to accomplish the requirement. Only one journal event handler can be assigned per application, but you can have multiple sections in the rule.

Nesting Security

Nesting security is a common OneStream practice to limit the number of security groups that an end-user is assigned to. For example, instead of assigning security groups A, B, and C to an end-user as three distinct groups, you can leverage nesting and assign one security group instead.

Nesting is the relationship between security groups where one is considered the parent, and the other is the child. Child security groups that are nested in a parent-level security group can access the data or artifacts that the parent group can – via the parent security group assignment (Figure 12.15). Removing a child security group from the parent group will revoke the access that the parent group provided.

The example below (Figure 12.15) shows that Users 1-3 are assigned to Security Group B. This assignment (Group B) also allows end-users to have Security Group A properties as well. In this example, Group B also represents the child security group, and Group A represents the parent group. The end-users in Group B will have access to any object that assigns Group A but will not have access to objects that assign Group C.

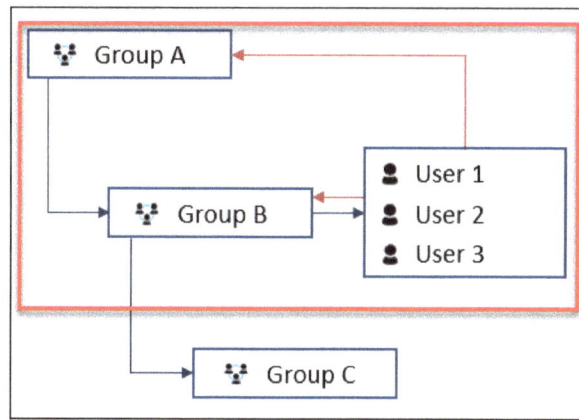

Figure 12.15

Common Security Practices Closure

As one can see, OneStream has a lot of flexibility when it comes to security. Often, an organization will need to decide how to handle common asks or requests, but a central theme is how to make life easier for the OneStream administrator. One of the ongoing aims of OneStream is to streamline processes, make life easier for all parties, and not put a huge burden on the administrator.

Common Security Frequently Asked Questions (FAQs)

This section is not intended to be an exhaustive list but rather a look at some of the more common questions that OneStream consultants and OneStream administrators get asked. When answering any question, the answer may be one of many possibilities. OneStream offers flexibility, and there can be different solutions for problems, after all!

Troubleshooting Cases

Why Can't I Access the System?

This one frequently comes up with new end-users. The end-user has access to the system approved and is ready to hit the ground running, but when they attempt to login, they either get an error or no access. A bulleted list of places to check:

- Validate that the Application Security Role setting of OpenApplication is set to Everyone or the correct access if changed.

- Validate the username they are using is correct.

- Validate that the correct security has been assigned.

- Ensure that the External Authentication Provider is properly selected.

- Ensure that SSO (Single Sign-On) providers have the end-user assigned to the proper SSO group(s) needed to access the OneStream application.

These are just some of the common reasons an end-user may be unable to access the system. It would be a daunting task to name every possible solution to validate against. These are designed to provide a starting point.

Why Can't I View Any Data in the System?

The end-user now has access to the system, but they are unable to view any data. The first place to check is the POV pane. Does that pane have any question marks, signifying that it hasn't been set for the user? If the end-user's POV is properly set, then does the artifact they are attempting to view data through have the proper security assignments? If the artifact security looks correct, then it is time to check the security assignment page. Does the end-user have any, or the proper, assigned security? Does the security assigned to the end-user make sense for the end-user's role? If yes, then I would ensure that security groups have been assigned throughout the application in the appropriate places. For example, make sure the designated security group is properly assigned to workflows, Cube Views, and access to metadata. Finally, validate that Security Roles under the Application tab has the OpenApplication and ViewAllData set to the correct security group as well.

Why Am I Receiving a No Access Message on my Report?

The end-user doesn't have sufficient security access to view a specific intersection. If the end-user should have access to the specific intersection, then the existing security will need to be adjusted. If your company has slice security, it warrants checking Cubes > Data Access and validating that the security is being properly sliced. If your company doesn't have slice security, then you should look to validate against the metadata security. This could be a combination of either entity or scenario security.

How Do I Limit Access by Workflows between Plan and Actuals?

The top-level workflows – Name_Act or Name_Plan – are defaulted to Everyone. If they need to be split by a security group, this can be set at the top workflow level. Figure 12.16 and Figure 12.17 show how this could be accomplished using security for the workflow cube root profile.

Figure 12.16

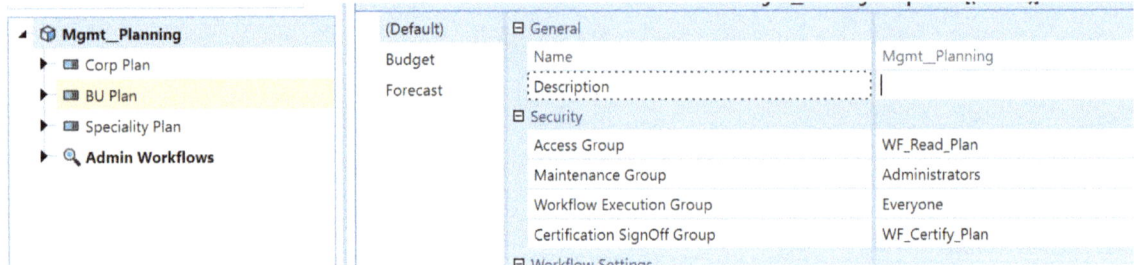

Figure 12.17

As you can see, by setting the proper security at the cube root profile, only users with WF_Read_Consolidation can see the actuals within that scenario, and users with the WF_Read_Plan can only see the budget and forecasting data.

> **Note:** Not every customer will have an extended workflow. Extended workflows mean having a suffix associated with the Scenario Type and creating a new workflow cube root profile. For additional details, refer to the workflow chapter. Remember, scenarios can be secured by the Scenario Type. Also, security can be applied to the specific scenario in the Scenario dimension.

Can Someone Other than the Administrator Handle Security Assignments?

Yes, under System > Administration, you will see System Security Roles (Figure 12.18). Adjust a combination of the following ManageSystemSecurityUsers, ManageSystemSecurityGroups and/or ManageSystemSecurityRoles to the desired group to control security. This page alters security assignments, although it is important to note that it impacts global settings and will affect all applications on that OneStream environment.

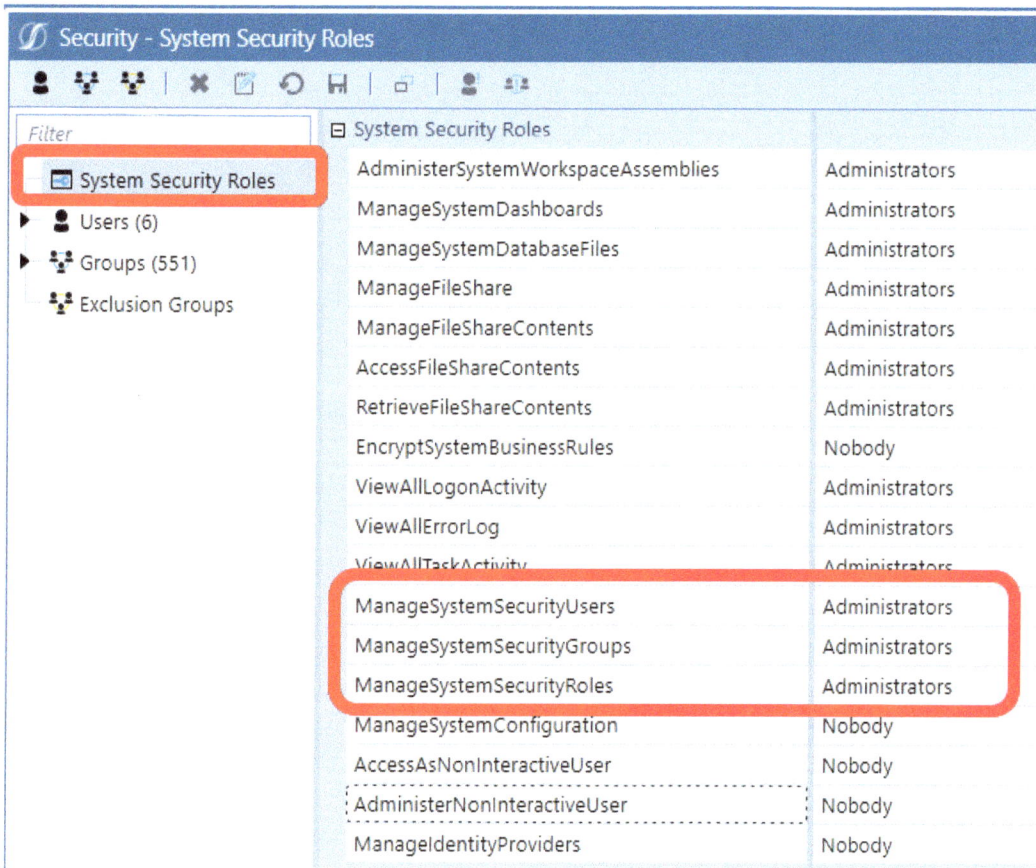

Figure 12.18

Common Security Maintenance

The below are maintenance suggestions, and administrators should always refer to company policy – first – when resolving matters. OneStream can be tailored to fit most (if not all) company policies.

Our End-User has Left the Company; How Should We Remove Security?

This is one of those instances where OneStream can handle the situation in many ways. The recommended approach would be to turn the end-user's account of Is Enabled from True to False. This will disable the ability to even log into the application.

Knowing that companies also have data retention policies, OneStream recommends never to delete an end-user. Deleting the end-user will remove the User ID, and all the audit logs that contain that user will be replaced with "OneStream User". It will be difficult for the auditing partners to understand why an unnamed OneStream user has performed an action or activity within the system.

Should Anything Security-related be Done with an Upgrade of the Application?

It is recommended to change OpenApplication from Everyone to Administrators only. The reason is that it allows administrators to login to the application prior to everyone else and perform any smoke testing or validations that need to take place before end-users run rules, jobs, or a consolidation. Upon validation, the administrator can re-enable security to Everyone.

Is there any Automation of Security Assignments or Security Processes?

OneStream has a MarketPlace solution to help handle the automation of security. **Application Control Manager (ACM)** is a solution designed to support and manage change requests and ensure the right level of control and governance over application changes. This pertains to mostly metadata-related changes, but also has a security element as well. ACM allows for the governance of user security creation and maintenance. Every OneStream customer has access to this solution. If your company is hesitant to implement this product, please reach out to your OneStream account manager to help procure an implementation consultant.

What Reporting Capability does OneStream offer for Security?

The out-of-the-box solution of **Security Audit Reports** should satisfy most audit requirements or requests from both internal and external audit partners. This reporting feature – if not already loaded to your application – can be downloaded from the OneStream Marketplace and uploaded to the OneStream environment. These reports include total end-user count, disabled end-users, added, deleted, updated, and inactive end-users. This report listing also includes security access changes, plus security group additions or deletions. All of this can be performed by date as well.

Conclusion

As stated multiple times in this chapter and in other books, the recommended security approach is to think holistically about security and slowly apply more security against the application. Going live with a minimal amount of security will make the transition from other systems to OneStream smoother and easier to digest. As your application matures, then you can begin to ramp up your security needs and really lock down the application to company-specific requirements.

Security is often viewed as the prevention of seeing some data or preventing access to certain parts of the application. If we flip the narrative of the idea of security, we actually begin to think of security as an additional tool to help guide our end-users on the data journey. Security often makes our auditing partners happy; it satisfies many IT controls and is a necessary part of the application.

Security will never be the most exciting topic for any OneStream implementation, but security is a necessary part of the implementation. OneStream can solve the most complex security needs or requirements with its multi-layered approach to security. The ability to prevent end-users from accessing workflow or entity or scenario – even down to certain reports – satisfies many companies' standards. Security can also take the burden of system ownership away from one system administrator and help them with dimension alterations.

13

Compliance and Audit

Compliance could be one of the least fun topics discussed in this book. However, as unfun as it may be, it is still important to any organization. The reason why – whether the company is a publicly traded company bound by SOX controls or a private company following GAAP standards – is that companies must still report, at some level, that they adhere to proper accounting principles.

This chapter aims to provide insight into MarketPlace solutions that offer reporting features for auditing purposes. These reports, armed with some basic naming convention consistency, can help any administrator provide the correct level of reporting to both internal and external auditing partners. The last section of this chapter aims to be a catch-all if none of the standard reports can successfully fulfill requests.

Standard Naming Conventions

Naming conventions, or nomenclature, play a large role in both application maintenance and enhancements. Naming conventions can take the guesswork out of what the named artifact is intended to be, or its role in the application. OneStream recognizes that its partners and customers may have their own naming conventions, and what is presented in this section are merely suggestions and not some hard and fast rules. This section will not cover every possible naming convention scenario but instead offer broad guidelines to help support the effort.

One general guideline is to include a prefix as all uppercase characters… *except* (specifically) for dashboard components. The prefix can be used to help identify the artifact (typically a customer, line of business, business unit, or some alternative identifying acronym). Typically, you will want to avoid using member properties in the name as they can occasionally change. Try to avoid abbreviations unless they are needed to limit the artifact name. If you are forced to use abbreviations, be consistent with them. For example, using FC instead of typing out Forecast every time. Be consistent and never try to mix the abbreviation. If you pick FC as the abbreviation for Forecast, don't change it to FOR or FORC or any other possible variation.

Moving on to good naming practices within the application, the first main item is when something appears in the OnePlace tab, either under Cube Views or Dashboards. Don't leave the artifact description blank; the artifact will be defaulted to the name of the artifact (as seen in Figure 13.1).

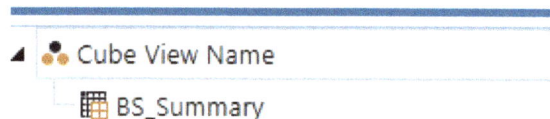

▲ ⚙ Cube View Name
⊞ BS_Summary

Figure 13.1

It is always recommended to populate the description on the artifact so that is what gets populated (see Figure 13.2).

My suggestion is to give the artifact a name that end-users will understand when searching for the report (see Figure 13.2). End-users could be confused if they only see BS_Summary, per the Figure 13.1 example above. However, the end-user is probably familiar with the naming convention of

Summary Balance Sheet, and by listing the report this way, it will be easier for them to find and use it.

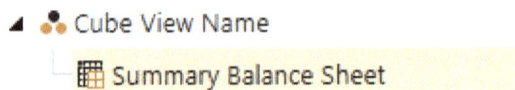

▲ ⚬⚬ Cube View Name

⊞ Summary Balance Sheet

Figure 13.2

The next tip is around MarketPlace solutions. If you need to alter something or add to an existing MarketPlace solution, it would be befitting for the administrator to maintain naming continuity while making clear that a *custom* addition to the MarketPlace solution has been made.

For example, if one needed to add a button to the PLP solution, they could use btn_custom_ButtonX_PLP. This would allow future admins to know that this button isn't part of the standard PLP solution. As always, documenting any customizations will also go a long way toward ensuring administrative continuity.

For something as robust as Cube Views, which tend to have a ton of alternate uses, it is beneficial to have something that identifies whether the Cube View is being used as a form or as a report. Putting a prefix at the start of the name of either frm_ or rpt_ will help existing and future administrators maintain the application.

Dashboard components are sometimes considered a free-for-all. In the reference guide, OneStream highly recommends using some type of prefix for any and all dashboard components. Below is the recommended prefix, if needed.

biv_	BI Viewer
bkv_	Book Viewer
btn_	Button
cbx_	Combo Box
chk_	Check Box
cht_	Chart (Basic)
chtn_	Chart (Advanced)
cv_	Cube View
da_	Data Adapter
das_	Date Selector (Windows App Only)
der_	Data Explorer Report
dex_	Data Explorer
fvw_	File Viewer
grd_	Grid View
gtv_	Gantt View
img_	Image
lbl_	Label
lbx_	List Box
logo_	Logo

lpg_	Large Data Pivot Grid (Windows App Only)
map_	Map
pbx_	Password Box
piv_	Pivot Grid (Windows App Only)
rbg_	Radio Button Group
rpt_	Report
sid_	State Indicator
spp_	Supplied Parameter
spr_	Spreadsheet (Windows App Only)
tbx_	Text Box
ted_	SQL Table Editor
tree_	Member Tree
trv_	Tree View
txd_	Text Editor (Windows App Only)
txv_	Text Viewer
web_	Web Content

Figure 13.3

For other specific naming conventions, please refer to the chapters associated with the artifacts themselves (e.g., the chapters on Cube Views or security). Naming conventions can be subjective, and customers often have their own naming convention standards. If you – as the administrator – are unsure, be consistent with *your* naming methodology.

Common Audit-Related Reports

Reporting has been extensively covered throughout many chapters of this book. As your auditing partners start to evaluate the application and the data within it, providing them with reports becomes pivotal for the success of the auditing process. This section will discuss the MarketPlace solutions' Standard Application Reports and Security Audit Reports.

Standard Application Reports

Standard Application Reports are a set of predefined reports that can be imported into OneStream. The reports are based on SQL data adapters or method queries, and used to help end-users understand data or the application in greater detail. One of the lesser-known features of application reports is the Reports Overview page. This page gives a brief description and purpose for each report. For this chapter, we will only focus on the reports that could be valuable for our auditing partners.

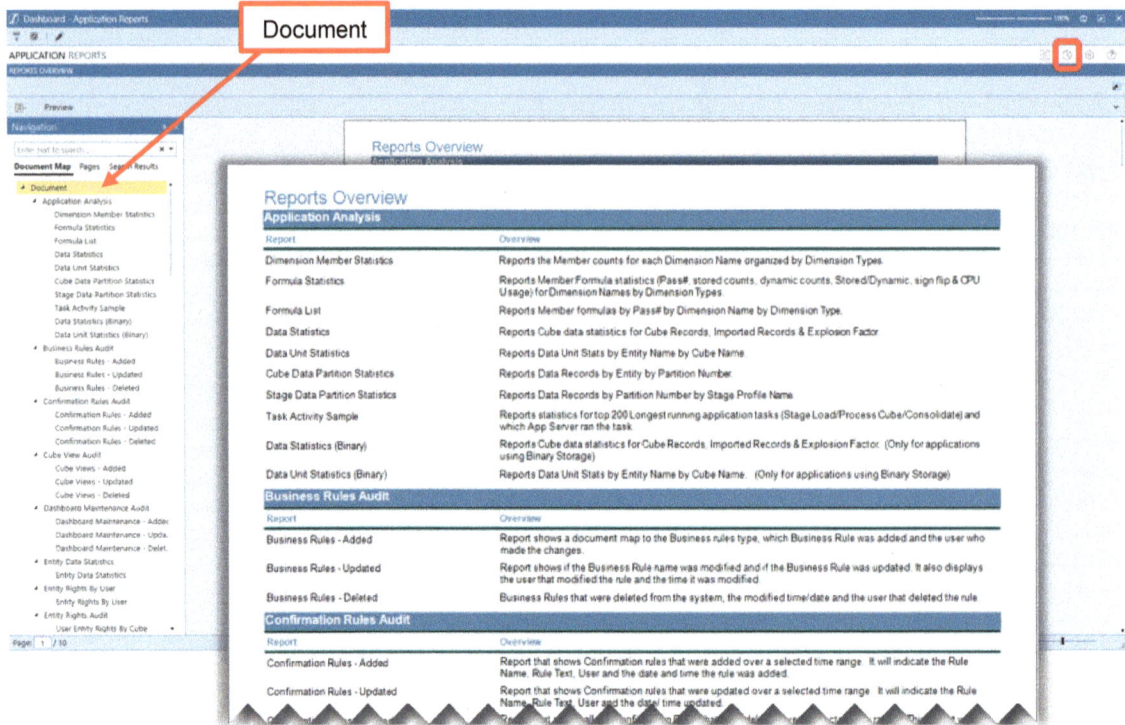

Figure 13.4

Business Rules Audit

The reason this report is valuable to our auditing partners is that they often need to validate that actuals data coming into the system hasn't been altered. This report allows auditors to determine that no changes to the rule have been made between specific time periods. Also, if rules were altered, the corresponding company should have the proper documentation to support the changes.

The rules can be viewed by what was added, updated, or deleted. You can also view the changes by specific business rule type and by the rule name. This type of reporting allows organizations to identify key rules for their application to continuously monitor during month-end or year-end documentation cycles. For example, with direct connections, the report would validate that the connector rules haven't been updated since go-live (or the last known agreed-upon change) and the sign-off on the rules during implementation.

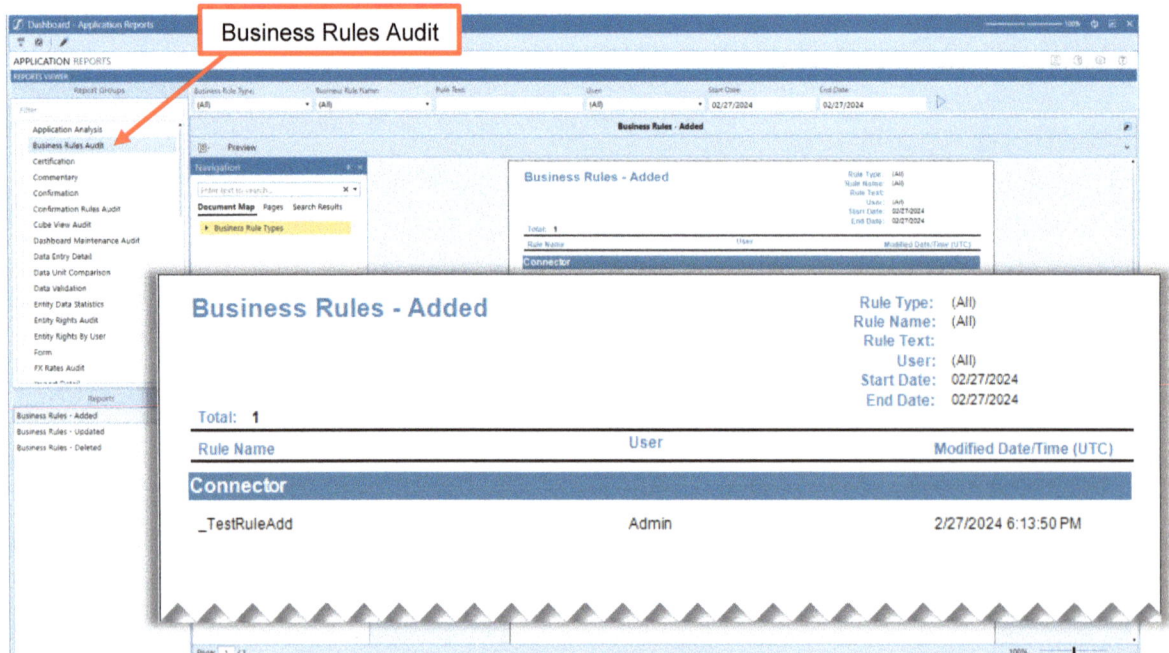

Figure 13.5

Certification

The Certification Check List report, Certification Status report, and Certification Detail provide information on workflow certifications. Any auditing partner might ask for proof regarding the certification of one, more, or all associated workflows. These reports can provide an overview if an auditor has put in such a request. These reports are Workflow POV driven, which requires you to change your Workflow POV to view the latest report. As seen in Figure 13.6, there are no reporting parameters to select.

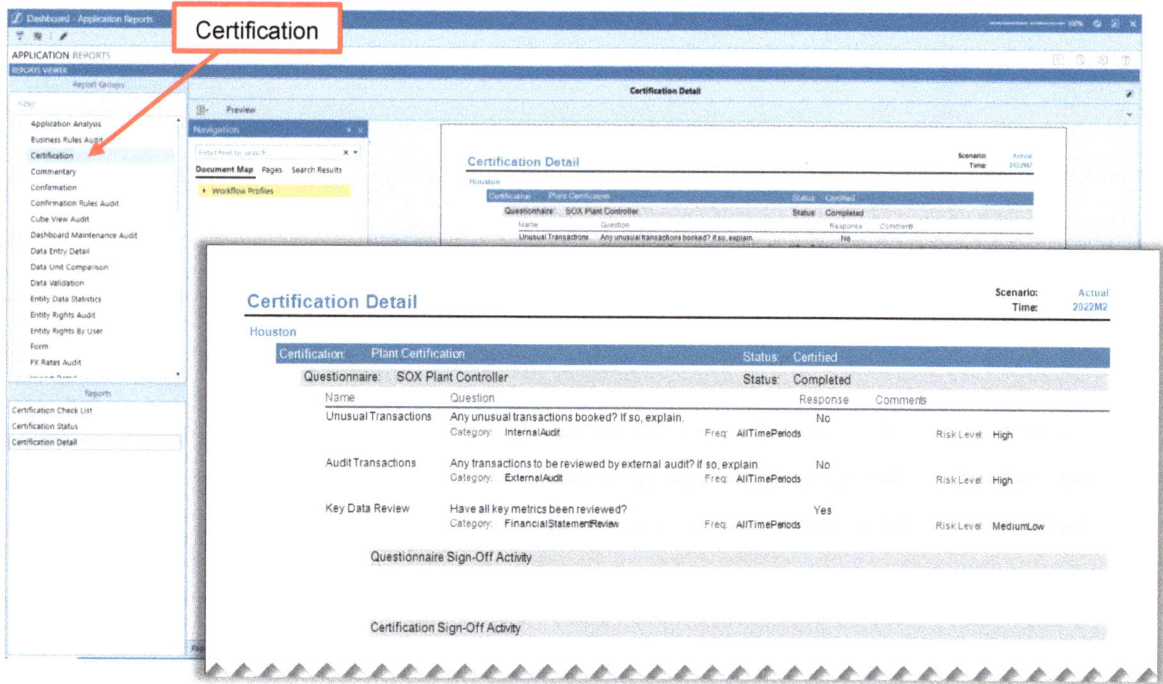

Figure 13.6

Dashboard Maintenance Audit

The Dashboard Maintenance Audit report allows an administrator to validate all things dashboard-related. An administrator can select which dashboard maintenance unit to audit and subsequently select the portion of the dashboard upon which they would like to focus. This can be the dashboard group to a group of components and even data adapters. This is beneficial for an organization that has listed dashboards as a key report or key control. This report can also be separated by a time filter and run by items that were added, updated, or deleted.

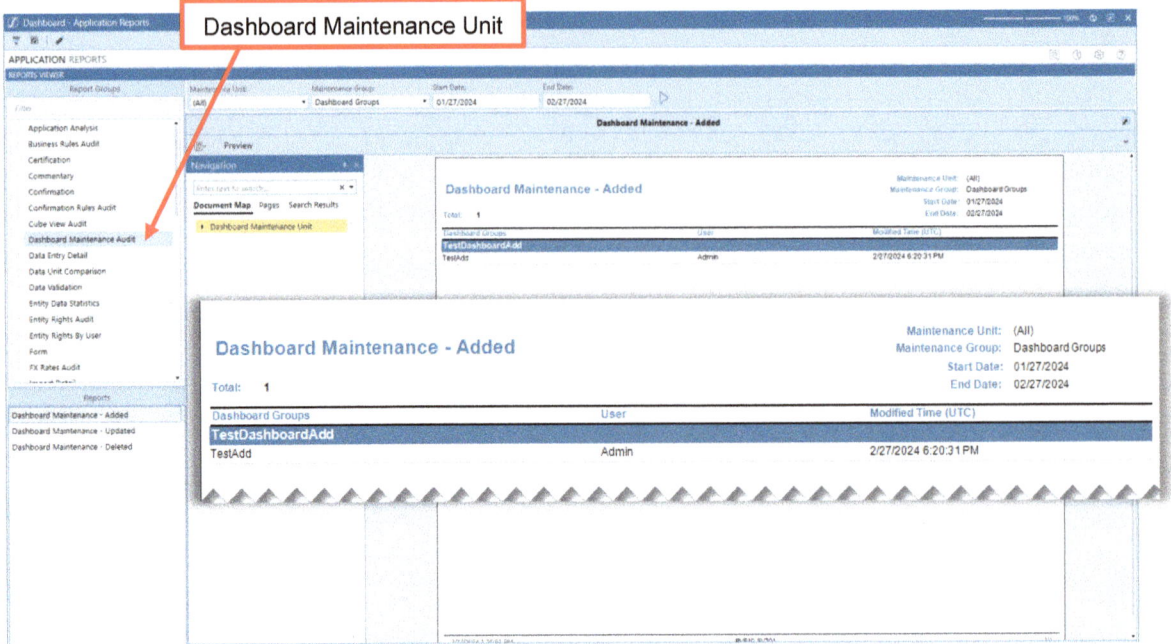

Figure 13.7

Map Change

As data is imported into the OneStream application, OneStream uses transformation rules. These rules are critical to an auditing partner and the auditing process. The customer usually provides the implementing partner with the transformation rules from the source system to OneStream early in any OneStream implementation project. Importantly, the customer will typically consider these mappings part of key controls and will need to report against them. With the Map Change report, the administrator can validate very specific transformation rule profiles for any updates, additions, or deletions of rules. These can also be completed using a time filter.

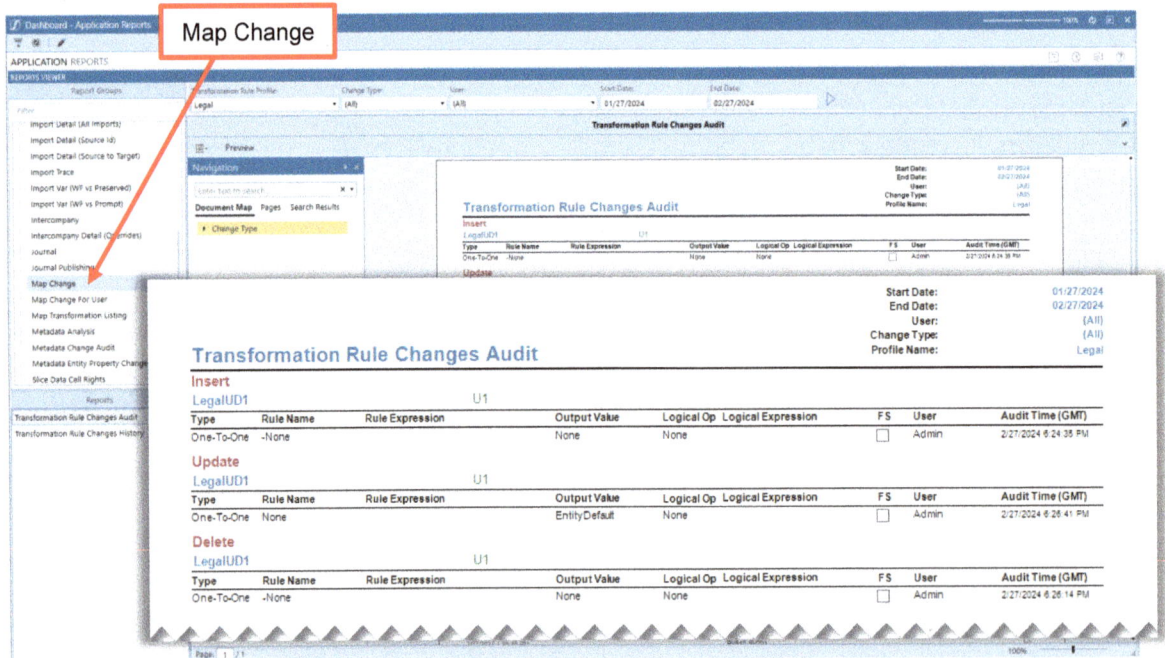

Figure 13.8

Journal

If the auditing partner has a requirement to audit or view specific journals, then the journal reporting section has two sub-reports: the Journal Checklist and the Journal Detail List. These reports are driven by the Workflow POV, and can retrieve the list of journals along with their status: Posted, Working, Submitted, Approved, or Rejected. These reports can be crucial for auditors wishing to examine all the journals posted by a specific period, or which journals are required by period. They also allow management to know which journals are still open before the month-end close can be finished.

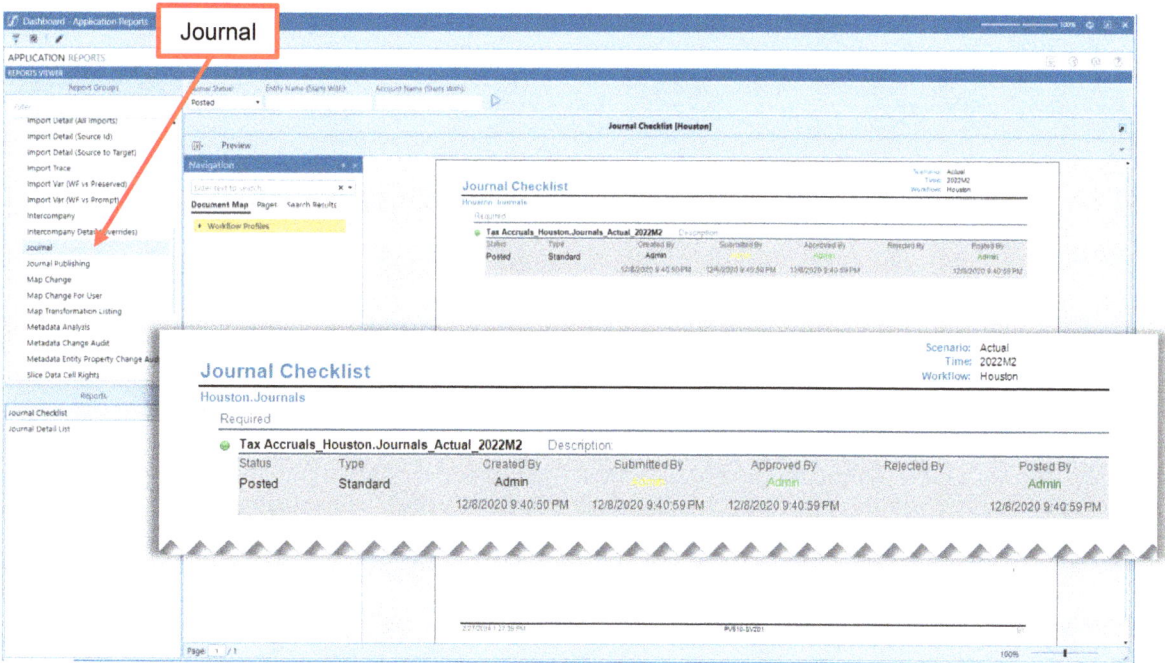

Figure 13.9

Metadata Change Audit

With metadata being one of the most critical components of the application, it would be no surprise that metadata is heavily audited. Metadata has a direct effect and correlation on a customer's actual reporting numbers, and within the Metadata Change Audit report, there are six active sub-reports that can help satisfy the most critical audit requirements. All six of these reports have the same reporting parameters, and they can be selected by change type (added, updated, or deleted) or by dimension to validate (all, or a specifically selected dimension) and, finally, a time filter.

Three of the reports can satisfy most (if not all) potential auditing questions. The first is the Member Changes Detail report. This report will list all the changes to a metadata member (including property changes) over a desired timeframe.

The next key report determines whether any metadata members have formulas attached to them. This becomes a key report when validating something such as a current year net income member for the balance sheet. This report can validate any changes against that member or any member that has a formula attached to the metadata member.

The final key report is the Relationship Detail Audit report. This report can validate that no relationship changes have occurred over a particular time period.

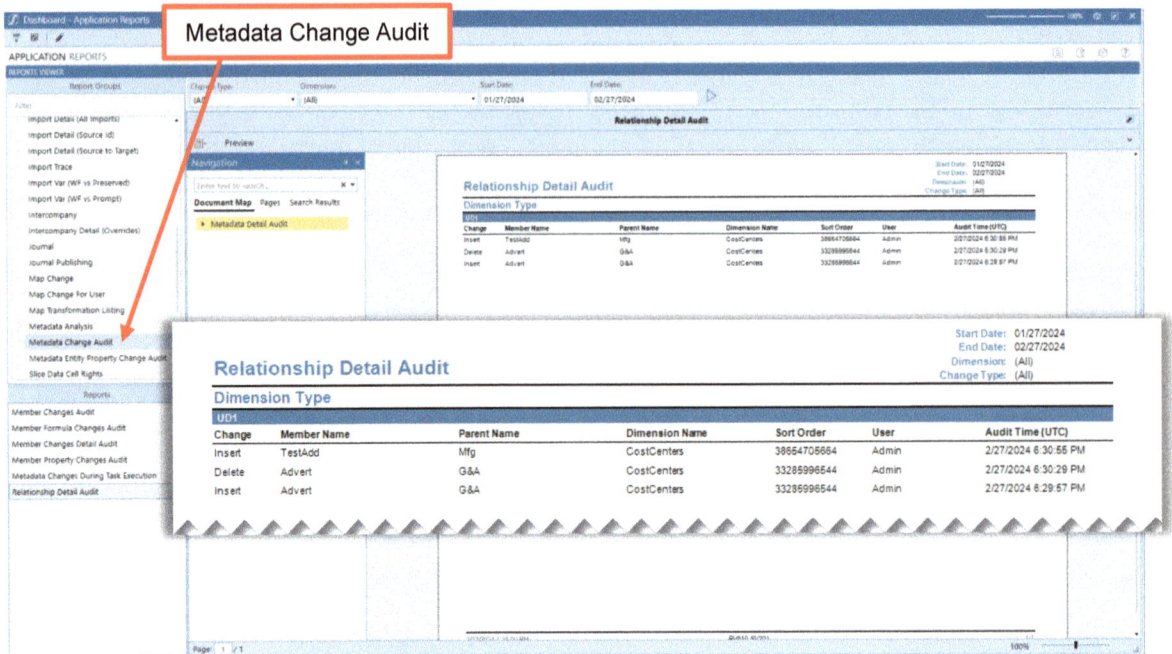

Figure 13.10

Although this is the last report discussed in this chapter's application reports section, one can see that there are a lot of reports for this Marketplace solution. You, as the administrator, are encouraged to explore and possibly find even more reports to help you through your OneStream journey.

Security Audit Reports

Security Audit Reports is another MarketPlace solution detailing user and group information. These reports can range from the total user count, to users in a specific security group assignment, down to the changes that were made to a security group. All the reports have a time span filter to allow the administrator to filter by period. Often, companies will have to provide a security access review on a quarterly basis. These reviews are typically by end-user along with their associated security group and role assignments (Figure 13.11).

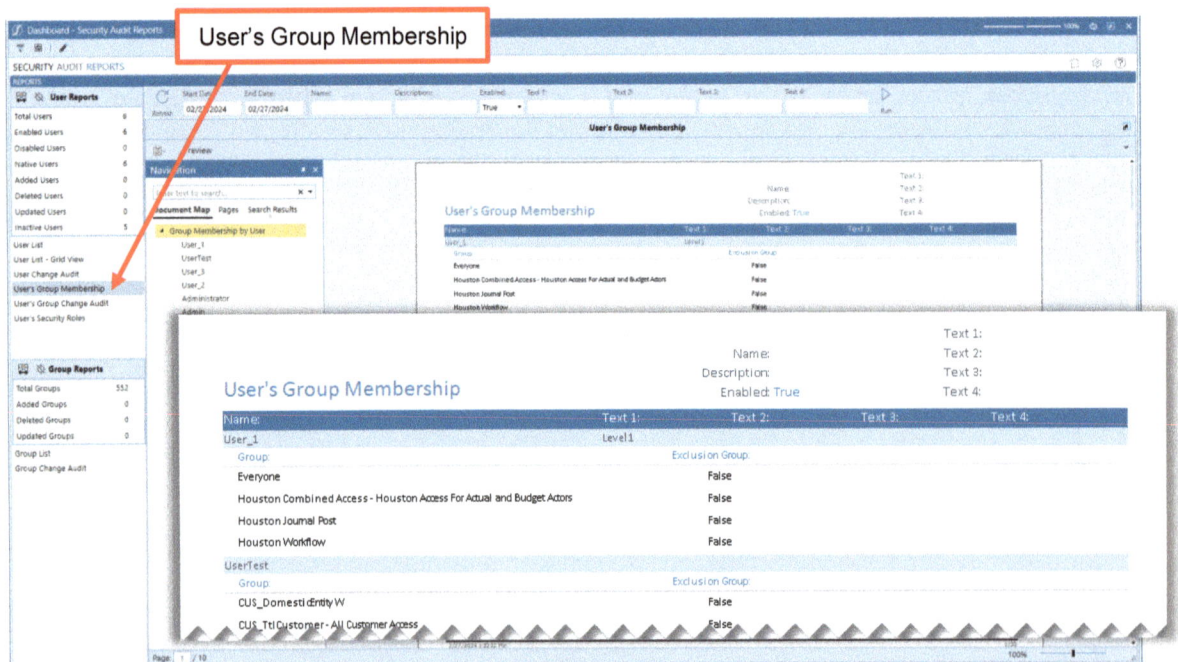

Figure 13.11

This security reporting package also offers a reverse view. Using the Group List and Administrator, an auditor can also see the total list of security groups and which users or other security groups are assigned to that specific group.

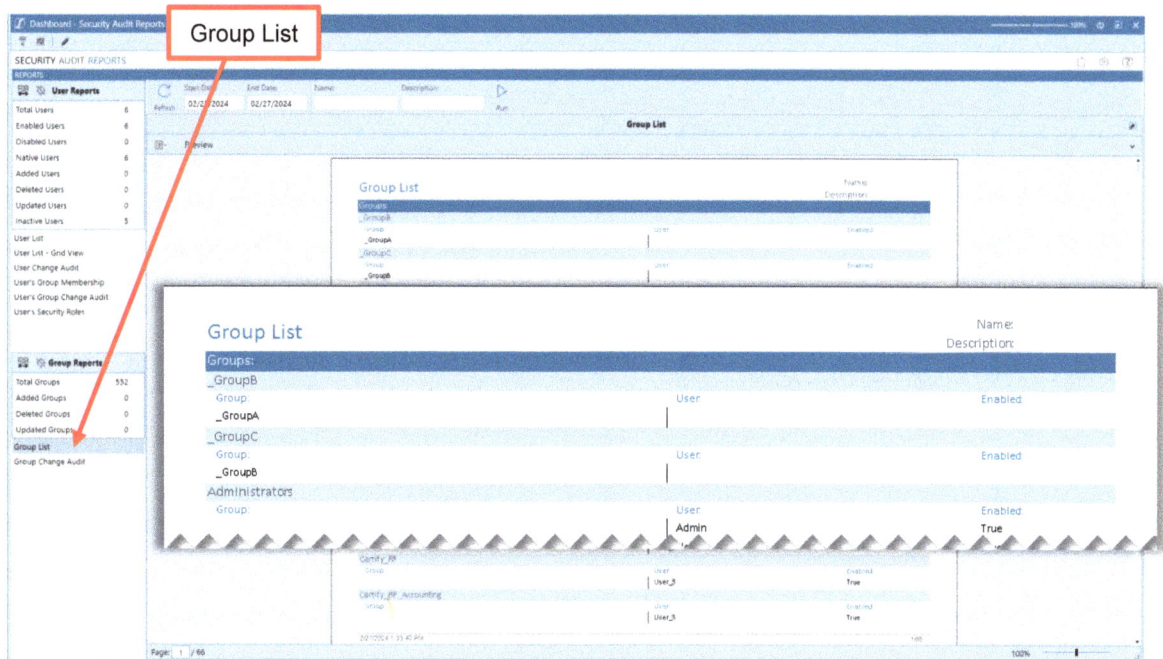

Figure 13.12

Of course, each of these reports (plus other reports) comes in a **Change Audit** report as well. You can see all the detailed changes for either users or groups in a specific report, too. This should give any auditor a full view of what is needed to complete any security access review request.

Custom Audit Reports

If the reports covered above are unable to satisfy an audit requirement, then OneStream has standard audit-specific tables. These tables can be found on the System tab under the Tools section in the Database selection. Both the Application Database (Figure 13.13) and the System Database (Figure 13.14) have audit tables.

With OneStream being a relational database, an administrator with moderate expertise in SQL could easily write any audit request from the auditing partners. If this type of custom report is required, write the query into a dashboard data adapter and then attach that to the report dashboard component before building a nice dashboard around that report.

> **Note:** The application database has over 70 audit tables, and the system database has 25 audit tables to choose from. This might seem intuitive, but the application audit tables are only applicable to the artifacts found in the Application tab. The system database audit tables are only applicable to the System tab.

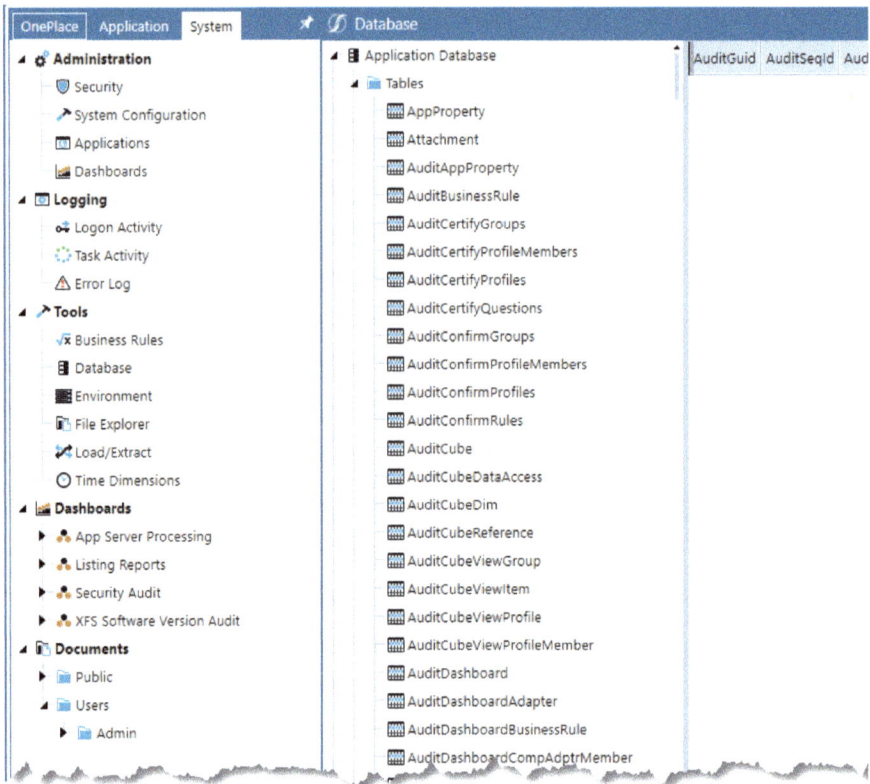

Figure 13.13

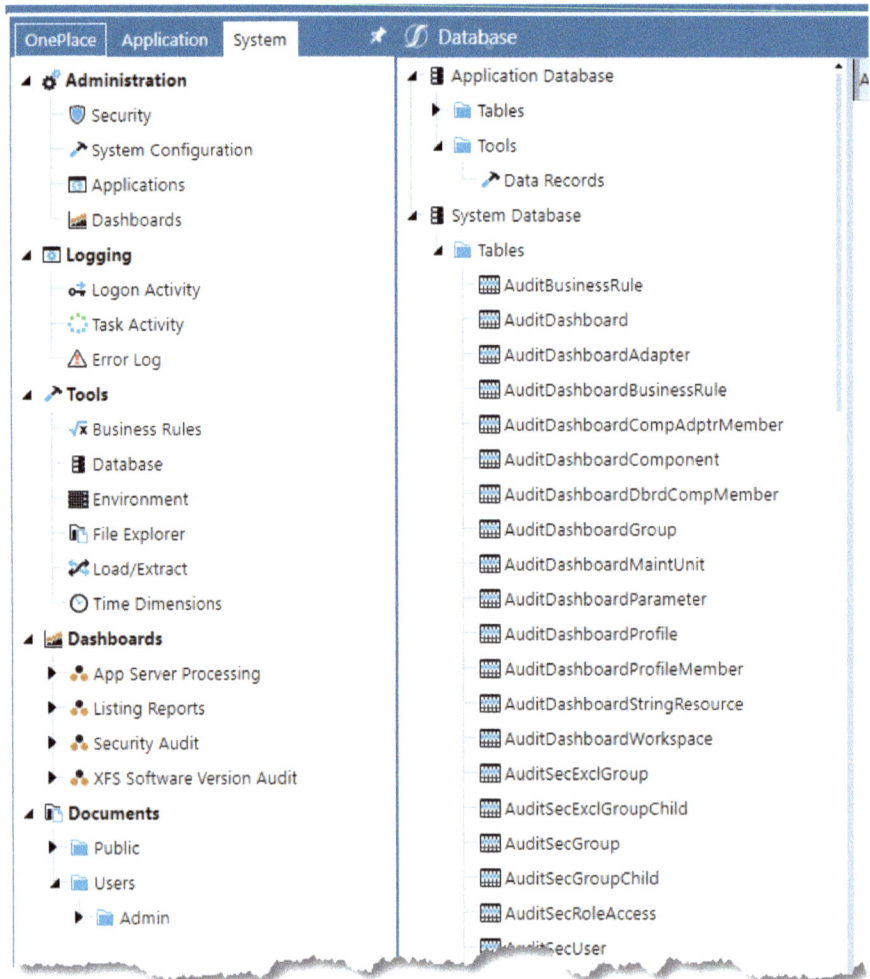

Figure 13.14

Conclusion

This chapter has provided an overview of how to assist an administrator in completing either month-end requirements (to ensure nothing has changed from the key controls) or in providing certain details to auditing partners. If a company's application has a strong naming convention, it is easy to filter down audit-specific reports to hand over to internal or external auditing partners. The chapter also offered broad oversight into common audit requests that OneStream has seen over many years and implementations.

14
Business as "Usual"

"It's business as usual," someone once said to me.

I am flabbergasted. Nothing about this seemed 'normal' to me.

"Well, you'll figure it out, and let me know if there are issues, right?"

Off I went into this known – yet unknown – abyss…

Introduction

This section holds a very dear place in my heart. The questions that administrators and end-users have asked me have enthralled me, and yet conjured tremendous stress for me when it comes to business process changes and how to incorporate them into OneStream. At some point, I noticed that these questions became iterative and repetitive, and I realized I had a baseline to work with; this was a baseline that I needed to share. As such, this chapter contains a compilation of use cases that occur as a company matures and grows.

I want to highlight that this chapter is not meant to be a step-by-step guide on what to do and how to go about handling business process changes. Instead, this chapter is meant to provide information and guidance that you can share with your stakeholders on the appropriate approach for your given application. These "business as usual" processes include:

1. Intercompany

2. Cash Flow

3. Journals

4. Org-By-Period

5. Business Acquisitions and Divestitures

6. New Chart of Accounts

7. Handling Historical Data Due to New Chart of Accounts

I hope this section helps you and lessens any heartburn you might experience when it comes to business process changes and the impact on OneStream. Pop an antacid and let's get right into this.

> **Disclaimer:** The case examples presented in this chapter may not be applicable to every company and its existing processes. Again, the purpose of this chapter is to ensure that the administrator is equipped with the appropriate technical understanding of the efforts behind each of the examples presented. The list of examples is not exhaustive, nor is it meant to be the only list or a complete list. It is recommended that the administrator works with process owners and/or consultants to determine the appropriate technical approach, especially as OneStream continues to add new capabilities or features with each version update.

"Business as Usual"

I am defining "business as usual" as business process changes that impact the OneStream application. Several of these business process changes could be:

- A change in which the system handles business processes with regard to intercompany and/or cash flow.

- An enhancement to existing processes such as journals. For example, your company has decided it now needs a separation of duties or additional topsides.

- A change in businesses that relates to acquisitions or divestitures.

- A fundamental shift in how one would view data going forward, which includes a new chart of accounts and the handling of historical data, as well as Org-By-Period.

I have categorized and organized these cases accordingly.

Intercompany

Intercompany is defined as an activity that occurs between two or more companies that ultimately roll-up to the same parent company. Usually, any sale or expense associated with intercompany is not counted – at the top – as a true sale and, as such, companies go through an intercompany reconciliation process where systems (or folks) verify and adjust these intercompany transactions to ensure that the amounts are properly eliminated when reporting on the overall company's financials.

This section will cover various intercompany cases (again, not exhaustive) in which the intercompany processes have shifted from an existing system to now being done in OneStream. Thus, the following sections will cover the use of the consolidation members, C#USD and C#Top, and how these members are used to view eliminations, as well as simple examples that showcase how amounts are eliminated going up the entity hierarchy. I hope these cases will give you some insight when you enable your intercompany processes in OneStream.

C#USD versus C#Top

Naturally, we need to address the first question – which consolidation member should I use for intercompany? The answer depends on what you are specifically reporting on or trying to research. If the report is intercompany-specific (e.g., checking that the elimination settings are correct with the proper plugs against the entities), then it is likely that C#Top will be better suited for your reporting needs, especially if you want to view the values at the base entity level in addition to the parent entities. If you do not care for the details at the base entities, then C#USD would be better suited as you would be referencing parent entities.

In the next sections, I will be covering different examples of intercompany and their views at C#USD and C#Top:

1. What intercompany would look like when the two base entities' first common parent is not the same as their immediate parent.

2. What intercompany would look like when two base entities' first common parent is the same as their immediate parent.

Remember, out-of-the-box elimination functionality in OneStream is to eliminate at the first common parent. The first two cases will show just that when going up the entity hierarchy.

3. For whatever reason, if your source data does not have intercompany partners associated with the records, but you still want to see elimination occur in OneStream, you may decide that the use of a temporary dummy intercompany entity in OneStream may be appropriate. You will still find eliminations using this dummy intercompany entity, but these eliminations will not be at the proper levels in the hierarchies that you would expect. Instead, the eliminations will be the first common parent at wherever you place this dummy intercompany entity in relation to the other entities.

Simple ICP Structure First Common Parent

This section covers a simple intercompany elimination, assuming the starting point has the correct intercompany partner and the entities' first common parent is not the same as their immediate parent. Below is the view from the debit and credit points of view.

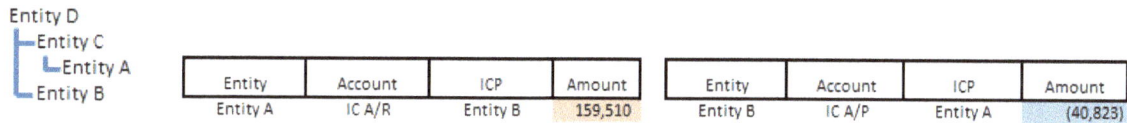

Figure 14.1

If Entity A has an intercompany amount with Entity B of 159,510 for accounts receivable, and Entity B has the payable equivalent of 40,823, then there is clearly a mismatch. The difference of 118,687 will be captured in the plug at the first common parent, which is Entity D in OneStream.

Figure 14.2

If OneStream was not used for intercompany eliminations, the journal equivalents would be:

Figure 14.3

View 1: C#USD

Taking the journal examples above, the following screenshot illustrates how OneStream handles eliminations at C#USD:

Figure 14.4

The first column represents the entity, while the second column represents the IC dimension. A consideration to keep in mind, depending on your application setup, is the reporting view versus the accounting debits/credits view. The example above has OneStream set to use the financial intelligence and reporting view.

- Yellow bolded cell: notice here ICP is I#Entity_A. This is interpreted as: E#Entity_D, 40,823 at A#[BS CLR] from the intercompany partner Entity_A

- Black bolded row: represents the use of C#USD at E#Entity_D, which is Entity A and Entity B's first common parent. Notice the amounts at O#Elimination for A#[IC Asset] and A#[IC Liability] are the opposite amounts of that at O#BeforeElim. Thus, at O#Top for A#[IC Asset] and A#[IC Liability], the amount is 0. The variance between A#[IC Asset] and A#[IC Liability] is captured in A#[BS CLR], which is the intercompany plug.

View 2: C#Top

C#Top represents the consolidation trail to track how the starting point – local amount – gets translated and consolidated up to Total Entity, which includes any topside journal entries and eliminations.

The screenshot below represents the two entities, Entity A and Entity B and their consolidation process. Notice that there is no elimination amount found for Entity A with parent Entity C since Entity C is not the first common parent between Entity A and Entity B, while there is an elimination amount for Entity B with Parent D.

View 2a — Entity_A:ICP_Entity_B, Parent: Entity_C

Consolidation	BS IC Asset BeforeElim	BS IC Asset Elimination	BS IC Asset Top	BS IC Liability BeforeElim	BS IC Liability Elimination	BS IC Liability Top	BS CLR (Plug) BeforeElim	BS CLR (Plug) Elimination	BS CLR (Plug) Top
Local	159,510.00		159,510.00						
Translated	159,510.00		159,510.00						
OwnerPreAdj									
Share	159,510.00		159,510.00						
Elimination									
OwnerPostAdj									
Top	159,510.00		159,510.00						

View 2b — Entity_B:ICP_Entity_A, Parent: Entity_D

Consolidation	BS IC Asset BeforeElim	BS IC Asset Elimination	BS IC Asset Top	BS IC Liability BeforeElim	BS IC Liability Elimination	BS IC Liability Top	BS CLR (Plug) BeforeElim	BS CLR (Plug) Elimination	BS CLR (Plug) Top
Local	40,823.00		40,823.00						
Translated				40,823.00		40,823.00			
OwnerPreAdj									
Share				40,823.00		40,823.00			
Elimination					(40,823.00)	(40,823.00)		40,823.00	40,823.00
OwnerPostAdj									
Top				40,823.00	(40,823.00)	-		40,823.00	40,823.00

Figure 14.5

Put differently, always keep in mind that the C#Elimination:O#Elimination view is dependent on the parent dimension reference. Even though the immediate parent of Entity_A is Entity_C, Entity C is not the first common parent between Entity_A and Entity_B. Thus, we would expect elimination at Entity_D. Refer to the yellow cells in Figure 14.5.

Continuing up the chain in Figure 14.6, the parent of Entity C is Entity D. Guess what? Entity D is the first common parent between Entity A and Entity B! Thus, at this view, you will find that the amounts are eliminated (View 2c) and that at C#Top, the amount is eliminated at O#Top (bolded orange cells in View 2c).

Lastly, at Entity D with the parent of Total_Entity, you will find the variance of 118,687 at the plug, A#[BS CLR] (yellow cell in View 2d), as well as the eliminations for the intercompany accounts (bolded orange cells in View 2d).

View 2c Entity_C:ICP Top Parent: Entity D	Consolidation	BS IC Asset BeforeElim	BS IC Asset Elimination	BS IC Asset Top	BS IC Liability BeforeElim	BS IC Liability Elimination	BS IC Liability Top	BS CLR (Plug) BeforeElim	BS CLR (Plug) Elimination	BS CLR (Plug) Top
	Local	159,510.00		159,510.00						
	Translated	159,510.00		159,510.00						
	OwnerPreAdj									
	Share	159,510.00		159,510.00						
	Elimination		(159,510.00)	(159,510.00)					(159,510.00)	(159,510.00)
	OwnerPostAdj									
	Top	159,510.00	(159,510.00)	-					(159,510.00)	(159,510.00)

View 2d Entity D:ICP Top Parent: Total Entity	Consolidation	BS IC Asset BeforeElim	BS IC Asset Elimination	BS IC Asset Top	BS IC Liability BeforeElim	BS IC Liability Elimination	BS IC Liability Top	BS CLR (Plug) BeforeElim	BS CLR (Plug) Elimination	BS CLR (Plug) Top
	Local	159,510.00	(159,510.00)	-	40,823.00	(40,823.00)	-		(118,687.00)	(118,687.00)
	Translated	159,510.00	(159,510.00)	-	40,823.00	(40,823.00)	-		(118,687.00)	(118,687.00)
	OwnerPreAdj									
	Share	159,510.00	(159,510.00)	-	40,823.00	(40,823.00)	-		(118,687.00)	(118,687.00)
	Elimination									
	OwnerPostAdj									
	Top	159,510.00	(159,510.00)	-	40,823.00	(40,823.00)	-		(118,687.00)	(118,687.00)

Figure 14.6

Simple ICP Structure Same Parent and First Common Parent

Let's look at another structure where Entity A and Entity B share the same parent and first common parent using the same amounts and accounts. The eliminations amount is at Entity C, the first common parent.

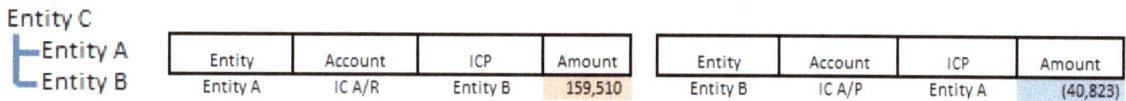

Entity C
 ├─ Entity A
 └─ Entity B

Entity	Account	ICP	Amount
Entity A	IC A/R	Entity B	159,510

Entity	Account	ICP	Amount
Entity B	IC A/P	Entity A	(40,823)

Figure 14.7

If Entity A has an intercompany amount with Entity B of 159,510 for accounts receivable, and Entity B has the payable equivalent of 40,823, then the difference of 118,687 will be captured in the plug at the first common parent, which is Entity C in this hierarchy setup.

Expected output (in debits and credits; natural sign of accounts)

	Entity C		
	Before Elim	Elimination	Total
IC A/R	159,510	(159,510)	-
Trade A/R	600	-	600
IC A/P	(40,823)	40,823	-
Plug Acct		118,687	118,687
Trade A/P	(400)	-	(400)

Figure 14.8

If OneStream was not used for intercompany eliminations, the journal equivalents would be:

Entries made:

Entity A	Plug Account	159,510	Debit
Entity A	IC AR	(159,510)	Credit

Entity B	IC AP	40,823	Debit
Entity B	Plug Account	(40,823)	Credit

Figure 14.9

View 1: C#USD

Taking the journal examples above, the screenshot below illustrates how OneStream handles eliminations:

View 1		BS IC Asset	BS IC Asset	BS IC Asset	BS IC Liability	BS IC Liability	BS IC Liability	BS CLR (Plug)	BS CLR (Plug)	BS CLR (Plug)
Entity, ICP	C#Local	BeforeElim	Elimination	Top	BeforeElim	Elimination	Top	BeforeElim	Elimination	Top
Entity A	Entity B	159,510.00		159,510.00						
Entity B	Entity A				40,823.00		40,823.00			
Entity C	Entity A				40,823.00	(40,823.00)	-		40,823.00	40,823.00
Entity C	Entity B	159,510.00	(159,510.00)	-					(159,510.00)	(159,510.00)
Entity C	Top	159,510.00	(159,510.00)	-	40,823.00	(40,823.00)	-		(118,687.00)	(118,687.00)
Total Entity	Entity A				40,823.00	(40,823.00)	-		40,823.00	40,823.00
Total Entity	Entity B	159,510.00	(159,510.00)	-					(159,510.00)	(159,510.00)
Total Entity	Top	159,510.00	(159,510.00)	-	40,823.00	(40,823.00)	-		(118,687.00)	(118,687.00)

Figure 14.10

The first column represents the entity, while the second column represents the IC dimension. A consideration to keep in mind, depending on your application setup, is the reporting view versus the accounting debits/credits view. The example above has OneStream set to use the financial intelligence and reporting view. Notice that Entity C and Total Entity will contain the eliminations for the intercompany account and the amounts found in the plug with this hierarchy. This is because the entities' immediate parent is also the first common parent.

View 2: C#Top

C#Top represents the consolidation trail to track how the starting point – local amount – gets translated and consolidated up to Total Entity, which includes any topside journal entries and eliminations.

The screenshot below represents the two entities, Entity A and Entity B, and their consolidation process to Entity C and finally Total Entity. Because both Entity A and Entity B share the first and immediate parent, you will find that the elimination amounts appear when parent Entity C is referenced for Entity A or Entity B (highlighted orange in Figure 14.11).

Thus, for instances where base entities share the same common parent, eliminations can be found at the base entity with the relevant parent dimension reference. Then, at the consolidation level, Entity C with the parent of Total_Entity, you will find the variance at the plug account as well as the eliminations for the intercompany accounts.

View 2a Entity_A:ICP_Entity_B Parent: Entity C	Origin in Col Consolidation in Row	BS IC Asset BeforeElim	BS IC Asset Elimination	BS IC Asset Top	BS IC Liability BeforeElim	BS IC Liability Elimination	BS IC Liability Top	BS CLR (Plug) BeforeElim	BS CLR (Plug) Elimination	BS CLR (Plug) Top
	Local	159,510.00		159,510.00						
	Translated	159,510.00		159,510.00						
	OwnerPreAdj									
	Share	159,510.00		159,510.00						
	Elimination		(159,510.00)	(159,510.00)					(159,510.00)	(159,510.00)
	OwnerPostAdj									
	Top	159,510.00	(159,510.00)						(159,510.00)	(159,510.00)

View 2b Entity_B:ICP_Entity_A Parent: Entity C	Origin in Col Consolidation in Row	BS IC Asset BeforeElim	BS IC Asset Elimination	BS IC Asset Top	BS IC Liability BeforeElim	BS IC Liability Elimination	BS IC Liability Top	BS CLR (Plug) BeforeElim	BS CLR (Plug) Elimination	BS CLR (Plug) Top
	Local	40,823.00		40,823.00						
	Translated				40,823.00		40,823.00			
	OwnerPreAdj									
	Share				40,823.00		40,823.00			
	Elimination					(40,823.00)	(40,823.00)		40,823.00	40,823.00
	OwnerPostAdj									
	Top				40,823.00	(40,823.00)	-		40,823.00	40,823.00

View 2c Entity C: ICP Top Parent: Total Entity	Origin in Col Consolidation in Row	BS IC Asset BeforeElim	BS IC Asset Elimination	BS IC Asset Top	BS IC Liability BeforeElim	BS IC Liability Elimination	BS IC Liability Top	BS CLR (Plug) BeforeElim	BS CLR (Plug) Elimination	BS CLR (Plug) Top
	Local	159,510.00	(159,510.00)	-	40,823.00	(40,823.00)	-		(118,687.00)	(118,687.00)
	Translated	159,510.00	(159,510.00)	-	40,823.00	(40,823.00)	-		(118,687.00)	(118,687.00)
	OwnerPreAdj									
	Share	159,510.00	(159,510.00)	-	40,823.00	(40,823.00)	-		(118,687.00)	(118,687.00)
	Elimination			-			-			
	OwnerPostAdj									
	Top	159,510.00	(159,510.00)	-	40,823.00	(40,823.00)	-		(118,687.00)	(118,687.00)

Figure 14.11

Simple Dummy ICP Structure

This section covers an example where, perhaps, you do not have true intercompany partners associated with your source data at the moment, but you want to leverage OneStream's intercompany process as you figure out how to source true intercompany partners in the future. If this option is used, keep in mind that the eliminations will not necessarily eliminate at the proper levels within the hierarchy as they would with true intercompany partners. Even though we are using a dummy intercompany partner, this does not change how OneStream will eliminate the accounts; OneStream, out-of-the-box, with the proper intercompany settings, will eliminate at the first common parent, which in this case will be found at `Entity E`. Notice that `Entity A`'s `IC A/R` and `IC A/P` is tagged with `Entity B` (dummy); this is different to the previous sections where we were assuming true intercompany partners.

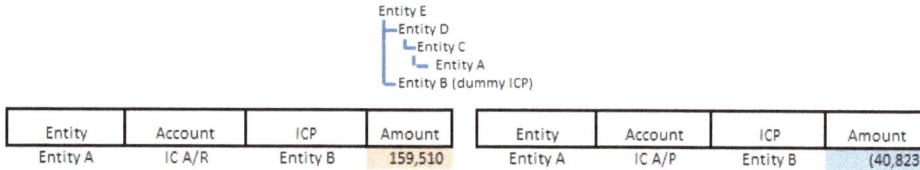

```
Entity E
 ├─Entity D
 │  └─Entity C
 │      └─ Entity A
 └─Entity B (dummy ICP)
```

Entity	Account	ICP	Amount
Entity A	IC A/R	Entity B	159,510

Entity	Account	ICP	Amount
Entity A	IC A/P	Entity B	(40,823)

Figure 14.12

Expected output (in debits and credits; natural sign of accounts)

	Entity E		
	Before Elim	Elimination	Total
IC A/R	159,510	(159,510)	-
Trade A/R	600	-	600
IC A/P	(40,823)	40,823	-
Plug Acct		118,687	118,687
Trade A/P	(400)	-	(400)

Figure 14.13

If OneStream was not used for intercompany eliminations, the journal equivalents would be:

Entries made:

| Entity A | Plug Account | - | Debit | Entity A (parent is Entity C) does not share the same immediate parent as Entity B (Entity E) |
| Entity A | IC AR | - | Credit | Eliminating entries are not made on Entity A |

| Entity C | Plug Account | - | Debit | Entity C (parent is Entity D) does not share the same immediate parent as Entity B (Entity E) |
| Entity C | IC AR | - | Credit | Eliminating entries are not made on Entity C |

| Entity D | Plug Account | 40,823 | Debit | Entity D and Entity B have the same parent, Entity E |
| Entity D | IC AR | (40,823) | Credit | Eliminating entries are made on Entity D (essentially, "topside" entries that encompass values from Entity C, which is from Entity A) |

| Entity D | IC AP | 159,510 | Debit |
| Entity D | Plug Account | (159,510) | Credit |

	Debit	Credit		Debit	Credit	
Plug Account	40,823	(159,510)		-	(118,687)	Entity D
IC AR		(40,823)			(40,823)	Entity D
IC AP	159,510			159,510		Entity D

Figure 14.14

View 1: C#USD

Taking the journal examples above, the following screenshot illustrates how OneStream handles eliminations:

View 1		BS IC Asset BeforeElim	BS IC Asset Elimination	BS IC Asset Top	BS IC Liability BeforeElim	BS IC Liability Elimination	BS IC Liability Top	BS CLR (Plug) BeforeElim	BS CLR (Plug) Elimination	BS CLR (Plug) Top
Entity, ICP	C#Local									
Entity A	Entity B	159,510.00		159,510.00	40,823.00		40,823.00			
Entity B	Top									
Entity C	Entity B	159,510.00		159,510.00	40,823.00		40,823.00			
Entity C	Top	159,510.00	-	159,510.00	40,823.00	-	40,823.00		-	-
Entity D	Entity B	159,510.00		159,510.00	40,823.00		40,823.00			
Entity D	Top	159,510.00	-	159,510.00	40,823.00	-	40,823.00			
Entity E	Entity B	159,510.00	(159,510.00)	-	40,823.00	(40,823.00)	-		(118,687.00)	(118,687.00)
Entity E	Top	159,510.00	(159,510.00)	-	40,823.00	(40,823.00)	-		(118,687.00)	(118,687.00)

Figure 14.15

Because Entity B (Dummy) and Entity A's first common parent is not until Entity E, you will not see any plug value or eliminations until you are at Entity E (last two rows), where you can drill into I#Top and see the elimination associated with the dummy intercompany partner.

View 2: C#Top

C#Top represents the consolidation trail to track how the starting point – local amount – gets translated and consolidated up to Total Entity, which includes any topside journal entries and eliminations. Because Entity B (Dummy) and Entity A's first common parent is not until Entity E, you will not see any plug value or eliminations until you reference an entity that has a parent as Entity E. In this case, you will not see elimination amounts until Entity D, with a parent of Entity E.

View 2a	Origin in Col	BS IC Asset BeforeElim	BS IC Asset Elimination	BS IC Asset Top	BS IC Liability BeforeElim	BS IC Liability Elimination	BS IC Liability Top	BS CLR (Plug) BeforeElim	BS CLR (Plug) Elimination	BS CLR (Plug) Top
Entity A:ICP_Entity B	Consolidation in Row									
Parent: Entity C	Local	159,510.00		159,510.00	40,823.00		40,823.00			
	Translated	159,510.00		159,510.00	40,823.00		40,823.00			
	OwnerPreAdj									
	Share	159,510.00		159,510.00	40,823.00		40,823.00			
	Elimination		-	-					-	-
	OwnerPostAdj									
	Top	159,510.00		159,510.00	40,823.00		40,823.00			

View 2b	Origin in Col	BS IC Asset BeforeElim	BS IC Asset Elimination	BS IC Asset Top	BS IC Liability BeforeElim	BS IC Liability Elimination	BS IC Liability Top	BS CLR (Plug) BeforeElim	BS CLR (Plug) Elimination	BS CLR (Plug) Top
Entity C:ICP Top	Consolidation in Row									
Parent: Entity D	Local	159,510.00		159,510.00	40,823.00	-	40,823.00		-	-
	Translated	159,510.00	-	159,510.00	40,823.00	-	40,823.00		-	-
	OwnerPreAdj									
	Share	159,510.00	-	159,510.00	40,823.00	-	40,823.00		-	-
	Elimination								-	-
	OwnerPostAdj									
	Top	159,510.00	-	159,510.00	40,823.00		40,823.00		-	-

View 2c	Origin in Col	BS IC Asset BeforeElim	BS IC Asset Elimination	BS IC Asset Top	BS IC Liability BeforeElim	BS IC Liability Elimination	BS IC Liability Top	BS CLR (Plug) BeforeElim	BS CLR (Plug) Elimination	BS CLR (Plug) Top
Entity D: ICP Top	Consolidation in Row									
Parent: Entity E	Local	159,510.00	-	159,510.00	40,823.00	-	40,823.00		-	-
	Translated	159,510.00	-	159,510.00	40,823.00	-	40,823.00		-	-
	OwnerPreAdj									
	Share	159,510.00	-	159,510.00	40,823.00	-	40,823.00		-	-
	Elimination		(159,510.00)	(159,510.00)		(40,823.00)	(40,823.00)		(118,687.00)	(118,687.00)
	OwnerPostAdj									
	Top	159,510.00	(159,510.00)	-	40,823.00	(40,823.00)	-		(118,687.00)	(118,687.00)

Figure 14.16

I thought it would be useful to cover a view that exists but which does not provide much added value (Figure 14.17). This is where we have Entity E representing Total Consolidated. Notice that Entity E does not have a parent; Entity E is, in fact, the Top Parent. Thus, you would not expect to see a consolidation trail for it; in other words, within C#Top only C#Local is valid, while the remaining consolidation members are considered invalid (as indicated by the red cells).

View 2d	Origin in Col	BS IC Asset BeforeElim	BS IC Asset Elimination	BS IC Asset Top	BS IC Liability BeforeElim	BS IC Liability Elimination	BS IC Liability Top	BS CLR (Plug) BeforeElim	BS CLR (Plug) Elimination	BS CLR (Plug) Top
Entity E	Consolidation in Row									
Parent: None	Local	159,510.00	(159,510.00)	-	40,823.00	(40,823.00)	-		(118,687.00)	(118,687.00)
	Translated									
	OwnerPreAdj									
	Share									
	Elimination									
	OwnerPostAdj									
	Top									

Figure 14.17

No ICP Tagged But Want to See IC Elimination

The most straightforward way is to create a dummy entity to do the elimination as we saw in the section above. This would allow for a transition when your ERP has true intercompany partners assigned.

Some non-straightforward ways are to have several elimination entities specifically created in the Entity dimension, or to have elimination centers as part of the UD. This would require custom elimination rules written into OneStream, which may be more complicated than any effort is worth, especially if you have plans to have a true intercompany partner assigned within your ERP. For these instances, it is highly recommended that you work with the relevant stakeholders, partners, and consultants on the approach.

Mapping Considerations

Because the source file would assume that there is no ICP associated with each relevant intercompany account record, there will be a need to leverage transformation rules or some sort of mapping logic to ensure all intercompany accounts are associated with a dummy ICP.

Plug Considerations

If there is a need to export or have an outbound integration from OneStream to another system, we will need to be mindful of plug naming conventions if they are not readily available or do not exist in the source file. One suggestion is to first identify the outbound integration requirements. Another suggestion is to leverage a similar naming convention associated with your accounts – for example, if your intercompany account starts with 234 and always has to be 5 characters, and you want all your balance sheet intercompany plugs to be associated with liability, you could consider calling a plug 2340A, and so forth.

Another consideration is the number of intercompany accounts associated with a plug. If you have entangled intercompany accounts, one suggestion is to have the +/- equivalent (two accounts) to one plug instead of having multiple accounts (two+ accounts) to a plug. This will make your research and ability to resolve the variances a little easier.

Common Errors

Common errors when updating the application for intercompany eliminations include, but are not limited to:

- **Transformation mappings:** for example, if you were to use **composites** to force an intercompany partner, you will need to make sure – with each new intercompany account – that you have transformation mappings included. If you are using explicit mappings, you will need to make sure that the intercompany account is captured as well.

- **Accounts**
    - Is `IC Account = False` instead of True? If you do not set an intercompany account to True, the account will not eliminate even if you have plug accounts assigned.
    - The plug account is missing when there should be a plug account assigned. If an intercompany account does not have a plug assigned, its variance will not be captured with the other pairings.

- **New intercompany plug accounts:** if you are using OneStream's out-of-the-box **Intercompany Matching Report**, you will need to update the workflows that are using the report to include the latest set of intercompany plug accounts.

- **Extensibility:** if you improperly extended your member (e.g., it should be in a different layer of the dimensions), you may not see the proper eliminations and/or consolidated amounts.

- **Entity:** Entity members that should never be ICP; ensure the `Is IC Entity` setting is set to `False`. This will limit the number of selectable intercompany partners for users.

Chapter 14

Intercompany Matching Report

The out-of-the-box Intercompany Matching Report is found on the workflow as part of the **Intercompany Matching Settings** section where `Matching Enabled` is set to `True` and the matching parameters are populated. If matching parameters need updating, click on the ellipsis icon and you will encounter a pop-up similar to the one below.

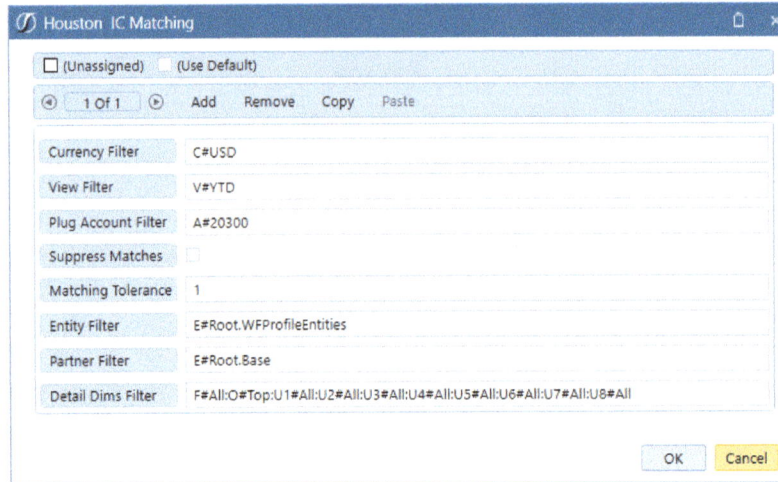

Figure 14.18

If assigned entities are present for the given workflow step, you can simply use the Entity Filter as `E#Root.WFProfileEntities`. Otherwise, you will need to be explicit with the entities. It is recommended to use Top for dimensions where the details are not important; all will use all details. Ensure that all plug accounts are assigned for every IC grouping.

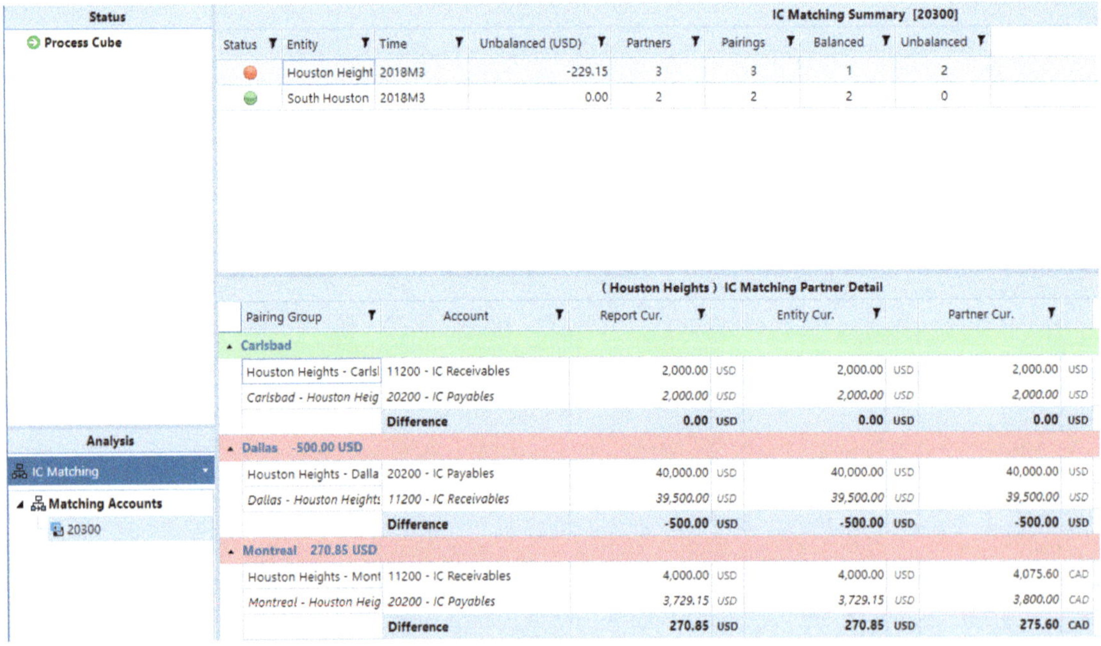

Figure 14.19

The matching report will evaluate the plug account. The report has the ability to translate on-the-fly, but historical/override accounts will not reflect the override for entities not yet translated. In versions 8.1+, the matching report will have a flag on balances that are stored versus translated on-the-fly.

> **Note:** If there is a matching tolerance assigned to the intercompany matching report, the matching tolerance is simply a number and does not translate. For example, if 100 is your threshold, this means 100 EUR, 100 Yen, 100 USD, etc. will be flagged.

Cash Flow

Cash flow, ahh, the final financial report that seems to instill a sense of drudgery. This section assumes that you are looking to reduce the manual efforts behind creating a cash flow and seeking to incorporate some sort of automation and transparency in OneStream. If you already have cash flow automated in OneStream, then continue to carry on!

Essentially, the goal of this section is to cover OneStream's capabilities, functionalities to be aware of, and the pros and cons of each situational case.

If you don't have the CPM Blueprint application already downloaded, I highly recommend that you do so via the Solution Exchange. It contains a good example of a possible cash flow solution that leverages text fields on the accounts and a business rule. This might be a good starting point if you have a situation where you are starting from scratch.

Starting from Scratch

Here, the assumption is that you have never really had the need to report on cash flow. How should you think about positioning OneStream to handle cash flow? This requires research on:

1. Determining mappings of balance sheet activity to cash flow line items.

2. What is the level of detail that you want users to enter rollforwards? For example, PP&E is common where you might want to describe – in more detail – that a portion related to Retirements goes to one cash flow line, but Additions goes to a different cash flow line.

3. At what level do you want to enter details for the entity? Do you care that every base entity is accounted for, or would you rather report at the parent level?

4. At what level do you want to enter account details? Do you want to enter at the base level or more of an aggregated level (which is where extensibility comes in handy)?

5. Do you plan to leverage the Flow dimension and add in the beginning balance, activity, and ending balance if you have not already done so? You will need `F#Activity`, as cash flow is all about the activity of balance sheet accounts!

As a reminder, you can refer to the CPM Blueprint application and its documentation on cash flow. You will find a cash flow business rule, which reads off the text fields of the balance sheet accounts with the corresponding source rollforward line items and target cash flow reporting line items.

When you look at the CPM Blueprint's Flow dimension, you will notice groupings dedicated to rollforward inputs. Keep in mind that these rollforward members will leverage the Switch Type of True for the portion that represents the details related to overall activity (e.g., `RF_PPE_Activity`) and `FX`. The `BegBal`, `FX`, `EndBal` are shared members and referenced in `F#BalSheetFlows`. Most importantly, for rollforward purposes, the aggregation weights are `-1` for `BegBal`, `RF_PPE_Activity` and `FX`, while it is `1` for `EndBal`. This allows you to use `RF_PPE` to represent any variances due to the aggregation.

You will also notice on the balance sheet accounts that there are values in the text field suited for cash flow purposes. The cash flow rule will parse based on the special characters used to differentiate which piece is the source and which piece is the target.

From here, you can work with the relevant stakeholders to identify your company's desired cash flow reports, rollforwards inputs, and mappings, which can then be handled as text fields and a business rule which is similar to that of the Blueprint. Below is a list of pros and cons to this approach; again, the list is not exhaustive.

Pros	Cons
You have an opportunity to create a less manual, more automated cash flow process within OneStream. You can review the cash flow setup of the Blueprint application and determine if that is a good fit for your company's requirements. If it is a fit, I consider this a pro as it would give you a framework to work with.	The research and effort required to identify the mappings and subsequent efforts to validate and test the cash flow process. This will require a deep understanding of the existing data set and how that should be used to produce the resultant cash flow statement.

Figure 14.20

Journals

This section covers common business cases on topside entries, setting up a separation of duties (if you have not done so already or are now considering a separation of duties), and other journal functionalities that will relate to the use of a **JournalsEventHandler** (extensibility rule).

Use of Journals for "Topside" Entries

Let's say you have a parent entity that needs to reflect an adjustment of $100 via a journal. Where do you put this amount? This $100 amount is considered a topside entry, and we have ways to handle this in OneStream:

- Entries booked to an existing base entity that changes what users want in the parent entity.

- Entries booked to a parent entity, which OneStream allows for adjustments to a non-base entity.

- Adjustment-only base entity that represents the entity to be used only for these adjustments.

With these three options, keep in mind that reorganizations of the entity structure (e.g., if base entities change parents, parent roll-ups change, or alternate structures change) will see users having to re-assess and validate existing journals and identify whether further updates and/or adjustments are needed. In an ideal world, topsides should be handled as adjustments to handle timing differences during the close process and then the journals should be made in the ERP such that they are already reflected for the next period.

Entering at Base Entity

The most straightforward way is to choose a base member as the representative entity for topside entries, and the amount will then get aggregated to the parent. You could have a journal template called Topsides to further differentiate cases where the journals represent topside adjustments.

Pros	Cons
This approach sees amounts and aggregations consistently make sense.	The entry isn't made at a true parent entity.
	The base entity will reflect this journal in its balances, depending on the POV.
	If you have entity assignments enabled on your workflow where this journal adj step resides, you may be required to unlock or uncertify completed workflows.

Figure 14.21

Entering at the Parent Entity

This represents an adjustment done at the parent level with no impact on the base entities. Parent entity adjustments are tracked through the Origin member where users can view the adjustments made at base entities and parent entities. See the example below in Figure 14.22:

	AdjInput	AdjConsolidated	Top
US Clubs	(1,000)	11,000	10,000
Houston		11,000	11,000
Houston Heights	5,000		5,000
South Houston	6,000		6,000

Figure 14.22

Observe the journal entries made to base entities Houston Heights and South Houston at AdjInput – and how they total 11,000. Notice, however, that they do not aggregate to Houston. Instead, this 11,000 will be reflected at O#AdjConsolidated at the parent entity, Houston.

If there is the need for a topside entry at US Clubs, this can be done through a topside journal entry and topsides will be found at the parent entity and O#AdjInput. When drilling down on the Origin member, users can determine which originated from journals (AdjInput), the values consolidated (AdjConsolidated), and how the values roll up to O#Top.

> **Note:** this approach will likely create confusion for users and will require training and change management. For example, if a user is at O#Top and E#[US Clubs] and drills down on this entity, they will pause, "Wait a minute, data isn't aggregating correctly!"
>
> For the correct view, the user would need to drill down on Origin instead and realize, "Oh! Okay, it looks like – at AdjInput – we had some journals for Houston Heights and South Houston and then there was the topside entry of -1,000.
>
> "So, if we took the AdjInput and the AdjConsolidated amount for US Clubs, it does make sense that it shows 10,000."

Pros	Cons
This approach represents a true topside parent adjustment, done at the parent entity. In other words, an entry here will not affect base entities' data and there will be no need for additional adjustment entities.	This will require user training and change management to prevent user confusion when users are querying intersections.

Figure 14.23

Entering at Adjustment-Only Entities

If you do not want these topside entries to co-mingle with your entities that have data from your source systems, another method is to create a group of adjustment-only entities. In other words, these would be dummy entities whose sole purpose is to store journal-related data.

Pros	Cons
An entry to the adjustment-only entity will not affect base entities' data, while aggregation to the parent makes sense.	The entry isn't made at a true parent entity.
	If you have entity assignments enabled on your workflow where this journal adj step resides, you may be required to unlock or uncertify completed workflows.

Figure 14.24

Updating the Journal Process

This section assumes that you have an application where you are actively using journals and it is either 1. set up with **Quick Post** and/or 2. users can be both the submitter and poster and/or 3. you have journals set up without a formal approval process in OneStream.

Now that your company has grown, however, there is an ask for a separation of duties and/or a new process where the submitter and approver cannot be the same person.

Separation of Duties and the Use of Workflow Security Groups

A separation of duties is differentiated with the workflow security groups found on the adj step. For versions 8.0+, a business rule is no longer needed to prevent self-posting or self-approving; they will be available as drop-down selections, as presented in Figure 14.25.

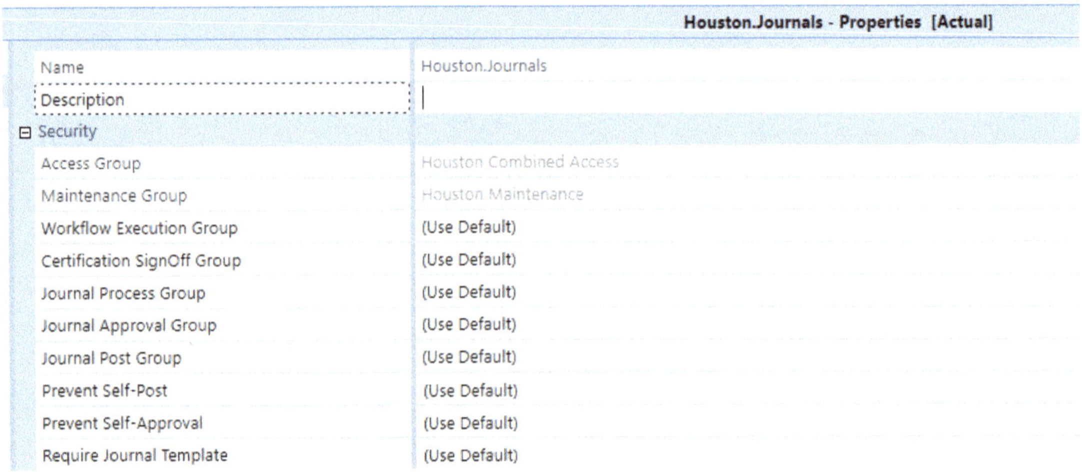

Figure 14.25

- **Access Group** is typically everyone or the group that should see the data in the assigned journal step.
- **Maintenance Group** should almost always be administrators.
- **Workflow Execution Group**: those who can complete the workflow.
- **Certification SignOff Group**: those who can certify (assuming that certify is part of the workflow).
- **Journal Process Group:** the group that can create journals.
- **Journal Approval Group:** the group that can approve journals.
- **Journal Post Group:** the group that can post the journals.

Submitter, Approver, Poster

If you want someone who can submit, approve, and post (no separation of duties), you will need to ensure that the person is within each of those groups (Journal Process Group, Journal Approval Group and Journal Post Group) or that the same group is used for all three settings.

Submitter + Poster, Approver

If you want someone who can submit and post but who cannot approve their own journals, then you will need to ensure that the person is within Journal Process Group and Journal Post Group; or if you know that every submitter will also be a poster, then you can use the same group for Journal Process Group and Journal Post Group. Furthermore, you will have the Prevent Self-Approve option in the Workflow Profile to prevent self-approvals.

Submitter + Approver, Poster

If you want someone who can submit and approve but cannot post his or her own journals, you will need to ensure that the person is within Journal Process Group and Journal Approval Group; or if you know that every submitter will also be an approver, then you can use the same group for Journal Process Group and Journal Approval Group. You will have the Prevent Self-Post option in the Workflow Profile to prevent self-posts.

Submitter and Approver Cannot Be the Same Person

If you need to ensure the submitter and approver cannot be the same person, this will likely have to be handled as part of the journal events handler for applications that are not on at least 8.0. For those on at least 8.0, a custom rule is no longer needed, and this functionality is assigned directly on the workflow.

I Want to Send Emails About These Journals

If there is a need to send emails about journals, this will require a setup on the users' settings, specifically those who should be receiving the emails. For example, if all approvers should receive an email that a certain journal is ready for their approval, then the `JournalEventHandler` rule needs some indication that the user should be receiving the journal (e.g., either the rule references the security group or a text field).

If you opt to include a PDF attachment of the journals to be sent, you will need to build this PDF out in the dashboard with the relevant components and then have it associated with the rule.

Org-By-Period

Org-By-Period is used to handle applications with periodic consolidation where you do not want historical data to be reflected with the latest hierarchical changes. This is distinct from reorganizations, which we commonly define as re-shuffling entities and their roll-ups, and where you want historical data reflected in the latest structure. Essentially, to enable Org-By-Period, you would need to maintain alternate entity structures with the relevant Percent Consolidation varied by the appropriate Scenario Type and time. In addition, **Org-By-Period Elimination** will be used as part of the Consolidation Algorithm Type instead of standard, as reflected in Figure 14.26. Furthermore, you will need to ensure that the Consolidation View on the scenario member is set to Periodic, which tells OneStream to consolidate into the parent on a monthly basis instead of moving its YTD balances.

Calculation	
Consolidation Algorithm Type	Org-By-Period Elimination
Translation Algorithm Type	Standard (Calc-On-The-Fly Share and Hierarchy Elimination)
Calculate None Cons Member If No Data	Stored Share
Calculate Local Currency If No Data	Org-By-Period Elimination
Calculate Translated Currencies If No Data	Stored Share and Org-By-Period Elimination
Calculate OwnerPreAdj If No Data	Custom

Figure 14.26

> **Note:** A business rule will need to be written to pull forward the elimination YTD when no data is loaded to an IC member.

Refer to the Design and Reference Guide and Foundation Handbook's Consolidation section for more information.

Business Acquisitions

Congrats! Your company has decided to acquire another company AND has tasked you with incorporating this new company into OneStream! This section will cover (at a high level) external reporting purposes and the common situations associated with a business acquisition; there is also a separate section dedicated to pro-rata management reporting. Remember, the situations described below are not considered to be an exhaustive or complete list.

Acquired Company Continues to Use Its Own Ledger

When I say "own ledger", what I really mean is that there is some agreement that the acquired company will continue to use its existing ERP system(s) and its existing chart of accounts structure, which could be entirely different to the parent company. Thus, I would assess the following:

1. Will this acquired company be handling its own data load to OneStream, or is this acquired company passing the file to your company to do the load?
    a. Regardless of who does what, it is good to *define the process* now that the acquired company will be reporting to your company.
    b. This approach would likely necessitate a separate data source, transformation profiles, and Workflow Profiles.
2. How different is this company's chart of accounts, and by "continues to use its own ledger" – what does that mean on the reporting front?
    a. Does this mean – for reports out of OneStream – the acquired company is expected to see the numbers in its chart of accounts?
    b. Or are we simply saying they want to load in their chart of accounts but are alright with the output in the parent company's chart of accounts?
3. Does the company use the same fiscal calendar year?

What OneStream can provide, again, is a lot of flexibility. The below list is not exhaustive but offers some options to consider when integrating this new business into OneStream:

- **New Extensibility and New Cube**: assess which dimensions should be extended. Adding extended dimensions would involve adding a new cube where you can apply the extended dimensions. This cube could be set for the acquired company to use. This could be an approach if there aren't any immediate or foreseeable plans that the acquired company's chart of accounts will be moving to the parent's chart of accounts for reporting.

- **New Data Source and Workflow to Existing Cube(s):** if it is determined that the acquired company will report using the parent's chart of accounts but will continue to use its chart of accounts for loads, perhaps adding a new data source with mappings and a Workflow step would be sufficient.

- **Creation of calendars:** this may involve a separate Entity dimension, separate Scenario dimension, and custom time profiles specific to this differing fiscal calendar.

Same Underlying ERP, But Acquired Company is Not Familiar with the Chart of Accounts

There are two main scenarios I see:

1. The acquired company is willing to change/update its ERP to align with your ERP and/or go onto your ERP. Where no one is familiar with the efforts of transitioning or combining

ERPs, you could provide them with an Excel helper that shows the mapping between acquired company charts and parent company charts as it updates its ERP.

2. The acquired company decides to keep its ERP as is, but will start using OneStream for all of its reporting in the new chart of accounts instead of its ERP or other EPM tool. This approach would be similar to what is already mentioned in the section above and dependent on the level of detail needed for reporting.

Generally, it takes time for the acquired company to acclimate to the acquisition and processes. The above suggestions are on the longer time horizon and the Acquired Company would not be expected to complete things quickly as part of reporting their financials to the parent company's totals.

Impact on OneStream Consolidation Process

Let's say that you have figured out how to source the new business acquisition, whether it's a flat file, direct connect to the ERP, inputs, or whatnot. Generally, I am assuming there is a process already in place to handle these changes in OneStream, so I'll cover the general changes needed at a high level:

- Has the proper metadata been set up for the new acquisition?

    o Entity: are the consolidation percentage and ownership set accordingly? Remember, you can use Vary by Scenario and Period.

    o Accounts: are the accounts from the acquisition's file already in OneStream with the proper settings?

    o Flow: if you are leveraging the beginning balance, activity and ending balance in the Flow dimension, do you have a beginning balance acquisition member or ending balance member to kick off the proper beginning balance/ending balance as of the date the acquisition's data comes in?

    o Remainder: are the remaining dimensions updated to accept the acquisition's data?

- If you have custom eliminations or advanced consolidation (e.g., complex ownerships), did you make those updates? Depending on how these rules were set up, you may need to make manual updates to the rules or update the metadata with certain text fields, etc.

- Are currency and FX rates accounted for?

- Are Workflow Profiles and security up to date?

- Are the remaining reports and inputs up to date? (e.g., consolidated financials, overrides, journals, etc.)

- Does management reporting include pro-rata reporting?

Business Divestitures

Congrats (again?). Your company has decided to sell a company and has tasked you with removing this company from OneStream!

What does this mean for you now that this company is off your books? Well, you have a few extra licenses on hand to distribute to folks within your company.

From your end, it is very likely that the divested company will still have data existing in your general ledger, which gets imported into OneStream, and you no longer want the data reflected in OneStream after some point in time. Within OneStream, I highly recommend leveraging the **In Use** settings and **Vary by Scenario Type** settings.

Each OneStream application is set up differently, so I'll cover some general setups I have seen:

- Some applications leverage text fields in the Entity dimension, and tag whether that entity is considered a discontinued operation. There could also be a custom dimension dedicated to data type (e.g., discontinued operations adj or something else) to handle reclasses. These reclasses, with the data type and Entity dimensions, allow users to view totals as if the entity were still operating for the selected period(s). There could also be a custom finance rule in the background to handle the reclasses.

- Set the entity's Percent Consolidation to 0% using Vary by Scenario Type; you can specify the specific date where Percent Consolidation will be 0% going forward. Depending on where this entity sits, you may need to update in the linked cubes and top cube.

    o If you decide to continue to load data, you may need to consider additional security (e.g., same balances as of X date until the end of the year). This may be relevant if you have additional MarketPlace solutions like Account Reconciliations.

    o If you decide not to load data after a point in time, then you may need to consider journal adjustments to the end of the year. This may be relevant if you have additional MarketPlace solutions like Account Reconciliations.

- Furthermore, if this divested company had associated Workflow Profiles, you would need to go ahead and update security groups and users who were part of the divested company. This means setting the users as inactive and setting the Workflow Profiles as inactive.

Impact on OneStream Consolidation Process

Overall, from the parent company's perspective, you want to ensure that the entity is no longer consolidating to the total after X date, and that relevant business rules that could contain this entity's data are updated. This can be done through the Percent Consolidation setting or by bypassing the data loads containing the entity reference.

Pro-Rata of Business Acquisitions and Divestitures for Management Reporting

With a business acquisition or business divestiture, your company's management may require some sort of pro-rata reporting that extends back 12-13 months for comparative reporting purposes. As mentioned repeatedly throughout this chapter, it is recommended that you work with the relevant stakeholders and consultants to determine the appropriate handling for pro-rata reporting.

At a high and general level, pro-rata reporting involves a separate set of data, handled by separate Scenario Types and/or if you already have a UD dedicated to data source or data type, you could have a member that sits as a sibling to the node that represents external/GAAP reporting; this way, you are able to view your data with or without the acquisition(s) or divestiture(s).

New Chart of Accounts

The chart of accounts refers to the naming convention that organizes your financial information. For example, you could have XXX-YYY-ZZZ, in which XXX represents your accounts, YYY could be your cost center, and ZZZ could be your country.

Depending on where your company is, and where your company wants to go, you might find yourself in a huge financial transformation, where your company decides to revamp everything related to your financial statements. Everything is going to change, from your ERP to your CPM. What do you do?

A few items to keep in mind and address:

- Do you have a plan to adequately test the new chart of accounts and compare it with your old chart of accounts?

- Is there a timeframe in which your company plans to transition to only the new chart of accounts?

- What about historical data in the old chart of accounts? Are there plans to "re-state" the data in the old chart of accounts into the new chart of accounts, or are people going to keep the old data in the old chart as is, and effectively have a time range where comparative reporting will not be possible?

- What about change management? Are your users ready? Are you ready?

- Do you have a design in mind, and do people agree with it?

- What could possibly go wrong?

With OneStream, we can look at a few considerations (remember, this is not an exhaustive list). These cases are options that companies have considered and had to assess the implications of. I have listed these cases based on complexity, from the most straightforward to the least.

1. Complete application redesign and build.

2. Use of separate dimensions and separate Scenario Types.

3. Keep everything in the same dimensions.

I am hoping that, at least with these cases, you can jot down a few ideas on how you want to approach your OneStream application and facilitate the transition from your current chart of accounts to a new chart of accounts. Again, I cannot emphasize enough that I highly recommend you work with your stakeholders and consultants on the appropriate approach.

Complete Application Redesign and Build

If you plan to use the new chart of accounts going forward, and the old chart of accounts is no longer going to be used, then starting out with a blank application is a viable option. Some folks have told me this is the preferred way, and I can see why… it is a pain to transition from an old chart to a new one because you essentially rebuild it anyway. If you must rebuild, you might as well start with a clean slate!

Use Separate Dimensions and Separate Scenario Types

This situation sees the creation of a completely new set of dimensions associated with a different Scenario Type. These dimensions will then exist in conjunction with the current set of dimensions.

Why would you want to consider this an option? Well, you could run into a situation where you have an active build that is still in the old chart of accounts, and management wants you to start considering the use of the new chart of accounts. You could have ongoing plans where new build items – as of a certain date – need to be in the new chart of accounts, all while you still need to figure out how to transition data from the old chart of accounts to the new one.

What does a new set of separate dimensions provide?

Pros	Cons
You can switch out Scenario Types on your scenario members.	You will have two sets of Actuals with different charts of accounts that will exist in your application until you decide to clear or re-state the old to the new chart of accounts.
If you need to compare old and new charts of accounts, you can do so by using Scenario Types and using the same application for comparison.	If you decide on one scenario to represent Actuals, you may need to consider a data copy or some mechanism to bring over the data the scenario used for the new chart of accounts; *or* if your company ultimately decides to convert all necessary historical data to the new chart, then you could take the old scenario and rename it as `Actual_Old` and rename the `Actual_New` as Actual – this may require communication and timing considerations for users active in the application.

Pros	Cons
Retains audit history of all submitted data if you decide to copy the amounts to the new chart of accounts' Scenario Type(s)	Metadata and data management will require vigilance. If your new chart of accounts ends up with a naming convention that exists in the old chart of accounts, you will need to go through all artifacts (e.g., Cube Views, transformation rules, business rules) and update accordingly.
	If you differ by Scenario Type and you have formulas by Scenario Type, they will all have to be updated to the appropriate Scenario Type.

Figure 14.27

Once all the relevant pieces are fully transitioned to the new chart of accounts, you will also need a cleanup period to remove all the old chart of accounts-related artifacts and data. This will include all historical data in the old chart, data sources, transformation rules, Cube Views, dashboards, etc. The complexity with this option comes down to tracking, organizing, and maintaining the flux of changes between the old chart and new chart for all pieces in the application.

Keep Everything in the Same Dimension(s)

When I say 'keep everything in the same dimension(s)', this is *not* the same thing as extending the dimensions that I mentioned above. What we are really talking about is using the existing dimensions and adding a **new hierarchy** that represents the new chart of accounts. Something that could look like this:

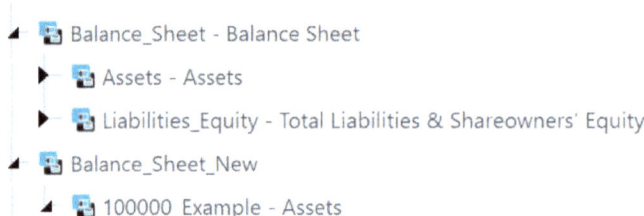

```
▲ 📋 Balance_Sheet - Balance Sheet
    ▶ 📋 Assets - Assets
    ▶ 📋 Liabilities_Equity - Total Liabilities & Shareowners' Equity
▲ 📋 Balance_Sheet_New
    ▲ 📋 100000_Example - Assets
```

Figure 14.28

What are the implications of this setup?

Well, what are you going to do with the old chart of accounts, which – in this case – would be Balance_Sheet? This Balance_Sheet structure will, at some point, be replaced with Balance_Sheet_New and all members, both base and parents, will need to have unique names that do not already exist in the given dimension. If you determine that there are a handful of members that will continue to use the same name, then you need to be mindful of data conversion.

Furthermore, you will need to decommission the old chart of accounts. You could do so by setting every single member as In Use = False and you could further specify the In Use by Scenario Type and time. However, this will *not* prevent the user from seeing the old chart when they select a member, whether that is in their POV or Quick View for ad hoc analyses. If you want to prevent users from not seeing these members *at all*, then the Display Member Group should be set to a group like Nobody instead of Everyone. Remember that you cannot vary the Display Member Group by time or Scenario Type, so this will be an all-or-nothing situation.

In Use = False can be varied by Scenario Type and time; existing data will remain, no new data will be allowed, and the cell goes invalid. Users will still be able to see the members in the hierarchy, though, if Display Member Group is not updated accordingly.

Alternatively, you could decide to remove the old hierarchy altogether but, again, this removal would be dependent on your company's decision on how to handle historical data (e.g., data continues to be old or did all the data convert to the new chart of accounts?).

This ultimately creates a concern: is this approach really going to be a clean transition from the old chart of accounts to the new one?

This approach presents a series of pros and cons (again, not exhaustive):

Pros	Cons
Minimal updates to the *dimension names* referenced in your artifacts (e.g., business rules, queries, Cube Views, etc.).	Even though you may not need to change the dimension name in which your new hierarchy resides, you will still need to go through all artifacts and update the member names that are part of the new hierarchy.
	Will increase query times for reports. For example, if you have a dimension of 10,000 cost centers and you added another 5,000 cost centers that will be in your new chart of accounts.
	This will also increase consolidation times.
	Comparative reporting becomes a pain. You could have issues comparing historicals (old chart) to the new chart, where there could be many-to-one mappings.
	Two charts of accounts exist in the same dimension and will be visible to users if you decide not to also update the Display Member Group.

Even if In Use is set to False for the old chart, users will still have the ability to view it. The In Use = False setting simply prevents future inputs and makes the cells invalid.

This could cause user confusion. A user could pull an old chart of accounts member and the query would return a 'blank' amount. The user might ask why, only to realize that the member is in the old chart of accounts. |

Figure 14.29

Handling Historical Data Due to New Chart of Accounts Changes

This section specifically covers the choices for handling historical data due to new chart of accounts changes. The historical data conversion significantly impacts data validation efforts.

Same Source File and New Transformation Rules

For this option, there are a few assumptions:

1. You have the flat file on hand, or the direct connect, enabling you to go back and reload the exact same source data for the given period.

2. The restatement is impacted at the base level where the amount was initially mapped to a certain base intersection, but now needs to be moved to a different base intersection.

If you meet the above conditions, you could leverage a new set of transformation rules and a new Workflow Profile, which denotes the historical restatement, or you can swap out the transformation rules profiles for the existing Workflow Profile. As always, any time there is a reload and revalidation with new mappings, you would need to validate that the output is correct.

Pros	Cons
You only need to create a new set of transformation rules and transformation rule profiles and attach them to the existing workflow import step.	If your source file or connector brings in a large volume of data, this could involve painful processing times for however many past periods are impacted.

Figure 14.30

Data Export and New Transformation Rules

This approach involves taking a data export of the existing cube data and then setting up a new data source to import this file with the new transformation mappings. This case would be straightforward and relatively quick if you know that the data volume within your application is not voluminous. Similar to the case above, you could have at least two sets of mapping profiles: 1. the existing transformation rules profile that represents the existing set of mappings, which would be considered the old chart of accounts, and 2. the new transformation rules profile that represents the new chart of accounts.

For this option, there are a few assumptions as well:

1. You have a OneStream application that has validated data that you are seeking to retransform into the new chart of accounts.

2. You do not require to have the true source files retransformed. In other words, whatever is in OneStream can be retransformed to the new chart of accounts.

3. After the data exports, you will be removing the data in the old chart of accounts. The application will not and does not use this data.

Pros	Cons
Exported historical data has already been validated, so you can limit validation errors to the mappings (this is a little different than the case above as the source files could contain several hundred mappings, whereas this case's mappings will likely be simpler).	This approach involves additional steps such as 1. creating the data export, 2. setting up a new data source to handle the import of the exported data file, 3. new transformation rules, 4. creating a new workflow import step and attaching the new data source and transformation rules profile, or leveraging the existing workflow import step and swapping out the data source and transformation rules profile.
	If your existing data per period in OneStream is of high volume, this approach could involve painful processing times for however many past periods are impacted.

Figure 14.31

Data Connector and Possible FDX Queries

This approach involves writing a connector rule, setting up the data source with the connector, creating new transformation rules, and then associating them with your relevant workflow import step. Depending on which cubes are impacted by the historical restatement, and the extent to which your cubes are extended, you may need to also include an FDX query.

FDX stands for **Fast Data Extract** and is only available for 5.3+ releases. An FDX setup also involves writing in VB.NET. The most common ones are covered in the Foundation Handbook. If existing FDX queries fit your restatement needs, you could leverage these rules as part of your overall connector rule(s).

Similar to the two cases above, you have at least two sets of mapping profiles: 1. the existing transformation rules profile that represents the existing set of mappings, which would be considered the old chart of accounts, and 2. the new transformation rules profile that represents the new chart of accounts.

Pros	Cons
Minimize human error as we have the system pull from Stage. We have the flexibility to set up the connector to pull pre-transformed data or transformed data.	Connector rules require you to know how to set one up (e.g., are you going to leverage Workflow Profile text fields or existing workflow import names?) and/or you have an existing connector rule to leverage, and you have a good understanding of VB.NET.
Extract and upload times are minimized because the connector is pulling directly from Stage. Reduces the level of manual loads.	You also have to be familiar with setting up FDX queries and know how to link possibly both the FDX queries with the connector rules.
	If you clear out the old data from Stage, then you can no longer use this as a valid method for re-import. This will be problematic if there is a point in time when you need to go back and re-import this data.

Figure 14.32

Conclusion

This was a big chapter, where we covered topics related to business process changes that could impact the OneStream application. These business process changes could involve alterations in the system for intercompany and/or cash flow (where you now want them in OneStream), enhancements to your existing processes (such as the separation of duties to your journals or additional topside capabilities or Org-By-Period), business acquisitions and/or divestitures, or simply a fundamental shift in how your company plans to view data going forward via a new chart of accounts and the handling of historical data.

After reading this chapter, you are now equipped with the knowledge to assess and work with your team and counterparts on how to incorporate various business processes into your OneStream application, all the while maintaining existing processes!

Index

Index

Index

Index

Index

Index

OneStream Foundation Handbook

The Definitive Reference to Design, Configure and Support Your OneStream Platform.

OneStream is a modern, unified platform that is revolutionizing corporate performance management. This proven alternative to fragmented legacy applications is designed to simplify processes for the most sophisticated, global enterprises. Hundreds of the world's leading companies are turning to OneStream to help with reporting and understanding financial data.

In this practical guide, The Architect Factory team at OneStream Software explains each part of an implementation, and the design of solutions. Readers will learn the core guiding principles for implementing OneStream from the company's top team of experts. Beyond offering a training guide, the focus of this book is on the 'why' of design and building an application.

- Manage your Implementation with the OneStream methodology
- Understand Design and Build concepts
- Build solutions for the Consolidation of financial data, and develop Planning models
- Create Data Integration solutions that will feed your models
- Develop Workflows to guide and manage your end-users
- Advance your solutions with Rules and Security
- Take advantage of detailed Data Reporting using tools such as Analytic Blend, Advanced Excel reporting, and Dashboarding
- Tune Performance, and optimize your application

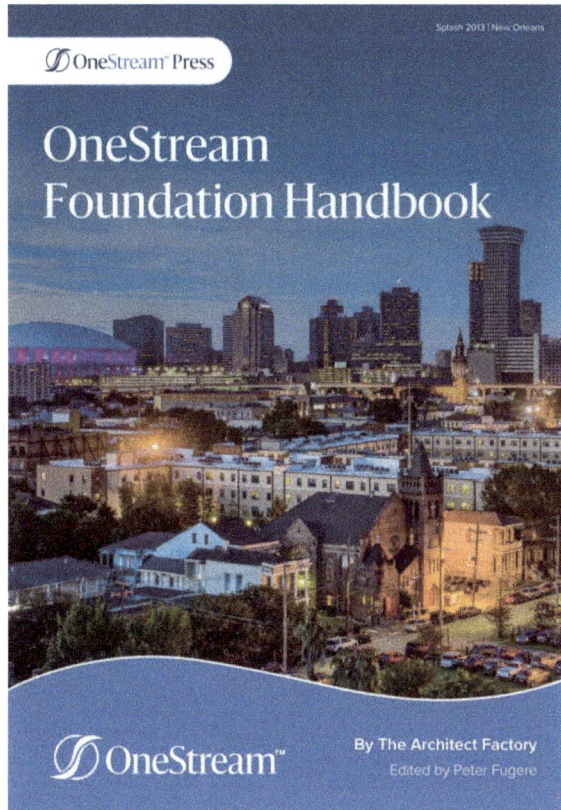

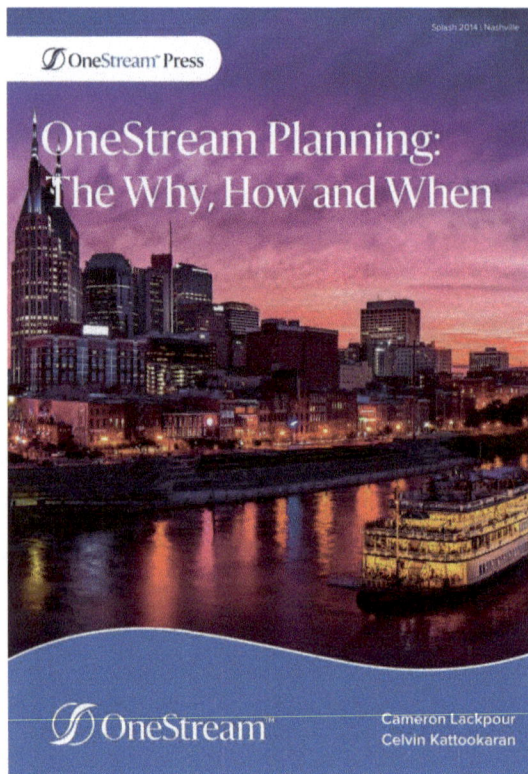

OneStream Planning: The Why, How and When

OneStream is a world-class Intelligent Finance Platform that handles the complex planning, consolidation, reporting and other requirements of mid-sized to large enterprises. Whether in retail, financial services, manufacturing or other industries, the OneStream platform provides the means to integrate multiple data sources and utilize a wide range of tools and methodologies to improve business processes and performance. Through OneStream, organizations benefit from unified, real-time, enterprise-wide planning and forecasting.

Aimed at OneStream Planning practitioners, administrators, implementors, and power users alike, as well as Financial close and consolidations practitioners, *OneStream Planning: The Why, How and When* is the first standalone book in the performance management space to cover the power and potential of Planning in OneStream. Drawing from real-world deployments, the book is rooted in easily understood business use cases, and explains approaches (with code) through a comprehensive exploration of the solution. All this is offered within a framework of top functional and technical practice as informed by the authors' decades-long consulting and application development experiences.

- Which should I do – Import or Direct Load, Consolidate or Aggregate?
- How do Data Buffers really work; what is Eval and why should I care? Which approach is fastest and does it really matter?
- Why Multiyear Scenarios should never be Yearly
- Can Thing Planning run in the Spreadsheet? (It can.)
- Combining REST API and Analytic Blend
- Slice Security down to the very tiniest slice
- Pivot Grid or Large Pivot Grid, that is the question
- A book filled with clear use cases
- Exhaustively tested and verified solutions, and extensive source code
- Undocumented features and functionality covered, along with functional and technical good practices

OneStream Finance Rules and Calculations Handbook

Hundreds of companies have turned to OneStream to solve complex planning, consolidation and operational reporting needs. OneStream's unique ability to provide a multitude of solutions across dozens of industries is largely due to its dynamic Finance Engine which provides the capability to add industry- and company-specific business intelligence to data. Employing the full power of the Finance Engine allows companies to extend the platform and fully exploit the power of their investment.

Aimed at everyone from novices to seasoned veterans, this handbook—by OneStream Distinguished Architect Jon Golembiewski—will break down the Finance Engine and outline how to write Finance Business Rules and Calculations. Its insights will help propel OneStream applications to the next level.

- Fundamentals of the Finance Engine
- Detailed breakdown of the Cube and Data
- A look under the hood of the api.Data.Calculate function
- Techniques for tackling complex calculation requirements
- How to use the Custom Calculate function to make calculations dynamic
- How to write calculations for optimal performance
- How to troubleshoot calculations
- How to solve and avoid common errors and pitfalls
- Real-world calculation examples with detailed explanations
- A full application with all referenced code examples is available to download

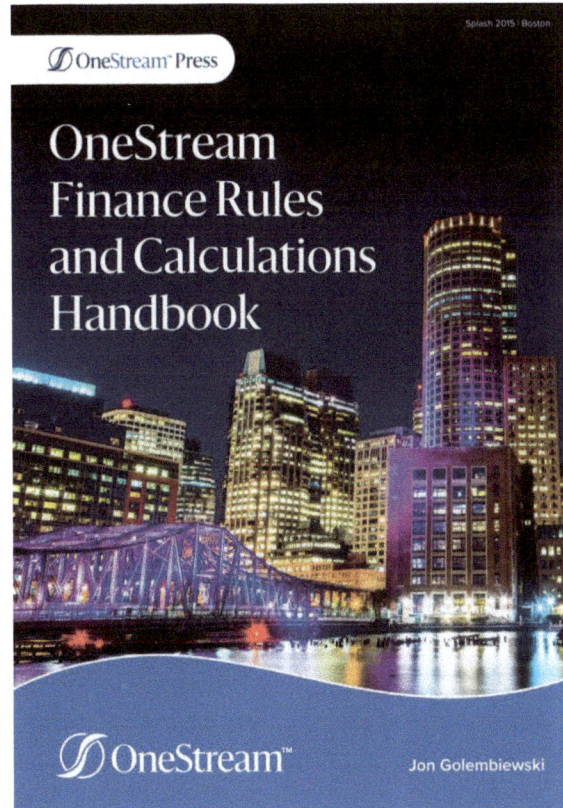

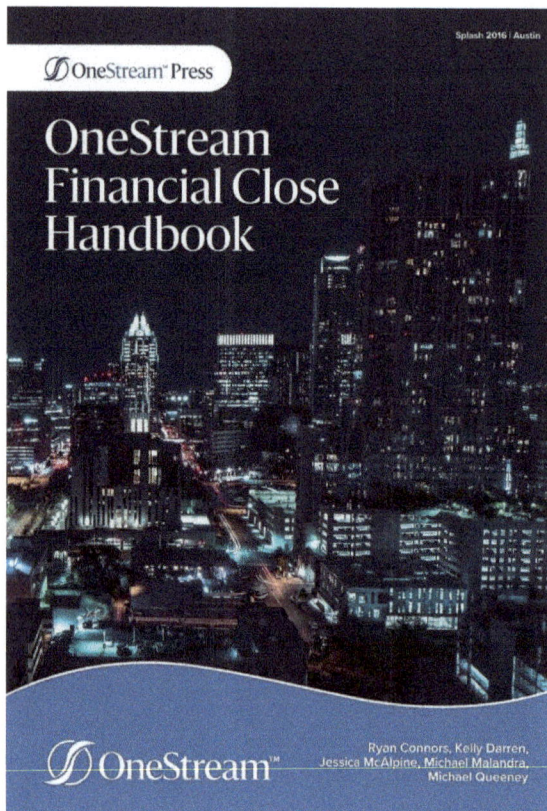

OneStream Financial Close Handbook

OneStream provides a market-leading Intelligent Finance Platform that reduces the complexity of financial operations. It unifies corporate performance management (CPM) processes such as planning, financial close & consolidation, reporting and analytics through a single, extensible solution.

The OneStream Financial Close Handbook – written by expert authors – is a practical book for implementors, administrators, and end-users, that dives into the Financial Close with a specific focus on the Account Reconciliations and Transaction Matching solutions.

The Account Reconciliations solution is a complete package that plugs into the Financial Close Workflow to leverage data that already resides within the consolidation application, whilst Transaction Matching helps accounting teams automate the collection and matching of large numbers of transactions across multiple sources.

With these solutions, OneStream Financial Close delivers the four key pillars of a good reconciliation process: Visibility, Standardization, Efficiency and Control.

In this book:

- Get a better understanding of the Financial Close process, and how OneStream delivers a streamlined, automated solution.
- Learn how to implement Account Reconciliations through detailed project phases, and accompanying case studies.
- Get to grips with the administration of Account Reconciliations, including settings, security, and auditing.
- Deep dive into the Account Reconciliation Solution from the End User's perspective, including how to prepare a Reconciliation, the sign-off and approval process, and overall reporting and monitoring capabilities.
- Learn what Transaction Matching is, plus how to build, test, and implement OneStream's highly automated system.
- Understand how to administer Transaction Matching through global options, access control, match sets, data sets, rules, and more!

OneStream Advanced Reporting and Dashboards

OneStream is a world-class Intelligent Finance Platform that empowers organizations to have confidence in their data and make decisions that maximize business impact. It is used by enterprises all over the world to streamline financial close, consolidation, planning, reporting and analysis, and drive effective business decisions – all based on near real-time data.

The user experience is the point of contact with the platform, and while OneStream comes with a powerful standard UI, one of its greatest strengths is its ability to create bespoke reports and custom dashboards. Like our customers, each OneStream application is unique – whether you're a novice or have experience with CPM solutions, OneStream provides the flexibility to tailor a solution to meet your needs. Concepts discussed in this book are intended to help you understand the unlimited possibilities of designing your ultimate user experience.

Written for administrators, dashboard and report designers, plus end users, and filled with background knowledge and step-by-step guides, this book deep dives into cube views, dashboards, reporting, and highlights the tools and tricks that will take user experiences to a new level. We examine how leveraging the full power of the OneStream Platform will help you move beyond the standard interface, align your end-user experiences with your business and process requirements, promote user adoption through efficiency and ease of use, and truly maximize the value of your OneStream implementation.

By the end of this book, you will have a deep understanding of the components that drive the user experience and how and when to use them. You'll walk away with a plethora of tools and ideas to incorporate into your application to deliver your very own user experience.

In this book, we will:

- Design and build cube views, based on data entry and reporting needs.
- Discuss the use of cube view extender business rules to expose advanced formatting capabilities.
- Explore how navigation links and drill to dashboard functionality provide intuitive analysis.
- Identify the benefits of configuring personalized home pages to ensure user adoption.
- Create working role-based dashboards inspired by real-world customer requirements.

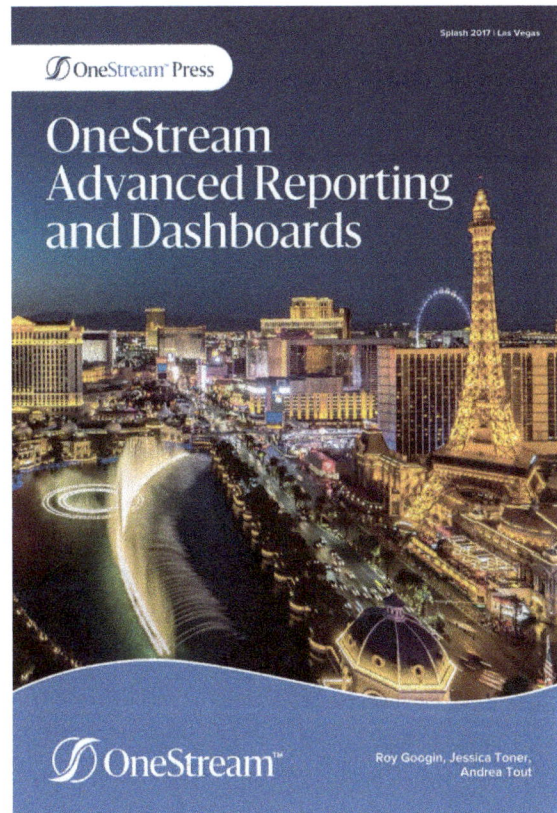

www.ingramcontent.com/pod-product-compliance
Lightning Source LLC
Chambersburg PA
CBHW041621220326
41598CB00046BA/7429

* 9 7 8 1 8 3 8 2 5 2 8 1 6 *